Leo Strauss

LEO STRAUSS

Leo Strauss

Political Philosopher and Jewish Thinker

Edited by
KENNETH L. DEUTSCH
and
WALTER NICGORSKI

Rowman & Littlefield Publishers, Inc.

ROWMAN & LITTLEFIELD PUBLISHERS, INC.

Published in the United States of America
by Rowman & Littlefield Publishers, Inc.
4720 Boston Way, Lanham, Maryland 20706

3 Henrietta Street, London WC2E 8LU, England

Copyright © 1994 by Rowman & Littlefield Publishers, Inc.

British Cataloging in Publication Information Available

Library of Congress Cataloging-in-Publication Data

Leo Strauss : political philosopher and Jewish thinker / edited by
Kenneth L. Deutsch and Walter Nicgorski.
p. cm.
Includes bibliographical references.
1. Strauss, Leo—Contributions in political science. 2. Strauss,
Leo—Contributions in Jewish philosophy. I. Deutsch, Kenneth L.
II. Nicgorski, Walter.
JC251.S8L45   1993   181'.06—dc20   92-44618   CIP

ISBN 0-8476-7837-7 (cloth : alk. paper)
ISBN 0-8476-7838-5 (paper : alk. paper)

Photo on frontispiece courtesy of The University of Chicago Press and
The Review of Politics (Notre Dame, Indiana).

Printed in the United States of America

 ™ The paper used in this publication meets the minimum require-
ments of American National Standard for Information Sciences—
Permanence of Paper for Printed Library Materials, ANSI Z39.48–
1984.

To the memory of LEO STRAUSS

In appreciation of his achievement in reviving political philosophy in political science and in clarifying the encounter between Jerusalem and Athens

Contents

Acknowledgments

We are especially grateful to the editor of the *Review of Politics*, Donald P. Kommers, for encouraging the development of this volume and granting the necessary permissions. Many of the essays in this collection initially appeared in the special issue on Leo Strauss published by the *Review of Politics* (Winter 1991). Our ability to publish here, and for the first time, Leo Strauss's lecture "Why We Remain Jews: Can Jewish Faith and History Still Speak to Us?" is due to permission granted by Joseph Cropsey, literary executor for Leo Strauss. His decision in favor of publication of this important, though informal, statement is a helpful aid to present and future students of Strauss's thought. We are also indebted to Peter Emberley, Barry Cooper, and Penn State Press for allowing us to publish in this collection Thomas L. Pangle's essay "On the Epistolary Dialogue Between Leo Strauss and Eric Voegelin," which was already committed—in a substantially similar version—to their book scheduled to appear in 1993 under the title *Faith and Political Philosophy: The Correspondence Between Leo Strauss and Eric Voegelin 1934–1964*.

We wish to thank Walter Soffer for his comments that contributed to the clarity and coherence of the Introduction and Elliot Bartky for his counsel and suggestions in the editing of Strauss's lecture. We are also much appreciative of the editorial skills exercised on much of the manuscript by Dennis W. Moran, managing editor of the *Review of Politics*; and for the typing and other assistance provided with accomplished skill and good cheer both by the *Review*'s secretary Roberta Ferkins and by Liz Ancker, secretary to the Department of Political Science of the State University of New York at Geneseo.

Introduction

All political action aims at either preservation or change. When desiring to preserve, we wish to prevent a change for the worse; when desiring to change, we wish to bring about something better. All political action is then guided by some thought of better or worse.
—Leo Strauss, *What Is Political Philosophy?*

It is surely nobler to be victim of the most noble dream than to profit from a sordid reality and to wallow in it.
—Leo Strauss, "Why We Remain Jews"

Leo Strauss is among the most influential thinkers of the generation of Americans that spanned the mid-point of the twentieth century. Both the impact of and the controversies over Strauss's legacy have greatly increased since his death in 1973. Perhaps the central controversy concerning Strauss is whether his scholarship and learned teachings are salutary or misguided in regard to living the good life in a liberal democracy. Characterizations of Strauss have ranged from moral absolutist to moral nihilist. His powerful impact and loyal following have lent themselves to portrayals of him as the founder of a cult of "godlike" philosophers and a "doctrinally fastidious sect."[1]

In fact, Strauss's most consequential students are in some disagreement about how best to characterize his legacy. Have they experienced different "sides" of Strauss? For Thomas Pangle, Strauss was an erotic and zetetic skeptic who was a "rational" and "sober" friend of democracy, refusing to be one of its "flatterers."[2] For Stanley Rosen, Strauss was an "atheist" who sought to be a "god" in order to create a form of rhetoric that would render the world safe for philosophy.[3] Yet George Anastaplo considers Strauss

1. Among the most important critical evaluations of Leo Strauss and his teachings are: M. F. Burnyeat, "Sphinx without a Secret," *New York Review of Books* 32:9 (May 1985): 30–36; Shadia Drury, *The Political Ideas of Leo Strauss* (New York: St. Martin's Press, 1988); John Gunnell, "Political Theory and Politics: The Case of Leo Strauss and Liberal Democracy," in Kenneth L. Deutsch and Walter Soffer, *The Crisis of Liberal Democracy: A Straussian Perspective* (New York: SUNY Press, 1987); and Sheldon Wolin, *The Presence of the Past: Essays on the State and the Constitution* (Baltimore: Johns Hopkins Press, 1989), pp. 50–53.
2. "Editor's Introduction," in Leo Strauss, *The Rebirth of Classical Political Rationalism*, ed. Thomas L. Pangle (Chicago: University of Chicago Press, 1989), p. xiii.
3. Stanley Rosen, *Hermeneutics as Politics* (New York: Oxford University Press, 1987), pp. 17 and 108.

1

to have been "a scholar who took seriously the problem between reason and revelation, perhaps more so than any other secular thinker since Hobbes, Locke and Spinoza."[4]

The controversy surrounding Strauss's work and impact can make it difficult for students and scholars to be open to the range and depth of Strauss's mind and to the substance of his intellectual odyssey. Undeniably, his incisive commentaries on the great texts of the Western political tradition have contributed to the revival of scholarly attention to the quarrels between Athens and Jerusalem, poetry and philosophy, the ancients and the moderns, the philosopher and the city, as well as the crisis of liberal democracy. His teachings that bear on the problem of liberal education have encouraged many of his students and followers to write and speak boldly about "the closing of the American mind."

In Strauss, we have witnessed a teacher who has stirred opposition on a scale rarely if ever seen in the American academy. Yet, in his classes and writings and at his study table, Strauss demonstrated the plain dignity of the life of the mind during which he grappled with the enduring questions about the human soul, about God, and about the good life, religion, and democracy. There is a conflict of images in the academic community between Strauss the kindly solitary scholar and Strauss the infallible academic cult leader. Which is the real Strauss?

Leo Strauss was born into an orthodox Jewish family in Kirchhain Hessen, Germany, on 20 September 1899. He had a classical education and served in the German army. By age seventeen, he became an advocate of "simple, straightforward political Zionism." The young Strauss turned to political Zionism out of a dissatisfaction with the general view in the Jewish community that a liberal "neutral" state—neutral to the difference between Christians and Jews or between non-Jews and Jews—could achieve true social and legal equality. After graduating from *Gymnasium*, he studied philosophy and natural science at the universities of Marburg, Frankfurt, Berlin, and Hamburg. In 1921 he received his doctor of philosophy degree from Hamburg. He had an opportunity to attend lectures by Edmund Husserl and Martin Heidegger at Freiburg. Strauss served as a research assistant in Berlin at the Akademie für die Wissenschaft des Judentums, where his primary

4. George Anastaplo, "Shadia Drury on Leo Strauss," *Vital Nexus* 1 (May 1990): 12.

interest in theology led him to explore the sources of the seventeenth-century "modern" attack by Benedict de Spinoza and Thomas Hobbes on traditional orthodoxy. His friend Jacob Klein reports that one of the two "primary interests" for Strauss as a young man was the question of God; Strauss himself says his predominant interest was in theology.[5] Much later in his career, Strauss would conclude *The City and Man* with the following statement:

> For what is "first for us" is not the philosophic understanding of the city but that understanding which is inherent in the city as such, in the pre-philosophic city, according to which the city sees itself as subject and subservient to the divine in the ordinary understanding of the divine or looks up to it. Only by beginning at this point will we be open to the full impact of the all-important question which is coeval with philosophy although the philosophers do not frequently pronounce it—the question *quid sit deus.*[6]

Understandably, then, one major pursuit of Strauss throughout his career was the recovery of the compelling nature of the call of both Athens and Jerusalem—reason and revelation—as well as of the "tension" between them and the bearing of that tension on the understanding of political life. At the end of his career, Strauss would claim that the core, the nerve, of Western intellectual history is the conflict between the biblical and the philosophic notion of the good life. He considered this unresolved conflict to be the secret vitality of Western civilization.[7] He thought that "revelation is looked for only if man needs it, that is to say if his own reason is not satisfactory for all questions."[8]

Strauss was a recipient of a Rockefeller grant to study in France in 1932. In Paris he did research on medieval Jewish and Islamic philosophy. This research led Strauss to the view that there is always a "fundamental tension between philosophy and the city"; there exists a permanent and even radical disproportion between philosophy and politics. This tension exists because "the element

5. Jacob Klein and Leo Strauss, "A Giving of Accounts," *College* (magazine of St. John's College), 22 (April 1970): 1 and 2.
6. Leo Strauss, *The City and Man* (Chicago: University of Chicago Press, 1964), p. 241.
7. Leo Strauss, "Progress or Return?" in *Rebirth of Classical Political Rationalism*, p. 270.
8. Emil Fackenheim, "Leo Strauss and Modern Judaism," *Claremont Review* 4 (Winter 1985): 21.

of society is faith or opinion," and pursuit of philosophy is the attempt to replace opinion by knowledge. Philosophy is subversive, and those who practice it have often experienced persecution. Strauss's study of Farabi (or Alfarabi) and Maimonides led him to conclude that many philosophers take care to distinguish the "true" teaching as the esoteric teaching and the "socially useful teaching" as the exoteric teaching. The exoteric teaching is intended to be accessible to virtually every reader, while the esoteric teaching is intended to be accessible to those who are well trained and careful readers and are capable of long and concentrated study.[9] His study of premodern Jewish and Islamic rationalism led Strauss to write circumspectly by employing a complexity of intentions and a certain opaqueness.

As Ralph Lerner has put it, Strauss "was a Jew by deliberation."[10] His thoughts on being Jewish in modern times focus on the challenge posed to Judaism by liberalism, and the challenge posed to Judaism by philosophy. Throughout his career, Strauss wrote on Jewish topics, namely, commentaries on Maimonides, Halevi, Spinoza, Hermann Cohen, Franz Rosenzweig, the Bible, and Zionism. According to Strauss, Cohen "sometimes writes like a commentator on a commentary on an already highly technical text and hence like a man whose thought is derivative and traditional in the extreme; and yet he surprises time and again with strikingly original and weighty thoughts."[11] Does Strauss imitate Cohen's example?[12]

Strauss's Jewish writings explore two problems and their interplay: first, whether liberalism or Zionism can solve the problem of the hatred and persecution of the Jews that is the most simple exemplification of the human problem, namely, of group hatred and antagonism; and second, whether the Torah's claim to wisdom can survive the modern intellectual critique of revelation. Given the limits of human nature and human finitude, how does the substance of Judaism—the abiding trust in God—provide for the

9. Leo Strauss, *What Is Political Philosophy? and Other Studies* (Glencoe, IL: Free Press, 1959), p. 222.

10. Ralph Lerner, "Leo Strauss (1899–1973)," *American Jewish Yearbook* (1976):95.

11. Leo Strauss, *Liberalism, Ancient and Modern* (New York: Basic Books, 1968), p. 251.

12. For a further exploration of the development of Strauss's career as a Judaic scholar, see Martin D. Yaffe, "Leo Strauss as Judaic Thinker: Some First Notions," *Religious Studies Review* 17 (1991):33–41.

"traditional Jewish hopes" for the survival and future of Judaism and the Jewish people? Strauss came to think that these problems can be best addressed in our time by a restoration of the study of both classical political philosophy and medieval Jewish and Arabic rationalism.

Because of Adolf Hitler, Strauss eventually migrated to the United States. His first teaching position in the United States was as a research fellow at Columbia University in 1937, but the following year he received an appointment at the New School for Social Research—an appointment he held until 1948. Then, from 1949 until 1968, Strauss taught political philosophy at the University of Chicago. After his retirement from Chicago, he taught briefly at Claremont Men's College in California and at St. John's College in Annapolis, Maryland. He died in Annapolis in 1973. Strauss published fifteen books and scores of articles during his career. Some of the most important of his books include commentaries on Machiavelli, Spinoza, and Hobbes and *Natural Right and History, On Tyranny, Persecution and the Art of Writing, Liberalism: Ancient and Modern, The City and Man, What Is Political Philosophy?* and *Studies in Platonic Political Philosophy* (which was published posthumously).

During the postwar decades, Strauss raised serious doubts about the dominant intellectual orthodoxies of our time, namely, the fact/value distinction, and historicism. Both orthodoxies were often propounded as if they were an obvious truth. The impact of these orthodoxies was to make it very difficult for political scientists to make principled judgments about political things or seek to validate those principles appropriate to the practical science of politics. As Strauss put it, "present-day social science admits and even proclaims its inability to validate any value-judgments proper. The teaching originated by modern political philosophy in favor of the universal and prosperous society has admittedly become an ideology—a teaching not superior in truth and justice to any other among the innumerable ideologies."[13]

Strauss's critical analysis of the dogmatic relativism of modern social science was a concomitant to his general critique of modern rationalism and his efforts to rethink the major quarrels of Western civilization. Having reflected on the crisis of the modern project,

13. *City and Man*, pp. 6–7.

the rise of early twentieth-century tyranny, and the inability of modern social science to provide rational distinctions between better and worse regimes, Strauss found himself compelled to take a fresh, direct, and serious look at the ancients; his focus on ancient thinkers and specifically on Socrates in his major writings after 1964 must be noted.

THE PHILOSOPHER AND THE CITY

Although Strauss came to distinguish himself as an interpreter of the history of political philosophy, it would be a mistake to conclude that he ever put the most fundamental and ultimate questions entirely aside or behind him. Strauss rarely speaks in his own name and generally presents himself as a commentator who is primarily concerned with recovering or explicating the teachings of a past philosopher. He leaves it to the reader to draw out the teachings for which he provides some hints. When Strauss does speak in his own name, we should give these comments considerable attention and allow them to serve as a starting point in seeking a genuine understanding of his thought.

Strauss chose the Socratic "way of life." As he states,

> In studying certain earlier thinkers I became aware of this way of conceiving the relation between the quest for truth (philosophy or science) and society: Philosophy or science, the highest activity of man, is the attempt to replace opinion about "all things" by knowledge of "all things," but opinion is the element of society; philosophy or science is therefore the attempt to dissolve the element in which society breathes, and thus it endangers society.[14]

Politics is to be understood from the point of view of both common sense and the search for knowledge about the nature of political things. The philosopher must write in such a way that he or she will improve rather than subvert the city. Though a philosopher's *thought* may be a certain kind of *mania*, the virtue of the philosopher's *public* speech is *sophrosyne*. Strauss's writings contain an "ironic superiority," which requires that Strauss be read with the kind of care he gave to his writings.

Strauss speaks thus about his vocation as a philosopher:

14. *What Is Political Philosophy?* p. 221.

Philosophy as such is nothing other than the real consciousness of the problems, that is to say, of the fundamental and comprehensive problems. It is impossible to think about these problems without being attracted to a solution, toward one or the other of certain rare typical solutions. However, as long as there is no wisdom, but only the search for wisdom, the evidence of all these solutions is necessarily smaller than the evidence of the problems. As a result, the philosopher ceases to be a philosopher from the moment that his "subjective certitude" of the truth of a solution becomes stronger than the consciousness that he may have of the problematic character of this solution. At this moment the sectarian is born.[15]

For Strauss, philosophy is a passion (or an *eros*) and the result of an act of the will in which the dominant passion is the desire for knowledge of the eternal order or the eternal cause or causes of the whole. Since philosophy has not provided "wisdom" or a final account of the whole, Strauss concludes that revelation is possible and political philosophy is necessary. Political philosophy emerges from the reflective citizen's concern for direction in action; it is inquiry in search of political wisdom. Political philosophy also has three political functions: it must protect the philosopher as questioner, lead the best citizens to philosophy, and "move with circumspection" concerning the salutary role of religious beliefs in society. Political philosophy, according to Strauss, has as its function "to persuade the city that philosophers are not atheists, that they do not profane all that the city holds sacred, that they respect what the city respects, that they are not subversives, finally, that they are not irresponsible adventurers but good citizens and even the best among the citizens."[16] As noted above, the philosopher's thought does have a certain mania associated with it; it cannot be satisfied with the "paltry," the "ephemeral," and the "sectarian." Yet the philosopher's public speech must reflect the virtue of prudence. For Strauss it is necessary to treat politics philosophically and philosophy politically. Philosophy necessarily challenges the core beliefs that make civil society possible. The philosopher must behave prudently if he or she is not to undermine the political order necessary for the philosophic life.

Because philosophy is subversive, good philosophical writing

15. Cited in Stanley Rosen, "Leo Strauss and the Quarrel between the Ancients and the Moderns," in *Leo Strauss's Thought*, ed. Alan Udoff (Boulder, CO: Lynne Rienner, 1991), p. 160.
16. Cited in ibid., p. 161.

will talk to some readers and be silent to others. A cautious writer would avoid mention of everything that would "displace the veil beneath which the respectable part of society dissembles its divisions."[17] Strauss had a definite method of inquiry in the study of political philosophy texts, and it reflected his common sense and probity. Herbert Storing once described it well, as follows:

> Strauss was not a methodologist, but he had a method. He sometimes described it as "content analysis." It is the method of careful reading. Assume that your writer may be telling the truth. Assume that he knows what he is doing. Read with the greatest of care and alertness that you can muster. If your writer falls into a contradiction that you can see, assume that he could see it and try to figure out his reason for arguing as he did. Remember (what we all know) that one does not say all one has to say to everyone, that for various reasons one may speak and write at different levels.[18]

Strauss relates this method to his own understanding of the vocation of the political philosopher when he states, "It cannot be the duty of a genuinely just man like Socrates to drive weaker men to despair of some order and decency in human affairs, and least of all those . . . who may have some public responsibility."[19] One should write and speak at different levels so that the "vulgar" can be enlisted in a good cause or at least prevented from jeopardizing the achievement of the highest good—the quest for knowledge. The wise can abide the truth, but must be required to read between the lines. Though philosophers must be prudent, their vocation as philosophers is primarily transpolitical, transreligious, and transmoral. There remains a radical and permanent tension or disproportion between the requirements of philosophy and the requirements of society.[20]

Strauss rediscovered the principles of "secret writing" as a result of his careful textual analyses of such classical political philosophers as Plato and such medieval rationalists as Farabi, a ninth-century Islamic philosopher. According to Farabi, secret writing

17. Leo Strauss, *Natural Right and History* (Chicago: University of Chicago Press, 1953), p. 206.
18. Herbert Storing, "The Achievement of Leo Strauss," *National Review* 25 (1973):1349.
19. Leo Strauss, *Persecution and the Art of Writing* (Glencoe, IL: Free Press, 1952), p. 177.
20. Leo Strauss and Alexandre Kojève, *On Tyranny* (Ithaca, NY: Cornell University Press, 1968), p. 26.

arose out of the philosopher's desire to avoid sharp confrontations between philosophical truth and received opinion such as resulted in the death of Socrates and the scandal of public opinion at Socrates' teaching. For Farabi and Strauss, Socrates' experience is typical of that of every truthful person who speaks too openly.

Strauss's revitalization of the study of premodern classical and medieval rationalism was also precipitated by the grave crises within Western civilization in which mere wishes and prejudices have usurped the place of reason. Strauss indicated that he considered classical political philosophy—the thought of Plato and Aristotle— to be true. Much of his later writings would seek to defend this claim by making accessible to others the self-understanding of Plato and Aristotle.

These ancients took their bearings from the naturally best regime; and since they held that what most determines the character of political life is the class of human beings that makes the laws, the matter of the best regime comes down to the question of who should rule. For the classical political philosopher, the highest title to rule was based on human excellence. Aristocracy—the rule of the best—was, in principle, the best political order. Strauss, in a letter to Karl Löwith, wrote concerning ancient wisdom:

> I really believe . . . that the perfect political order, as Plato and Aristotle have sketched it, *is* the perfect political order. Or do you believe in the world-state? If it is true that genuine unity is only possible through knowledge of the truth or through the search for the truth, then there is a genuine unity of all men only on the basis of the popularized final *teaching* of philosophy (and naturally this does not exist) or if all men are philosophers (not Ph.D.'s, etc.)—which likewise is not the case. Therefore, there can only be closed societies, that is, states. But if that is so, then one can show from political considerations that the small city-state is in principle superior to the large state or to the territorial-feudal state. I know very well that it cannot be restored; but the famous atomic bombs—not to mention at all cities with a million inhabitants, gadgets, funeral homes, "ideologies"—shows that the contemporary solution, that is, the completely modern solution is *contra naturam*.[21]

Nonetheless, Strauss does agree with Aristotle's distinction between the feasible, or legitimate, regime and the best regime, given the

21. Letter to Karl Löwith, 15 August 1946, "Correspondence concerning Modernity: Karl Löwith and Leo Strauss," *Independent Journal of Philosophy* 4 (1983):107–8.

heterogeneity of political communities, traditions, and circumstances.

BETWEEN ATHENS AND JERUSALEM

Strauss states that many Jews have traditionally been attracted toward Athens, which is to say, philosophical wisdom. Others have "returned" to Judaism. However, the claims to wisdom made by Athens and Jerusalem are mutually exclusive. As Strauss observes,

> We see at once that each of the two claims to be true wisdom, thus denying to the other its claim to be wisdom in the strict and highest sense. According to the Bible, the beginning of wisdom is fear of the Lord; according to the Greek philosophers, the beginning of wisdom is wonder. We are thus compelled from the very beginning to make a choice, to take a stand.[22]

In the face of their mutual exclusivity, the sensible thing to do, it would appear, would be to postpone a choice until arguments advanced for each side were listened to. By the very act of listening to each side prior to deciding, however, "we have already decided in favor of Athens against Jerusalem." To engage in philosophic wondering is to question the very authenticity of revelation.

In his careful manner, Strauss also presented his view that neither philosophy nor revealed religion have refuted one another: "The Bible refuses to be integrated into a philosophical framework, just as philosophy refuses to be integrated into biblical dogma."[23] In other words, they disagree about the very basis of refutation: the principles or criteria of proof. Religion has not refuted philosophy, for all alleged refutations of philosophy already presuppose faith in revelation, that is, faith in accounts of what God promised and has done. Religion refuses to accept the refutations of those sources that contain the revelation of God, because religion refuses to accept the tribunal of human reason as an acceptable basis for the justification of prophetic faith. Therefore, it is necessary for philosophy to grant the possibility that wisdom is to be found in Jerusalem.

22. Leo Strauss, "Jerusalem and Athens: Some Preliminary Reflections," in *Studies in Platonic Political Philosophy* (Chicago: University of Chicago Press, 1983), p. 149.
23. *Ibid.*

But to grant that revelation is possible means to grant that the philosophic account and the philosophic way of life are not necessarily, not evidently the true account and the right way of life: philosophy, the quest for evident and necessary knowledge, rests itself on an unevident decision, on an act of the will, just as faith does. Hence the antagonism between Spinoza and Judaism, between belief and unbelief, is ultimately not theoretical but moral.[24]

Strauss insisted that, because there is no third or higher standpoint, no one can be both a philosopher and a theologian or a third that is beyond the conflict between philosophy and theology or a synthesis of both. He opposed Christian attempts to create a synthesis of Greek philosophy and biblical faith that only corrupted both. Strauss seems to have decided that for himself the philosophic life—the pursuit of the good of the intellect—was more virtuous than a life of faith entailing ritual and simple moral action. Strauss had chosen, by an act of his will, not to have faith in any doctrine, opinion, or any of the conflicting traditions of divine revelation, but to pursue a quest for wisdom by means of his own unaided reason. He seems to make this choice even though he realized it is virtually impossible for human beings to become genuinely wise, for this would require the success of the philosophic system whereby the merely given world is replaced by man as its theoretical and practical master.[25] This success is not possible because it would require that humans become genuinely divine. Yet, as we shall see, Strauss as a *political* philosopher and a Jew was concerned with both ways of life: that of reason and that of faith.

Strauss did provide some solace to those facing this "irresolvable antagonism" between philosophy and revelation when he stated that "the core, the nerve of Western intellectual history, Western spiritual history, one could almost say, is the conflict between the Biblical and philosophical notions of the good life."[26] It seemed to Strauss "that this unresolved conflict is the secret vitality of Western civilization."[27] We should live the life of this fundamental tension, and we ought to be either "the philosopher open to the challenge

24. Leo Strauss, "Preface to the English Translation" (commonly known as "the autobiographical preface"), *Spinoza's Critique of Religion*, tr. Elsa M. Sinclair (New York: Schocken Books, 1965), p. 29.
25. *Ibid.*
26. "Progress or Return?" p. 270.
27. *Ibid.*

of theology or the theologian open to the challenge of philosophy."[28]

Strauss was especially critical of modern dogmatic atheism, which he considered to be unreasoned unbelief totally lacking in sobriety. He finds Maimonides more profound than Spinoza. Modern dogmatic atheism cannot be truly philosophical because the philosopher must be sober in deed in order to be liberated in thought. Modern unbelief fails to recognize that philosophy can be pursued only by the *aristoi* and that sobriety requires that the contradictory religious opinions of the vulgar must not be destroyed. The modern unbelief effected by Hobbes, Machiavelli, and Spinoza led to "the epoch making change" of "political atheism." Such political atheists have "grown active, designing, turbulent and seditious."[29] Premodern atheists never "doubted that social life required belief in, and worship of God, or gods."[30] According to Strauss, modern unbelief—by undermining those comforting "religious delusions"—leads to the recognition that human beings can become "the master and owner of nature. But this whole enterprise requires, above all, political action, revolution, a life and death struggle."[31]

> For the understanding of that antagonism [between belief and unbelief] the Jewish designation of the unbeliever as Epicurean seemed to be helpful, especially since from every point of view Epicureanism may be said to be the classic form of critique of religion. . . . Epicureanism is hedonism, and traditional Judaism always suspects that all theoretical and practical revolts against the Torah are inspired by the desire to throw off the yoke of the stern and exacting duties so that one can indulge in a life of pleasure. Epicureanism can lead only to a mercenary morality whereas traditional Jewish morality is not mercenary. . . . Epicureanism is so radically mercenary that it conceives of its theoretical doctrines as the means for liberating the mind from the terrors of religious fear, of the fear of death, and of natural necessity. Characteristically, modern unbelief is no longer Epicurean. It is no longer cautious or retiring, not to say cowardly, but bold and active. Whereas Epicureanism fights the religious "delusion" because of its terrible character, modern unbelief fights it because it is a delusion.[32]

28. *Ibid.*
29. *Natural Right and History*, p. 196.
30. *Ibid.*, p. 169.
31. "Preface to the English Translation," p. 29.
32. *Ibid.*

The philosophic enterprise, as Strauss teaches, requires temperance. Strauss claimed that one cannot hoot with owls at night and still soar with the eagles in the morning, one cannot be drunk all the time and still think well, and one cannot boldly advocate atheism and expect to engage in the philosophic quest in a decent society. The philosopher's knowledge of the legitimate claims of "unwisdom" precluded all pretension to omnicompetence. For Strauss, wisdom cannot "be divorced from moderation or to the sacrifices which we must make so that our minds may be free."[33]

Strauss's pursuit of the philosophic enterprise included a Judaic dimension and a kind of "openness" to revelation in the Torah. Judaism has always been more attuned to the things of this world, to "worldly" wisdom, than Christianity. Strauss, throughout his career, emphasized the significance of the wisdom found in the Mosaic law with its concerns for family life and public duty—the kind of concerns that are fundamental to political philosophy. This is demonstrated by how he cherished Deuteronomy 4:6: "Keep therefore and do [these statutes and judgments]; for this is your wisdom and understanding in the sight of the nations, which shall hear all these statutes and say, Surely this great nation is a wise and understanding people." Furthermore, it was Strauss's Jewishness, open to the Jewish tradition of revelation, that gave his political teachings and his understanding of political philosophy a moral earnestness—a dedication to justice and mercy—not readily found in classical political philosophy.[34] Although Strauss was not an observant Jew, he "remained" a Jew.

On 4 February 1962 he gave a lecture on "Why We Remain Jews: Can Jewish Faith and History Still Speak to Us?" at the Hillel Foundation of the University of Chicago. His lecture is published for the first time in this volume. Strauss's answer to the question was an ambiguous yes. In his prefatory remarks, Strauss made it quite clear that his lecture was to be grounded in "social science [or political philosophy] rather than divinity." Notwithstanding these initial remarks, he did take the opportunity to discuss movingly the "substance" of the Jewish faith and its contribution to Western

33. Leo Strauss, *The Political Philosophy of Hobbes* (Chicago: University of Chicago Press, 1952), p. xvii.
34. For a more extensive discussion of Strauss's "Jewishness," see the following essays by George Anastaplo, "The Challenge of Leo Strauss," unpublished essay; and "On Leo Strauss: A Yahrzeit Remembrance," *University of Chicago Magazine* 67 (Winter 1974): 30–38.

civilization, as well as the theologico-political predicament of Jewish survival in the context of both Zionism and modernity. With considerable public candor, he actually presented an example of how the "truth" that serves the good of the intellect can be harmonious with the salutary "truth" that involves the contribution of Jewish law and moral teaching to our civilization.

Strauss boldly confronted Heinrich Heine's characterization of Judaism as a "misfortune" and, by implication, Heine's suggestion that Jews should abandon their religion and assimilate. Strauss also explored the proffered Zionist and liberal solutions to the Jewish theologico-political predicament.

Strauss argued that assimilation does not completely work: even converts from Judaism, he claimed, are often seen by Gentiles as remaining Jews, remaining distinctive in a manner. Liberal society with its public/private distinction has protected freedom of religious worship while it also has permitted social discrimination against Jews by private organizations. It offers legal equality and private discrimination. Finally, Strauss viewed the political Zionist solution to hatred of Jews to be contrary to the spirit of the Jewish religion and a "radical break with the principles of the Jewish tradition"—which call for trust in God, not in human "hardware." Political Zionism is not enough to sustain the Jewish people. Nor will a return to cultural Zionism, such as folk dances, do what is necessary. A "return" to the Talmud and Midrash provides the "rock bottom" of any Jewish culture. The "substance" of Judaism is divine revelation. Religious Zionism is a better answer to the survival of the Jewish people. If a Jew cannot believe in miracles and all of the "old faith," he or she can still be dedicated to what can be seen as "the noblest of all delusions."

For Strauss, Judaism is not a misfortune, but possibly a "heroic delusion." It is characterized by a "righteousness or charity" that provides "the one thing needful," but that is "not defensible if the world is not the creation of the just and loving God, the holy God." No nobler dream than "the Lord shall be king over all the earth" has ever been dreamt. Such a dream or aspiration involves "the truth of the ultimate mystery." For Strauss, "it is surely nobler to be victim of the most noble dream than to profit from a sordid reality and to wallow in it." Because a Jew who does not believe in miracles can still be dedicated to "the noblest of dreams," Strauss seemed to be claiming that there is a third way of life that can be chosen other than strict philosophy or simple religious orthodoxy.

Emil Fackenheim captures much of Strauss's position in this:

> The fundamental point about Jewish tradition which comes out again and again in . . . meetings I had with him [Strauss], was that Torah is either the Word of God or else it has no essential significance. If the whole tradition was mistaken on this fundamental point, and if Torah is just a part of culture (and maybe a minor part), to treat it as mere culture would revolutionize the whole past. But perhaps the tradition was right? This was the obvious question, but there was also an underlying question: How does one know that to get back to either the Greeks or the Jews, Athens or Jerusalem, is possible? It must be possible because it is necessary! And why is it necessary? Because the shadow of Nazism hung over us all.[35]

Leo Strauss attracted a fairly large number of Roman Catholic students to his classes, including a few priests. To be sure, the Catholic students—along with other Christians—were attracted to his teachings concerning the crisis of modernity, his serious textual analysis, and his genuine openness to and respect for the fundamental alternative of divine revelation. Strauss also praised the survival of philosophy in contemporary Roman Catholic colleges and universities.

Strauss was, nonetheless, ambivalent about the status of philosophy in the Roman Catholic tradition. In *Persecution and the Art of Writing*, Strauss noted that there is a difference in the status of philosophy in Christianity on the one hand and Islam as well as Judaism on the other.

> For the Christian, the sacred doctrine is revealed theology, for the Jew and the Muslim, the sacred is, at least primarily, the legal interpretation of the Divine Law (talmud or fiqh). The sacred doctrine in the latter has, to say the least, much less in common with philosophy than the sacred doctrine in the former sense. It is ultimately for this reason that the status of philosophy was, as a matter of principle, much more precarious in Judaism and in Islam than in Christianity: in Christianity philosophy became an integral part of officially recognized and even required training of the student of the sacred doctrine.[36]

The negative effect of this "official recognition" of philosophy in the Christian world has been that it became subject to ecclesiastical supervision, which ultimately produced bureaucratic restraints

35. Fackenheim, "Strauss and Modern Judaism," p. 22.
36. *Persecution and the Art of Writing*, p. 19.

over philosophy. Furthermore, Strauss appeared to think Christian medieval philosophy played a part in the change that occurred in the character of philosophy in the passage from ancient to modern rationalism. Strauss wrote that "philosophy was certainly in the Christian Middle Ages deprived of its character as a way of life."[37] Strauss seems to have thought that "Christian philosophy" insisted too much on completeness and, in effect, on removing the mystery that both biblical religion and the best of ancient philosophy acknowledged at the ultimate horizon.

While many in the Catholic tradition celebrate the achievement of Thomas Aquinas in terms of a synthesis of faith and reason, Strauss questioned the possibility of such a synthesis. Strauss appeared reluctant to accept the view that revelation need not contradict reason. He also stated that "in Thomas . . . philosophy is divorced from the conviction [of the classics] that happiness can be achieved only by, or essentially consists in, philosophy."[38] Strauss's view of Thomas has a positive side: "Thomas studied the teachings of his predecessors with an exclusive regard to their truth or falsehood, . . . for Thomas, only argument and not 'history' could legitimately decide the fate of any philosophic thesis."[39] The Roman Catholic reaction to Strauss ranges from Frederick D. Wilhelmsen's distancing characterization of Strauss as a "Hellenized Jew"[40] to Ernest Fortin's accommodating portrait of Strauss's teachings, which he considers to be "close to, if not actually identical with, those of any number of orthodox theologians, beginning with Thomas Aquinas, who insists that un-aided human reason is powerless to establish the possibility, let alone the truth of divine revelation."[41] Likewise, non-Catholics have also proffered dramatically opposed views of what Strauss meant by "living" the tension between religion and reason, ranging from Stanley Rosen's view "that Strauss's own respect for and attention to the detailed statements on behalf of revealed religion were primarily intended as extensions of his own elusive propaganda for philosophy, or what

37. Leo Strauss, "The Mutual Influence of Theology and Philosophy," *Independent Journal of Philosophy* 3(1979):113. See also "Letter to Karl Löwith," p. 106.
38. *What Is Political Philosophy?* p. 286.
39. *Ibid.*
40. Frederick Wilhelmsen, *Christianity and Political Philosophy* (Athens: University of Georgia Press, 1978), chap. 8.
41. Ernest Fortin, "Dead Masters and Their Living Thought: Leo Strauss and His Friendly Critics," *Vital Nexus* 1 (May 1990): 68.

he would have preferred to call his philosophical rhetoric" to Harry Jaffa's view of Strauss's basic teaching as being that, even though reason and revelation were in theoretical disagreement as to the end or ends served by the moral virtues, they "had agreed substantially on what in practice morality was."[42] Such commentaries may lead the reader to the many significant passages in Strauss's texts, and thereby he or she may be induced to think more profoundly about the fundamental alternative of faith and reason.

THE CRISIS OF LIBERAL DEMOCRACY

Strauss was quite ambivalent about liberal democracy and the American regime. As a political philosopher in the classical sense, Strauss could appreciate American liberal democracy as a decent but flawed regime (perhaps even the best available regime, given present conditions), yet he could not suspend criticism of its weaknesses. His judgments were governed by the notion of "essential differences," which claims "that the whole consists of heterogeneous beings; that there is a noetic heterogeneity of beings, this common sensible notion on which we fall back all the time, and this has in no way been refuted [by evolutionism]."[43] This understanding of the character of the whole provides support for the apparent natural inequality of human beings, especially in terms of intellectual capabilities, and for judgments on a spectrum of the naturally high and intrinsically low. Strauss, then—given his aristocratic perspective—could offer only qualified praise of American liberal democracy. Such principles of the Declaration of Independence as natural political equality, individual rights on a universal scale, the pursuit of idiosyncratic happiness, and the use of political institutions rather than character development to promote political success could only be viewed as problematical by him.[44] Although he provides an edifying reference to the Declaration of Independence in *Natural Right and History*, his position on American liberal

42. Rosen, *Hermeneutics as Politics*, p. 112; and Harry Jaffa, "Leo Strauss, the Bible, and Political Philosophy," in this volume.
43. Leo Strauss, "The Crisis of Political Philosophy," in *The Predicament of Modern Politics*, ed. Harry J. Spaeth (Detroit: University of Detroit Press, 1964), pp. 92–93.
44. John Agresto, "Leo Strauss and the Resurgence of American Conservatism," paper delivered at the American Political Science Association Meeting, Chicago, 1983, p. 10.

democracy is best characterized as "friendly" criticism. As friendly critic, he recognized that "liberal or constitutional democracy comes closer to what the classics demanded than any other alternative that is viable in our age."[45] Supporting liberal or constitutional democracy was seen to require an understanding of the Founders' natural rights principles, which served as the foundation for a regime that did not leave exclusively to the courts and legislatures the determination of what is right or just.[46]

Leo Strauss considered liberal democracy to be in "crisis" and the American regime to be an endangered one. Liberal democracies displayed an inner loss of purpose and a diminished conviction that there exists certain moral obligations binding on all who are committed to the survival of a free society.[47] He was especially concerned that contemporary liberal democracies have not sufficiently recognized the dependence of private freedom in a limited state on the virtues the public (or the voter) must exercise to remain free from oppression.

Although Strauss was convinced that human beings will never create a society free of contradictions, he noted rather pointedly serious "contradictions" in contemporary liberal democracy with regard to the qualities of the citizen and voter.

> Liberal democracy claims to be responsible government, a political order in which the government is responsible to the governed. . . . [I]n order to be responsible, the government must have no secrets from the governed. Of course, liberal democracy also means limited government, the distinction between the public and the private. Not only must the private sphere be protected by the law, but it must also be understood to be impervious to the law. . . . The true place of secrecy is not the home but the voting booth. We can say the voting booth is the home of homes, the seat of sovereignty, the seat of secrecy. The sovereign consists of individuals who are in no way responsible, who can in no way be held responsible: the irresponsible individual. This was not simply the original notion of liberal democracy. The original notion was that this sovereign individual was a conscientious individual, the individual limited and guided by his conscience.
>   . . . You cannot limit voting rights to conscientious people as you limit voting rights by property qualifications, literacy tests and the

45. *What Is Political Philosophy?* p. 113.
46. *Natural Right and History*, pp. 1–2.
47. For a fuller discussion of the "crisis of liberal democracy" in Strauss's thought, see Deutsch and Soffer, *Crisis*, pp. 1–4.

like. Conscientiousness can only be fostered by non-legal means, by moral education. For this no proper provision is made, and the change in this respect is well known to all. This change which has taken place, is still taking place, may be called the decline of liberal democracy into permissive egalitarianism. Whereas the core of liberal democracy is the conscientious individual, the core of permissive egalitarianism is the individual with his urges. . . . The man who wants to indulge his urges does not have the slightest intention to *sacrifice* his life and hence also his urges. . . . This is the moral decline which has taken place.[48]

What predominates today with liberal democracies is the lack of a philosophical grounding or justification of the central principles of this type of regime. As Strauss stated, "The crisis of liberalism [is] a crisis due to the fact that liberalism has abandoned its absolutist basis and is trying to become entirely relativistic."[49] The one thing needful in contemporary liberal democracies is a viable notion of natural right. In the absence of a concept of natural right, the alternative confronting liberal democracy is nihilism.

The problem posed by the conflicting needs of society cannot be solved if we do not possess knowledge of natural right. . . . If our principles have no other support than our blind preferences, everything a man is willing to dare will be permissible. The contemporary rejection of natural right leads to nihilism—nay, it is identical with nihilism.[50]

In the face of such nihilism as well as the rise of totalitarianism in this century, Strauss was moved to consider a reexamination of the principles of classical natural right and premodern Arabic and Jewish rationalism. The modern notions of nature and freedom have to be reexamined in light of the ancient classical dependence of morality on purposive nature. The exaltation of human creativity along with the concomitant despair of finding a rational source of ends to guide that creativity is the "deepest" reason for the crisis of liberal democracy. A "return" to ancient philosophy is not a nostalgic return to Athens. Rather, it is a contemporary reflection on the fundamental alternative of ancient and modern natural

48. Leo Strauss, "Political Philosophy and the Crisis of Our Time," in *The Post-behavioral Era*, eds. George Graham and George Carey (New York: David McKay, 1972), pp. 222–23 (emphasis added).
49. Leo Strauss, "Relativism," in *Relativism and the Study of Man*, eds. Helmut Schoeck and James Wiggins (Princeton, NJ: Van Nostrand, 1961), p. 140.
50. *Natural Right and History*, pp. 2–3 and 4–5.

right in the context of the contemporary crisis of liberal democratic regimes. It is required by the present crisis since the progression in the history of the West from nature to reason to history to will as the standard of thinking and acting has produced an intellectual and moral vacuum. Emblematic of this crisis is the contemporary liberal democrat's view of tolerance. According to Strauss, the contemporary liberal appears to believe that the human failure to secure genuine knowledge of what is intrinsically good or right obligates us to be tolerant of every opinion about good or right or to accept all preferences or all civilizations as equally respectable.

Politics concerns human decisions about courses of action. Since politics is ever called to resolve competing claims regarding the right or best course of action, it "must be guided by some thought of better or worse." Strauss was quite concerned about the capacity of contemporary American liberal democrats to think in terms of better or worse, and his ambivalence on liberal democracy came to the fore when he stated:

> We are not permitted to be flatterers of democracy precisely because we are friends and allies of democracy. While we are not permitted to remain silent on the dangers to which democracy exposes itself as well as human excellence, we cannot forget the obvious fact that by giving freedom to all, democracy gives freedom to those who care for human excellence.[51]

THE INSOUCIANT WORLD OF POLITICAL SCIENCE

Strauss claimed that contemporary political scientists were fiddling while Rome (liberal democracy) was burning. Political scientists have failed to develop standards of political morality by which to judge and influence actions that affect the character and preservation of the regime itself. The moral neutrality of contemporary political science has concealed the fact that the ever-present experience of politics at all times and places is an experience involved with unavoidable moral discriminations and judgments. Strauss sought to demonstrate to contemporary political scientists that they were faced with a dilemma. While most of them remain liberal democrats, they do so despite the apparent inconsistency between their alleged value neutrality and their liberal democratic convictions. As Strauss puts it, the fact/value distinction implies "that

51. *Liberalism, Ancient and Modern*, p. 24.

before the tribunal of reason all values are equal." Most contemporary liberal political scientists assume that "the rational society will be egalitarian, or democratic and permissive or liberal: the rational doctrine regarding the difference between facts and values rationally justifies the preference for liberal democracy—contrary to what is indicated by the distinction itself."[52] Political scientists, actually, have no criterion for distinguishing specious from authentic claims upon sympathy in liberal democratic society, because the fact/value distinction subjects them to the kind of moral suasion that becomes little more than manipulative appeals to sympathetic emotions. Contemporary political science contributes to the fecklessness of American public life. What is lost is the appreciation that any political order must establish a hierarchy of values which represses some values so that others may flourish.

Strauss concluded that the effect of an ostensibly value-free conception of politics would be to mask the differences of opinion from which controversy arose, and thus to attempt to neutralize politics or to create the "neutral" liberal state. Strauss was particularly critical of the term *life-style* as it was linked to the neutral state because this bespeaks a "value-free" politics that denies the human being's political nature, namely, the human need for community and the concomitant need for a hierarchy of values. By denying the distinction between the naturally high and the intrinsically low, contemporary liberal political scientists, argues Strauss, have unwittingly contributed to the victory of the low and its attendant "life-styles" along with the formation of a nonconscientious electorate and an irresponsible government.

For Strauss, political science as well as all the disciplines of the academy, insofar as they would be philosophical, tend to be disabled and rendered incoherent at their foundation by a historicism that dogmatically cuts off access to universal truth and confines inquiry in all forms to the limits of the given "culture" or a *geist.* Strauss did not overlook the evidence for the historical conditioning of the political teaching of political philosophers but protested against the pervasive and gratuitous assumption that "the relation between doctrines and their 'times' is wholly unambiguous." Strauss added on this occasion, "The obvious possibility is overlooked that the situation to which one particular doctrine is related,

---

52. Leo Strauss, "An Epilogue," in *Essays on the Scientific Study of Politics,* ed. Herbert Storing (New York: Holt, Rinehart, and Winston, 1962), p. 324.

is particularly favorable to the discovery of the truth, whereas all other situations may be more or less unfavorable."[53] Joseph Cropsey—who collaborated with Strauss on the important collection *History of Political Philosophy*—drew out the implications of an interpretation of history that denies the philosophic character of the history of political philosophy, and observed that such an interpretation "leads away from philosophy of history altogether, thus depriving the history as such of a peculiar philosophic gravity."[54]

Strauss's most stinging charge against contemporary political science was his claim that "it rests on dogmatic atheism."[55] He expressed his sharp criticism as follows:

> The new science rests on dogmatic atheism which presents itself as merely methodological or hypothetical. For a few years, logical positivism tried with much noise and little thought to dispose of religion by asserting that religious assertions are "meaningless statements." This trick seems to have been abandoned without noise. Some of the adherents of the new political science might rejoin with some liveliness that their posture toward religion is imposed on them by intellectual honesty: not being able to believe, they cannot accept belief as the basis of their science. . . . Yet just as our opponents refuse respect to unreasoned belief, we on our part, with at least equal right, might refuse respect to unreasoned unbelief; honesty with oneself regarding one's unbelief is in itself not more than unreasoned unbelief, probably accompanied by a vague confidence that the issue of unbelief versus belief has long since been settled once and for all. It is hardly necessary to add that the dogmatic exclusion of religious awareness proper renders questionable all long-range predictions concerning the future of societies.[56]

Contemporary political scientists such as John Schaar and Sheldon Wolin were strongly stung by Strauss's criticism. They argued that Strauss was in no position to demonstrate the actual connection between a political scientist's religious beliefs and his work as a political scientist. "On what basis, then, can Professor Strauss confidently assert the dogmatic atheism which underlies the new science. What is the relevance or the propriety of such a charge in a work which presents itself as an academic and professional

53. *What Is Political Philosophy?* p. 64.
54. "Leo Strauss," *PS* (Winter 1974): 79. See Leo Strauss and Joseph Cropsey, *History of Political Philosophy*, now in its 3rd edition (Chicago: University of Chicago Press, 1963, 1972, and 1987).
55. *Liberalism, Ancient and Modern*, p. 218.
56. *Ibid.*, pp. 218–19.

work."[57] Schaar and Wolin have quite simply misread Strauss's criticism. Strauss was calling into question the "dogmatic exclusion" of the possibilities of biblical faith by contemporary political scientists.

Quite clearly, Strauss's teaching represented a deep concern for the health and vitality of American liberal democracy. Relativism, historicism, and dogmatic atheism in the political science profession and elsewhere have contributed to a loss of conviction in the American regime. Though he favored the theoretical politics of the ancients, he was appreciative of the practical wisdom of the American Framers. Perhaps on questions of American practical politics we could term Strauss an "aristocratic liberal"—an advocate of including the aristocratic dimension respecting human excellence within modern liberal democracy. His hopes for the stability and durability of American liberal democracy were founded on the development and recognition of prudent statesmen—an endeavor to be supported by liberal education.

EDUCATION: THE PRACTICAL CENTER OF STRAUSS'S TEACHING

What Strauss had found in premodern rationalism was not philosophy as a doctrine, understood as one or another school's compendium of answers; nor was it, to be sure, a definitive understanding of the whole. It was primarily philosophy as a way of life, and this way was defined—later one might say it was exemplified—by Socrates. The primary experiences, the key questions, and the ultimate openness that characterize this Socratic way of life appeared to shape both Strauss's practice and theory of education.

Not surprisingly, given the Socratic model, Strauss acted and wrote as if his task as teacher or educator was the central activity of his vocation.[58] His research, whether into medieval or ancient thought, was given focus and meaning by his concern with the modern context that he saw enveloping himself as well as his listeners and readers. That focus, constantly in evidence through-

57. John H. Schaar and Sheldon S. Wolin, "Review Essay," *American Political Science Review* 57 (March 1963): 128.
58. Martin Diamond, "Leo Strauss," *PS* (Winter 1974): 77. For Strauss's interest in students rather than faculty affairs, see Edward C. Banfield, "Leo Strauss," in *Remembering the University of Chicago*, ed. Edward Shils (Chicago: University of Chicago Press, 1991), p. 497.

out his work, was perhaps most memorably formulated in those opening lines to *The City and Man*:

> It is not self-forgetting and pain-loving antiquarianism nor self-for-getting and intoxicating romanticism which induces us to turn with passionate interest, with unqualified willingness to learn, toward the political thought of classical antiquity. We are impelled to do so by the crisis of our time, the crisis of the West.[59]

Yet, Strauss did not see his work as educational primarily because of his apparent reaching out to people where they are, of his being relevant—however much, in practice, he in fact was relevant and insisted on being so. Strauss opened one of his rare direct writings on education with the confession, "I own that education is in a sense the subject matter of my teaching and my research."[60] Strauss's "in a sense" properly alerts the reader to qualifications of the statement that begin to unfold in the very next sentence and that differentiate what Strauss has done on education from most writing and talks about education. In that next sentence Strauss reports that he has given "very little" attention to the "conditions" and "how" of education. Instead, he was "almost solely concerned with the goal or end of education at its best or highest—of the education of the perfect prince as it were." In light of the promi-nent positioning and unambiguity of this statement, it is reasonable to conclude that whatever might be gleaned from Strauss's words about the conditions and means of education is not at the center of his attention and can be presumed to be secondary to and derivative from what he understands about "the goal or end of education at its best or highest." This goal and end of education *at its highest or best* appears to be the philosophical way of life, the Socratic way. And the art of education would appear to be in making practical judgments about the how and when of drawing people toward that peak.

This explanation by Strauss of the way in which education is the subject matter of his teaching and research provides a basis for understanding a dimension of his life as well as the pattern of life for many of his students. The same Strauss who is so centrally concerned with education is notably disinterested in faculty affairs

59. *City and Man*, p. 1.
60. "Liberal Education and Responsibility," in *Liberalism, Ancient and Mod-ern*, p. 9.

and the ordinary politics of the university; he held no administrative positions and appeared not to aspire to the conventional leadership positions in higher education. He could hardly be said to have imparted to his students the "highly professional orientation" that characterizes many prominent scholars' formation of their graduate students. He did orient them to a love of wisdom, to a life of teaching and learning rather than to a mere career. His students—both direct and indirect, and however academically outstanding—learn the lessons of professionalization slowly and painfully in most cases. No doubt, this has something to do not only with what Strauss emphasized, but also with the kind of people he attracted.

Strauss's self-confessed focus on the human peak as his way of discoursing on education appears to be the same perspective from which he considers politics. Is it possibly the case that "education," as Strauss's subject matter *in a sense*, is taken to encompass politics? However, if we approach the topic of education in its more usual and constricted sense, we find all the large themes of Strauss's thought appearing in important ways in what he says about it. In other words, Strauss's consideration of education cannot be isolated from, and opens to, his positions on the philosopher and the city, the philosopher and the person of religious faith, the crisis of liberal democracy, and the limitations of modern science. Nowhere in Strauss's statements directly on education are certain of his larger themes more evident than in what he says about liberal education.

Liberal education was the chief topic whenever Strauss spoke or wrote directly about education; that is sufficiently evident in the title of each of his published works on education.[61] That this was his central topic in considering education is not at all surprising, for it is a favorite theme in higher education and especially so

61. Prior to the appearance of "Liberal Education and Responsibility," cited in footnote 60 and originally delivered as an address in 1960, Strauss had prepared and delivered a 1959 commencement address under the title "What Is Liberal Education?" This essay is published as the first selection and immediately preceding "Liberal Education and Responsibility" in *Liberalism, Ancient and Modern*. Both of these essays were initially published in 1961 and 1962, some years before their appearance in *Liberalism, Ancient and Modern*. In 1967 Strauss prepared a single essay from substantial portions of the two earlier addresses and published it under the title "Liberal Education and Mass Democracy," in *Higher Education and Modern Democracy*, ed. Robert A. Goldwin (Chicago: Rand McNally, 1967), pp. 73–96.

around the University of Chicago. Whatever conventional expectations might have contributed to his taking up the topic of liberal education, Strauss probably regarded it as a useful point of entrée, if not leverage, in discourse with the contemporary world. He once wrote that "especially in the expression 'liberal education,' " the term *liberal* continues to be used "in its premodern sense."[62] Thus "liberal education is not the opposite of conservative education, but of illiberal education." He seemed to relish bringing to attention the classical roots of the concept, doing so with precision uncharacteristic of most discussions of liberal education in higher education.

In the language of freedom, Strauss spoke of liberal education as "liberation from vulgarity," recalling on this occasion the beautiful Greek work for vulgarity, *apeirokalia*, and its literal meaning of "lack of experience in things beautiful."[63] The idea of freedom that originally informed the concept of liberal education was traced by Strauss to a context of slavery where the slave, in contrast with the free man or master, "has in a sense no life of his own: he has no time for himself."[64] Strauss at once acknowledged that this notion of freedom implies release not simply from the formal state of slavery, but even from those states of enslavement to work which are sometimes necessitated for the poor and sometimes chosen by the well-to-do in their pursuit of wealth. Liberation from vulgarity is connected then with a certain leisure; it appears that both the process of such liberation or liberal education, and the end of the process in the practices of a free way of life, require leisure.

Such practices are implied in the affirming language Strauss uses at times to discuss the goal of liberal education. Liberal education is not simply a release or "freedom-from" or mastery for its own sake. Rather, Strauss writes of liberal education as "supplying us with experience in things beautiful," as being "education in and toward culture"—which means "the cultivation of the mind," which in turn is associated with the fullness of virtue, including the practice of the virtue of liberality.[65] The practices of human virtue require the freedom—hence the leisure—for politics and philosophy.[66] Understanding this positive conception of liberal

62. *Liberalism, Ancient and Modern*, p. vii.
63. "What Is Liberal Education?" p. 8.
64. "Liberal Education and Responsibility," p. 10.
65. "What Is Liberal Education?" pp. 8 and 3; *Liberalism, Ancient and Modern*, p. vii.
66. "Liberal Education and Responsibility," p. 10.

education allows one to appreciate the meaning of Strauss's provocative and memorable observation that "liberal education is the necessary endeavor to found an aristocracy within democratic mass society."[67]

For Strauss, liberal education—considered as an "endeavor," as movement "toward culture"—has a dynamic and open-ended dimension. It does not appear to be citizen education as often understood, that is, education that takes its bearings from the conventions and widely evident needs of the city; if it can be called "citizen education," it is more reflective and restless than the common form. It is more questioning and less trusting. Even less trusting is the philosophical life that represents the peak toward which liberal education tends. Thus, liberal education is presented as mediating between the citizen's horizon and that of the philosopher. Liberal education proceeds from the common or citizen horizon; it seems, then, that liberal education would consist largely in thinking about the basic questions of moral and political philosophy—such as, what is just? what is honorable? what is the best constitution? The liberally educated person—the classical "gentleman," in Strauss's terms—is not necessarily and not yet the philosopher. The philosopher's life is formed by the "*quest* for the truth about the most weighty matters or for the comprehensive truth."[68] The fully cultured human being is the end of philosophy—the perfected philosopher. Liberal education, in moving toward culture, is on the same line or quest toward the goal of philosophy, but appears to reach a viable terminus at some point—variable according to each individual—along this continuum toward full culture or wisdom.

At the other side of the continuum on which liberal education stands as preparation for philosophy, Strauss places an initial education dominated by the poets and religious education. The former is explicitly presented as preparation for liberal education and as consisting "above all in the formation of character and taste."[69] Religious education, as understood by Strauss, seems also formative of qualities of character potentially helpful to liberal education as well as useful for an orderly society. Strauss understood religious education to be "based on the Bible," and to effect

67. "What Is Liberal Education?" p. 5.
68. "Liberal Education and Responsibility," p. 13, emphasis added.
69. *Ibid.*, p. 11.

the result that people saw themselves as "responsible" for their actions and thoughts to a God Who would judge them.[70] Strauss in fact once analyzed the crisis of modern democracy as "caused by the decay of religious education of the people and by the decay of liberal education of the representatives of the people."[71] He thought it mistaken to look primarily to liberal education for the character formation that liberal education largely presumed and that religious education had traditionally provided. Liberal education and religious education were both seen as necessary to improving the modern situation, but they needed to be properly distinguished and employed. To do so would be to recognize a tension between them, not unlike the tension that must exist between a character formation wrought chiefly by the poets and liberal education. Strauss describes the tension between religious education and liberal education as a "fruitful and ennobling" one.[72]

Does Strauss's aligning of religious education with education by the poets, and his seeing both in tension with and propaedeutic to liberal education and potentially the philosophical life, mean that he disparages religion? That he regards it merely as popular myth, a necessary "opium of the people"? First, it might be said that a part of what Strauss's analysis reveals—namely, the once effective and still potentially effective power of religious education for character formation on a widespread scale—can in every way be accepted by a religious believer. Need it be said that the psychological appeal or suitability of a religious explanation, or the effectiveness of a religious sanction, is hardly evidence of the essential falsehood of a religious understanding of the whole and might reasonably be taken as a consideration toward establishing its truth. Second, however, the framework in which Strauss discusses religious education is decisively that of philosophy. Though there is no disparagement or, to be sure, ridicule of the ultimate ground of religious education by Strauss—in fact, religious education is an ingredient in a "fruitful and ennobling" tension—Strauss views the potential of Jerusalem from the perspective of Athens. Strauss's own ultimate trust and faith is so placed.

Liberal education is then for Strauss both an opening to the life of philosophy and the fullness of virtue as well as the chief means

70. *Ibid.*, pp. 15–16.
71. *Ibid.*, p. 18.
72. *Ibid.*, p. 22.

of securing a genuinely *liberal* democracy. "Liberal education," he writes, "is the ladder by which we try to ascend from mass democracy to democracy as originally meant."[73] Liberal education is a means, however modestly it might necessarily be employed, of conjoining philosophy and power.

Strauss was acutely aware that education—whether character formation or liberal education—was ever subject to and encroached upon by politics and specifically by the now-pervasive kind of politics, those of the modern democratic regime. He thought formation of character likely to be lost as an educational objective amid "instruction and training," and that insofar as such formation was yet intended, "there exists a very dangerous tendency to identify the good man with the good sport . . . an overemphasis on a certain part of social virtue and a corresponding neglect of those virtues which mature, if they do not flourish, in privacy, not to say solitude."[74]

Strauss appeared to balance his great hope for liberal education against his recognition of the uncongenial conditions for its success in colleges and universities of the day. In those places there was too often found not only a dominant mixture of positivism, historicism, and uncritical egalitarianism that militated against serious and patient inquiry into knowable principles for the good life, but also tendencies of the larger mass culture to mass and machinelike education, to "harried labor" rather than the necessary leisure, and to specialization "without spirit or vision" rather than true education of the human soul.[75] In two of Strauss's most eloquent moments, he seems to have revealed what he thought about the conventional contentions and ambitions of higher education. In the last paragraph of his first essay on liberal education, Strauss wrote of liberal education as demanding "from us the complete break with the noise, the rush, the thoughtlessness, the cheapness of the Vanity Fair of the intellectuals as well as their enemies."[76] He concluded his second essay on liberal education with the observation that such education "consists in learning to listen to still and small voices and therefore in becoming deaf to loudspeakers. Liberal education seeks light and therefore shuns the limelight."[77]

73. "What Is Liberal Education?" p. 5.
74. *What Is Political Philosophy?* pp. 37–38.
75. *Ibid.*, p. 234. Also, "What Is Liberal Education?" p. 5.
76. "What Is Liberal Education?" p. 8.
77. "Liberal Education and Responsibility," p. 25.

Just as what precedes says much about the *conditions* for liberal education, Strauss was not without convictions as to the best *methods*. The critical consideration, for Strauss, was the personal qualities of teacher and learner; and where these were of the highest quality, the clear rule was no rule, or no interference with this relationship. In general, Strauss thought liberal education consists "in studying with the proper care the great books which the greatest minds have left behind."[78] Those books are to be studied with full attention to the important differences between great minds; students and teachers are to bring the great minds into dialogue as they think through those differences. Aware that this great-books focus would not always be attainable, Strauss fell back to the "modest, pertinent and practical" course of urging teachers of all subjects to teach with an emphasis and approach that encourages "whatever broadens and deepens the understanding," as opposed to that which at best "cannot as such produce more than narrow and unprincipled efficiency."[79]

Strauss was no overt revolutionary in the world of education, however searing and colorful his language could be in censuring higher education. His devotion to moderation and therefore modest expectations in politics extended to his approach to education. One could fairly substitute "education" for "politics" in his discerning observation that "moderation will protect us against the twin dangers of visionary expectations from politics and unmanly contempt for politics."[80]

There is ample evidence in his statements—not to speak of his way of life—about Strauss's noncontempt for and prudent elevation of education. The great philosophers, he once concluded, saw education as "the only answer to the always pressing question, to the political question par excellence, of how to reconcile order which is not oppression with freedom which is not license."[81] Strauss's hope for liberal democracy was tied to that for the liberal education which that democracy allowed. This appeared to be what he was talking about when he noted that democracy "gives freedom to those who care for human excellence," and added, "No one prevents us from cultivating our garden or from setting up out-

---

78. "What Is Liberal Education?" p. 3.
79. "Liberal Education and Responsibility," p. 19.
80. *Ibid.*, p. 24.
81. *Persecution and the Art of Writing*, p. 37.

posts which may come to be regarded by many citizens as salutary to the republic and as deserving of giving to its tone."[82] This view of liberal education and liberal democracy accords well with Socrates' example of a devotion to the freedom to teach and to persuade that a flawed but corrigible Athens allowed.

Strauss saw in the informing of modern liberal democracy by classical political philosophy the best possible way to establish the kind of public life and liberal education that would permit the unfinished dialogue concerning the fundamental alternatives—that dialogue being philosophy—to survive. Perhaps ancient and modern liberalism could be made to complement each other in theory and practice. Only then, thought Strauss, might those souls who inhabit contemporary liberal democracies yearn for the end of tyranny and the recovery of excellence in human community, instead of the joyless quest for joy.[83]

The Leo Strauss beyond many of the contemporary images and caricatures was extraordinarily fair-minded and magnanimous. Strauss would light up with enthusiasm and appreciation when in some writer whom he might rank low in his comprehensive view there would be found a point of remarkable insight and ingenuity. He was not afraid to leave a seminar with problems that honest inquiry into a text could not resolve.[84] J. Winfree Smith, who knew Strauss at the end of his life, rightly observed of him that "he knew how to present two sides of a general argument in such a way that one could see the strength of the case on each side.[85]

The great legacy of Leo Strauss has been to stir the minds and souls of numerous contemporaries to seek a much richer understanding of the substantive and procedural requisites of living the good life in a liberal democracy.

All the essays in this collection provide, from a variety of perspectives, an opportunity to explore the range and depth of

82. "Liberal Education and Responsibility," p. 24.
83. Kenneth L. Deutsch, "Leo Strauss on Liberal Democracy and Modern Political Science," paper delivered at the Northeastern Political Science Association Meeting, Philadelphia, November 1989.
84. Walter Nicgorski, "Leo Strauss," *Modern Age* 26 (Summer/Fall 1982): 270.
85. J. Winfree Smith, "Leo Strauss," *College* (magazine of St. John's College), 25 (January 1974): 2.

Strauss's mind and the nature of his intellectual odyssey. Those that follow his own lecture bear witness to his extensive and profound impact on students and scholars, and throw light on the most significant controversies concerning his thought and the school to which it has given rise. These essays are best read in aid of studying the writings of Strauss himself. They could not possibly simply reflect the editors' views, for they differ among themselves and thus draw attention not only to key points in exchanges between Strauss's appreciators and critics but also, though less evidently so, to differences in understanding and application of Strauss's teaching among those who have come to look to it for direction and inspiration.

The essays of Steven B. Smith, John G. Gunnell and Hillel Fradkin approach Strauss with a special interest in exploring the role of the "Jewish themes" in his early writings and in understanding the relationship of his thought to Judaism. Smith, in his piece "Leo Strauss: Between Athens and Jerusalem," claims it is arguable that Strauss's interests were not "in Judaism per se but with Judaism insofar as it was an illustration of a more general problem, what he called 'the theological-political' problem." Smith discusses Strauss's view of Judaism as based on the claim that particular providence will always be at odds with the liberal Enlightenment urge to unify all humankind by the overcoming of each particular faith. Smith also explores Strauss's concern that unequivocal support for the liberal state may come at the cost of a loss of Jewish self-identity. Gunnell in "Strauss before Straussianism: Reason, Revelation and Nature" historicizes Strauss in order to recapture his thought before the emergence of "Straussianism." He places Strauss in the historical context of the Weimar conversation in which Strauss is shown to grapple with the crisis of Jewish theology in his exchange with Carl Schmitt on the concept of the political.

Hillel Fradkin considers Strauss's writings on medieval Jewish texts to have remained significant for him throughout his entire career and to constitute an important part of Strauss's legacy. Fradkin understands Strauss's teaching as calling upon students of Western civilization to come to terms with the fact that law presents itself as the framework of the original experience of Western man and may be the key to the revitalization of the West. For Fradkin, Strauss's primary inspiration was not mere historical curiosity, but concern with the contemporary fate of both rationalism and Judaism. Medieval Jewish thought is seen to entail both the most radical examination of the ground of Socratic philosophy and a like radical examination of the alternative provided by the Bible. Fradkin reviews Strauss's encounter with Moses Maimonides, the greatest defender of philosophy in medieval Judaism, and with Judah Halevi, its greatest critic.

Walter Soffer and Susan Shell give sustained and careful attention to Strauss's encounter with Spinoza. Noting that the young Leo Strauss, in the grip of the theologico-political predicament, saw a refutation of Benedict de Spinoza as the prerequisite for a possible return to Jewish orthodoxy that would be consistent with intellectual probity, Soffer presents Strauss's hermeneutics for the reading and rejecting of Spinoza's critique of revealed religion. Soffer examines and tests Spinoza's positive and metaphysical critiques and also discusses Strauss's analysis of the limitations of critiques that approach the possibility of the inscrutable biblical God on the basis of moral experience and the principle of noncontradiction. In an attempt to indicate the direction of Strauss's thought regarding the possibility of a resolution of the conflict between philosophy and theology, Soffer concludes with a discussion of the meaning of Strauss's return to premodern rationalism subsequent to his realizing the self-destructive character of the arguments on behalf of both modern rationalism and religious orthodoxy.

Shell's essay on "Taking Evil Seriously" takes up aspects of Strauss's work on Spinoza as part of an effort to understand Strauss's consideration of Carl Schmitt. Noting that "recent suggestions" that Strauss's attention to Schmitt compromises him intellectually and morally "gain an at least superficial plausibility from the fact that both Strauss and Schmitt criticize liberalism in the name of politics or the political," Shell approaches Strauss's published "Comments on Carl Schmitt's *Concept of the Political*" by tending to Strauss's two chronologically flanking works: *Spinoza's Critique of Religion* and *Philosophy and Law*. The role of Maimonides in the two works is specifically examined; and through Maimonides and Plato, politics or the Law is seen as a guiding theme for philosophy. Schmitt's concept of the political—in contrast with Strauss's "true politics"—is found outside of this tradition. Strauss is shown as seeking to learn from Schmitt in the pursuit "of understanding Hobbes and thereby criticizing liberalism radically."

The seeming conflict of reason and revelation in Strauss is approached from different perspectives in the pieces by Harry V.

Jaffa, Father James V. Schall, and Thomas L. Pangle. Jaffa disclaims Strauss's authority for his reflections on the need for the "continuing dialogue" between Jerusalem and Athens and the "insolubility" of their opposition, while saying that he offers simply what he believes to be true and "what in Strauss's writings has led" him to think as he does. Jaffa argues that it is impossible "to restore the claims" of Socratic political philosophy without restoring those of the Bible, for "Socratic skepticism and biblical faith stand on the same epistemological foundation," that is, "the awareness of ignorance." Jaffa is drawn to comment on how faith and law may operate differently in the Judaic and Christian traditions and how the establishment of Christianity in the fifth century resulted in a "theological despotism" that threatened the "vitality" of the West, depending, as its vitality does, on the free theoretical encounter of Athens and Jerusalem.

In his essay concerning Strauss on St. Thomas, Schall examines Strauss's claim that the higher tensions between Jerusalem and Athens could not be harmoniously mitigated by a third strand: Rome. No such third strand, Strauss apparently thought, could establish their mutual insufficiency or mutual compatibility. Yet, Strauss is seen as admitting that St. Thomas was a philosopher who could bring theology before the court of philosophy. Although Strauss wanted to uphold revelation and not rule it out of consideration, it is not clear why he took the position that, when philosophy demonstrates a claim of revelation not to be "contrary to reason" (the Thomistic proposition), what philosophy learns by this exercise is not, as Strauss held, philosophy. Though St. Thomas may have saved Aristotle for posterity, Strauss persistently excluded any possible "improvement" on Aristotle found in St. Thomas's reflections on theology. Schall also finds in Strauss's thought a rejection of St. Thomas's "natural law" deprivation of a certain "latitude" for statesmen in dealing with morals and politics, and a desire to return to Aristotle's "natural right" position, which gives statesmen the "latitude" to deal with evil without themselves becoming corrupted through their own actions. In this respect, Schall wonders whether "Strauss's dance with Machiavelli . . . is . . . almost too close."

Thomas Pangle, reflecting primarily on the Strauss–Voegelin correspondence that extended over thirty years, notes the significant common ground of the correspondents and explores some important differences that appear to turn on a fundamental divergence concerning the nature of philosophy. Eric Voegelin's understanding of philosophy as a "historical philosophizing" that accounts for the "historically changing in humanity's consciousness" in terms of "faith or faithful intimation through the symbolization of moral-religious experience" is set against Strauss's seeing philosophy—quintessentially present in "Platonic-Socratic-Aristotelian philosophy"—as rigorously seeking science or universal nonhistorical knowledge. Voegelin is further seen by Strauss to obscure the distinction and tension between reason and revelation, which Strauss finds himself understanding in harmony with the Catholic tradition. Voegelin is found, in contrast with Strauss, not to do justice to the experience of doubt as fundamental to human existence and as ever animating philosophy. Strauss is shown conceding that Platonic-Aristotelian science "culminated" in great difficulties related to "the *nous*," and appreciating Edmund Husserl's lead in overcoming these difficulties. Pangle finds Strauss pointing to a dialectical, nonhistorical political philosophy, exemplified in Plato's *Laws*, as an apparent way to "ascend from the quarrel between reason and revelation to its resolution."

In the second part of the collection that follows, the focus of attention shifts to Strauss's project on classical political philosophy, including his effort and methods in distinguishing modernity from the classical tradition, the implications for modern democracy and specifically the American regime, and the major contemporary controversies concerning Strauss's thought and its impact. Nathan Tarcov's "On a Certain Critique of 'Straussianism' " attends in a surprising way to Strauss's self-consciousness of his project in its early stages. Here readers will be exposed to a young reviewer acutely alert to the often alleged flaws of what came to be called "Straussianism."

Stewart Umphrey in "Natural Right and Philosophy" provides a probing commentary on Strauss's influential book *Natural Right and History*. He explores the work through its surface tension between Strauss's apparent defense of natural right and his skepticism about the knowability of natural right. Umphrey suggests that the tension in Strauss is similar to that in Socratic philosophy, which fathered both Stoicism and Academic skepticism. Our inability to resolve the tension, argues Umphrey, cannot be taken as determinative of the incoherence of Strauss's political philosophy.

Dante Germino, in "Blasphemy and Leo Strauss's Machiavelli," claims that Strauss makes "one of the great attempts" at a serious portrayal of Niccolò Machiavelli. Germino takes a critical look at Strauss's view that Machiavelli was a deliberate, covert blasphemer. He offers a very close textual analysis of Strauss's interpretation of *Discourses* I, 26, along with Machiavelli's "Exhortation to Penitence." Germino concludes, against Strauss, that Machiavelli was not guilty of "impious irreverence" but instead explicitly condemned blasphemy. Though Germino views Machiavelli to be in love with the tangible, the concrete, and the comical, he also takes seriously a Machiavelli who could conclude his exhortation by quoting the following lines from Petrarch:

> to repent and to know clearly
> that everything which pleases the world is
> but a brief dream.

Thomas G. West and Christopher Bruell explore how the work of Strauss inspired many of his students to develop "a deepened interest in the American Founding." The precise character of the bearing of Strauss's work on the Founding "is a matter of some ambiguity." West understands Strauss's recovery of classical political philosophy to be a response to the contemporary "crisis of the West." He acknowledges that Strauss never wrote thematically on American democracy, but that he did show qualified confidence in American liberal democracy because it derived some powerful support from the premodern thought of our Western tradition—a tradition teaching that wisdom cannot be separated from moderation and that wisdom requires "unhesitating loyalty to a decent constitution." Yet, West reveals that Strauss did fear the possibility of a new Dark Age in which "politically relevant natural differences" are to be "abolished or neutralized by progressing scientific technology." West concludes that Strauss would not "surrender" to the forces of such a Dark Age.

Christopher Bruell wonders how Strauss's return to classical political philosophy was thought to relate to the American Founding. Though he sees Strauss's project as concerned with helping students of the Founding to take the Founders' claims of universal truth seriously, he cautions that this is not necessarily to say that such claims would ultimately be found valid. Strauss's "return" to classical political philosophy offers a critique of both aristocracy and democracy that is quite severe. Bruell understands Strauss to take the position that it would be "unwise to say farewell to reason" and that the self-destruction of reason may be "the inevitable outcome of modern rationalism."

The essays by David Lewis Schaefer and David Lawrence Levine represent developed responses to the most widely noted critiques of Strauss and "Straussians" in the English-speaking world in the late 1980s, those of Stephen Holmes in the *Times Literary Supplement* and of Gordon Wood and Myles Burnyeat in the *New York Review of Books*. These responses can assist readers in coming to appreciate the actual distance of Strauss's thought from many of the contemporary points at issue and to weigh the roles of misunderstanding and political partisanship in the conflict over Strauss and his teaching.

David R. Lachterman's "Strauss Read from France" provides readers in the English-speaking world with a substantial introduction to recent scholarship on Strauss's thought in France, where the reception of Strauss has "not been beclouded by the phenomenon of 'Straussianism' and the accompanying rancor of internal debate among disciples and external fusillades against political 'cultism' and elitism." It is with regret that we report the death of Lachterman in 1991. His piece here, the final one in this collection, is more than a dutiful report on a segment of relevant European scholarship; it displays his own subtle understanding of Strauss's thought and its bearing on the most significant of contemporary questions. In reflecting on the issue of esotericism, Lachterman concludes that "in our present circumstances the defense of premodernity can and ought to be philosophically outspoken."

SELECT BIBLIOGRAPHY: WORKS ON LEO STRAUSS

Anastaplo, George. "On Leo Strauss: A Yahrzeit Remembrance." *University of Chicago Magazine*, vol. 67 (Winter 1974), pp. 30–38.

Benardete, Seth. "Leo Strauss's *The City and Man*." *Political Science Reviewer*, vol. 8 (Fall 1978), pp. 1–20.

Bloom, Alan. "Leo Strauss: September 20, 1899–October 18, 1973." *Political Theory*, vol. 2, no. 4 (November 1974), pp. 372–92.

Burnyeat, M. F. "Sphinx without a Secret." *New York Review of Books*, vol. 32, no. 9 (30 May 1985), pp. 30–36.

Caton, Hiram. "Explaining the Nazis: Leo Strauss Today." *Quadrant* (October 1986), pp. 61–65.

Cropsey, Joseph. "Leo Strauss: A Bibliography and Memorial, 1899–1973." *Interpretation*, vol. 5, no. 2 (1975), pp. 133–47.

Dannhauser, Werner J. "Leo Strauss: Becoming Naive Again." *American Scholar*, vol. 44 (1974/75), pp. 636–42.

Deutsch, Kenneth L. and Walter Soffer, eds. *The Crisis of Liberal Democracy:*

A Straussian Perspective, corrected edition. Albany: State University of New York Press, 1987.

Drury, Shadia. *The Political Ideas of Leo Strauss.* New York: St. Martin's Press, 1988.

East, John P. "Leo Strauss and American Conservatism." *Modern Age*, vol. 21 (Winter 1977), pp. 2–19.

Fackenheim, Emil. "Leo Strauss and Modern Judaism." *Claremont Review of Books*, vol. 4 (Winter 1985), pp. 21–22.

Fortin, Ernest. "Between the Lines: Was Leo Strauss a Secret Enemy of Morality?" *Crisis* (December 1989), pp. 19–26.

Frisch, Morton. "Leo Strauss and the American Regime." *Publius: A Journal of Federalism*, vol. 17 (Spring 1987), pp. 1–5.

Germino, Dante. "The Revival of Political Theory." *Journal of Politics*, vol. 25 (August 1963), pp. 437–60.

Gourevitch, Victor. "Philosophy and Politics: I." *Review of Metaphysics*, vol. 22, no. 1 (September 1968), pp. 58–84.

Gourevitch, Victor. "Philosophy and Politics: II." *Review of Metaphysics*, vol. 22, no. 2 (December 1968), pp. 281–328.

Gunnell, John. "Political Theory and Politics: The Case of Leo Strauss." *Political Theory*, vol. 13, no. 3 (August 1985), pp. 339–61.

Harbison, Warren. "Irony and Deception." *Independent Journal of Philosophy*, vol. 2 (1978), pp. 89–94.

Himmelfarb, Milton. "On Leo Strauss." *Commentary*, vol. 58, no. 2 (May 1974), pp. 60–66.

Holmes, Stephen. "Truths for Philosopher Alone." *Times Literary Supplement* (December 1–7, 1989), pp. 1319–24.

Jaffa, Harry V. "Leo Strauss's Churchillian Speech and the Question of the Decline of the West." *Teaching Political Science*, vol. 12, no. 2 (Winter 1985), pp. 61–68.

Lampert, Laurence. "The Argument of Leo Strauss in 'What Is Political Philosophy?' " *Modern Age*, vol. 22 (Winter 1978), pp. 39–46.

Lawler, Peter A. "Leo Strauss, Platonic Political Philosophy, and the Teaching of Political Science." *Teaching Political Science*, vol. 13, no. 4 (Summer 1986), pp. 179–83.

Lerner, Ralph. "Leo Strauss (1899–1973)." *American Jewish Yearbook* (1976), pp. 91–97.

Liebich, Andre. "Straussianism and Ideology." In Anthony Parel, ed., *Ideology, Philosophy, and Politics.* Waterloo, Ontario, Canada: Wilfred Laurier University Press, 1983.

Lowenthal, David. "Leo Strauss's Studies in Platonic Political Philosophy." *Interpretation*, vol. 13, no. 3 (September 1985), pp. 297–320.

Maaranen, Steven A. "Leo Strauss: Classical Political Philosophy and Modern Democracy." *Modern Age*, vol. 22 (Winter 1978), pp. 47–53.

MacCormack, John R., ed. "A Leo Strauss Symposium." *Vital Nexus* (Halifax, Canada), vol. 1, no. 1 (May 1990).

McCoy, C. N. R. "On the Revival of Classical Political Philosophy." *Review of Politics*, vol. 35 (April 1973), pp. 161–79.

Miller, Eugene F. "Leo Strauss: The Recovery of Political Philosophy." In Anthony de Crespigny and Kenneth Minogue, eds., *Contemporary Political Philosophers*. New York: Dodd, Mead, 1975.

Nicgorski, Walter. "Leo Strauss and Liberal Education." *Interpretation*, vol. 13, no. 3 (May 1985), pp. 233–50.

Niemeyer, Gerhart. "What Is Political Knowledge?" *Review of Politics*, vol. 23 (January 1961), pp. 101–7.

Pangle, Thomas L. "Editor's Introduction." In Leo Strauss, *The Rebirth of Classical Political Rationalism: An Introduction to the Thought of Leo Strauss*. Chicago: University of Chicago Press, 1989, pp. vii–xxxviii.

Pines, Shlomo. "On Leo Strauss." *Independent Journal of Philosophy*, vol. 5/6 (1988), pp. 169–71.

Pippin, Robert B. "The Modern World of Leo Strauss." *Political Theory*, vol. 20, no. 3 (August 1992), pp. 448–72.

Pocock, J. G. A. "Prophet and Inquisitor." *Political Theory*, vol. 3, no. 4 (November 1975), pp. 385–401.

Schaefer, David L. "The Legacy of Leo Strauss: A Bibliographic Introduction." *Intercollegiate Review*, vol. 9, no. 3 (Summer 1974), pp. 139–48.

Schall, James. "Revelation, Reason, and Politics: Catholic Reflections on Strauss: I" and "Revelation, Reason, and Politics: Catholic Reflections on Strauss: II." *Gregorianum* (1981), pp. 349–65 and pp. 467–97, respectively.

Schall, James. "Sense and Nonsense: Leo Strauss on Prayer." *Crisis* (July 1984), pp. 46–47.

Staal, Rein. "The Irony of Modern Conservatism." *International Political Science Review*, vol. 8, no. 4 (1987), pp. 343–53.

Steintrager, James. "Political Philosophy, Political Theology, and Morality." *Thomist*, vol. 32 (1968), pp. 307–32.

Tarcov, Nathan and Pangle, Thomas L. "Epilogue: Leo Strauss and the History of Political Philosophy." In Leo Strauss and Joseph Cropsey, eds., *History of Political Philosophy*. Chicago: University of Chicago Press, 1987, pp. 907–38.

Tarcov, Nathan. "Philosophy and History: Tradition and Interpretation." *Polity*, vol. 16, no. 1 (Fall 1983), pp. 5–29.

Tolle, Gordon J. "Modernity, Nobility, Morality: Leo Strauss's View of Nietzsche." *Commonwealth: A Journal of Political Science*, vol. 5 (1992), pp. 1–15.

Udoff, Alan, ed. *Leo Strauss's Thought: Towards a Critical Engagement*. Boulder, CO: Lynne Rienner, 1991.

Ward, James F. "Experience and Political Philosophy: Notes on Reading Leo Strauss." *Polity*, vol. 13, no. 4 (Summer 1981), pp. 668–87.

40   *Kenneth L. Deutsch and Walter Nicgorski*

Yaffe, Martin. "Leo Strauss as Judaic Thinker: Some First Notions." *Religious Studies Review*, vol. 17, no. 1 (January 1991), pp. 33–41.
Yaffe, Martin. "On Leo Strauss's *Philosophy and Law*: A Review Essay," *Modern Judaism*, vol. 9 (1989), pp. 213–25.

Part One

Strauss: Judaism, Reason, and Revelation

Why We Remain Jews: Can Jewish Faith and History Still Speak to Us?

Leo Strauss

This was presented as a lecture to a small audience at the Hillel Foundation of the University of Chicago on 4 February 1962. The text that follows was not prepared for publication, or reviewed, by Leo Strauss. It was prepared by the editors from a transcription of a tape recording. The spontaneous and informal aspects of the statement by Strauss and especially of the question period should be duly noted. One of the editors, Walter Nicgorski, was present at the lecture and the discussion that followed. All notes are those of the editors. Material in brackets [ ] has been supplied or moved to such places by the editors in an effort to clarify the prose of the text at points where that seemed necessary. Ellipsis points in brackets [. . .] indicate material lost or seriously garbled in transcription. The lecture as presented below begins after omitting only Strauss's formal greeting to the audience and an acknowledgment of his introduction, which was given on this occasion by Joseph Cropsey.

. . . I have to make two prefatory remarks. . . . When Rabbi Pekarsky first approached me and suggested this title I was repelled by it, not to say shocked by it. But then on reflection I found one could say something about it. At any rate I must say that to the extent to which I prepared this paper, I prepared it on the assumption that I was going to speak on the subject "Why Do We Remain Jews?" I learned of the subtitle only a few days ago, when thanks to some mishap in the printing division of the Hillel Foundation I saw for the first time the subtitle, on which I could not with propriety speak because, after all, everyone is a specialist and my specialty is (to use a very broad and nonspecialist name) social science rather than divinity. Now, social science demands from us, as we all know—and the gentlemen from the social science division I see here, some of whom take a very different view than I, would agree with me—[that we] start from solid if low facts and remain as much as possible on that ground. No flights of fancy, no science fiction, no metaphysics will enter. That is clear.

The second point which I have to make in my introduction is of a more private nature, which I am sad to have to make: I could not prepare this lecture, for entirely private reasons, as I would have wished to prepare it. But nevertheless I did not cancel the lecture

43

because I thought I am prepared, if not indeed for this lecture, for this subject. I believe I can say, without any exaggeration, that since a very, very early time the main theme of my reflections has been what is called the "Jewish Question." May I only mention this single fact, perhaps, going very far back in my childhood. I believe [that when] I was about five or six years old in some very small German town, in a village, I saw in my father's house refugees from Russia, after some pogroms which had happened there, women, children, old men, on their way to Australia. At that time it could not happen in Germany. We Jews there lived in profound peace with our non-Jewish neighbors. There was a government, [perhaps] not in every respect admirable, but keeping an admirable order everywhere; and such things as pogroms would have been absolutely impossible. Nevertheless the story which I heard [on this occasion] made a very deep impression on me, which I have not forgotten until the present day. It was an unforgettable moment. I sensed for a moment that it could happen here. That was overlaid soon by other pleasing experiences, but still it went to my bones, if I may say so. Now this and many other experiences which would be absolutely boring and improper to rehearse are the bases of my lecture. You will not expect, then, a lucid presentation. On the other hand I will promise to give, as I indicated by the reference to the fact that I am a social scientist, what one would call a "hard-boiled" one. I prefer to call it a "frank" one. I will not beat around the bush in any respect. At the same time I hope that I can reconcile what not necessarily all social scientists do: the avoiding of beating around the bush with a treatment which we would call *bekavod* or, to translate it, "honorable." I think such would be possible. Now I turn to my subject.

The main title taken by itself implies that we could cease to be Jews [and] that there might be very good reasons for not remaining Jews. It even suggests this possibility. The clearest expression of this view, of this premise, was given by Heinrich Heine, the well-known poet: "Judaism is not a religion but a misfortune." The conclusions from this premise are obvious. Let us get rid of Judaism as fast as we can and as painlessly as we can. If I may now use an almost technical word, complete "assimilation" is the only help. Now this solution to the problem was always possible, and it was always somehow suggested because at all times it was very difficult to be a Jew. Think of the Middle Ages. Think of the Reformation—to say nothing of other times. In a way, that solution was even easier in the past than it is now. It was sufficient in the Christian countries for a Jew to convert to Christianity and then he would cease to be a Jew, and no statistician will ever be able to find out how many Jews took this easy way out of what Heine calls "misfortune." Yet it was not quite easy even then. I will not speak of the obvious things like the separation from one's relatives and friends. There was a big experiment made with this solution in Spain, after 1492, when the Jews were expelled from Spain. What I say about these things, of course, is entirely [based on] authorities I have read.

Spain was the first country in which Jews felt at home, although they knew they were in exile. Therefore the expulsion from Spain was an infinitely greater misfortune for the Spanish Jews than the expulsion from France in 1340 (if I remember well) or the expulsion from England in 1290 or so. Quite a few Jews simply could not tear themselves away from Spain. This difficulty was enhanced if the individuals in question were wealthy, had large possessions, especially landed possessions; some of them, some leaders of Jewish communities converted to Christianity. And they stayed in Spain. But [here at] this time it was different because there were so many converts at the same time, not one here and another there. As a consequence there was a reaction to these many new Christians. And the reaction showed itself in distrust of them. Many Christians thought that these converts were not sincere believers in Christianity but simply had preferred their earthly fortunes to their faith. So the Inquisition entered, and all kinds of things which are most horrible to read; and of course, in some cases, even if the Inquisition did its worst, it could not give a legal proof of the fact that some former Jew had engaged in Jewish practices or whatever it may be, and so quite a few survived. But one thing was done which was extralegal but not illegal: the Spaniards made a distinction between the old Christians and the new Christians, and they began to speak of Spaniards of pure blood—the old Spaniards—and, by implication, of Spaniards of impure blood, meaning the *conversos*. The Jews who had converted to Christianity were forced to remain Jews, in a manner.

This is ancient history. Assimilation now does not mean conversion to Christianity, as we know, because assimilation now is assimilation to a secular society, a society which is not legally a Christian society, a society beyond the difference between Judaism and Christianity, and—if every religion is always a particular religion

(Judaism, Christianity)—an areligious society, a liberal society. In such a society there are no longer any legal disabilities of Jews as Jews. But a liberal society stands or falls by the distinction between the political, or the state, and society, or by the distinction between the public and the private. In the liberal society there is necessarily a private sphere with which the state's legislation must not interfere. It is an essential element of this liberal society, with its essential distinction between the public and private, that religion as a particular religion, not as a general religion, is private. Every citizen is free to adhere to any religion he sees fit. Now, given this—the necessary existence of such a private sphere—the liberal society necessarily makes possible, permits, and even fosters what is called by many people "discrimination." And here in this well-known fact the "Jewish problem" (if I may call it that) reappears. There are restricted areas and in various ways, [. . . .] I do not have to belabor this point, any glance at [a] journal of sociology or at Jewish journals would convince you of the fact if you have any doubt about its existence. Therefore the practical problem for the individual Jew on the low and solid ground is this: how can I escape "discrimination"? (A term which I beg you to understand as used always with quotation marks. I would not use it of my own free will.) The answer is simple: by ceasing to be recognizable as a Jew. There are certain rules of that which everyone can guess, I would say, *a priori*; and I would not be surprised if there were an Ann Landers, and other writers of this type, who had written perhaps a long list of these techniques. The most well known are mixed marriages, changes of name, and childless marriages. It would be a worthy subject for a sociological study to enlarge on this theme and to exhaust it if possible. I do not have to go into it because it is not truly important, for this solution is possible at most only for individuals here or there, not for large groups. I once heard the story of some Jews in Los Angeles who tried to solve the "discrimination" problem by becoming Christian Scientists; there were first four and then ten and then more. Then at a certain moment the chairman (I don't know whether they call him "chairman") said, well, that is really nice, but why don't you make another group—a group of your own—of Christian Scientists, meaning former Jews. I would say that this possibility [assimilation by ceasing to be recognizable] is refuted by a very simple statistical phenomenon not known to me statistically but only by observation: the Jewish birthrate.

A broad solution would require the legal prohibition against "discrimination" in every manner, shape, or form. And I have seen people—Jews—who just wanted that. Fraternities must not be permitted to pick their own people; and strictly speaking, no man can pick his own company. The prohibition against every "discrimination" would mean the abolition of the private sphere, the denial of the difference between the state and society—in a word, the destruction of liberal society—and therefore it is not a sensible objective or policy. But some people would say, "Why not the destruction of liberal society if this is the only way in which we can get the abolition of discrimination (or what they call the 'abolition of injustice')?" Now, we have empirical data about this fact—the abolition of a liberal society and how it effects the fate of Jews. [An] experiment [was] made on a large scale in a famous country, a very large country, unfortunately a very powerful country, called Russia. We all are familiar with the fact that the policy of communism is the policy of the communist government, and not of a private fraternity like other organizations, and this policy is anti-Jewish. That is undoubtedly the fact. I have checked it by some information I receive from certain quarters. I asked a gentleman whom I know very well, a friend of mine, who is very much in favor of a deal with Russia. He is a Jew. I asked him, "What did you observe about Jews in Soviet Russia?" And he said, "Of course, it is true: Jews are discriminated against, as a matter of principle, by the government." And he gave me a striking example. Some of you will say, all right, that is the policy of the present Russian government; it is not essential to communism. In other words, it is possible to abolish liberal society, to abolish the difference between state and society, without having to become anti-Jewish. I would like to discuss this objection—that it is not essential to communism to be anti-Jewish. I would say it is very uncommunistic to seek for the essence of communism outside of what they call the "historic reality of communism," in a mere ideal or aspiration. Trotsky's communism, which was different and which was surely not anti-Jewish in this sense, has been refuted by his highest authority: history. A Trotskyite is a living, a manifest, contradiction. There is no longer a Western revolutionary proletariat, to put it on a somewhat broader basis, and that settles this issue perfectly. Only thanks to Stalin could the communist revolution survive. Stalin was a wiser statesman from this point of view than Trotsky—and to some extent, than Lenin—by demanding socialism within a single country. Only thanks to Stalin could the communist revolution survive Hitler.

But in order to survive Hitler, Stalin had to learn from Hitler. That is always so: in order to defeat an enemy you have to take a leaf from his book. Stalin learned two grave lessons from Hitler. The first, which has nothing to do directly with our issue but should be mentioned, is that bloody purges of fellow revolutionaries are not only possible, but eminently helpful. The old communist theory (as you surely know) was: no repetition of the bad experiences of the French Revolution, where the revolution ate its own children. And then Hitler showed by [his] classic act against Roehm that this can be done; it makes governing much easier.[1] Hence, the big Stalin purges.

Second (and here I come back to our immediate subject), in pre–First World War socialism where the distinction between Bolshevism and Menshevism was not so visible—at least not in the Western countries—it was an axiom, "Anti-Semitism is the socialism of the fools," and therefore incompatible with intelligent socialism. But again, one can state the lesson which Hitler gave Stalin in very simple words, as follows. The fact that anti-Semitism is the socialism of the fools is an argument not against, but for, anti-Semitism; given the fact that there is such an abundance of fools, why should one not steal that very profitable thunder. Of course, one must not become a prisoner of this like that great fool Hitler who believed in his racial theories; that is absurd. But judicially used, politically used, anti-Jewish policies make governing Russians and Ukrainians, and so on, much easier than if one would be strictly fair to Jews. I do not have to point out the obvious fact that we must think not only of the Russians, the Ukrainians, but also of the Arabs; and everyone can easily see that there are many more Arabs in the world than there are Jews. I mean, a sober statesman for whom the end sanctifies every means has no choice. Khrushchev (I think one can say) abandoned lesson number one regarding the desirability and usefulness of bloody purges of party members—let me add, for the time being—but he surely kept lesson number two, and it has come to stay.

1. Ernst Roehm, longtime associate and supporter of Hitler and the key leader of the paramilitary brownshirts, was killed in an extremely vicious general purge of the Nazi movement in late June 1934; the purge appeared to Hitler politically necessary to secure his rise to full political control in Germany.

I draw a conclusion. It is impossible not to remain a Jew. It is impossible to run away from one's origins. It is impossible to get rid of one's past by wishing it away. There is nothing better than the uneasy solution offered by liberal society, which means legal equality plus private "discrimination." We must simply recognize the fact, which we all know, that the Jewish minority is not universally popular, and the consequences which follow from that. We all know that there is in this country an entirely extralegal, but not illegal, what we can call "racial hierarchy" coming down from the Anglo-Saxons, down to the Negroes; and we are just above the Negroes. We must face that. And we must see that there is a similarity between the Jewish and the Negro question. There are quite a few Jewish organizations which are very well aware of this; but also, in order to keep the record straight, we must not forget the difference. When we Jews fight for something which we may fairly call "justice," we appeal to principles ultimately which (if I may say so) were originally our own. When the Negroes fight for justice, they have to appeal to principles which were not their own, their ancestors' in Africa, but which they learned from their oppressors. This is not an altogether negligible difference, which should be stated by someone who does not want to beat around the bush.

I begin again. There is no solution to the Jewish problem. The expectation of such a solution is due to the premise that every problem can be solved. There was a famous writer, a great mathematician in the sixteenth century, as I read somewhere—Vieta—who literally said that there is no problem which cannot be solved. This is, in application to social matters, a premise of many well-meaning men in the West in the nineteenth and twentieth centuries. I disagree with them entirely. It is not self-evident that every problem can be solved, and therefore we should not be altogether surprised if the Jewish problem cannot be solved.

Let us briefly survey the solutions which have been suggested. The first is the assimilation of individuals, which I disposed of before. The second would be assimilation in a different form: Judaism would be understood as a sect like any other sect; I say advisedly a "sect," and not as a "religion." A sect is a society that is based on an entirely voluntary membership—so that today you belong to sect A, and if you change your mind you leave sect A and enter sect B; and the same applies, of course, to all members of your family. The fact that the man stems from Jewish parents would be entirely irrelevant from this point of view. I do not believe that this opinion can be reconciled with anything ever understood as Jewish, regardless of whether it is orthodox, conservative, or reform.

There is a third solution—the only one [of those] mentioned which deserves our serious attention—and that is assimilation as a nation. Here the fact that the Jews are an ethnic group is honestly faced. But it is also implied that Judaism is a misfortune, and hence that we must do something about the problem. But the problem cannot be solved except on a national scale. We Jews are a nation like any other nation; and just as any other nation, we have the right to demand self-determination. It leads necessarily to the demand for a Jewish state. This was the view taken by the strictly political Zionists. I emphasize the word *strictly* because in fact there are all kinds of combinations which are by no means due to accident but to one of the deepest principles of human nature—which is that man is the animal who wishes to have the cake and to eat it. To make clear what I mean, I remind you of the motto of the most impressive statement of political Zionism: Pinsker's *Auto-emancipation*, written in the eighties of the last century.[2] Pinsker's motto is this: if I am not for myself, who will I be for? and if not now, when? That is, don't expect help from others, and don't postpone your decision. This is a quotation from a well-known Jewish book, *The Sayings of the Fathers*; but in the original, something else is said which Pinsker omitted: "But if I am only for myself, what am I?"[3] The omission of these words constitutes the definition of pureblooded political Zionism. There was, long before Pinsker, a man who sketched the principles of political Zionism—a great man, but not a good Jew—and that was Spinoza. Towards the end of the third chapter of his *Theologico-Political Treatise*, he said (I am speaking from memory), "If the principles of their religion did not effeminate the Jews, I would regard it as perfectly possible that one day, if the political constellation is favorable, they might succeed in restoring their state."[4] I don't believe he said "in Palestine" because,

2. Leon Pinsker (1821–91) was a Polish-born Russian Jew whose influential Zionist tract *Autoemancipation* appeared in 1882.
3. This "saying" as presented in a widely used translation by R. Travers Herford reads, "If I am not for myself who is for me? and when I am for myself what am I? and if not now, when?" *The Ethics of the Talmud: Sayings of the Fathers* (New York: Schocken Books, 1962), p. 34.
4. The relevant sentence in the commonly used R. H. M. Elwes translation reads, "Nay, I would go so far as to believe that if the foundations of their

from his point of view, Uganda would have been as good as Palestine. I did not explain what he meant by the effeminating character of the Jewish religion. He meant by that trust in God instead of trust in one's own power and "hardware." But in spite of the undeniable fact that political Zionism, pure and simple, is based on a radical break with the principles of the Jewish tradition, I cannot leave the subject without paying homage to it. Political Zionism was more passionately and more soberly concerned with the human dignity of the Jews than any other movement. What it had in mind ultimately was that the Jews should return to their land with their heads up, but not by virtue of a divine act but rather of political and military action—fighting.

Yet it is impossible to settle all Jews in that very small land. Political Zionism was a very honorable suggestion, but one must add that it was also merely formal or poor. I would like to illustrate this. I was myself (as you might have guessed) a political Zionist in my youth, and was a member of a Zionist student organization. In this capacity I occasionally met Jabotinsky, the leader of the revisionists.[5] He asked me, "What are you doing?" I said, "Well, we read the Bible, we study Jewish history, Zionist theory, and, of course, we keep abreast of developments, and so on." He replied, "And rifle practice?" And I had to say, "No."

In this [student] group, when I talked to my friends—some [of whom] are now very high officials in Israel—I made this observation. They were truly passionate Zionists and worked very much and were filled with enthusiasm. But, after all, you cannot always make speeches and have political discussions, or do other administrative work: you also have to have, so to say, a life of your own. I was struck by the fact that the substance of the intellectual life of some of these estimable young men—to the extent that it was not merely academic and therefore of no particular interest outside of academic halls—consisted of their concern with people like Balzac. The main point is that this Zionism was strictly limited to political action. The mind [—or even the heart—] was in no way employed in matters Jewish.

Now this led very early to a reaction and opposition to political

religion have not emasculated their minds they may even, if occasion offers, so changeable are human affairs, raise up their empire afresh, and that God may a second time elect them." *The Chief Works of Benedict De Spinoza*, vol. 1 (New York: Dover Publications, 1951), p. 56.

5. Vladimir Jabotinsky (1880–1940) was a Russian Jew who founded and led the Revisionist movement in Zionism.

Zionism by cultural Zionism. Cultural Zionism means simply that
it is not enough to have a Jewish state; the state must also have a
Jewish culture. In other words, it must have a life of its own. Jewish
culture means the product of the Jewish mind, in counterdistinc-
tion to other national minds. If we look, however, at what this
means in specific terms, we see that the rock bottom of any Jewish
culture are the Bible, Talmud, and Midrash. And if you take these
things with a minimum of respect or seriousness, you must say
they were not meant to be products of the Jewish mind. They were
meant to be ultimately "from Heaven," and this is the crux of the
matter: Judaism cannot be understood as a culture. There are folk
dances and pottery and all that. But you can't live on that. The
substance is not culture, but divine revelation. Therefore the only
consistent solution, clear solution, is that which abandons, which
goes beyond, cultural Zionism and becomes clearly religious Zionism. Return to the Jewish faith, to the faith of our ancestors.

But here we are up against a difficulty which underlies the very
title of the lecture and everything I said before. What shall those
Jews do who cannot believe as our ancestors believed? So while
religious Zionism is the only clear solution, it is not feasible,
humanly speaking, for all Jews. I repeat: it is impossible to get rid
of one's past. It is necessary to accept one's past. That means that
out of this undeniable necessity one must make a virtue. The virtue
in question is fidelity, loyalty, piety in the old Latin sense of the
word *pietas*. The necessity of taking this step appears from the
disgraceful character of the only alternative, of denying one's
origin, past, or heritage. A solution of a man's problem which can
be achieved only through a disgraceful act is a digraceful solution.
But let us be detached; let us be objective, scientific. Is this universally true? We must bust the case wide open in order to understand
the difficulty; I am not interested in preaching up any solution. I
try to help myself and (if I can) some of you in understanding our
difficulty. Let us take a man by nature very gifted for all excellences
of man—of the mind and of the soul—who stems from the gutter.
Is he not entitled to run away from the gutter? Surely, one could
even say that by being silent about his gutter origins he acts more
decently than by displaying them, and thus annoying others with a
bad smell. Yet, however this may be, this interesting case (which
deserves all our compassion, I think) is surely not our case. Our
worst enemies admit this in one way or another. Our worst enemies
are not called—since I don't know how many years—"anti-Sem-

ites," a word which I shall never use, which I regard as almost obscene. I think that if we are sensible we abolish it from our usage. I said in a former speech here that it was coined by some German or French pedant: I smelled them. But then I learned, a few weeks ago, it was coined by a German pedant, a fellow called Marr. The reason was very simple: "anti-Semitism" means hatred of Jews. Why not call it as we Jews call it? *Rismus*, "viciousness"? "Hatred of Jews" is perfectly intelligible; "anti-Semitism" was coined in a situation in which people could no longer justify their hatred of Jews by the fact that Jews are not Christians. They had to find another reason; and since the thirteenth century was almost as proud of science as the twentieth century, the reason had to be scientific. Science proves that the Western World consists of two races—the Aryan and the Semitic race—and therefore, by speaking of anti-Semitism, our enemies could claim that they acted on a spiritual principle, not mere hatred. The difficulty is that the Arabs are also Semites. One of my Arab friends was occasionally asked in the Chicago suburbs, "You are, of course, an anti-Semite." And he would say, "I can't be that."

So I speak of our enemies, and I want to show that they recognize that we are not from the gutter. Let us take the latest and crudest and simplest example: the Nazis. The Nazis' system was based on the notion of the Aryan. I mean, it was no longer a Christian Germany; it was to be an Aryan Germany. But what does "Aryan" mean? The Nazis were compelled, for example, to give the Japanese the status of Aryans, and quite a few others. In a word, "Aryan" had no meaning but "non-Jewish." The Nazi regime was the only regime of which I know which was based on no principle other than the negation of Jews. It could not define its highest objective except by putting the Jews into the center; that is a great compliment to us, if not intended as such. I take more serious cases: the anti-Judaism of late classical antiquity, when we (and incidentally also the Christians) were accused by the pagan Romans of standing convicted of hatred of the human race. I contend that it was a very high compliment. And I will try to prove it.

This accusation reflects an undeniable fact. For the human race consists of many nations or tribes or, in Hebrew, *goyim*. A nation is a nation by virtue of what it looks up to. In antiquity a nation was a nation by virtue of its looking up to its gods. They did not have ideologies at that time; they did not have even ideas at that time.

At the top there were the gods. And, now, our ancestors asserted *a priori*—that is to say, without looking at any of these gods—that these gods were nothings and abominations. That the highest of any nation was nothing and an abomination. (I cannot develop [the basis for this] now. [For that] we would have to go into broader [considerations]—into that metaphysical, science-fiction thing which I have tried to avoid—but I must make one remark.) In the light of the purity which Isaiah understood when he said, of himself, "a man of unclean lips in the midst of a nation of unclean lips," the very parthenon is impure.[6] This is still alive in Judaism today—not among all Jews, but among some. I heard the story that, when Ben-Gurion[7] went to Thailand for negotiations or something, he went to a Buddhist temple and there was quite an uproar in Israel about that on the old, old grounds. And I suggested to the man who told me that he should wire to Ben-Gurion that he should say that what he was meditating upon in that Buddhist temple was the foreign policy of Israel, which might be pleaded as an attenuating circumstance.

Now, the fight of our ancestors against Rome was unique. We have the two greatest cases: the Jewish fight against Rome and the German fight against Rome. The Germans were more successful from the military point of view: they defeated the Romans; we were defeated. Yet, victory or defeat are not the highest criteria. And if we compare these two actions, we see that the fight of our ancestors was not merely a fight against foreign oppression, but it was a fight in the name of what one should very provisionally call an "idea"—the only fight in the name of an idea made against the Roman Empire.

The next great anti-Jewish body was the Christian republic. The hatred of Jews persisted, but changed; in some respects it was [even] intensified. For the Jewish people's posture toward the God-man was the same as that against the manlike god of the Greeks and Romans. And since there are many Christians today who are no longer Trinitarians, one difference surely remains between Judaism and Christianity which was never, never taken back. The Christian assertion that the redeemer has come was always counted by our ancestors with the assertion that the redeemer has not

6. Isaiah 6:5.
7. David Ben-Gurion (1886–1973) was the first prime minister of the State of Israel; he retired from his leadership post in 1963.

come. One can perhaps say (and I say this without any animus) that *the* justification of Judaism in its fight with Christianity was supplied by the Crusades. One only has to read that history as a Jew to be satisfied with the fact that one is a Jew. The Crusades consisted partly of a simple orgy of murder of Jews. Wherever the Crusaders went—above all, in Jerusalem itself—how did our ancestors act? Permit me to read a few lines from the writings of the greatest living Jewish historian, Yitzhak F. Baer's *Galut.*

> The best description left us of the persecutions that took place at the time of the First Crusade are to be found in Hebrew records. These were constructed from shorter reports describing the happenings in individual places and provinces, and encountered similar pamphlets with opposite tendencies that were circulated by the Christians. In this age religious-national martyrdom reaches its highest expression. These martyrs are no seekers after death like the early Christians, no heroes challenging destiny. Violence and death come unsought. And the whole community suffers—old and young, women and children, willing or not. At first they fight for the preservation of the community, and they hold off their enemies before the walls of the episcopal palace or the fortress just as long as defense is possible.[8]

One must add here the remark, which Baer of course does not deny, that the higher clergy behaved on the whole much better than the lower clergy. You know the peasants' sons who became priests were much more fanatical and savage than [. . .] the famous case of Bernard [de Clairvaux] who tried to prevent that. But they did not prevail.

> [Strauss then continues reading from Baer's *Galut.*] But then, when all hope for safety is gone, they are ready for martyrdom. No scene is more stirring than the sabbath meal of the pious Jews in [Xanten] Rumania (1096): Hardly had the grace before the meal been recited when the news came of the enemy's approach; immediately they fulfilled the ceremony of the closing grace, recited the formula expressing faith in the oneness of God, and carried out the terrible act of sacrifice that was renewed again and again, generation after generation from the time of Macedon [Massada] in the Roman rule.

8. The reading by Strauss from Baer's *Galut* corresponds almost in its entirety to a translation of *Galut* by Robert Warshow that first appeared in 1947. The passage read has been checked against the current version of the Warshow translation (Lanham, MD: University Press of America, 1988), where it appears on pages 24–25. Punctuation was done in accord with this current edition.

The martyrologies here described in frightful clarity and ritual of voluntary mutual slaughter (not the sacrifice of enemies falsely ascribed to the Jews), and have glorified it in poetry modeled after the sacrifice of Isaac.

The Reformation abolished bloody persecution. But the unbloody persecution which remained was in some respects worse than the bloody persecution of the Middle Ages because it did not call forth the fighting qualities which were still so powerfully visible in that glorious time for us of the Crusades. I summarize. Our past, our heritage, our origin is then not misfortune as Heine said—still less, baseness. But suffering indeed; heroic suffering; suffering stemming from the heroic act of self-dedication of a whole nation to something which it regarded as infinitely higher than itself—in fact, as the infinitely highest. No Jew can do anything better for himself today than to live in remembering this past.

But someone might say, "Is this sufficient if the old faith has gone? Must the Jew who cannot believe what his ancestors believe not admit to himself that his ancestors dedicated themselves to a delusion—if to the noblest of all delusions? Must he not dedicate himself to a life in a world which is no longer Jewish, and by the same token no longer Christian, but, as one could say, post–Judeo-Christian? However repulsive the thought of assimilation must be to any proud man, must he not accept assimilation as a moral necessity and not as a convenience? Is not the noblest in man his capacity to assimilate himself to the truth?" Very well, let us then reconsider assimilation.

We will be helped in that reconsideration in this statement by a non-Jew, by a German. By a German, in addition, who has a very bad reputation in many quarters—and that is Friedrich Nietzsche. I would like to read to you an aphorism which will not please every one of you, from Nietzsche's *Dawn of Day*, aphorism 205.

Of the people of Israel. To the spectacles to which the next century invites us belongs the decision of the destiny of the European Jews. That they have cast their die, crossed their Rubicon, is now quite obvious: it only remains for them either to become the lords of Europe or to lose Europe, as once in olden times they lost Egypt, where they confronted a similar either-or. In Europe, however, they have gone through a schooling of eighteen centuries such as no other people here can show, and in such a way that the experiences of this terrible time of training have benefitted not merely the community but even more the individual. As a consequence of this the psychic and spiritual resources of today's Jews are extraordinary; they, least of all those who inhabit Europe, reach, when in distress, for the cup or for suicide in order to escape a deep dilemma—as the less gifted are so prone to do.[9]

Every sociologist knows that, regarding suicide, the situation is terribly changeable. That was still the old sturdy Jews of Europe he means.

[Strauss continues reading from Nietzsche.] Every Jew has in the history of his fathers and ancestors a treasure of examples of coldest self-possession and steadfastness in dreadful situations, of bravery under the cloak of wretched submission, their heroism in *spernere se sperni* (despising that one is despised) surpasses the virtues of all the saints. One has wanted to make them contemplate by treating them contemptibly for two millennia, and by barring them access to all honors, to everything honorable, and by all the more deeply pushing them down into the more sordid trades—and indeed, under this procedure they have not become cleaner. But contemptible? They themselves chosen for the highest things, nor have the virtues of all sufferers ever ceased to adorn them. The way in which they honor their fathers and children, the reason in their marriages and marriage customs, distinguish them among all Europeans. In addition they have understood how to create a feeling of power and eternal vengeance out of the very trades that were left to them (or to which one left them); one must say in the excuse even of their usury that without this occasionally pleasant and useful torture of those who hold them in contempt, they could hardly have endured holding fast to their self-respect for so long. For our self-respect is tied to our ability to retaliate in good and evil. In all this their vengeance does not easily carry them too far, for they have all that liberality, also of the soul, to which frequent changes of place, climate, customs of neighbors and oppressors, educates man; they possess by far the greatest experience in all human intercourse, and [even in their passions they practice the caution taught by this experience. They are so sure in the] exercise of their spiritual versatility and shrewdness that they never, not even in the most bitter circumstances, find it necessary to earn their bread by physical force as manual laborers, porters, or farmhands. [Strauss remarks, "Well, we knew only Germany."] Their manners still show

9. If Strauss in this reading used a translation other than his own, the editors have not yet located it. The transcription of the reading from Nietzsche appears, at one point, to be missing a line, which is supplied in brackets from the recent translation by R. J. Hollingdale published under the title *Daybreak: Thoughts on the Prejudices of Morality* (Cambridge, England: Cambridge University Press, 1982), see pp. 205–6. The translation read by Strauss was found to correspond quite closely to that of Hollingdale, so that the two set side by side present no significant interpretative differences.

that one has never put noble chivalric feelings into their soul and
beautiful weapons about their body: something obtrusive alternates
with an often tender and almost always painful submissiveness. But
now that they unavoidably intermarry more and more, from year to
year, with the noblest blood of Europe, they will soon have a good
heritage of the manners of soul and body so that in a hundred years
already they will appear noble enough so that as lords they will not
awaken the *shame* of those subdued by them. And that is what matters!
Therefore a settlement of their case is still premature! They themselves best know that there can be no thought of a conquest of Europe
or of any violence whatsoever; but also that at some time Europe may
fall like a perfectly ripe fruit into their hand, which only casually
reaches out. In the meantime it is necessary for them to distinguish
themselves in all the areas of European distinction and to stand among
the first, until they will be far enough along to determine themselves
that which distinguishes. Then they will be called the inventors and
guides of the Europeans and no longer offend their shame. And how
shall it issue forth, this abundance of passions, virtues, resolutions,
renunciations, struggles, victories of every kind how shall it issue forth
if not at last in great spiritual men and works: Then, when the Jews
will be able to exhibit as their work such precious stones and golden
vessels as the European people of shorter and less profound experience neither can nor could bring forth, when Israel shall have
changed its eternal vengeance into an eternal blessing of Europe, then
that seventh day will once again be here when the old Jewish God will
be able to *rejoice* in Himself, his creation, and his chosen people—and
we all, all will rejoice with Him!

This is the most profound and most radical statement on assimilation which I have read. It does not lose any of its significance by
the fact that Nietzsche has not written without irony. In other
words, he had no hopes in this respect; he only thought something
through. Assimilation cannot mean abandoning the inheritance,
but only giving it another direction, transforming it. And assimilation cannot be an end; it could only be a way toward that. Assimilation is an intermediate stage in which it means distinguishing
oneself in pursuits which are not as such Jewish but, as Nietzsche
would say, European—as we would say, Western. After having
received a notion of what assimilation in the highest could mean—
and only in this way can we understand any assimilation—we must
look at the actual assimilation. After one has heard such a passage,
one trembles to look at the actual assimilation. There exists a kind
of Jewish glorification of every clever or brilliant Jewish mediocrity—which is as pitiable as it is laughable. It reminds me of
villagers who have produced their first physicist and hail him for

this reason as the greatest physicist that ever was. I refuse to quote chapter and verse, but when I read statements in Jewish periodicals about Jewish celebrities I am always reminded of that. I became so distrustful of it [at one time, that I did not] believe that Einstein was of any significance. I am not a theoretical physicist and, therefore, I was as entitled to my opinion as any other ignoramus. Then I asked a trustworthy friend of mine—a physicist, a Jew. I told him my opinion [about the matter, and] I had the feeling that this was really a propaganda machine organized by Einstein's wife. I believe that was, by the way, true; I had heard that [there was such an effort]. But then he told me,

> You are mistaken. He [Einstein] was presently at a seminar in Berlin, and that was tops in physics: Planck and other such men were present. And it was simply so. Einstein had the defect that he didn't know elementary mathematics. I mean that was his genuine defect, but his conceits, his inventions, were surpassing that of all the others there. You must believe it. He is really a first-rate physicist, and surely the greatest physicist of this epoch. It is an empirical fact.

So I accepted that. But I must say I am still proud of my resistance, because this inclination to self-glorification in things in which there is no reason for self-glorification is a disgrace. That we have today so many outstanding Jews is due—let us not deceive ourselves about that—to the general decline, to a general victory of mediocrity. It is today very easy to be a great man. "Among the blind, the one-eyed is king" goes the proverb.

[Nietzsche's analysis has some defects though] his statement, which is almost dithyrambic, is based on a very deep analysis—perhaps on the deepest analysis ever made—of what assimilation could possibly mean. Now, the most patent defect of Nietzsche's analysis seems to be this: the regeneration or cleansing which he had in mind as part of the process proved to be insufficient as a work of individuals—however numerous, dedicated, or gifted. It required and requires an act of national cleansing or purification; and this, in my mind, was the establishment of the state of Israel. Everyone who has seen Israel—nay, everyone who has witnessed the response to that act in New York—will understand what I mean. But this fact refutes Nietzsche's dream. For the establishment of the state of Israel means, while it may be a progress in a way of Jewish assimilation—as it surely is—is also a reassertion of the difference between Jews and non-Jews. Since I said "an act" of assimilation, may I tell another story from my youth? I had a friend who was not a Zionist, and his father was an old-fashioned liberal Jew. They called themselves in Germany "German citizens of Jewish faith." And what he said when he goes to fetch his father from the synagogue and sees him together with his other assimilationist friends, and then he sees these young generations of Zionist boys, then he must admit that this older generation which is so un-Jewish by refusing any national character of Judaism is much more Jewish than this young generation is which was [. . .] Jews. It's undeniable.

Judaism is not a misfortune (I am back to my beginning) but, let us say, a "heroic delusion." In what does this delusion consist? The one thing needful is righteousness or charity; in Judaism these are the same. This notion of the one thing needful is not defensible if the world is not the creation of the just and loving God, the holy God. The root of injustice and uncharitableness, which abounds, is not in God but in the free acts of his creatures—in sin. The Jewish people and their fate are the living witness for the absence of redemption. This, one could say, is the meaning of the chosen people: the Jews are chosen to prove the absence of redemption. The greatest expression surpassing everything that any present-day man could write is that great Jewish prayer which will be known to some of you and which is a stumbling block to many: *Olenu leshabeach*. It would be absolutely improper for me to read it now.[10]

10. The transcribers supplied the following version of the prayer that Strauss referred to but did not read. Unable to locate the source of this translation, the editors checked it against a recently published version and found no significant variations. The anglicized title of the prayer in this version is *Aleinu*.

It is our duty to praise the Lord of all things, to ascribe greatness to him who formed the world in the beginning, since he hath not made us like the nations of other lands, and hath not placed us like other families of the earth, since he hath not assigned unto us a portion as unto them, nor a lot as unto all their multitude. For we bend the knee and offer worship and thanks before the supreme King of kings, the Holy One, blessed be he, who stretched forth the heavens and laid the foundations of the earth, the seat of whose glory is in the heavens above, and the abode of whose might is in the loftiest heights. He is our God; there is none else; in truth he is our King; there is none besides him; as it is written in this Law, And thou shalt know this day, and lay it to thine heart, that the Lord he is God in heaven above and upon the earth beneath: there is none else.

We therefore hope in thee, O Lord our God, that we may speedily behold the glory of thy might, when thou wilt remove the abominations from the earth, and the idols will be utterly cut off, when the world will be perfected under the kingdom of the Almighty, and when thou wilt

Now let us reflect for a few moments more—be patient—about delusion. What is a delusion? We also say a "dream." No nobler dream was ever dreamt. It is surely nobler to be victim of the most noble dream than to profit from a sordid reality and to wallow in it. Dream is akin to aspiration. And aspiration is a kind of divination of an enigmatic vision. And an enigmatic vision in the emphatic sense is the perception of the ultimate mystery, of the truth of the ultimate mystery. The truth of the ultimate mystery—the truth that there is an ultimate mystery, that being is radically mysterious—cannot be denied even by the unbelieving Jew of our age. That unbelieving Jew of our age, if he has any education, is ordinarily a positivist; [if he is without an education, he is, if not a positivist, a believer in science]. As scientist he must be concerned with the Jewish problem among innumerable other problems. He reduces the Jewish problem to something unrecognizable: religious minorities, ethnic minorities. In other words, you can put together the characteristics of the Jewish problem by finding one element of it there, another element of it here, and so on. I am speaking from experience. I had once a discussion with some social scientist in the presence of Rabbi Pekarsky where I saw how this was done. The unity, of course, was completely missed. The social scientist cannot see the phenomenon which he tries to diagnose, analyze, as it is. His notion, his analysis, is based on a superficial and thoughtless psychology or sociology. This sociology or psychology is superficial and thoughtless because it does not reflect on itself, on science itself. At the most it raises the question "What is science?" Nevertheless—whatever may follow from that—I must, by God, come to a conclusion.

Science, as the positivist understands it, is susceptible of infinite progress. That you learn in every elementary school today, I believe. Every result of science is provisional and subject to future

---

return unto thyself all the wicked of the earth. Let all the inhabitants of the world perceive and know that unto thee every knee must bow, every tongue must swear. Before thee, O Lord our God, let them bow and fall; and unto thy glorious name let them give honor; let them all accept the yoke of thy kingdom, and do thou reign over them speedily, and for ever and ever. For the kingdom is thine, and to all eternity thou wilt reign in glory; as it is written in thy Law, The Lord shall reign for ever and ever. And it is said, And the Lord shall be king over all the earth: in that day shall the Lord be One, and his name One.
See p. 197 of *A Prayerbook for Shabbat, Festivals, and Weekdays*, ed. and trans. Rabbi Jules Harlow (New York: Rabbinical Assembly, 1985).

62 *Leo Strauss*

revision, and this will never change. In other words, fifty thousand years from now there will still be results entirely different from those now, but still subject to revision. Science is susceptible of infinite progress. But how can science be susceptible of infinite progress if its object does not have an inner infinity? In other words, the object of science is everything that is—being. The belief admitted by all believers in science today—that science is by its nature essentially progressive, and eternally progressive—implies, without saying it is, that being is mysterious. And here is the point where the two lines I have tried to trace do not meet exactly, but where they come within hailing distance. And, I believe, to expect more in a general way, of people in general, would be unreasonable.

QUESTION AND ANSWER PERIOD[11]

The title of the lecture "Why Do We Remain Jews?"—am I correct that your answer is that we have no choice?

As honorable men, surely not.

Well, even one step back from that, even if we wish to be dishonorable, do we have a choice?

Yes. I tried to show that even then it wouldn't work because you have to have a very, very special [. . .] like a murderer, you know, who thinks that the easiest thing is to get the money he wants by murder, and then he lives his whole life with that murder. I mean, that is not a practical thing. And this fellow who tries to do that will live for the rest of his life with his solution. In other words, his solution will prove to be a problem. I made this reservation only for this reason: one cannot look into human beings, and of human beings one only knows a limited number. There may be somewhere, perhaps in Alaska, a man of Jewish origin who no one knows as a Jew and who lives happily ever after. That I cannot exclude. But you get my point.

I tend to be not quite as pessimistic temperamentally as you and perhaps younger and more foolish, but it seems to me that one of the things that could contribute to a better outlook for the problem of discrimination is just

11. The questions addressed to Strauss or comments from members of the audience are presented in italics.

the best of sciences. If we as Jews can better come to understand the Christians and non-Jews sociologically, culturally, as well as just in terms of theological doctrine, and they can come to understand us better sociologically, culturally, and historically—and so also with the Negroes—we can yet remain Jews, non-Jews, and Negroes and yet win some mutual respect.

Well, sure: I would say I deplore the word *pessimism* because that means the belief that this world is the worst of all possible worlds; and that, I think, very few people believe. It is impossible to maintain. But you think I am more apprehensive than you are?

Can we not hope at least? Let us not hope for winning an end to discrimination. I mean, everyone has his friends, everyone has his likes and his dislikes, and we don't wish to take that away from anyone although we can certainly hope for increasing the mutual respect of peoples of different religious and different races.

Sure! Sure! I mean, everyone should try to educate himself and, if he can, educate others to behave as decent human beings. But whether the so-called prejudices, meaning the erroneous opinions, are so important—in some cases they may be important—but whether they are universally so important can be doubted. You see, knowledge of another group—a nation or whatever it might be—is not necessarily conducive to good relations. The cultural exchange between Germany and France shortly before the First World War surpassed everything which the most sanguine man could expect now to take place from cultural exchange with Soviet Russia. And there was no security officer at the elbow of every German in Paris or of every Frenchman in Berlin. And yet when the thing came to the test, all these cultural relations which were much more intimate than the cultural relations between the United States' scientists and Soviet scientists meant absolutely nothing for the fate. In other words, in political matters the stronger and lower is more powerful than the higher and weaker; that is well known. But, by all means, go on! There is no question that if there are misconceptions—that if people think (to pick a somewhat neutral example) that every Negro is given to violence—of course it is good to tell him that "you are absolutely mistaken; that is a false generalization." Surely! I'm all in favor of that. But I don't believe that [. . .] By the way, I would not regard my view as apprehensive in particular, but it is only if you expect the possibility of perfect harmony among human beings in general; then, indeed, it would be disappointing. But what right do we have to expect that, short of divine intervention? In other words, if that day would come where there would not be a trace of "discrimination" against Jews and perfect amity between all non-Jews and all Jews in this country, I'll bet there will be another line of "discrimination" drawn. Man needs that, I believe.

In the discussion as to why we remain Jews I don't know that I heard a definition of what a Jew is. I bring this up because [I am] going back to the historical treatment [and to] whatever similarities there may be between Jews of today and our Jewish ancestors. And I wonder, reflecting on this, if with this change we can't think of something that we are progressing toward? Perhaps something which we can't define today, but still a progression? And also, looking at people in the world in general, if all people aren't progressing toward some goal?

I believe I understand your position; it has a long and very respectable ancestry also. But I would say this. That there is a change from our ancestors to us is the massive fact which is underlying my whole paper. Otherwise we would sit here and perhaps listen to a homiletic interpretation of some biblical verse, and not discuss that; or discuss some subtlety of the religious Law, and not do what we do. Surely things have changed. And you ask, "Could there not be further progress?" This means that the change from our ancestors to us was unqualifiedly a progress. A very grave assertion. If you take as the standard the absence of pogroms or other bloody things of this kind, a standard of living and many conveniences, legal security, and other greater things even, it is undeniable. Also science. I mean, there is no question that today science is much more advanced as science than it was centuries ago. But is this sufficient? Can we simply speak of progress?

Expanding on question above, I think there has also been a progress theologically speaking.

What is that?

A change. It might be individualistic, but it's a progress.

Yes, but you see, when you say "Let the individual decide," you say it is absolutely arbitrary preferences; and then we can no longer speak of progress. So why don't you stick to your guns? That would then mean that the theology written in our century—Jewish theology—is in fact superior (if you assert progress) to, say, the theology of Jehudah Halevi, Maimonides, or someone else. I mean, prior to investigation that is surely possible, but let me only draw your attention to one thing, one point. The enormous progresses which have been achieved in every respect—in the standard of living and even politically—have very much to do with modern technology, which itself is based on modern science. This same science and technology has also made it possible for the first time, or is about to make possible, the destruction of the human race. The most wicked and vicious human beings who ever were—Nero himself— could not, even if they wished, think of such devices as the atomic bomb. In other words, his killing capacity did not reach the state of what some people call "over-kill." That is exactly the other side. I mean, when we speak of progress, positive progress, we must also say that this progress is essentially, not accidentally, accompanied by a progress in destructiveness. And if we look at Jewish history— we look at that history as Jews—we must say that such a thing—we have gone through terrible things—but such a thing as the Nazis has never happened before. Before the twentieth century. If you look at the terrible persecution of the Middle Ages, you have to admit that this was not the *government* which demanded it. The government represented by the higher clergy was opposed to it. I mean, one can prove this by a simple picture. In some medieval churches, especially in the Muenster in Strassburg, there is a presentation of the church and the synagogue. The church: eyes open. The synagogue: blindfolded. "Blindness," as the Christians call it. But there is nothing whatever mean and degrading in that— nothing whatever. It is a dogmatic assertion to which the Christians from their point of view are entitled; but it has nothing in itself, it has nothing whatever, to do with a debasement, degradation, and so on as a *government* policy as it was pursued in Nazi Germany. Even the tsarist regime, although it was surely abominable, did not reach that degree of abomination which the Nazis reached. And that is in the twentieth century. So I believe that [is why there are] many people who have become doubtful whether it is wise to speak of "progress." Progress in certain respects; regress in other— perhaps more important—respects. And therefore, that we are different, that there was a change from our ancestors to us, is undeniable. And it is also prudent to assume that there will be further changes from us to Jews a hundred years from now. But that this should be a progress is an unwarranted assumption. There would be possibly, if everything goes well, a reduction in

what is now called "discrimination." That, I believe, is for the time
being very possible. [. . .]

*I'm afraid I didn't make my question very clear. I think you pointed out
some things which aren't exactly to our taste, only the Nazis and the
Russians—the possibility but not the definite direction of nuclear destruction. The point of my question was not the discussion of progress or not
progress, but rather there has been an undeniable change from Judaism as
it was designed many centuries ago and what it is today. And it seems to me
that this change is continuing, and therefore will continue in the future;
and I think it's reasonable.*

Aha! That's the key point. I mean, change is undeniable. But for
better or for worse, that is the question.

*Well, I bring the question back to the basic discussion: why do we remain
Jews? In view of this continuing change going on, we have to define—what
is a Jew, and what are we remaining, what have we changed from, what
are we changing to? And isn't there a possibility that the various beliefs
might eventually come a little closer to something that is not what we call
today "Jewish"?*

Well, that was exactly the dream of the eighteenth century. Lessing
put it this way in a letter to Moses Mendelssohn, if I remember
well. Lessing was absolutely sick and tired of religious controversy,
you know. He was not an orthodox Lutheran, and he got into all
kinds of troubles. And he said, "I wish I could go to a country
where there were neither Jews nor Christians." That was his simple
epistolary formulation of what a very broad political movement
intended. There are people who say that this notion underlies the
American Constitution. You know that that is controversial, [and
that it involves the meaning of the First Amendment]. It is surely
at first glance a possible view: a secular society. But this is no longer
an aspiration. Now we have some experiences with a secular society.
And if we are sensible we must consider that experience. We have
also the experience in an alternative secular society, namely, the
communist society. I mean, a religious man who is sure on the
basis of divine revelation that this will be the future—namely, that
the Messianic Age will come—he is consistent if he believes in the
face of all evidence to the contrary. But someone who bases his
hopes not on divine revelation must show some human grounds
for it. And I think you cannot show any. Because, you see, even
granting what some people suspect—that a hundred years from

now there will no longer be religious people in practical terms; that the members of religious communities, churches, synagogues, and so on will become a tiny minority—even that would of course not mean that the distinction between Jews and Christians, between Jews and non-Jews rather, would disappear. Because a Jewish community is of this peculiar character that it is indeed what we now call a "religious community"—"religion" not being a Jewish word. But at the same time it is the people, the seed of Abraham; that goes together. How this goes together in the thought of the Jewish tradition—that is a very deep and very old question, but the fact is undeniable. You see, all practical questions must be settled here and now. The way in which your great-grandchildren might settle it cannot determine the way in which you settle it now, because you cannot possibly know under what circumstances your great-grandchildren will live. If social science claims to predict, it does not mean that it can predict the circumstances in which Jews will live a hundred years from now. The predictions of social scientists are much more circumscribed and, if I may say so, irrelevant. I mean, from a practical point of view. They are theoretically very interesting.

I have both uneasiness to express and a question to ask you. The uneasiness that I want to express firstly has to do with the fact that in the contemporary world—and I am directing my comment to the rather easy way in which you talked about the Christians on the one hand, and then the non-Jews on the other—in the contemporary world the outstanding anti-Jews or Jew haters have not been Christians, but have been Nazis on the one hand who have not been Christians and communists who have not been Christians. [Strauss: "That is correct."] *The question that I ask is: what implications do you see, if any, in the growth in the kind of friendliness—at least theologically, and in other areas too—which prevails say between people like Tillich on the one hand and Martin Buber on the other. Where, if you will, the leading theologians both Jewish and Christian have referred to each other, read each other with a considerable amount of friendliness, and quote each other. Do you see any Judaizing in the contemporary world of Christianity, or Christianizing of Judaism?*

No. Surely not. I mean, I don't know whether the examples you chose were the ones I would have chosen—I mean, the individuals you mentioned. But that is truly irrelevant. You are right. There are such figures: Parkes in England is a good example.[12] There are

12. Strauss is evidently referring to James W. Parkes (1896–1981), historian

Leo Strauss

quite a few Christians now who deplore the decision originally made by Augustine in favor of forcible persecution. I know that. And I would assume that there are at all times deep Christians who in their heart of hearts saw the same thing: that this is incompatible with Christianity. Glad as I am about these developments, I must not give up a certain (how shall I say?) sobriety to which I am obliged by virtue of the fact that I belong to a political science department. In other words, I must also speak of the seamy side of the matter. By this I do not wish for one moment to impugn the motives of any individual concerned with these matters. For example, I know Professor Finkelstein of the Theological Seminary, and he is on (as you know) excellent terms with Reinhold Niebuhr of the Union Theological Seminary; and I know other such examples. No question. But you cannot be blind to the fact that for a hundred years, gradually building up and now coming to the fore in our century, there is a very powerful movement which is both anti-Christian and anti-Jewish. And this of course leads [. . .] and here it is not entirely legitimate to adduce examples from straight politics. You know, when a new party arises—very powerful—the older parties who were in a dogfight up to this point might be compelled to make peace among themselves. That this could be, in the case of Judaism and Christianity, in the spirit of the noblest aspirations of the noblest Jews and Christians—you know, we Jews find all kinds of statements to this effect in Halevi, Maimonides, and so on. I do not wish to question the theological legitimacy [of such rapprochement], but I would like to say that we must also look at the other side. And here I come to my point. This was exactly what I tried to show. I could show it sensibly only in the case of communism—that this new power or powers which are both anti-Jewish and anti-Christian still make the distinction between Jews and Christians. The Greek Church and Islam are treated by the Soviet government very differently from the way in which (to use a Christian expression) the synagogue is treated. You see the point? Only someone completely ignorant would say that anti-Jewish things are a matter of Christianity. Of course not. The Romans and Greeks in Alexandria and other places were as much anti-

---

and theologian whose work focused on the history of anti-Semitism and of Jewish–Christian relations. Parkes, a Gentile, was president of the Jewish Historical Society of England at one point (1949–51), and in 1960 his book *The Foundations of Judaism and Christianity* was published in Chicago.

Jewish as the most wicked monks in Germany or in Italy or wherever it was. In other words, this fact that quite a few Christians—and I mentioned Nietzsche advisedly, from this point of view, although Nietzsche was surely not a Christian, as you all know; but Nietzsche surely was very German, and he is held partly responsible for the Nazis. And there is a certain animosity against Germany among Jews—which I shared, I believe, as much as anyone could have shared it, but which is also in need of rethinking, I believe. And we find other cases: for example, Max Weber, a man very well known in the social sciences; the philosopher Schelling, much less known; and there were some other famous cases—*precisely* in Germany—who were not only friendly to Jews but showed a very profound understanding of what one would call the "substance" of Judaism, which a man who is friendly to Jews does not as such possess, as you all know. Surely that exists. But we must not forget the background of this reconciliation. A new power has arisen: Marxist communism, which promised—by a break, a radical break, with the whole past—to destroy the very possibility of anti-Jewish feelings and thoughts. Marx's well-known anti-Jewish utterances were, of course, not inspired by anti-Jewish feelings in the common sense of the word. Yet, Marx's present-day successors like Khrushchev have restored anti-Jewish policies on a communist basis. However this may be, communism in principle threatens Judaism and Christianity equally. As a consequence, the Jewish–Christian antagonism—just as the intra-Christian antagonisms—tend to disappear. I would say, in proportion as Jewish–Christian antagonism disappears, other antagonisms come to sight; and these antagonisms cannot be presumed to be indifferent to the difference between Jews and non-Jews, and [are likely] to exploit it [the difference] for their purposes. But it is most important to realize, as I tried to show by the comparison of the Greek Orthodox Church and the synagogue, that the actual policies of that common enemy are much more anti-Jewish than anti-Christian. I know the facts you mention. My reference to the terrible times in the Middle Ages was intended only to dispel Heine's crude and simplistic view: misfortune. That was not mere misfortune; that was something much greater than misfortune.

Do you agree that there is a basic difference between discrimination against Jews and discrimination against Negroes—in that those who discriminate against Negroes are glad to have some people that they can look down on or

Leo Strauss

around, whereas those who are against Jews would rather have no Jews at all, and therefore have their property belong to Christians or belong to some other sect of which they happen to be members?

I never have considered it. I don't know. I mean, in the first place I would say that the desire to have someone to look down on is not limited to anti-Jewish people. I have known Jews who have had the same desire. I mean, every man who has "ambition"—in the vulgar sense of the word—has this desire. So let us not be self-righteous at this point. But, you know, every chaser after badges doesn't have to be vicious, but the element of the viciousness is in that. But as for this point which you have made, I am not so familiar with the details of anti-Jewish and anti-Negro propaganda. The facts as you stated them—if they are facts—would simply prove there is more Jewish property to distribute easily than the Negroes have.

As a non-Jew I find that one of my greatest problems is, as you mentioned at the very end of your lecture, the fact of being and the infinity which underlies and holds up the idea of progress. And I find myself—before this idea of being—looking at a Jew as if the difference between him and me was irrelevant. The one thing that seems to distinguish us in our attitudes is that ([and] I suppose you could call me a "humanist") before the fact of being I acknowledge that all our symbols are relevant and that we all stand under the same dispensation. But the Jew will not admit that. He will never merely say, "You are a man as I." And I find this a real difficulty. [Strauss: "Oh, that is not true; I mean, that is simply not true."] No, I find that he insists, you see, in saying that he is a Jew. And this question of self-definition creates real difficulties in communication.

Oh God! That is, I think, really unfair. That is as if you would blame a Christian for saying that he is a Christian. Would you say that a Christian as Christian denies to non-Christians the qualities of men? Or a Muslim or Buddhist? Or if a man says "I am an American," does he deny that the people who are not Americans are not human beings?

No. But the Christians make certain assertions about dogma. I find that there are certain people [such as] you dealt [with] to some extent [when you raised] the problem of the Jew who cannot believe as his fathers believed. Now, I am inclined to think also that the question of race as a Nazi problem is merely a residual one. That is, there may continue—out of choice—to be people who choose to stay in the tradition and race, may continue for so long as there is a human race, a seed, which is what we would call a "distinctive race."

Well, race not in any particular biological sense. That is, I suppose, sheer nonsense. But people who—to put it very cynically—people who believe [themselves] to be descended from Abraham, Isaac, and Jacob? Yes, sure. That could be. But I would say I don't see where there is anything wrong with that.

Yes. But the whole point is that given this fact that race as such [. . .] I mean one has only to go to New York and watch, for instance, the Maccabbee soccer team, which has come from Israel to play soccer on the fields of Yonkers, to realize that the whole business of race is irrelevant. All these peoples call themselves Jews, and the idea of physical race [. . .].

"Race" as it is used in any human context is not a subject about which biologists can say anything. This is clear.

Right. Granted. So this then is my point. We have the Jew who cannot identify himself with any dogmatic fixation of his fathers. And yet withal he insists on calling himself a Jew. Now, he may be a Jew, but his Jewishness consists in a myth. Which can be a reality, I grant you, in the human consciousness, but I can't lay my hands on it.

Well, that is very, very nice of you to say that it might exist, although you cannot lay your hands on it. But I would say I have tried to explain that. I took the extreme case of a Jew who feels—I did not take your particular humanist, but I could also have taken him— who thinks that this was all, well, perhaps a noble belief, but it is not a true belief. He cannot share it. And then he sees no reason whatever for perpetuation of this old community. All right. But what is he going to do? How does it look in practice? You see, in all practical matters it is not sufficient to state merely the ends; you must also show the way to the end. And the simplest thing you can show is the first step. Now, if you tell this man, "All right, you don't wear a beard"—today beards have changed their meanings, I have been told; there was a time when the beard was a sign by which you could recognize a Jew. So, in other words, all other things which he can possibly change in his external appearance he will change. He may even change his name. He may even marry a non-Jewish woman, and the children will not be brought up as either Jews or Christians; they will not be circumcised or baptised. I mean, let us go into this; if we want to commit the act of treason

we must go into it. Good, now how do we go from here? I would
say you will discover—except in extremely rare cases—somewhere,
flies in the ointment. For example, this very liberal Jew and this
very liberal non-Jewess are not descended from rocks or oaks (to
quote an old poet) but from human beings. By which I mean they
belong to families. And the families do not necessarily see eye to
eye with their most liberal members. The Jew may be willing to say,
"All right, I will never see my father, mother, brother, and sister
again." But the non-Jewish wife—owing to an amiable weakness of
the female sex—may perhaps say, "Well, it is too hard. I will see my
mother." And then they (the family) will always say, "Why did you
do it? Why did you marry that Jew?" Then the children must also
see the grandmother, and the same difficulty arises again. I mean,
you cannot wish away these things. Then you would have to form
colonies in which only people who have broken with their Jewish
heritage, past origins, and with their Christian past origins would
live together. People have made such small communities for other
purposes—for example, for trying out socialism and communism.
But they are mentioned in the histories of social movements as
amiable but wholly ineffective. It doesn't work. If you take it on the
lowest ground of practice—I mean, just Machiavellian recipes for
getting rid of their misfortune—it doesn't work. It can work in
individual cases. If one may speak of a living man in this connection, perhaps Bernard Baruch is an example where it worked. I
have heard this at some time; but I don't know the gentleman, and
I don't know how it works in practice. But this is a very old man
now, in addition, living in the South. That I have heard; I do not
know that. There may be other cases of this kind. But if it is a
problem of a social kind—meaning not a problem peculiar to him,
but to other people of his kind—[I] would think of the other
people of his kind. And I would say that a solution which is even
perfect for me is imperfect because of these bonds. And the fundamental point seems to me to be this. Again speaking detachedly,
hard-boiledly, and disregarding all of the deeper issues, why do
you want perfect solutions?

*But that's the whole point. I'm not looking for a solution. You see, I don't
want Jews to cease to exist.* [Strauss: "Oh!"] *That is why a man who is a
religious Jew—that this is a position before the mystery of being for which I
have respect. Rather more, let me say in passing, than many [others] with
which I am acquainted. But I meet people who do not have this orientation.*

I recognize that the race question is irrelevant; and yet withal, this individual creates a special orientation for himself which seems to me to have just the quality of a myth.

No. That is, I believe, empirically wrong. I mean, if you mean by "myth" something fabricated, merely figured out [. . .] and that was the word *galut*, "exile." In other words, the recollection, the notion, that there is something—a deep defect—in our situation as Jews, and this deep defect in our situation as Jews is connected with the deep defect with the situation of man. That was an implication of the traditional Jewish faith. This implication—disregarding the theological premises, and so on, and its consequences—is, I think, an empirically tenable assertion. And that the Jews know—most of them, I mean, it is perfectly clear: this difficult position in which modern Jews are I have not brought out fully because I thought everyone knows it. Every Jew surely knows it, and every thoughtful non-Jew who knows any Jews also doesn't have to be told. These are things which are partly very painful if no useful purpose is served—in other words, merely for the sake of the record. That is, I would not do that. But, on the other hand, one cannot deny it, and deny, as you call it, its "reality." It is not a myth. The theories of this or that Zionist ideology—these can be said to be myths. When I was still studying these things with intensity many decades ago, I always made a distinction between Pinsker as the clearest case, on the one hand, and Nordau, on the other.[13] Pinsker really starting from the Jewish Question as it was hitting him directly; and Nordau, having a general theory of nationalism of which the Jewish case was only a special case. And I always went more for the more direct people—you know, who started from what everyone could know. And there are all kinds of things, and I don't wish to go into intra-Jewish polemics. You are aware of the fact that there are Jews, a minority in this country, who regarded the state of Israel as—to use a mild expression—as a pain in the neck. I know these people, but one can simply say that they are the delusionists. One can also say it as follows (also on the lowest denominator): that the "Jewish problem," as it is called, is the most simple and available exemplification of the human problem. That is one way of stating that the Jews are the chosen people. If that is properly developed,

13. Max Nordau (1849–1923) was a Hungarian-born writer and physician as well as Zionist who lived much of his adult life in Paris.

the whole of the other things would come out. The clean solutions of which people dream and dreamt have led either to nothing or to a much greater beastiality than the uneasy solutions with which sensible people will always be satisfied.

Well, if I were to try to draw a general principle from what you have said— I don't know if this is right—but I would say something like this: a man is being dishonorable if he chooses to disagree with, break away from, his origins, what his family believes.

I qualified that. I said that I could visualize a man stemming from absolute degradation and simply having a nobler thing in himself tending away, as it were. And I could only say he acts wisely. [And] if the singular qualities ascribed to him [were indeed present], he would not go around and peddle them and say, "Look what I achieved." But what I said is that this is not the case of the Jews. However degraded we had to live for centuries in all various countries, we were not degraded. Surely we were maltreated; all kinds of things were inflicted upon us. But for the average Jew it was perfectly clear that we did not deserve it at the hands of these people. Perhaps we deserved it at the hand of God—that is another matter—but not at the hands of the people as such. I could give you some childhood stories which—and older people or people of my age here could also give examples of what the traditional posture was. I remind you of only one essay which is still worthy to be read by everyone who is interested in this. That is an essay by Achad Ha'am. You know who he was? Asher Ginsberg. An essay by Achad Ha'am which he called "In External Freedom and Internal Slavery"—and he compared the situation of the Jews in the Russian ghetto to the chief rabbi of France, the head of the Sanhedrin, you know—an institution founded by Napoleon himself—and highly respectable, with badges and all. And then he showed him on the basis of what this man said, this chief rabbi—that he was a slave, not a free man. Externally he was free: he could vote, and do many other things—acquire property, whatever kind he liked. But in his heart he was a slave. Whereas the poorest Polish Jew—if he did not happen to be an individual with a particularly lousy character, which can happen in any community—was externally a man without rights and in this sense a slave, but not in his heart. And that is of crucial importance in this matter.

My point of view is this: if a person who is an average Jew comes to me and says, "On the basis of my latest thinking, I had a real struggle, but I have

*decided that I can no longer in conscience remain a Jew. I have decided I
will become a positivist; I will suspend judgment, etcetera." I would say
that, even though I realize this is going to cause trouble with his family, it's
going to be dysfunctional for him*—[Strauss: "Do you mean 'inconvenient' "?] *yes, inconvenient for him. I would say that if this man remains a
Jew he would be dishonorable.*

Oh! That is another question. You mean to say: is it not morally
necessary for certain Jews not to go to synagogue, not to pray, and
not to participate in other communal activities?

*I mean even more than that—take over, say, the trappings of another
religion completely if he so decides that this is the correct thing to do.*

Yes, prior to any deeper argumentation one would have to say yes.
I was still brought up in the belief, in a very old fashioned country,
that no Jew who ever converted to Christianity was sincere. That
was what I learned and which I believed until I met, as a student, a
professor and son of a rabbi who told me of his conversion to
Christianity. I must say I was not impressed by his story; and if I
could speak of living people here among more or less strangers, I
could tell the story, which was more pitiable than an object of any
indignation. But I would have to admit that he was subjectively
sincere, and no calculation entered into it. I can't say anything
more about that. I know there is a real disproportion between my
primitive feelings—which I learned from my wet nurse, as a much
greater man put it—and my rational judgment. But as I said at the
beginning, conversion was always possible. But the question was
simply whether not to be a member of a Jewish congregation, with
all its implications. Quite a few Jews do that; you know what the
statistics say about that. Nevertheless, the interesting point is this:
the Jewish Question remains. I gave you the example of those
people who became Christian Scientists. I assume—because everyone must be regarded innocent until proven guilty—that they did
it out of conviction. In other words, they didn't want to get rid of a
"misfortune," but they were convinced of the truth of Christian
Science. All right, but what happened to them without any doings
on their side? After all, other Jews had also come to this conviction—all pure convictions. The chairman of this group came to
them and said, "Why don't you form a group of Christian Scientists
of your own?" You can say, "Well, for people who are *only* concerned with the religious truth—in this case, Christian Science—it

doesn't make any difference whether they or their fellow workers are former Jews or not." Surely. That is, however, very unfair and, I would say, almost cruel, because these people suffered from that. While they did not become Christian Scientists in order to get rid of the Jewish disability, they felt a "discrimination" was committed. They are right from their point of view—only it is of no use to get indignant about individual occurrences or symptoms, and one must view the whole situation.

In a sense, and I guess with some pain, I really think that I—as a Jew who is very concerned with finding some meaningful answer as to why I remain a Jew and how to do so—must really repeat the question that was asked by the non-Jew. I think that you give us really little reason to want positively to remain Jewish. At best, you tell us that an empirical, hard-boiled analysis of the situation—which is your position tonight [Strauss: "Absolutely and always."]—*would constrain one in this direction. At second best, you tell us there are various flies in the ointment which we might idealize.* [Strauss: "No! I didn't say that. No, no."] *Well, I guess really I'm reacting, and I think I'm permitted to react.* [Strauss: "Yes, sure, get it out of your system."] *But basically I think what you are really suggesting—if you talk to the young people here, of whom I number myself* [Strauss: "Rightly."]—*is that you are really challenging us, you're really forcing us to say that this is just another one of the things that "we shall overcome." Because, even if we fail, it is worthwhile from the way you paint the picture. And I think, and I would hope—although this is not my evening to lecture—that I have different reasons for positively wanting to remain a Jew and for having an answer to in what ways one might be meaningfully different from a Christian. But partly my difference stems from my inability to accept your basic premise. I think at least that—now, maybe we are deluded—but Americans in my situation, I think, pretty well feel that it is a revolutionary thing; that your anecdotes are out of date, so to speak; that the Christian Science story has no compelling meaning to people of our generation. And I think much of your interpretation of the American scene is based on such anecdotal material which I feel is not compelling, although it may be true that it has happened somewhere else and quite recently. But basically, accepting your premise, I would say that all you offer me positively is to be a religious Zionist. But failing that, you give me the quite comfortable solution—but which I find inadequate because not challenging enough and not different enough—to be a scientist who somehow can reconcile his scientific positivism with the eternal mystique, which, after all, derives from Judaism.*

Thank you very much for your statement. You misunderstood certain points; but since I know you, I can only say that that must be due to certain defects of my presentation. When you say that my knowledge of American Jewry (and there is a question there) is defective, I simply have to grant that. I came to this country only about twenty-three years ago. (I have not figured that out at the moment, but roughly.) But I have also some training in seeing, by which I do not necessarily mean the social science training.

You see, what I tried to show is this: I think clarity or honesty about the most important matters is a most important thing. That was my premise. Therefore I rejected—partly explicitly and partly implicitly, because I couldn't develop the whole thing—all attempts to interpret the Jewish past, in terms of a culture. Therefore the emptiness of which you complain. In other words, for me the question is truly either the Torah, as understood by our tradition, or, say, unbelief. And I think that is infinitely more important than every cultural interpretation which is based on a tacit unbelief and cannot be a substitute for the belief it has given up. That is, I believe, the basis of our disagreement as far as I can see it. Let me add one point. When I say "the Jewish faith as our ancestors held it," I do not mean that every particular belief—even if entertained by the majority of Jews or by the large majority of Jews for centuries—must necessarily be binding. I happen to know a bit of the Jewish medieval thinkers, and I know that quite a few very powerful and important changes were made even by them. I believe, and I say this without any disrespect to any orthodox Jew, that it is hard for people—for most Jews today—to believe in verbal inspiration, in verbal inspiration of the Torah, and in the miracles—or most of the miracles—and other things. I know that. My friend Rabbi Harris is not here, but I am in deep sympathy with what he means by a "post-critical Judaism." I think that offers a perfectly legitimate and sensible goal, namely, to restate the essence of Jewish faith in a way which is by no means literally identical, say, with Ram Bam's "Creator of the world," or something of this kind—I mean, of any traditional statement of principles. That's not the point. But a Judaism which is not belief in the "Creator of the world"—that has problems running through it.

Now, I tell you another story, and this story has a somewhat greater dignity. One of the most outstanding Jews in Germany was Hermann Cohen, the founder of the neo-Kantian school. And he was concerned very much with how he could be both a philosopher and a Jew, in the sense of a believing Jew. That was a lifelong struggle, and what he said is by no means irrelevant and [is] I think worthy of the study of everyone who is concerned with that question. At a certain point of his life he read to an Orthodox and educated Jew a brief statement of what he thought to be the essence of Judaism. And then the old-fashioned man, [simple] of birth and education, said, "And where remains the Creator of the world?" I have heard that in this very building at some time someone said, "I believe in God as a symbol." Then I would say that a man who says "I do not believe in God" is, other things being equal, a better man. Now I do not deny that a man can believe in God without believing in Creation, and particularly without believing in creation out of nothing. After all, the Bible itself does not explicitly teach Creation out of nothing, as one might see. But still, Judaism contains the whole notion of man's responsibility and of a final redemption. I mean, you can say "All right, abolish the personal Messiah and have only a Messianic Age"—which is done by most liberal Jews, as you know—and add many more of these things. But the very notion of the certainty of final redemption [is] untenable without belief in a God concerned with justice. And this is such a most important issue. And I would say that it seems to me that the proper posture of a man who does not believe in that is to enter into this mystery, into this mysterious belief. And [I think] he will come out of it—even if he will not come out with belief in this— with some understanding he did not have before.

One of the deepest Jewish thinkers now, in my private opinion (which doesn't count in these matters much), is Gershom Scholem of the Hebrew University. Now, in his most recent book, which is in German only[14] (I suppose it came out in Hebrew, but don't even remember the German title), he shows to what amazing lengths some of our mystics went by thinking through these beliefs and their coming out with views [indicating that] many of the objections which many of us would have to such traditional beliefs [can] no longer be tenable, that is, be the kind of thing which I would regard as satisfactory. But, I believe, by simply replacing God by

14. Gershom Scholem (1897–1982) was a prolific scholar whose central interest was Jewish mysticism. Strauss was no doubt referring to one of three books by Scholem that appeared in German in the period 1960–62. These three books are all concerned with facets of Kabbala. See *Bibliography of the Writings of Gershom G. Scholem* (Jerusalem: Magnes Press of the Hebrew University, 1977), pp. 35–38.

the creative genius of the Jewish people, one gives away, one deprives oneself—even if one does not believe—of a source of *human* understanding. Let us also not forget [to ask]—what does it mean [that] one does not believe? How much of the unbelief now existing is as much a matter of hearsay, or what someone of your profession would call "social pressure"? Belief and unbelief are not such simple states: here's a camp of the believers; here's a camp of nonbelievers. Politically it may very well appear this way on many occasions; but for most of the more *thoughtful* people in both camps, things would be different. Now, I do not wish to minimize folk dances, Hebrew speaking, and many other things. I do not want to minimize them. But I believe that they cannot possibly take the place of what is most profound in our tradition.

But however this may be, I have had my day in court. I have said what I thought about it, and I must say that I am surprised that you are still here.

Leo Strauss: Between Athens and Jerusalem

Steven B. Smith

Harold Bloom, the Yale literary critic, once described Leo Strauss as "political philosopher and Hebraic sage."[1] This always seemed to me unusually prescient. For Strauss is most frequently understood as an interpreter and critic of a number of thinkers, both ancient and modern, who belong to the history of political philosophy. But far less often is he regarded as a contributor to Jewish thought. It is neither as a historian nor as a philosopher but as a Jew that I want to consider him here.

At first blush this approach to Strauss seems relatively unproblematical. Even a superficial perusal of his major works shows that Jewish themes were a continual preoccupation of his from the earliest times onwards. His first book *Spinoza's Critique of Religion* (1930) was written as a researcher at the Akademie für die Wissenschaft des Judentums in Berlin.[2] His second book *Philosophy and Law* (1935) looked to Spinoza's most illustrious predecessor, Moses Maimonides, and his conception of law.[3] Furthermore, a number of later essays and lectures return to these early themes, especially his Frank Cohen lecture on "Jerusalem and Athens."[4] Finally, in a semi-autobiographical introduction to the English translation of his book on Spinoza,

An earlier draft of this article was presented at the Benjamin Cardozo School of Law. My thanks extend to the National Endowment for the Humanities for their financial support of the research upon which this article is based.

1. Harold Bloom, Foreword to Yosef H. Yerushalmi, *Zakhor: Jewish History and Jewish Memory* (New York: Schocken, 1989), p. xiii.

2. Leo Strauss, *Die Religionskritik Spinozas als Grundlage seiner Bibelwissenschaft* (Berlin: Akademie-Verlag, 1930); English translation by E. M. Sinclair, *Spinoza's Critique of Religion* (New York: Schocken, 1965).

3. Leo Strauss, *Philosophie und Gesetz: Beitrage zum Verstständnis Maimunis und seiner Vorläufer* (Berlin: Schocken, 1935); English translation by Fred Baumann, *Philosophy and Law: Essays Toward an Understanding of Maimonides and his Predecessors* (Philadelphia: Jewish Publication Society of America, 1987).

4. Leo Strauss, "Jerusalem and Athens: Some Introductory Reflections," *Commentary* 43 (1967): 45–57; reprinted in *Studies in Platonic Political Philosophy*, ed. Thomas Pangle (Chicago: University of Chicago Press, 1983), pp. 147–73; see also "The Mutual Influence of Theology and Philosophy," *Independent Journal of Philosophy* 3 (1979): 111–18; "Progress or Return?" *Modern Judaism* 1 (1981): 17–45; reprinted in *The Rebirth of Classical Political Rationalism*, ed. Thomas Pangle (Chicago: University of Chicago Press, 1989), pp. 227–70; "On the Interpretation of Genesis," *L'Homme* 21 (1981): 5–20.

Strauss spoke in no uncertain terms about the various currents of
neo-orthodoxy, political, and cultural Zionism within which he came
to maturity.[5]

Nevertheless, at a deeper level Strauss's relation to Judaism seems
considerably more ambiguous. It is arguable that Strauss was not
interested in Judaism per se but with Judaism insofar as it was an
illustration of a more general problem, what he called "the theological-
political" problem. But since this problem, as Strauss himself recognizes, is not peculiar to Judaism but is central to the experiences
of the Christian and the Islamic worlds, there is no reason to believe that Strauss's concern was with Judaism as such.

Perhaps more significantly, to say that Strauss is not just a historian
but a contributor to Jewish thought presupposes that there is some
meaningful sense in which we can speak of something called Jewish
political thought. But what, for instance, does the thought of men
such as Akiba, Rashi, Halevi, and Maimonides have in common
with the thought of such "non-Jewish Jews" as Spinoza, Heine, Marx,
and Freud? While there might be some reason to believe that the
political problems faced by Jews are no different from those faced
by any other peoples, a moment's reflection is all that is necessary
to reveal that this is emphatically not the case. At the risk of ar-
bitrariness I would like to suggest that Jewish political thought is
marked by a preoccupation with such themes as exile, homelessness, marginality, and a need to retain some sense of ethnic or historical identity. Since Judaism, for much of its history, has existed
as a "despised religion" (Halevi) among non- or even anti-Jewish
peoples, the twin aspirations for assimilation and the assertion of
separateness are the bipolarities within which Jewish thought has
developed.

The position of the Jews in modern, enlightened, liberal society
is only the most tangible contemporary expression of the theological-

---

5. Leo Strauss, "Preface to Spinoza's Critique of Religion," *Liberalism: Ancient
and Modern* (New York: Basic Books, 1968), pp. 224–59. In a letter to Gershom
Scholem dated 2 December 1962, Strauss explained his decision to publish this
autobiography as follows: "When studying Hobbes, I observed that what he said
and did not say was a function of the heresy laws obtaining at the time of publication of his various works. But then I saw that in one of his works published at
the time of considerable restriction he was more outspoken than ever before. I
was baffled until I noted that this book was published when he was already very
old, with one foot in the grave and I learned that this condition is conducive to
courage. As for me I have had my first two heart attacks, Ergo." I would like to
thank Professor Joseph Cropsey for allowing me access to the Strauss-Scholem
correspondence.

political problem. Strauss traces his own preoccupation with this problem back to his experiences as "a young Jew born and raised in Germany." The Germany to which he alludes here was Weimar Germany, the Germany that came into being in that all-too-brief period between the Treaty of Versailles and the Reichstag fire. Weimar was, of course, a liberal democracy, one which could trace its name back not only to the residence of Goethe but to a preference for things Western and, above all, French and English. The Weimar republic was of a "moderate, nonradical character," determined to maintain "a balance between the dedication to the principles of 1789 and the dedication to the highest German tradition."[6] This Germany offered both unusual opportunities as well as dangers for the Jews.

On the one hand, liberal democracy traces its origins in continental Europe back to the French Revolution's claim to be entirely neutral on the religious issue. Liberalism, as articulated in the philosophy of such men as Locke, Montesquieu, and Kant, to say nothing of such official documents as the American Declaration of Independence and the French Declaration of the Rights of Man and the Citizen, was based on a universal morality of natural rights that was indifferent to the differences between Jews and Gentiles.[7] Liberalism was thus the first European political settlement to offer the Jews "emancipation" from the tyranny of state-sponsored religious intolerance.

On the other hand, the emancipation of the Jews was conceived by liberalism along the model of assimilation. Jews would henceforth forego their claims to exclusivity and adherence to a specific tradition and become one with the non-Jewish majority. Even Zionism of the type sponsored by Herzl and Pinsker did no more than offer a political or civil solution to the so-called Jewish Question. It promised the Jews a state of their own which, like the modern European states, would be a liberal state, that is, indifferent to or above religion. Strauss described as "blasphemous" the very suggestion that liberalism or Zionism be regarded as the solution to the Jewish Question. He could write in 1965 that:

> The establishment of the state of Israel is the most profound modification of the Galut [Exile] which has occurred, but it is not the

6. "Preface to Spinoza's *Critique of Religion*," p. 224.
7. Leo Strauss, *The City and Man* (Chicago: University of Chicago Press, 1964), pp. 2–4.

end of the Galut: in the religious sense, and perhaps not only in the religious sense, the state of Israel is a part of the Galut. Finite, relative problems can be solved; infinite absolute problems cannot be solved. . . . From every point of view it looks as if the Jewish people were the chosen people, at least in the sense that the Jewish problem is the most manifest symbol of the human problem insofar as it is social or political problem.[8]

The Jewish problem, then, is of interest because it is "the most manifest symbol of the human problem." But what is the human problem of which the Jewish problem is but a symbol? In a phrase it is the problem of the universal and the particular or, in Platonic language, the one and the many. This is a problem with many branches and tributaries. But in purely social or political terms this problem presents itself as a conflict between universalistic commitments and particularistic identifications. For Strauss, this problem became a conflict between assimilation and eventual absorption in a universal humanity or the assertion of stubborn loyalty to a particular tradition. When the particular tradition in question is one like Judaism which claims divine or revealed origins, this conflict is made all the more difficult. It was precisely his choice to stand outside of or above this conflict as a sort of mediator between fidelity and assimilation that, I would argue, constitutes the uniqueness of Strauss's answer to the Jewish Question.

I

The core of Strauss's thought is the famous "theological-political problem," a problem which he would say "remained *the* theme of my studies" from a very early time.[9] The question *quid sit deus*, first raised in his study of Spinoza was later described by him as "the all-important question" of philosophy "although the philosophers do not frequently pronounce it."[10] This problem reveals a number of distinct aspects which it is necessary to untangle.

In the first place, the theological-political problem represents for Strauss the "core" or "nerve" of the West. The conflict between biblical faith and Greek philosophy is said to be "characteristic of the

---

8. "Preface to Spinoza's Critique of Religion," p. 230.

9. Leo Strauss, New Preface to *Hobbes politische Wissenschaft* (Berlin: H. Luchterhand, 1965), p. 7.

10. *Spinoza's Critique of Religion*, p. 194; *City and Man*, p. 241.

West" and "the secret of its vitality."[11] This conflict, symbolized by the eternal archetypes of Jerusalem and Athens, indicates the two great antitheses of the Western tradition. The Bible and philosophy represent two fundamentally different "codes" or ways of life which defy final reconciliation. In the final analysis one can be either a philosopher or a theologian but one cannot be both, even though Strauss argues that each should be open to the challenge of the other.

What exactly is that challenge? Philosophy, as Strauss claims, is the attempt to replace opinion about all things by knowledge about all things.[12] By its nature, philosophy is the effort to understand the whole or cosmos by means of one's unaided reason alone. Philosophy must submit, and submit ruthlessly, everything to the bar of its own critical rationality. It was their relentless emphasis on reason, their own reason, that led the philosophers to believe that contemplation, *theoria*, is the highest or best life for a human being. Biblical thought, by contrast, begins not from the experience of intellectual curiosity about all things but from a sense of awe or fear of the Lord. According to the Bible, human life is characterized not by self-sufficiency but by a radical sense of our dependence upon God. Not contemplation but piety, obedience, and the need for divine mercy are what is most characteristic of us.[13]

This conflict, then, between revelation and reason, the Bible and philosophy, took on from the beginning a predominantly secular or political character. Philosophy, as represented in the person of Socrates, finds its natural home in the city. Philosophy presupposes a context of urbanity, wealth, and leisure to sustain it. The life of simple piety and humble awe, as extolled by the Bible and its most authoritative interpreters, by contrast, is unequivocal in favor of the rustic or pastoral life. According to the Bible, the first murderer was also the founder of the first city and the arts necessary for civilized life. It is no accident that it was not Cain, the tiller of the soil, but Abel, the keeper of sheep, who found favor in the eyes of God.[14]

But this secular conflict has another dimension as well. The conflict between philosophy and the Bible is ultimately a conflict about how

11. "Mutual Influence of Theology and Philosophy," p. 113; "Progress or Return?" p. 270.
12. Leo Strauss, *What Is Political Philosophy and Other Studies* (New York: Free Press, 1959), p. 11.
13. "Progress or Return?" p. 246.
14. *Ibid.*, p. 251.

political and ecclesiastical authority should be divided. In earlier times communities were held together by powerful moral and legal codes said to be derived from God or the gods. The *theos nomos*, divine law, is said to constitute the foundation of all society. Accordingly, the ideal regime was a theocracy governed by priests or kings claiming priestly authority. The problem is the conflict, or potential conflict, between divine laws.

Over time this monopoly of power was challenged by those philosophers seeking to carve out a sphere of freedom of thought and opinion over which clerics should have no say. Strauss attaches enormous significance to this fact. Apparently belief in the gods or religion is found wherever men live together. Philosophy, by contrast, is a late and relatively rare phenomenon. Philosophy was made possible, however, only with the discovery of "nature." There is, Strauss likes to remind his readers, no word in biblical Hebrew that approximates the Greek term *physis*. The Hebrew *mishpat* meaning "way" or "custom" is at best a prephilosophic anticipation of nature.[15] To inquire into nature is to seek for principles or first causes. However, the discovery of nature was only a necessary and not a sufficient condition for the possibility of political philosophy. It was only when Socrates applied the idea of nature to the study of the human and political world that political philosophy proper was born. It is, again, no coincidence that Plato's *Republic*, the greatest work of ancient political philosophy, culminated in the claim that there would be no cessation of evils until kings became philosophers or philosophers became kings.

To be sure, despite the obvious and important differences between biblical thought and classical philosophy, Strauss was not blind to their areas of agreement. In particular he points to two. In the first place, there is broad agreement regarding the place of morality in the overall economy of human life. Furthermore, both Greek philosophy and the Bible agree that the locus of morality is the patriarchal family which is the basic cell of society. And second, both agree that the core of morality is justice. By justice is meant primarily obedience to law. Law is understood here to mean not just civil law but divine or religious law, law with some transcendent sanction.[16] Strauss is not altogether clear about the precise content of justice

    15. *Ibid.*, pp. 253–54; see also *History of Political Philosophy*, ed. Leo Strauss and Joseph Cropsey, 2nd ed. (Chicago: Rand McNally, 1972), pp. 2–3.
    16. "Progress or Return?" pp. 246–47.

or the penalty for its transgression. However, it entails a fundamental intuition about certain restraints upon our behavior or, as he put it, "a kind of divination that not everything is permitted."[17] Indeed, Strauss claims that what Plato says about the power of divine retribution in the *Laws* is "literally identical" with certain verses of Amos and Psalm 139.[18]

The conflict or tension between the Bible and philosophy which has been the "nerve" of the Western world is today on the verge of extinction. While many would, no doubt, regard this as a sign of progress, Strauss takes it as symptomatic of a "crisis." The "crisis of the West," as Strauss sometimes calls it, is the direct result of a new kind of philosophy, the philosophy of the Enlightenment, which is based on the idea of progress.[19] This idea is neither clearly of Greek or of biblical heritage. Unlike the biblical prophets who chastised their contemporaries by invoking an earlier time of piety and obedience, the modern philosophers beginning with Machiavelli, Descartes, and Hobbes turned away from the past and looked toward the future. Between the past and the future one could discern progress understood as the conquest of nature for the relief of man's earthly estate. Strauss even toys with the idea that the Enlightenment conception of science as a universal technique was known to the ancients but rejected by them in advance as "unnatural" or "destructive of humanity."[20]

The cause of this crisis can be discovered in the attempt of the Enlightenment to abolish or truncate the roots of the West. Whatever the differences between ancient philosophy and the Bible alluded to above, pre-Enlightenment thought was "conservative" in the sense that it did not seek a solution to the human problem through unaided human effort. The best city of the *Republic* just like the messianic kingdom of Isaiah was to be an object of fervent wish or prayer but not of political activism. This awareness served to impose some limitations on what was deemed politically possible. It was because ancient political philosophy and the Bible understood that "evil cannot be eradicated" from the soul and that"one's expectations from poli-

17. Leo Strauss, *Natural Right and History* (Chicago: University of Chicago Press, 1953), p. 130; see also *On Tyranny* (Ithaca: Cornell University Press, 1975), p. 205.
18. "Progress or Return?" pp. 247–48.
19. *City and Man*, pp. 1–12; *Liberalism: Ancient and Modern*, pp. v–ix; "The Crisis of Our Time," *The Predicament of Modern Politics*, ed. Harold Spaeth (Detroit: University of Detroit Press, 1964), pp. 41–54.
20. *On Tyranny*, p. 190.

tics must be moderate" that allowed it to escape the "fanaticism" of destruction.[21] All of the revolutionary movements of our day, on both the left and the right, can be traced back to the Enlightenment's forgetfulness of this and other such pieces of prudential advice. The French Revolution's demand to establish justice here and now was just the first act in a political drama that would seek to overcome all otherworldliness or transcendence.[22] It is no accident, then, that the Enlightenment appears in Strauss's thought as nothing less than an unprecedented "propaganda" seeking to advance itself through a combination of ridicule and intimidation.[23]

The crisis of the West reveals itself today as the attempt of modern philosophy or the Enlightenment to vanquish, once and for all, the claims of revealed religion or what Strauss calls simply "Orthodoxy."[24] At the core of Orthodoxy—whether Christian, Jewish, or Muslim—is a belief in the revealed or mysterious character of the law. Even later claims regarding the natural law represent a falling away from the standards of strict orthodoxy by suggesting that law can be understood or discovered by unaided human reason. Obviously, the attack upon Orthodoxy is as old as philosophy itself. The official charge brought against Socrates by the court of Athens was that he was *atheos*, a disbeliever. What Strauss disputes is that any premodern thinker ever seriously doubted the necessity of religion as a prerequisite for social order.[25] The belief that God or the gods are in some sense "first for us" and that consequently the city is subservient to divine or revealed law constitutes the original form of political self-understanding.[26]

It was only with the modern Enlightenment that we find for the first time the intransigent demand that philosophy replace Orthodoxy as the foundation for social order. "Political atheism," Strauss remarks, "is a distinctly *modern* phenomenon."[27] Accordingly, the claims of religion were reviled in the works of the Enlightenment as produc-

---

21. *What Is Political Philosophy?* p. 28.

22. *Natural Right and History*, p. 15.

23. *Philosophy and Law*, pp. 11–12; *What Is Political Philosophy?* p. 45; see also Leo Strauss, *Thoughts on Machiavelli* (Glencoe, IL: The Free Press, 1958), pp. 297–98.

24. *Philosophy and Law*, pp. 3–20.

25. "Boldness formerly was not the character of atheists as such. They were even of a character nearly the reverse; they were formerly like the old Epicureans, rather an unenterprising race. But of late they are grown active, designing, turbulent, and seditious" (Edmund Burke, cited in *Natural Right and History*, p. 169).

26. *Natural Right and History*, pp. 81–83; *City and Man*, p. 241.

27. *Natural Right and History*, p. 169; emphasis mine.

tive only of error, distortion, and superstition.[28] The underlying premise of the Enlightenment was that the truths of philosophy were "harmless," that is, beneficial to society as a whole and that henceforth philosophers should be regarded not as threats to but as benefactors of the public good.[29] To be sure, the early founders of the Enlightenment wrote works with titles like the *Tractatus Theologico-Politicus*, the *Reasonableness of Christianity*, and *Religion within the Limits of Reason Alone* precisely to defend themselves from allegations of public atheism. The early or moderate Enlightenment still regarded some kind of rationalized religion as a necessary basis for securing a just and stable social order. However, it became part of the modern demand for "probity" that religion, just like politics, defend itself against the bar of reason.[30] For later more radical thinkers like Marx, Nietzsche, and Heidegger the terrors and harshness of existence or history were to be preferred to the comforts and illusions offered by the religious imagination.[31]

The question Strauss asks us to consider, then, is this. Was the Enlightenment successful in banishing religion or at least pushing it to the very periphery of civilization? Has the progress of culture witnessed an abatement of hostility toward philosophy? Or can we expect to see a "return of the repressed"? Is religion a permanent need of man, a permanent response to the human condition, or is it a remnant left over from a prerational, prescientific age? These are questions to which we shall return.

II

Strauss's views on the theological-political problem did not arise full blown. Rather they emerged only gradually in his writings and according to some interpreters underwent a profound modification over time.[32] The earliest evidence of Strauss's concern with this

28. *Spinoza's Critique of Religion*, pp. 172–82.
29. René Descartes, *Discourse on Method*, Part VI.
30. Immanuel Kant, *The Critique of Pure Reason*, trans. Norman Kemp Smith (New York: St. Martin's, 1965): "Our age is, in especial degree, the age of criticism, and to criticism everything must submit" (p. 9).
31. *Philosophy and Law*, p. 18.
32. Alan Bloom, "Leo Strauss," *Political Theory* 4 (1974): 383, speaks of "three phases" in Strauss's development while Seth Benardete, "Leo Strauss' 'The City and Man,'" *Political Science Reviewer* 8 (1978): 1, speaks of a "fundamental change" taking place in his thought.

Steven B. Smith

problem occurs in a review article of Max Nordau's Zionism published in Martin Buber's journal *Der Jude* in 1923.[33] In this article the young Strauss makes clear his differences with the policies of both liberal assimilationists and Zionists respectively. He deplores especially the "self-destructive" tendencies of assimilationist Jews with their naive belief in the liberalizing principles of the French Revolution and their willingness to abandon the traditional grounds of Judaism, namely, the idea of chosenness and faith in the Messiah. For Strauss, the experience of the *galut* — the history of the Jews during the Diaspora — has had the positive effect of strengthening the traditional faith. "This is the essence of the *galut*," Strauss writes. "It gives the Jewish people a maximum possibility for existence by means of a minimum normality."[34]

The policy of assimilation seeks to reverse the historical relationship of the Jews with their host nations. Its goal could be stated as providing a minimum possibility for existence by ensuring a maximum normality. Strauss takes this policy to be illusory. It deprives the Jews of "the self-assurance of ghetto life" by promising "the illusory surrogate of trust in the humanity of civilization."[35]

As for political Zionism, Strauss regards it as merely "continuing and intensifying the dejudaizing tendency of assimilation." This dejudaizing tendency is revealed in Zionism's attribution of the distress of the Jews not to divine punishment for the sins of the fathers but to "the many minor facts of politics and economics."[36] And likewise Zionism understands the amelioration of this distress as having nothing to do with the coming of Messiah but everything to do with the secular, political struggle of the Jewish people for a homeland. While for tactical reasons Strauss felt closer to the representatives of German Zionism than to the representatives of assimilation, he recognized that Zionism too was but another form of assimilation premised on the belief that the Jews should become a people no different from any other.

In other words, Zionism offers the Jews nothing more than a pale imitation of the liberal secular state —"a state for a people

33. Leo Strauss, "Der Zionismus bei Nordau," *Der Jude* 7 (1922–23): 657–60; English translation by Joachim Neugroschel "Zionism in Max Nordau," *The Jew: Essays from Martin Buber's Journal "Der Jude" 1916*–1928, ed. Arthur Cohen (University: University of Alabama Press, 1980), pp. 120–26.
34. *Ibid.*, p. 124.
35. *Ibid.*
36. *Ibid.*, p. 125.

without a state." Nordau's particular form of Zionism with its lofty appeal to a politics of honesty, sincerity, and candor has no other aim than to appeal to "the Jewish heart which is always open to innocent suffering and disillusioned idealism." But a Jewish state divorced from traditional Jewish beliefs and practices could be only an empty shell. Consequently, Nordau's quasi-Hegelian belief that European civilization is moving toward a more rational solution to the Jewish problem is itself evidence of a gross philistinism. "Nordau," Strauss writes, "has the attitude of the apothecary Homais [in Flaubert's *Madame Bovary*] who makes his splendid scientific knowledge universally useful for improving cider-making and always emphasizes his virtue."[37]

Strauss's identification of the delusions of German Jewry (or at least its most prominent representatives) led him to search out the roots of this attitude. His book on Spinoza was the result of that search. Spinoza was, after all, the founder of the so-called higher criticism of the Bible with its search for more accurate historical and philological evidence about the dates of composition. But even more importantly Spinoza gave decisive impetus to the twin currents of Zionism and assimilationism mentioned above. Strauss's book was, in large part, an answer to Hermann Cohen, the founder of the Marburg School of neo-Kantianism and "a faithful warner and comforter to many Jews"[38] who had savagely attacked Spinoza at a time when the latter's reputation was being rehabilitated among educated German Jews.[39]

Cohen had routinely attacked Spinoza's *Ethics* throughout his long career, but it was only when he turned to the *Tractatus theologico-politicus* that his criticisms turned hateful. Cohen's attack stemmed from the belief that Spinoza's entire philosophy represented a kind of "revenge" upon Judaism for the edict of excommunication he had received from the rabbinate of Amsterdam.[40] Cohen denounced Spinoza first and foremost as a "renegade to his people" and an "apostate" who preferred Christianity to Judaism. Spinoza's cardinal sin was his

37. *Ibid.*, p. 126.
38. Leo Strauss, "Introductory Essay," in Hermann Cohen, *Religion of Reason out of the Sources of Judaism*, trans. Simon Kaplan (New York: Ungar, 1972); reprinted in *Studies in Platonic Political Philosophy*, p. 246.
39. Hermann Cohen, "Spinoza uber Staat und Religion, Judentum und Christentum," *Jüdische Schriften*, ed. B. Strauss (Berlin: Schwetschke, 1924) 3: 290–372.
40. *Ibid.*, pp. 298, 360.

92

Steven B. Smith

depiction of Judaism as a purely political legislation which had the function of denying the universalism and "ethical idealism" of the prophets. Consequently, not only did Spinoza willfully misrepresent Judaism before a predominantly Christian and hence hostile world, but his work became a source of anti-Semitism for those who later took his depiction of Judaism as authoritative.[41] For all of these reasons, not to mention others, Spinoza stood condemned as a "base traitor" to his people, guilty of a "humanly incomprehensible betrayal."[42]

In an early article entitled "Cohens Analyse der Bibelwissenschaft Spinozas," Strauss denied that Spinoza's philosophy could be understood simply as motivated by the desire for revenge.[43] He attacked Cohen's psychologistic method of attempting to explain a thinker's ideas by reference to motives like hatred or a desire for revenge. In fact the emphasis that Cohen had put upon Spinoza's excommunication is at best a "conjecture" since the main lines of his biblical criticism had been worked out prior to his expulsion from the synagogue.[44] Further, Strauss doubted the authenticity of Cohen's claim that Spinoza's "sacrilege" consists in his politicization of Judaism. For Cohen the social democrat, it would not have been "satanic" but rather "godly" if Spinoza had said that the religion of Moses was the foundation of the socialist state.[45] Finally, Strauss maintains, as he did almost forty years later, that Spinoza's biblical exegesis is motivated not by a hatred of Judaism but by a desire to free scholarship (*Wissenschaft*) from ecclesiastical supervision.[46] His critique of the prophets is not "completely incomprehensible" once we realize that it is directed not to any specifically Jewish matters but to the sect-filled Netherlands of the seventeenth century. Strauss concludes that Spinoza's biblical scholarship is "adequately motivated" by "objective considerations" which are not reducible to his "frame of mind" or any other "personal motives" stressed by Cohen.[47]

Cohen's reasons for repudiating Spinoza are tied not only to his commitment to Judaism but to his ethical theory and especially the

41. *Ibid.*, pp. 371–72.
42. *Ibid.*, p. 361.
43. Leo Strauss, "Cohens Analyse der Bibelwissenschaft Spinozas," *Der Jude* 8 (1924)): 295–314.
44. *Ibid.*, p. 298.
45. *Ibid.*, p. 299.
46. *Ibid.*, p. 302.
47. *Ibid.*, pp. 309, 311.

Kantian idea of rational autonomy.[48] Cohen's argument proceeds in two stages. In the first place, he accepted Kant's view that for a moral law to be binding—a "categorical imperative" in Kant's terms—it had to be universal. A universal law is one whose determining ground is the rational will (*vernünftige Wille*) and not simply the agent's arbitrary whim or caprice (*Wilkür*). Indeed, for Cohen as for Kant, there can be no other source of law than man's practical rationality itself; any other incentive for obeying the law would, strictly speaking, be outside of reason and therefore not a reason at all.

But while Cohen accepted the Kantian demand for universality, he had to reject Kant's specific views on Judaism. For Kant, Judaism was nothing more than a collection of "statutory" laws and therefore "really not a religion at all."[49] Kant accepted Spinoza's view (although he lacked Spinoza's profound knowledge of Jewish law and tradition) that Judaism was a purely political or civil legislation and as such indifferent to the higher moral or spiritual needs of mankind. The religious practices and rituals of Judaism—the entire domain of *Halakha*—are no more than an historical contingency and thus lacking in moral necessity. Judaism was for Kant the religion of sheer heteronomy, that is, of externally imposed command. Thus did Kant regard the *Akedah*, the binding of Isaac, as a "deception" contrary to the moral law.[50]

Cohen's conception of Judaism seemed to owe more to Kant's greatest Jewish contemporary, Moses Mendelssohn. For Mendelssohn, Judaism was the original repository of a rational monotheism. Belief in God, providence, and the immortality of the soul were rational precepts not dependent upon revelation. The beauty of Judaism's ethical monotheism is that it is independent of any special revelation or particular providence, but is available to man as such. After all, did he not write in his *Jerusalem* that:

> According to the concepts of true Judaism, all the inhabitants of the earth are destined to felicity; and the means of attaining it are as widespread as mankind itself, as charitably dispersed as the means of warding off hunger and other natural needs?[51]

48. See especially, Hermann Cohen, *Kants Begründung der Ethik* (Berlin: F. Dummlers, 1877), pp. 272–73.

49. Immanuel Kant, *Religion Within the Limits of Reason Alone*, trans. T. M. Greene and H. H. Hudson (New York: Harper and Row, 1960), p. 116.

50. Immanuel Kant, *Der Streit der Facultäten*, *Werke*, ed. Ernst Cassier et. al. (Berlin: B. Cassirer, 1922), 7: 375.

51. Moses Mendelssohn, *Jerusalem or on Religious Power and Judaism*, trans. Allan Arkush (Hanover, NH: University Press of New England, 1983), p. 94.

And did not Talmudic Judaism itself declare that "the righteous of all nations have a share in the world to come"? For Cohen as for Mendelssohn, the essence of Judaism is that it is a "religion of reason" in which all men, so long as they be rational, are invited to participate.

This leads to a second difference between Spinoza and Cohen, namely, their treatment of the messianic theme in Judaism. For Spinoza, the prophets were not philosophers but "men of great imaginative power" and "unusually vivid imaginations" but as such "less fitted for abstract reasoning."[52] In contrast to Maimonides for whom Moses' prophecy was raised above that of all other prophets, Spinoza argued that "it is hardly likely that men accustomed to the superstitions of Egypt . . . should have held any sound notions about the Deity" and that the Mosaic prophecy, far from representing a liberation merely substituted one form of oppression for another.[53] Indeed, the alleged election of the Jewish people had less to do with their wisdom or tranquility of mind than with their social organization and the means by which they acquired and maintained political hegemony. Accordingly, the gift of prophecy was limited to the period of Jewish national sovereignty and after that lost forever.[54]

For Cohen, however, the messianic idea in Judaism is not of a purely national or political character. The Messiah is not just a national savior but a universal redeemer. But for Cohen, messianism was tied to the idea of the progress or perfection of the human race to be attained not through God's grace but through the historical process itself.[55] Cohen goes so far as to suggest that the messianic idea of a united humanity living under self-chosen laws was already implicit in the teachings of the prophets. Messianism is only another term for socialism which envisages a perfect unity of all mankind raised above petty national vanities and rivalries. Indeed, Cohen's passionate attack on Zionism was undertaken out of the belief that the reassertion of Jewish nationalism would only affirm what the anti-Semites had believed all along.[56]

Cohen believed that there was a peculiar affinity between Ger-

52. Baruch Spinoza, *A Theologico-Political Treatise*, trans. R. H. M. Elwes (New York: Dover, 1951), p. 27.

53. *Ibid.*, pp. 38–39.

54. *Ibid.*, p. 46.

55. *Jüdische Schriften* 1: 105–24; partial English translation Eve Jospe, *Reason and Hope: Selections from the Jewish Writings of Hermann Cohen* (New York: W. W. Norton, 1971), pp. 122–27.

56. *Ibid.*, 2: 319–27, 328–40; *Reason and Hope*, pp. 164–71.

many and Judaism which it was the unique contribution of his work to explore. In a wartime pamphlet entitled "Deutschum und Judentum" he argued that the essence of "Germanism" (*Deutschum*) was its "ethical idealism" by which he meant the humanistic culture of Kant, Schiller, and Beethoven. It was also this cosmopolitan (*Weltbürgerlich*) outlook that informed the prophetic teachings of Judaism. The combination of Germanism and Judaism, then, would bring out the best of both "the nation of Kant" and the people of the book.[57] To be sure, Cohen understood that this "German-Jewish symbiosis" was not yet an actuality. It remained for him an "idea" in the precise Kantian sense of the term, a legitimate object of moral aspiration. For this reason, he feared the over hasty tendency of many of his contemporaries toward assimilation. Until a cosmopolitan culture had been realized, Jews have an obligation to remain separate if only because he believed the very future of monotheism was at stake.[58]

While remaining an admirer of Cohen, Strauss did not share either his rationalistic conception of Judaism or his optimistic assessment of its future. In the first place, he believed there was a kind of unreality in Cohen's conception of Judaism as the religion of reason. This conception depended for its validity upon a distinction between what is rational and hence morally obligatory and what is merely historical and contingent in Judaism. But this distinction is itself a product of the modern Enlightenment and as such not endogenous to Judaism itself. Cohen's method of "idealization" thus led him to distort the very thing he tried to understand and defend.

Strauss's conception of Judaism always remained closer to Cohen's younger partner Franz Rosenzweig to whose memory Strauss's Spinoza book was dedicated and "whose name," he would later remark, "will always be remembered when informed people speak about existentialism."[59] Strauss was especially impressed by Rosenzweig's claim that Judaism is not about law (*Gesetz*) in the Kantian sense of universality but command (*Gebot*).[60] The *mitzvot* are com-

---

57. *Jüdische Schriften*, 2: 73.
58. *Ibid.*, pp. 310-11; see also *Jerusalem*, p. 133ff.
59. *Rebirth of Classical Political Rationalism*, p. 28; for a sustained examination of Rosenzweig's relation to Heideggerian existentialism see Karl Löwith, "M. Heidegger and F. Rosenzweig or Temporality and Eternity," *Philosophy and Phenomenological Research* 3 (1942): 53–77; for Strauss's relation to Löwith see their "Correspondence Concerning Modernity," reprinted in *Independent Journal of Philosophy* 4 (1983): 111–18.
60. Franz Rosenzweig, *The Star of Redemption*, trans. William Hallo (New York: Holt, Rinehart, and Winston, 1970), pp. 176–77.

mandments in the primordial and most revealing sense of the term:
God speaks, man listens. But this emphasis on command did not
entail a return to a religion of sheer heteronomy or otherness. God's
first command to "love me" is followed by another to "love thy
neighbor."[61] According to Rosenzweig, the command to love is superior to the Kantian demand for rational autonomy for two reasons.
First, it provides some "content" to the Kantian moral imperative
which Rosenzweig, following Hegel, regards as an "empty for-
malism."[62] And second, the Kantian emphasis upon formal laws or
rules makes unintelligible the highest form of moral action, namely,
saintliness which is only possible with the assistance of divine love.[63]

Even here, it must be admitted, Strauss did not find Rosenzweig's
reconstruction of Judaism altogether convincing. Rosenzweig himself
admitted that he could not believe all the commandments revealed
in the Torah. A number of them remained "alien" to him. At the
heart of his Judaism, then, Rosenzweig imposed a conception of
free choice which Strauss regarded as contrary to the spirit of genuine orthodoxy.

Further, for all of his efforts to avoid the excessive rationalism
of the philosophers, Rosenzweig still regarded his work as "a system
of philosophy." Despite his claim to develop a "new thinking" (*neue
Denken*)[64] different from both the philosophers and the rabbis, Rosenzweig remained in some sense dialectically dependent upon the
thought he tried to supersede. Concerning this point Strauss wrote:
"Whereas the classic work of what is called Jewish medieval philosophy, the *Guide of the Perplexed*, is primarily not a philosophic book,
but a Jewish book, Rosenzweig's *Star of Redemption* is primarily
not a Jewish book, but 'a system of philosophy.'"[65] The failure of
Rosenzweig to produce a "Jewish book" merely showed the difficulty
of recovering orthodoxy in the face of modernity.

Second, Strauss did not share Cohen's optimistic forecast for an
eventual synthesis of Germanism and Judaism. Cohen believed that

---

61. *Ibid.*, p. 213.
62. *Ibid.*, p. 213: "The [Kantian] moral law is necessarily purely formal and
therefore not only ambiguous but open to an unlimited number of interpretations. By contrast the commandment to love one's neighbor is clear and unambiguous in content." The classic of this critique of Kant is still Hegel's *Philosophy of
Right*, trans. T. M. Knox (Oxford: Clarendon Press, 1967), para. 135, pp. 89–90.
63. *Star of Redemption*, p. 217.
64. See Nahum Glatzer, ed., *Franz Rosenzweig: His Life and Thought* (New York:
Schocken, 1961), pp. 190–208.
65. "Preface to Spinoza's Ctiritque of Religion," p. 237.

this synthesis was made possible because of the inherent perfectibility of human nature. Interpreting Moses's exclamation "Would that all the Lord's people were prophets" (Numbers 11:29) in the light of Kant's perfectibilian philosophy of history, Cohen predicted an eventual end of war and human suffering.[66] In contrast to Cohen's prophetic idealism, Strauss emphasized the constancy of human nature and especially man's propensity for evil.[67] Cohen's belief in progress which relegated hatred of Jews to a thing of the past was itself refuted by subsequent events. Cohen's synthesis of Greek classicism, German idealism, and Jewish messianism did not survive beyond 1933. In his lecture on "Jerusalem and Athens" Strauss wrote:

> Cohen's thought belongs to the world preceding World War I. . . . The worst things he experienced were the Dreyfus scandal and the pogroms instigated by Czarist Russia: he did not experience Communist Russia or Hitler Germany. . . . Catastrophes and horrors of a magnitude hitherto unknown, which we have seen and through which we have lived, were better provided for, or made intelligible, by both Plato and the prophets than by the modern belief in progress.[68]

According to Strauss, Cohen sought to replace both historical Judaism and Christianity with a religion of reason. This religion would provide the basis for a new culture which would be secular in its scholarship, democratic in its politics, and individualistic in its ethics. This belief in the redemptive or transformative power of culture reached its high water mark in Germany in the years immediately prior to and following World War I. At that time "the faith in the power of Western culture to mold the fate of mankind" was considerably greater than it is today. The fact that this kind of culture — modern, secular, and democratic — soon became the object of the murderous hatreds of both the left and the right proved to Strauss that the Enlightenment's solution to the Jewish question was deeply flawed.

III

The flaws with the Enlightenment came to light only in the course of Strauss's studies of Maimonides' *Guide of the Perplexed*, a work, he

---

66. *Jüdische Schriften* 1: 306–30; *Reason and Hope*, p. 76.
67. *Pirke Aboth*, III, 2; see also "Cohens Analyse," p. 305; "Preface to Spinoza's Critique of Religion," p. 247.
68. "Jerusalem and Athens," p. 168.

would say later, that occupied "about twenty five years of frequently interrupted but never abandoned study."[69] What, exactly, were the fruits of this study?

Strauss discovered that the modern Enlightenment of which Spinoza was one of the chief proponents had been preceded by a "medieval Enlightenment" whose greatest representative was Maimonides. Unlike the modern Enlightenment which had as its public goal the "Epicurean" intention to banish fear of invisible powers of the religious imagination, the medieval Enlightenment was characterized precisely by its esoteric teaching. The medieval philosophers by contrast were, in the original understanding, precisely not Enlighteners. They were not concerned with spreading knowledge but with preventing its vulgarization.[70]

The difference between modern and medieval rationalism can be traced back to their different views regarding the relationship of reason to civil society. The esoteric mode of utterance was necessary, in the first place, to protect the philosopher from the accusations of impiety and atheism that inevitably attend the utterance of unpopular truths. The popular suspicion of philosophy derives from the belief that knowledge is power and that philosophers must aspire to tyranny. Strauss does not believe that this allegation is simply false. It is because, as a practical matter, philosophers lack the power to attain their ends that they are forced to resort to esoteric rhetoric. Esoteric teaching, therefore, was widely practiced as a matter of practical necessity in pre- or nonliberal societies that do not guarantee the absolute right of freedom of speech.[71]

At the same time, esoteric writing was practiced by those writers who wished not just to protect themselves from persecution but who wish to protect society from the dangers always inherent in philosophy. Accordingly, premodern thinkers presented a purely edifying teaching that could be grasped by any relatively intelligent reader and another, esoteric, teaching wrapped up in enigma, contradic-

69. Leo Strauss, "How to Begin to Study 'The Guide of the Perplexed,'" in Maimonides, *The Guide of the Perplexed*, trans. Shlomo Pines (Chicago: University of Chicago Press, 1963), p. xi; for some of Strauss' other writings see "Quelques remarques sur la science politique de Maimonide et de Farabi," *Revue des Etudes Juives* 100 (1936): 1–37; "Maimonides' Statement on Political Science," *What Is Political Philosophy?* pp. 155–69; "The Literary Character of the 'Guide of the Perplexed,'" *Persecution and the Art of Writing* (New York: Free Press, 1952), pp. 38–94.

70. *Philosophy and Law*, pp. 82–83.

71. *Persecution and the Art of Writing*, p. 36: "This literature is essentially related to a society which is not liberal."

tion, and paradox that would have quite another meaning for the initiated.[72] The distinction between esoteric and exoteric writing is not, as a recent interpreter has maintained, simply a convenient medium through which the philosopher can put forward a shocking, nihilistic teaching.[73] There is rather a public or political purpose to this distinction. The distinction is necessary so that the philosopher's proposals for political reform are phrased in a language or rhetoric that his audience will be able to understand. "Exoteric teaching is *political* philosophy," as Nathan Tarcov has said.[74]

Strauss found ample evidence of the esoteric character of medieval rationalism in Maimonides' *Guide*. In the Introduction to the work Maimonides notes that the two main subjects to be taught there *Maaseh Bereshit* and *Maaseh Merkavah*, the Account of Creation and the Account of the Chariot, are equivalent to physics and metaphysics respectively. Furthermore, he notes, that there is a rabbinic injunction against the public discussion of these teachings. "The Account of the Chariot," the injunction reads, "ought not to be taught even to one man, except if he be wise and able to understand himself, in which case only the chapter headings may be transmitted to him."[75] And Maimonides goes on to remark that these teachings will not be set down by him in order but will be " scattered and entangled with other subjects" so that "the truths be glimpsed and then again concealed."[76]

From passages such as these, Strauss became convinced that Maimonides practiced a mode of writing that revealed different things to different people with different levels of competence. The *Guide*, he tells us, is a book "sealed with many seals" and "an enchanted forest."[77] The exoteric or public premise of the work is that reason and revelation are mutually compatible, but to the careful reader Maimonides indicated that there was a profound, perhaps unbridgeable, gulf between them. Thus to vouchsafe the freedom to philosophize Maimonides had to present philosophy as something commanded by the Torah or within the traditional framework of Jewish

72. See *ibid.*, pp. 22–37.
73. See Shadia Drury, *The Political Ideas of Leo Strauss* (New York: St. Martin's, 1988).
74. Nathan Tarcov, "Philosophy and History: Tradition and Interpretation in the Work of Leo Strauss," *Polity* 16 (1983): 19.
75. *Guide of the Perplexed*, p. 6.
76. *Ibid.*, pp. 6–7.
77. "How to Begin to Study the *Guide*," pp. xiii, xiv.

law. There was, Maimonides argued, a legal obligation to philosophize laid down by Moses "our Master." Only in presenting philosophy within the context of law could it acquire respectability within
the community of the orthodox.

Maimonides' attribution of a secret teaching to Scripture and especially to the story of Creation in Genesis 1–3 is scarcely unique
in medieval literature.[78] The so-called Gnostic heresy of late antiquity took the account of creation not as a literal story of God's work-
manship but as a tissue of symbols and allegories that had to be
properly decoded if Scripture was to reveal its deeper meaning. Christian writers of the second century like Valentinus completely inverted the literal meaning of the story. No longer was the world seen
as the creation of a just and loving God, but the Gnostic deity was
something "wholly other" who stands in no positive relation to the
finite, sensible world. Indeed, thanks to Gershom Scholem we now
know that Gnosticism was not just a Christian phenomenon but
had deep roots in early Jewish mysticism as well. The school of Mer-
kabah mysticism incorporated important Gnostic elements in its
interpretation of Ezekiel's vision of the throne as a kind of apocalyptic
disclosure of God's knowledge of the end of days.[79]

The idea, then, that Scripture contained a deeper, richer allegorical substructure than had been thought had potentially explo-
sive implications. As Hans Jonas, Strauss's friend and colleague from
the New School for Social Research, argued, Gnosticism contained
latent nihilistic and antinomian implications that bear a striking
resemblance to certain contemporary movements of thought.[80] For
if God is withdrawn from human affairs as the Gnostics assert, then
man is permitted an unprecedented freedom to dispose of his powers
as he sees fit. The paradoxical result, as Jonas demonstrates, are
the revolutionary extremes of asceticism and libertinage. Both are
equally valid (but also equally groundless) replies to a cosmic order
that has become evacuated of telos and where the only legitimate
source of value is the pneumatic self. From here, one can see, it

78. See Elaine Pagels, *Adam, Eve, and the Serpent* (New York: Random House,
1988), pp. 57–72.

79. Gershom Scholem, *Major Trends in Jewish Mysticism* (New York: Schocken,
1961), pp. 40–79.

80. Hans Jonas, *The Gnostic Religion* (Boston: Beacon Press, 1963), pp. 320–40;
for some of the literary uses of Gnosticism see Paul Cantor, *Creature and Creator:
Myth-Making and English Romanticism* (Cambridge: Cambridge University Press,
1984).

is not far to the infamous doctrine of "redemption through sin" according to which those who have been initiated into gnosis (knowledge) are encouraged to abrogate the laws of the Torah in order to hasten the end of time.[81]

The adequacy of Strauss's interpretation of Maimonides and other medieval writers is obviously too large a topic to be treated here.[82] Suffice it to say that Strauss's attribution of an esoteric teaching to them has important implications for his understanding of the theological-political problem. For if his reading is correct, it follows that Maimonides regarded the whole of rabbinic Judaism (including his own *Mishneh*) as of exoteric value only. The exoteric level of a text consists of those writings that are commonly and constantly reiterated and which adhere to conventional opinions, while the esoteric level consists of those relatively rare or isolated remarks found in out-of-the-way passages in which the author reveals his innermost purposes. The purpose of such writing is to approximate as closely as possible in written form the direct "oral" character of communication between teacher and student. The novelty of Strauss's hermeneutic is not, as is vulgarly believed, his discovery or rather "recovery" of esoteric writing as such. For the existence of an esoteric tradition there is more than ample evidence.[83] Rather Strauss's novelty resides in the claim that philosophers of one generation can speak with those of another without the benefit of direct oral communication.

Strauss was aware that his interpretation of the *Guide*, like the *Guide* itself, was rich with paradox. For if the *Guide* contains a hidden teaching, Strauss appears to be violating the first rule of that teaching, namely, discussing publicly what is best left wrapped in silence or enigma. By recovering, and what's more publicizing, this "forgotten kind of writing," Strauss seems to be in "flagrant transgression" of the law. How does he justify this act?

Strauss is not unaware of this paradox and offers two solutions

81. Gershom Scholem, *The Messianic Idea in Judaism and Other Essays in Jewish Spirituality* (New York: Schocken, 1971), pp. 78–141.

82. See I. Twersky, *Introduction to the Code of Maimonides: (Mishneh Torah)* (New Haven: Yale University Press, 1980); David Hartman, *Maimonides: Torah and Philosophic Quest* (Philadelphia: Jewish Publication Society, 1976); Rémi Brague, "Leo Strauss et Maimonide," *Maimonides and Philosophy*, ed. S. Pines and Y. Yovel (The Hague: Martinus Nijhoff, 1986), pp. 246–68.

83. See Helmut Holzhey and Walther C. Zimmerli, eds., *Esoterik und Exoterik der Philosophie. Beiträg zur geschichte und Sinn philosophischer Selbstbestimmung* (Basel: Schwabe, 1977).

to it. In the first place he says, "the historical situation today is *fundamentally different* from that of the twelfth century."[84] It suggests that while public opinion at the time of Maimonides was ruled by a belief in the divine or mysterious origin of the law, today this is simply no longer believed. The modern Jew has become a disciple of Spinoza with his belief in the historical or merely contingent character of the Torah. The modern scholar, unlike Maimonides, need not fear persecution at the hands of the Jewish community because both scholar and layman are likely to share the same basic beliefs. Consequently, Strauss feels justified in transgressing the rabbinic injunction because the law itself no longer has a hold upon the lives of modern Jews. The esoteric tradition can today become a subject of scholarly research and even public debate because it is a dead tradition, one which, like political philosophy itself, is in a state of "decay" or "putrefaction."[85] Thus what earlier generations could only whisper or hint at through indirection, Strauss feels justified in revealing fully to the light of day.

But there is another reason justifying Strauss's apparent transgression of the law. Commentary, even on an esoteric work, need not imply disobedience to the law. There are commentaries, and there are commentaries. Strauss himself hints at the possibility of an esoteric commentary on Maimonides.[86] Such a commentary may be today the only way of keeping alive the philosophical tradition of which Maimonides was the greatest representative. It is not inconceivable that Strauss's manner of writing sought to wed modern scholarly research with the function of the traditional commentator as a keeper and transmitter of tradition. Strauss suggests that the historical recovery of works from the past "takes on philosophical significance for men living in an age of intellectual decline."[87] Commentary on an ancient author, then, becomes a way of recovering certain "fundamental problems" or questions, questions like the proper relation of order and freedom.[88] If the author in question is one like Maimonides who operated within a tradition of revealed

---

84. *Persecution and the Art of Writing*, p. 55; emphasis mine.
85. *What Is Political Philosophy?* p. 17.
86. *Persecution and the Art of Writing*, p. 56; for the possibility of an esoteric commentary see Aviezer Ravitzky, "Samuel Ibn Tibbon and the Esoteric Character of the 'Guide of the Perplexed,'" *AJS Review* 6 (1981): 87–123.
87. Leo Strauss, "On Collingwood's Philosophy of History," *Review of Metaphysics* 5 (1952): 585.
88. *Persecution and the Art of Writing*, p. 37.

law, it falls to the scholar to recover the meaning of the law and how it was understood both by the author and his audience. It is a suggestive possibility that in his emphasis on scholarly commentary and the close reading of texts Strauss was fulfilling, not abrogating, the function of the law.

IV

To return, then, to our original question: how does Strauss's handling of the Jewish Question help us understand the more general theological-political problem? Where do we stand vis-à-vis the universal and the particular?

At one level Strauss defends the integrity of Judaism from the skeptical assaults of philosophy. He denies that reason can ever simply refute Orthodoxy. The only way that Orthodoxy could be refuted would be to prove that the cosmos is perfectly intelligible without recourse to the workings of a mysterious God. Spinoza and Hegel were in Strauss's view the two thinkers who made the grandest efforts to refute the very possibility of biblical revelation on the basis of reason alone. But their philosophies reveal themselves, on close examination, to rely on arbitrary premises or on premises no more rational than the claims of revelation. Thus from a strictly epistemological or scientific angle, modern philosophy remains no more certain than the view of Orthodoxy that it set out to refute.[89]

On the other hand, however, Strauss seems to believe that Orthodoxy is no longer a viable option for ourselves as citizens of the modern enlightened world. By Orthodoxy Strauss means such things as the belief in an omnipotent and inscrutable God, the creation of the world *ex nihilo,* and the possibility of miracles. Any modification of these fundamental tenets or "roots," as the medieval Jewish tradition would call them, would be a corruption of the original spirit of Orthodoxy. Despite Strauss's repeated assertions that we must remain "open" to the claims of both reason and revelation, I do not believe that he considered Orthodoxy to be a feasible alternative in the final analysis. The suspension of critical judgment needed for such things as belief in the resurrection of the dead is no longer a living possibility for modern man. Indeed, Strauss himself often warned of the dangers in attempting to reoccupy earlier positions. He even remarks that every modern attempt to return to an earlier

89. *Natural Right and History,* pp. 74–76; *Philosophy and Law,* pp. 13–14.

position has unwittingly resulted in "a much more radical form of modernity."[90] The attempt to restore Orthodoxy in its pristine form today could only lead to obscurantism and fanaticism.

The question becomes, then, what posture ought a Jew to take living in a skeptical age. Here Strauss delineates two attitudes. The first was that of Spinoza, the most consistent and uncompromising critic from within Judaism. His was the rationalistic criticism of the Enlightenment which everywhere juxtaposed philosophic detachment or freedom from the tradition of his own people. Spinoza as well as other *Aufklärer* of his age rejected not only Judaism but all tradition as incompatible with the alleged freedom and dignity of man.

The second form of criticism Strauss, following Hermann Cohen, calls "idealizing." Rather than rejecting tradition in toto, the idealizing critic begins from a posture of "fidelity" or "sympathy" toward one's tradition. This does not mean uncritical or blind acceptance of tradition but rather the interpretation of a tradition in the light of its highest possibilities. To idealize is not just to praise or flatter but to use what one regards as the best or highest aspects of one's tradition as a norm to criticize others. It is this method of criticism that is at the basis of Strauss's oft-quoted remark: "It is safer to try to understand the low in the light of the high than the high in the light of the low."[91] It is this kind of idealizing criticism that Strauss practiced himself in his treatment of the Jewish Question.

At long last this brings us to the relation between Judaism and liberal democracy. Are they compatible? There is surely much evidence for an affirmative answer to this question. It is arguable that the liberal democracies of the West with their guarantee of full civil rights and universal suffrage have provided the only decent solution to what Strauss called the theologico-political problem. The liberal solution to this problem can be described as a combination of legal equality plus private discrimination. Liberalism is based on the distinction between public and private. Thus while the liberal state has by and large eradicated the worst forms of state-sponsored religious bigotry and persecution, it cannot and has not sought to abolish social hierarchies and private forms of religious and ethnic discrimination. The attempt to use political power as a means of

90. *What Is Political Philosophy?* p. 50.
91. "Preface to Spinoza's Critique of Religion," p. 225.

abolishing all private discrimination has resulted in a cure worse than the disease.

At the same time Strauss believed that it was base and unconscionable for Jews to abandon their ancient faith for the sake of assimilation to the mainstream. As the early critique of Nordau indicated, the price of assimilation came at the cost of a loss of Jewish self-identity and Jewish pride. The result of assimilation was inevitably "the bog of philistinism . . . a most inglorious end for a people which had been led out of the house of bondage into the desert with careful avoidance of the land of the Philistines."[92] While there is no reason to doubt that Strauss was not profoundly grateful to the United States for the opportunities it had bestowed on the Jews to live safely and securely from the worst forms of European anti-Semitism, this by no means blinded him to a frankly realistic assessment of the problem:

> It is very far from me to minimize the difference between a nation conceived in liberty and dedicated to the proposition that all men are created equal, and the nations of the old world, which certainly were not conceived in liberty. I share the hope in America and the faith in America, but I am compelled to add that that faith and that hope cannot be of the same character as that faith and hope which a Jew has in regard to Judaism and which the Christian has in regard to Christianity. No one claims that the faith in America and the hope for America are based on explicit divine promises.[93]

This brings us close to Strauss's core belief about the essence of Judaism. The core of Judaism was its belief in the reality of a supernatural revelation. The fundamental Jewish experience in history was God's revelation of the Torah on Mount Sinai. This revelation had the function, to some degree, of insulating and protecting the Jews from the cultures of other nations. Unless it can somehow be demonstrated that this revelation demanded the unification of all mankind by the overcoming of each particular faith, Jews will be justified in remaining stubbornly attached to their own particularity. To the extent that the liberal Enlightenment has urged the abolition of a particular providence, it will always be at odds with Judaism.

---

92. "Progress or Return?" p. 232.
93. *Ibid.*, p. 233.

Strauss Before Straussianism: Reason, Revelation, and Nature

John G. Gunnell

> Rationalism itself rests on nonrational, unevident assumptions; in spite
> of its seemingly overwhelming power, rationalism is hollow.[1]
> —Leo Strauss

I

Despite the impact of Leo Strauss on American political science
and political theory, where, exactly, Strauss was "coming from," in
both senses of that phrase, has been far from clear. Carl Friedrich,
reviewing the, at that point, unknown author's book on Hobbes,
noted that Strauss might have been more forthcoming about his
own position, but he believed th... it was safe to conclude that he
was a "historical relativist."[2] Friedrich may have been closer to the
mark than many subsequent commentators realized, but in order
to understand Strauss's work, it is necessary to return to the universe he inhabited before "coming to America." Since Strauss's death,
his enterprise has been subject to careful scrutiny,[3] but his early
life and work have remained opaque.

---

1. Strauss, *The Rebirth of Classical Political Rationalism*, ed. Thomas Pangle
(Chicago: University of Chicago Press, 1989), p. 43.

This essay is the final version of a long paper originally presented at a symposium on Leo Strauss sponsored by the Institute of Human Values at the annual
conference of the Canadian Learned Societies, Laval, Quebec City, June 1989.
The proceedings of the symposium were printed in the first issue of *The Vital Nexus*,
May 1990. Two subsequent revisions were the basis of presentations at the University
of Chicago (November 1989) and Princeton University (April 1990). Although
the focus, argument, length, and content have been substantially transformed,
I have retained the original main title, since the subject has remained "Strauss
Before Straussianism." I wish to acknowledge valuable conversations with Shadia
Drury over a period of several years as well as her considerable aid in obtaining
material, such as Strauss's dissertation, to which I did not have initial access. I
also thank my colleague Peter Breiner for helping me work through passages in
the untranslated dissertation.

2. Carl Friedrich, "Thomas Hobbes: Myth Builder of the Modern World," *Journal
of Social Philosophy* 3 (1938): 25–57.

3. See, for example, Kenneth L. Deutsch and Walter Soffer, eds., *The Crisis
of Liberal Democracy: A Straussian Perspective* (Albany, NY: State University of New
York Press, 1987); Shadia Drury, *The Political Ideas of Leo Strauss* (New York: St.
Martin's Press, 1988).

Like so many of the emigres from Germany who had such a profound effect on political theory in the United States,[4] Strauss's arguments, and even his intellectual identity as a political theorist or
political philosopher, evolved in the context of the American academy
and the matrix of issues that constituted the conversation in which
he found himself. It would indeed be difficult to extrapolate either
the form or substance of his major work from his early writings.
Yet what he contributed to that conversation were ideas and concerns that were fundamentally formed in the world of Weimar
Germany.

Recent critical commentary on Strauss has raised radical questions about the manner in which his work has been conventionally
understood, and even among his most dedicated followers, there
are notorious divisions of opinion. There are, however, limits to
an interpretation pursued in terms of an analytical examination of
Strauss's post-emigration writings. My goal is to historicize Strauss
and recapture "Strauss before Straussianism."

I am concerned with the Strauss who came to intellectual maturity while grappling with a crisis in Jewish theology and who first
ventured directly into the discussion of politics in his reply to Carl
Schmitt, the same year that he fled Germany. More specifically, I
wish to explore the roots of Strauss's critique of liberalism, the formulation of his historical/philosophical project, his persistent concern about the tension between philosophy and politics, and his conception of natural right.[5]

II

Leo Strauss was born in Kirchhain, Hessen, Germany on 20 September 1899. He was raised in an assimilated but orthodox Jewish
family (his father sold farming supplies). He attended the gymnasium
in Marburg where, in his words, he "became exposed to the message of German humanism" and "furtively read Schopenhauer and
Nietzsche." By age 16, he had decided that he would be content to
enter a humble occupation and spend his life "reading Plato and

4. See John G. Gunnell, "American Political Science, Liberalism, and the Invention of Political Theory," *American Political Science Review* 82 (1988): 71–87.

5. For a more analytical treatment of these issues based primarily on Strauss's
later work, see John G. Gunnell, *Political Theory: Tradition and Interpretation* (Cambridge, MA.: Winthrop, 1979; University Press of America, 1987). "Political Theory
and Politics: The Case of Leo Strauss," *Political Theory* 13 (1985): 339–61.

breeding rabbits." But at age 17, he became a convert to "straight-forward political Zionism."[6] The problem of the relationship between philosophy, theology, and politics would circumscribe his intellectual world. As he noted later, "I believe that I can say without any exaggeration that since a very early time the main theme of my reflections has been what is called the Jewish question."[7]

After serving in the German army during World War I, Strauss studied philosophy at the University of Marburg among the remnants of the neo-Kantian school that had been founded by the late Hermann Cohen. Cohen's work appealed to Strauss, since it was devoted to the complementarity of philosophy and Judaism and the reconciliation of reason and revelation. But he had problems with Cohen's approach and remained a "doubting and dubious adherent of the Marburg school."[8]

Strauss eventually took his doctorate in philosophy at the University of Hamburg in 1921 where he wrote a short, primarily expository, dissertation on the epistemology of F. H. Jacobi.[9] Although in his subsequent work Strauss had little to say about Jacobi, some of the similarities between their concerns and arguments are indeed striking. Jacobi is no longer a well-known figure, but he was the protagonist in a late eighteenth-century debate that had a profound effect on the evolution of German philosophy.[10] Much of the idealist tradition, from Kant to Hegel, was an attempt to salvage rationalism from Jacobi's critique.

Jacobi was a philosophical realist who criticized Kant's concept of the "thing-in-itself" as contradictory, but he initially pressed his arguments through an attack on Spinoza and the German Enlightenment. Although Spinoza had been almost universally reviled during the first three-quarters of the eighteenth century, his influence was unsurpassed in Germany by the late 1700's. The rehabilitation of Spinoza had begun in mid-century with Moses Mendelssohn, but

6. Jacob Klein and Leo Strauss, "A Giving of Accounts," *The College* 25 (1970): 2.
7. Leo Strauss, "Why We Remain Jews: Can Jewish Faith and History Still Speak to Us?" in this volume.
8. Leo Strauss, *Studies in Platonic Political Philosophy* (Chicago: University of Chicago Press, 1983), p. 31.
9. Leo Strauss, *Das Erkenntnisproblem in der philosophischen Lehre Fr. H. Jacobis*, dissertation, University of Hamburg, 1921. This manuscript, and the possible impact of more than one dimension of the work of both Jacobi and his friend and contemporary J. G. Hamann, deserve more attention than can be rendered here.
10. Frederick Beiser, *The Fate of Reason: German Philosophy from Kant to Fichte* (Cambridge, MA.: Harvard University Press, 1987).

his fame was principally the product of a dispute between Mendelssohn and Jacobi—the so-called Pantheist controversy.

Mendelssohn had been about to write a tribute to G.E. Lessing, the leading representative of the *Aufklarunq*, when Jacobi, in 1785, undercut him by publishing an account of a conversation between himself and Lessing which intimated that the latter had been influenced by Spinoza. This suggested an abandonment of many of the values with which Lessing had been associated and particularly the idea that religious beliefs could be rationally justified. What transformed the event into a major intellectual issue was Jacobi's claim that religion must be based on faith rather than reason, since Spinoza, the quintessential liberal rationalist, ended up an atheist and fatalist.

Jacobi argued that rationalism inevitably led, as Hume demonstrated, to skepticism. Scientific naturalism, founded by Spinoza, undercut practical belief and entailed relativism and eventually *Nihilismus* (a concept that Jacobi introduced into the vocabulary of modern philosophy). Jacobi, a Christian, argued for a return to orthodoxy. The dilemma of skepticism created by the pursuit of reason could only be solved by a leap in faith. Either follow reason and become an atheist or renounce reason and choose faith. The Jacobian dilemma and the critique of modern rationalism would remain fundamental for Strauss's perspective.

After finishing his degree, Strauss went to the University of Freiburg (1922) to seek out Husserl whose "ontological turn," and phenomenology, presented a challenging alternative to neo-Kantianism. But Husserl seemed to offer him little, since Strauss's "predominant interest was in theology" and the problem of orthodoxy in Judaism.[11] Theology, however, was being revived by individuals such as Franz Rosenzweig in reaction to Enlightenment ideas, and it was Rosenzweig's return to revelation that formed the pivot of much of Strauss's early thought. But it was here, in "Husserl's entourage," that he also first encountered Martin Heidegger.

Strauss sensed that Heidegger's lectures dealt with something of the "utmost importance to man as man," and he was in awe of Heidegger's interpretation of Aristotle's *Metaphysics* which he remembered in terms of having "never heard or seen such a thing—such a thorough and intensive interpretation of a philosophical text."

---

11. Klein and Strauss, "A Giving of Accounts," p. 2.

Strauss commented to Rosenzweig that, compared to Heidegger, Max Weber was only "an orphan child."[12]

Jacob Klein, his friend from Marburg and later fellow exile, recalled that Strauss's principal concerns at this time were "God" and "politics."[13] Orthodoxy still suffered from the attack of the Enlightenment, and it was this problem, Strauss recalled, that brought him, in 1922, like Jacobi before him, to confront Spinoza's *Theological Political Treatise* which was "the classic document of the attack on orthodoxy." Since he was not satisfied with Cohen's "fierce criticism" of Spinoza, he undertook a "fresh study" in order to form an "independent judgment."[14]

From 1925 through 1932, Strauss held a post at the Academy of Jewish Research in Berlin. Here, between 1925 and 1928, he wrote his book on Spinoza (1930), but the involvement with Heidegger's ideas continued. In 1925, Heidegger came to Marburg where Klein attended his classes regularly. Klein and Strauss spent much time together, often at the Prussian state Library in Berlin and nearby coffee houses, and Heidegger, as well as Nietzsche, became principal objects of their conversation. Strauss later noted that

> nothing affected us as profoundly in the years in which our minds took their lasting direction as the thought of Heidegger . . . who surpasses in speculative intelligence all his contemporaries and . . . attempts to go a way not yet trodden by anyone or rather to think in a way which philosophers at any rate have never thought before. Certain it is that no one has questioned the premise of philosophy as radically as Heidegger.[15]

Strauss recalled that "gradually the breadth of the revolution in thought which Heidegger was preparing dawned upon me and my generation" as he replaced Hegel and "dethroned" everything else.[16] It was, however, Klein who, according to Strauss, first "saw why Heidegger is truly important: by uprooting and not simply rejecting the tradition of philosophy, he made it possible for the first time after many centuries . . . to see the roots of the tradition and thus perhaps to know, what so many merely believe, that those roots are

---

12. *Ibid.*, p. 3.
13. *Ibid.*, p. 1.
14. *Ibid.*, p. 3.
15. Leo Strauss, "An Unspoken Prologue to a Public Lecture at St. John's," *Interpretation* 7 (1978): 2.
16. Strauss, *The Rebirth of Classical Political Rationalism*, p. 28.

the only natural and healthy roots." Klein discerned in Heidegger's disinterral of the ancients an unintentional opening to "the possibility of a genuine return to classical philosophy, to the philosophy of Plato and Aristotle."[17]

Heidegger's *Destruktion* of the philosophical tradition was a "taking down" which served to "uproot" and "lay bare" Greek philosophy and make it possible to see it "as it was in itself and not as it had come to appear in the light of the tradition and of modern philosophy." What was needed was a "return to, and recovery of classical philosophy."[18] Strauss attributed to Heidegger the discovery that "with the questioning of traditional philosophy, the traditional understanding of the tradition becomes questionable."[19]

Strauss had only begun to entertain these ideas as he worked through his analysis of Spinoza, from which, he noted, he was "led to Hobbes, on the one hand, and to Maimonides on the other."[20] Both foci became the subject of books that emerged shortly after he left Germany.[21] Strauss noted that when he undertook his study of Spinoza, he was in the "grip of a theological-political predicament."[22] The problem Strauss referred to was the "Jewish problem" in the context of Weimar Germany.

III

Although it is difficult to determine Strauss's original assessment of the situation, he later claimed that Weimar was an "option against Bismarck," against the traditional *Rechtstaat*, and a "leaning" toward the liberal democratic regimes of France and England. It had a "moderate nonradical character" which was a balance between 1789 and "the highest German tradition," but unlike the "old Germany" which was "stronger in will," it was "weak" and amounted to "justice without a sword." In this situation, the man with the "strongest will or single-mindedness, the greatest ruthlessness, daring, and power over his following and the best judgment about the strength of the

17. Strauss, "An Unspoken Prologue to a Public Lecture at St. John's," p. 2.
18. Klein and Strauss, "A Giving of Accounts," p. 3.
19. Leo Strauss, *Spinoza's Critique of Religion* (New York: Schocken Books, 1965), pp. 9–10.
20. Klein and Strauss, "A Giving of Accounts," p. 3.
21. Leo Strauss, *Philosophie und Gesetz* (Berlin: Schocken, 1935); *The Philosophy of Thomas Hobbes: Its Genesis and Its Basis* (Oxford: Clarendon Press, 1936).
22. Strauss, *Spinoza's Critique of Religion*, p. 1.

forces in the immediately relevant political field was the leader of the revolution."[23]

Strauss argued that, following the principle of understanding "the low in light of the high," it was necessary to explain the new Germany in light of the old. Germany had never been "distinctly in favor of liberal democracy," there was a general political weakness consequent to Germany's defeat in the war, and there had been a betrayal by the liberal democratic allies in the form of a treaty which "discredited liberal democracy in the eyes of Germany." The weakness of Weimar made the situation of the Jews "precarious."[24] Strauss recalled that in the old Germany, "we Jews there lived in profound peace with our neighbors. There was a government, not in every respect admirable, but keeping an admirable order everywhere, and such things as pogroms would have been absolutely impossible."[25]

Even though it understood itself as a great advance over medievalism, by its relegation of religion to the private sphere and by its adoption of "a universal human morality," Weimar nevertheless provided conditions conducive to repression and eventually totalitarianism. While the split between the public and private realms insured political rights, the independence of the social sphere offered a relatively unrestrained space for the pursuit of egoism and material interest which often eventuated in discrimination. For Strauss, it was no accident that Weimar, which for the first time in Germany gave political rights to the Jews, "was succeeded by the only German regime — the only regime anywhere — which had no other clear principle than murderous hatred of the Jews." Hitler, after all, Strauss noted, did not emerge from Prussia or Bismarck's Reich but from a liberal democracy.[26]

The general sentiment in German society was that Judaism was in conflict with the basic, and Christian, spirit of the culture. Thus, for Strauss, and many other young Jews who wanted to avoid "spiritual dependency," this led to a form of social alienation which made Zionism popular. Political equality did not produce "social equality" and "honor." But although Zionism was a "blessing," it did not ultimately solve the Jewish problem. It did not deal adequately

23. *Ibid.*

24. *Ibid.*, p. 2.

25. Strauss, "Why We Remain Jews: Can Jewish Faith and History Still Speak to Us?" in this volume.

26. Strauss, *Spinoza's Critique of Religion*, p. 3.

with the issue of Jewish culture and its basis in revelation and a divine dispensation. In the most fundamental sense the Jewish problem was "insoluble," by human and political means, even in the state of Israel.[27] Strauss always maintained that there ultimately was "no solution to the Jewish problem," and this was both because of the inevitable tension between the divine and temporal, and because "the human species consists by nature of tribes or nations, *ethne*."[28]

In the context of liberal democracy, a partial solution to the Jewish problem was to return to the Jewish community and reject cultural assimilation. Yet, Strauss argued, this often tended to conflict with the demands of reason which transcended any *"ethnos."* Although it seemed to many that Jewish theology had succeeded in meeting secular challenges, it had done so, as in the case of Cohen, by understanding Judaism as a "religion of reason" and seeking the identity of reason and revelation, philosophy and prophecy, which Cohen believed was adumbrated in medieval Jewish philosophy and its turn to Plato.

Strauss "grew up in an environment in which Cohen was the center of attraction for philosophically minded Jews who were devoted to Judaism." He was "the greatest representative of German Jewry and spokesman for it," but, at the same time, "the most powerful figure among the German philosophers of his time." In his life and his ideas, he represented, like Mendelssohn before him, a synthesis of reason and religion, ethics and science, and Judaism and German society. All this "assumed indeed that the state is liberal or moving toward liberalism."[29]

Strauss claimed that these arguments "suddenly lost all their force." Both tradition and experience demonstrated the autonomy of faith and revelation. Modern reason had reached its high point in Hegel whose work exemplified all the "limitations" of reason. In the perennial battle between reason and revelation, the latter, Strauss concluded, had won out. This position seemed to reflect Jacobi, but it also found support in the "new thinking" represented by Rosenzweig (to whom Strauss dedicated his book on Spinoza).[30]

27. *Ibid*, p. 5.
28. Strauss, "Why We Remain Jews: Can Jewish Faith and History Still Speak to Us?" in this volume. "The Problem of Socrates," Lecture at St. John's College, Annapolis, 1970, p. 5.
29. Strauss, *Studies in Platonic Political Philosophy*, pp. 168, 233, 247.
30. Strauss, *Spinoza's Critique of Religion*, pp. 8-9.

In his early attempt to deal with the Jewish predicament, Rosenzweig nearly converted to Christianity, but then made a radical turn
toward the Judaic tradition and away from the "curse of historicity"
that plagued both Christianity and philosophy. In *The Star of Redemption* (1921), the enemy was Hegel and German idealism. Rosenzweig
was drawn to Kierkegaard and Nietzsche and the idea of faith in
the face of nihilism. Although a student of Cohen, Rosenzweig rejected humanism and embraced the tradition of the Kabbalah and
classical theology where man was not the measure. He rejected epistemology and metaphysics in favor of a philosophy grounded in natural reason and the temporality of life and speech.

Rosenzweig's position, Strauss claimed, was paralleled by another
trend of "new thinking" represented by Heidegger which offered an
even deeper understanding of what was involved in the "insight or
demand" that modern rationalism must be superseded. A problem
with Rosenzweig's position was that his return was not, in the end,
an unqualified return to the days before Mendelssohn, for example,
to Maimonides. The new thinking was still an heir to elements of
the old thinking. It historicized the Torah and was not a return to
faith as it had been understood in the past. Rosenzweig, like Cohen,
was still halfway between orthodoxy and liberalism.[31]

All this, Strauss said, "made one wonder if whether an unqualified
return to Jewish orthodoxy was not both possible and necessary—
was not at the same time the solution to the problem of the Jew
lost in the non-Jewish modern world and the only course compatible with sheer consistency and intellectual probity." These issues
eventually led to a confrontation with Spinoza—"the greatest man
of Jewish origin who openly denied the truth of Judaism and had
ceased to belong to the Jewish people without becoming a Christian." It was this defender of modern rationalism who must be proved
"wrong in every respect" if there was to be a return to orthodoxy.[32]

IV

Spinoza, Strauss argued, was "the first philosopher who was both
a liberal and a democrat. He was the philosopher who founded liberal
democracy, a specifically modern regime."[33] In his conception of the

31. *Ibid.*, pp. 9–10.
32. *Ibid.*, p. 15.
33. *Ibid.*, p. 16.

polity, there was more freedom for the passions. Everything was understood as natural, and consequently, as opposed to the classics, the life of passion was not against nature. There was no natural end for man. The end of man was conceived and created by reason, and thus emerged the modern notion of an "ideal" and of man as a human project. Spinoza's philosophy entailed a liberal society that promised an end to the tension between Christians and Jews by transforming the latter into the former and the former into "cultured human beings" who transcended religion through art and science and achieved secular redemption. It was, in short, a society from which Hitler could emerge.[34]

Strauss concluded, however, that Spinoza refuted orthodoxy only if orthodoxy depended on *knowing* such things as the occurrence of miracles — not if it was simply based on a belief in such things. Spinoza never demonstrated, and could not in principle demonstrate, that the premise of God's existence was refutable by reason, logic, or experience. Since Spinoza could not deny the possibility of revelation, he could not demonstrate that the philosophical account was necessarily the true one. In the end, it "rests itself on an unevident decision, on an act of will, just as faith does. Hence the antagonism between Spinoza and Judaism, between unbelief and belief, is ultimately not theoretical but moral," that is, based on faith.[35]

Beginning at least from the point of his encounter with Jacobi, Strauss was convinced that reason ultimately rested on irrational decisions. Reason and revelation were rooted in irreducible commitments. His encounter with Nietzsche and Heidegger only confirmed this idea. But there were consequences to embracing reason; it was not simply a neutral choice.

Modern rationalism, as opposed to more ancient skepticism and Epicureanism, led man to "making himself the master and owner of nature," and this in turn required political action, revolution, and a life and death struggle directed toward "the systematic attempt to liberate man completely from all non-human bonds." Yet in the end this "really leads to man becoming . . . smaller and more miserable in proportion as the systematic civilization progresses." Eventually the idea of pushing back nature in order to achieve freedom began "to wither" and a "new fortitude" and harsher view of life set in. Religion was rejected not because it was hard, but because it

34. *Ibid.*, p. 20.
35. *Ibid.*, p. 29.

was comforting—a "final atheism" based on "intellectual probity" but in the end grounded on "belief" and an "act of will," a position which is "fatal to any philosophy."[36]

Thus Strauss, like Jacobi, found himself forced to conclude that orthodoxy won out, both theoretically and practically, because of the "self-destruction of rational philosophy" and its religious and political manifestations. This, however, he could not accept as an "unmitigated blessing," since it entailed not only the victory of Jewish orthodoxy but of any orthodoxy. These matters and

> other observations and experiences confirmed the suspicion that it would be unwise to say farewell to reason. I therefore began to wonder whether the self-destruction of reason was not the inevitable outcome of modern rationalism as distinguished from pre-modern rationalism, especially Jewish-medieval rationalism and its classical (Aristotelian and Platonic) formulation.[37]

V

In the early 1930's, Strauss pursued the recovery of medieval Jewish thought and focused on Maimonides. Just as his later work would be devoted to reawakening the quarrel between the ancients and moderns with respect to political philosophy, this book continued to attack the idea that modern rationalism had refuted Jewish orthodoxy and to confront "modern rationalism" with "medieval rationalism."[38] Although Strauss assumed that in principle the Enlightenment had been discredited, its residue in Mendelssohn, Cohen, and even Rosenzweig continued to undermine the revelatory "foundation of the Jewish tradition." He concluded that the only path was to "repeat" the "classical quarrel between Enlightenment and orthodoxy."[39]

Strauss argued that the Enlightenment had not so much refuted orthodoxy as mocked it and dismissed it. It "left in its rear the uncapturable fortress of orthodoxy" as it turned to the practice of "civilizing the world and man," or pushing back "natural limits," and eventually embraced the ideal of "freedom, understood as the autonomy of man and his culture." Then (through Hegel) the "ideal

36. *Ibid.*, p. 30.
37. *Ibid.*, p. 31.
38. Strauss, *Philosophy and Law* (New York: Jewish Publication Society, 1987), p. 3.
39. *Ibid.*, pp. 5, 7, 8.

118   *John Gunnell*

of culture, understood as the sovereign creation of the spirit" and the "self-assertion of man against an over-powerful nature" became dominant.[40]

In his discussion of the conflict between the ancients and the moderns, Strauss argued that Maimonides "rational critique of reason" approached the problem of the tension between revelation and philosophy through the idea of the "grounding of philosophy" in revealed law which in turn commanded reflection on revelation and issued in the "philosophical grounding of the law." Ultimately, however, revelation was paramount, since the philosopher was forced to admit the "inadequacy of human reason to know the truth" of things beyond the "lower world."[41]

Strauss also found in Maimonides another dimension of the answer to the tension between reason and revelation and between Greek philosophy and Judaism. Both the philosophers and the prophets recognized "man's being by nature a political form" and were guided by the idea of natural right as a law addressing the total order of human life as well as by the idea that "the human race needs laws and thus a lawgiver." The prophet is at once a teacher, leader, philosopher, and lawgiver. The medieval Jewish and Islamic philosophers understood revelation in light of Platonic philosophy, but Plato also "foretold" revelation. The prophet is like Plato's founder of the ideal state who knows the upper world and solves the problem of theory and practice by acting as a mediator between the two worlds.[42]

Strauss's conclusion, however, was that medieval Jewish philosophy's answer to the problem of the relationship between philosophy and religion was, in the end, a tenuous one. For the Jews, philosophy faced religion and divine law much like philosophy faced politics in Greece—something without, on its face, public authority. Only in the figure of the prophet cum lawgiver, modeled on the philosopher-king, could there be a resolution. But this did not offer a solution in the practical modern world, and Strauss would eventually see the tension between revelation and reason as something that could not be overcome.

This tension was a vital dialectic in the Western tradition, but it did ultimately require a "choice." In Jewish thought, the law, although philosophically grounded, was not open to question. Thus,

40. *Ibid.*, pp. 13, 16.
41. *Ibid.*, pp. 40–41.
42. *Ibid.*, pp. 50–51.

in the end, this position "does not have the sharpness, originality, depth, and ambiguity of Platonic politics."[43] Strauss, eventually a nonbelieving Jew, chose philosophy or "Greek wisdom" over "biblical wisdom." By adopting the philosophical attitude, "we have already decided in favor of Athens against Jerusalem."[44] He would eventually conclude that "no one can be both a philosopher and a theologian" and that revealed divine law and rationally discerned natural order present fundamental alternatives which can be neither transcended nor synthesized.[45]

Strauss noted that when he wrote his critique of Spinoza, he had proceeded on the "premise, sanctioned by a powerful prejudice, that a return to premodern philosophy is impossible." But he had found that a return to orthodoxy required coming to terms with "traditional philosophy, which is of Greek, pagan origin." This "change of orientation found its first expression, not entirely by accident," in his reply to Carl Schmitt's *Concept of the Political*.[46]

VI

This "change" involved, in part, the idea, which was largely the product of his encounter with Heidegger, that philosophy was bound up with historical deconstruction and that

> the enlightenment critique of the tradition must be radicalized, as it was by Nietzsche, into a critique of the principles of the tradition (the Greek as well as the biblical); thereby the original understanding of these principles may again become possible. The "historization" of philosophy is therefore, and only therefore, justified and necessary. Only the history of philosophy makes possible the ascent out of the second, "unnatural" cave (into which we have fallen, less through the tradition than through the tradition of the polemic against the tradition), into the first, "natural" cave that Plato's image depicts, and the ascent from which, to the light, is the original meaning of philosophizing.[47]

What Strauss had come to accept by the time that he addressed Schmitt was the idea that the critique of religion and politics were two basic and entwined projects. He found in these realms, and

43. *Ibid.*, p. 55.   44. Strauss, *Studies in Platonic Political Philosophy*, p. 150.
45. Strauss, *The Rebirth of Classical Political Rationalism*, p. 270.
46. Strauss, *Spinoza's Critique of Religion*, pp. 8–9, 31.
47. Strauss, *Philosophy and Law*, p. 112.

the tension between them, irreducible aspects of human existence. Religion and politics were the *"original facts,"* the natural dimensions of life.[48] Thus a critique of modernity was necessarily theological-political in character and based on elements that stood outside the pluralistic horizon of the philosophy of culture. It was in his discussion of Schmitt that Strauss announced the naturalness of the political and most explicitly extended his critique of liberalism and modernity from religion to politics.

Although Schmitt eventually became an apologist for the Third Reich, he was generally recognized as a brilliant legal theorist. Despite his increasingly right-wing associations and his defense of the use of emergency powers and executive authority in the Weimar constitution, he continued, through 1932, to have considerable influence on thinkers across the political spectrum. Few of the emigres were innocent of Schmitt's work and his transformation of the term "political" into a noun. Much of his influence derived from his focused attack on liberalism — which was an object of disapprobation on the part of both the left and right.

Through the 1920's, Schmitt mounted an attack on the pluralist theory of the state and on the party politics and parliamentary practice of Weimar which he claimed failed to recognize the "objective nature and autonomy of the political." He argued that "the concept of the state presupposes the concept of the political," but this equation failed when there was an interpenetration of state and society and a loss of a distinct center of sovereignty.[49] For Schmitt, political actions and motives were reducible to the relationship between "friend and enemy," in the same manner that good and evil defined the sphere of morality or that competition defined economic relations. But politics, morality, and economics were different realms. The problem with liberalism was that it conflated these distinctions and obscured the nature of politics by reducing or subordinating it to these other dimensions of life.

Schmitt's claim was that while the state had the role of defining friend and enemy — both internally and externally, "liberal individualism" and pluralism tended, in theory and practice, to deny the sovereignty of the state and the existence of the political as a decisive entity. Furthermore, states were fundamental in the sense that

48. *Ibid.*
49. Carl Schmitt, *The Concept of the Political,* trans. and ed. George Schwab (New Brunswick, NJ: Rutgers University Press, 1976), pp. 27, 19.

there were necessarily multiple states. The idea of a world state and a transpolitical natural law was a contradiction, because the very idea of the state and law, based on the notion of friend and enemy and the concept of sovereignty, presupposed others and otherness."[50]

All genuine political theories, according to Schmitt, saw man as evil or at least saw human nature as problematic in the sense of self-seeking. Thus, as Hobbes indicated, the state is concerned with protection and obedience and must be clearly distinguished from society. The liberal hope for the disappearance or sublimation of the state and the political was misplaced. "The state and politics cannot be exterminated."[51]

There is a great deal of Schmitt's argument that Strauss embraced: the emphasis on the autonomy and irreducibility of the political, the impossibility of a world state, and the danger of the encroachment of society and a technological materialistic culture. Strauss's principal disagreement with Schmitt was quite simply that his critique of liberalism did not go far enough and that he failed to recognize that the roots of liberalism were deeper than the Enlightenment and that Hobbes was actually a "founder of liberalism," of the "idea of civilization," and, ultimately, of the notion of a rational universal society.[52]

Hobbes was the initiator of modern natural right theory and the idea that the individual preceded, temporally and in priority, the state and politics. He did not present the state as a natural entity. It was to Hobbes's credit that he saw the fundamental problem of politics in human nature and not merely in corrupt institutions. And it was his successors who moved to the idea of man's "natural goodness" and eventually to the "philosophy of culture" which was the final "self-consciousness of liberalism." But it was nevertheless Hobbes who started the whole process by denying the naturalness of the political and suggesting that the human world was entirely open to artifice.[53]

Strauss praised Schmitt for his affirmation of the political and his defense of the state in the face of the liberal negation. "Whereas Hobbes living in an illiberal world, lays the foundation of liberalism,

50. *Ibid.*, pp. 45, 53.
51. *Ibid.*, p. 78.
52. Leo Strauss, "Comments on Carl Schmitt's *Der Begriff des Politischen*, " in Schmitt, *The Concept of the Political*, p. 89.
53. *Ibid.*, p. 90.

Schmitt living in a liberal world, undertakes the critique of liberalism."[54] And it was this project with which Strauss fully identified. His quarrel with Schmitt centered on the fact that Schmitt was still bound by a residue of liberal assumptions and did not sufficiently demonstrate the naturalness of the political as distinct from specific historical institutions such as the state. In a subsequent letter to Schmitt, Strauss emphasized once more that Schmitt's formulation, despite the recognition that politics was grounded in human nature, still left room for the implication that the political was in some way "derivative."[55]

Schmitt affirmed the political, Strauss claimed, because he realized that "when the political is threatened, the seriousness of life is threatened. The affirmation of the political is in the last analysis nothing other than the affirmation of the moral." But "in order to launch the radical critique of liberalism that he has in mind, Schmitt must first eliminate the conception of human evil as animal evil, and therefore as 'innocent evil,' and find his way back to the conception of human evil as moral depravity," that is, back to a conception of human nature that antedates Hobbes and liberalism.[56]

Strauss, agreeing with Schmitt, stressed that politics "remains constantly determinative of man's fate," but it also was "always dependent on what is at any given time man's ultimate concern." And, he claimed, today, in Weimar, that concern had been reduced, both domestically and internationally, to the liberal ethic of "neutralization" and "agreement at any price." Humanity entails the question of what is right, and this often means choices about life and death which justify a division between friend and enemy and require a rejection of a "humanitarian pacifist morality."[57]

Since, in Strauss's view, Schmitt was still in part bound by the liberal vision, his "affirmation of the political as such can therefore not be other than merely the first word from Schmitt against liberalism. It can do no more than prepare the way for a radical critique of liberalism." Rather "it is undertaken only to clear the field for the decisive battle against the 'spirit of technology,'" the "'mass faith

54. *Ibid.*, p. 91.
55. Leo Strauss, letter to Carl Schmitt, in Heinrich Meier, *Carl Schmitt, Leo Strauss, und "Der Begriff des Politischen"* (Stuttgart: J. B. Metzlersche Verlagsbuchhandlung, 1988), pp. 132–33.
56. Strauss, "Comments on Carl Schmitt's *Der Begriff des Politischen*," pp. 99, 97.
57. *Ibid.*, pp. 100–101.

of an antireligious, this worldly activism' and the opposite spirit and faith, which it seems, does not yet have a name" but which looks forward to the "order of human things" which was Schmitt's "last word."[58]

This language, in retrospect at least, sounds indeed ominous — particularly in light of the manner in which the revised 1932 version of Schmitt's essay, on which Strauss was commenting, was being understood. Within the next year, Heidegger would be personally inviting Schmitt to join him in theoretically underwriting the new Reich. Strauss was flirting with philosophical doctrines that were much more proximate to the political demise of Weimar than the liberalism, positivism, existentialism, and relativism on which he later focused.

In the end, Strauss stressed still once again that the principal problem with Schmitt's argument was that he was still constrained by liberal premises, and he repeated once more that Schmitt's

> critique of liberalism takes place within the horizon of liberalism; his illiberal tendencies are arrested by the as yet undefeated "systematic of liberal thinking." The critique of liberalism that Schmitt has initiated can therefore be completed only when we succeed in gaining a horizon beyond liberalism. Within such a horizon Hobbes achieved the foundation of liberalism. A radical critique of liberalism is therefore possible only on the basis of an adequate understanding of Hobbes.[59]

This sentence points forward to Strauss's exile in England, his book on Hobbes, and the more familiar world of Straussianism.

VII

What this excursion into Strauss's early work most clearly reveals is the manner in which the structure of his critique of liberal theology was transformed into a critique of liberal politics and how his repudiation of modern rationalism and liberalism propelled him toward the historical recovery of a different ground of judgment and conception of political phenomena. Exactly where he had arrived intellectually by the time that he came to the United States may be a more contentious issue, but I offer the following conclusions.

Strauss's naturalism had little to do with natural law as commonly

58. *Ibid.*, pp. 102–104.
59. *Ibid.*, p. 105.

understood. What was natural was not some particular moral principle or ethic. Natural right involved demands that were coincident with the naturalness or givenness of the political and its relationship to other orders of existence such as the social and religious. It could be abrogated, but this invited retribution. The political, in some historical form such as the *polis* or the modern state, was rooted both in human nature and humanity's place in nature. Strauss remained emphatic in his claim that "there can only be closed societies, that is, states." The "contemporary solution, that is, the modern solution," with all its technological complexity, which is "the fruit of rationalism," and its drive toward the goal of a universal homogeneous order, was "*contra naturam*."[60]

Strauss was concerned with what was by nature the best regime, but although the "perfect political order, as Plato and Aristotle sketched it," might not be possible, or even desirable, it was an intellectual construct that constituted the logical opposite of what was minimally, and maybe practically, required.[61]

> Natural right is that right which must be recognized by any political society if it is to last and which for this reason is everywhere in force. Natural right thus understood delineates the minimum conditions of political life, so much so that sound positive right occupies a higher rank than natural right.[62]

What was natural was "the floor and the ceiling, the minimum condition and maximum possibility of political society." Thus he could agree with what he took to be Aristotle's teaching to the effect that "all natural right is changeable" and that "it is just to deviate even from the most general principles of natural right" under certain circumstances.

Morality in any positive sense was derivative from and relative to the political, but also a necessary aspect of it. Yet morality, as a set of specific dictates, and by definition conventional, could not transcend the political order. It was the beliefs and opinions of, hopefully, the best (most prudent, wise, realistic, just) men in a regime. It was not something discovered by philosophy.

His conception of philosophy offered little in the way of a posi-

60. Leo Strauss, letter to Karl Lowith, 10 January 1946, in "Correspondence Concerning Modernity," *Independent Journal of Philosophy* 4 (1983): 107–108; *The Rebirth of Classical Political Rationalism*, p. 42.
61. *Ibid.*
62. Strauss, *Studies in Platonic Political Philosophy*, p. 140.

tive vision. He could hardly have been more pointed when he said that for "the philosopher, what counts is thinking and investigating and not morality."

> Philosophy is the attempt to replace opinion with knowledge; but opinion is the element of the city, hence philosophy is subversive, hence the philosopher must write in a way that he will improve rather than subvert the city. In other words, the virtue of the philosopher's thought is a certain kind of *mania* while the virtue of the philosopher's public speech is *sophrosyne*. Philosophy is as such trans-political, trans-religious, and trans-moral but the city is and ought to be moral.[63]

He did not mean that the philosopher was not concerned with morality (understanding it, supporting it, undermining it), but philosophy, as for Nietzsche, was beyond good and evil.

What philosophy could know was something about the nature of the political, but one of the things that it knew was that everyday political life was based on opinion. And this was the fundamental source of the inevitable, and natural, tension and "gulf" between philosophy and politics that could be bridged neither by philosophical practice nor practical philosophy. Like the difference between reason and revelation, this breach was part of the human condition.

Since philosophy could not say in any specific historical context what was transcendentally right, its function was almost necessarily critical and destructive if practiced in an open and unrestrained manner. It could not but reveal the partiality and historicity of political opinion. Although philosophy could and should contribute to sustaining a decent regime and although the philosopher and the city are "attached" through mutual "care," the philosopher, as questioner, is necessarily "detached" and transcends politics. The philosophical quest creates a "conflict between the philosopher and the city," and philosophy necessarily becomes a kind of "political action."[64]

All this is not to say that Strauss was not in some sense a foundationalist, but this is a term best applied to modern rationalism and the epistemological tradition sprung from Descartes which Strauss rejected very early in his life. The notion of foundations of knowledge, the very essence of modern rationalism, is what Strauss so vehemently repudiated. The philosopher who embraces "certainty"

---

63. Klein and Strauss, "A Giving of Accounts," p. 4.
64. Leo Strauss, *On Tyranny* (Glencoe, IL: The Free Press, 1963), pp. 208, 219.

is no longer a philosopher. Certainty belongs to politics and practical life.[65] And here he was at one with Nietzsche and Heidegger. From the time of his encounter with Jacobi, Strauss embraced the view that modern rationalism, and its practical manifestations, was self-destructive. It could not justify itself, and it ultimately either ended in nihilism or rested on an orthodoxy of its own. "This basis of rationalism proves to be a dogmatic assumption."[66]

Thus Strauss returned to what he understood as premodern Socratic rationalism which he conceived as something of a different sort that was not, despite how later commentators may have read Plato, based on an idealist and foundationalist epistemology. And it did not, in his view, necessarily underwrite a particular practice of morals, politics, or any form of conventional life. What it grasped was the fundamental character of the human condition and the manner of human being in the world.

For Strauss, religion, morality, politics, science and most other conventional dimensions of life were in the end grounded in commitment. And philosophy could not offer a substitute for such practical belief. The pursuit of philosophy, the Socratic quest, also involved commitment, but it was primarily a deconstructive activity. Philosophy was potentially dangerous for society, just as society was dangerous for philosophy. Although Strauss saw Husserl as holding on to the idea of "philosophy as a rigorous science" against the forces of historicism, he also noted that "he did not go on to wonder whether the single-minded pursuit of philosophy as rigorous science would not have an adverse effect on *Weltanschuungsphilosophie* which most men need to live by."[67]

There can be no doubt that Strauss saw the dominant tendency in modern philosophy as rendering political philosophy impossible. Even Hegel and Marx held on to the idea of an "absolute moment" in history, and Nietzsche at least saw something transhistorical in the idea of the "over-man." It was Heidegger, however, who surrendered to the "homelessness" of human historicity and who severed "the connection . . . with politics more radically than either Marx or Nietzsche" and who left "no place for political philosophy."[68] But it is important not to misunderstand what Strauss was saying.

65. *Ibid.*, p. 210.
66. Strauss, *The Rebirth of Classical Political Rationalism*, p. 43.
67. Strauss, *Studies in Platonic Political Philosophy*, p. 37.
68. *Ibid.*, pp. 32–34.

Although historicism had led to the demise of "rigorous philosophy," Strauss was not calling for a return to political philosophy based on rationalism. His basic quarrel with Heidegger was, first, that he denatured politics. He no longer allowed for a political moment or for politics as a fact of the human condition or a structure of human existence. But, second, the real problem with Heidegger, as with Nietzsche, was not so much that they were philosophically wrong as practically dangerous. Strauss's criticism was essentially that their overt teaching rent the fabric of public life. They revealed the awful truth that no conventions were philosophically vouchsafed.

For Strauss, existentialism, typified by Heidegger, was the epitome of historicism. He later argued that there was "an intimate connection" between Heidegger's philosophy and National Socialism.[69] He claimed that there was also "an undeniable kinship between Nietzsche's thought and fascism" rooted not only in his critique of philosophy but in his rejection of both constitutional monarchy and democracy, yet Strauss did not believe that in the end Nietzsche, "a European conservative," would have sided with Hitler.[70] Strauss argued that Heidegger's turn toward the Nazi regime was more deeply determined.

It was not, as Arendt would suggest, a mere "error of judgment" on the part of a naive scholar but something rooted in a fundamental "kinship in temper and direction." He asked "what was the *practical*, that is to say, serious meaning of the contempt for reasonableness and the praise of resoluteness except to encourage the extremist movement?"[71] An uncharitable commentator might very well say the same about Strauss's support of Schmitt's ontologizing of "the political," but more to the point is the fact that Strauss's quarrel with Heidegger was in large measure one about the practical role and implications of philosophy.

What Heidegger had done was to declare "that ethics was impossible, and his whole being was permeated by the awareness that this fact opens up an abyss.[72] The "abyss" had two dimensions, and both involved the relationship of philosophy to politics.

---

69. Strauss, *Studies in Platonic Political Philosophy*, p. 30.
70. Strauss, *The Rebirth of Classical Political Rationalism*, p. 31, 40.
71. *Ibid.*, p. 30, emphasis added.
72. *Ibid.*, p. 28.

If a rationally grounded ethics was impossible, philosophy lost its authority vis-à-vis politics. But for Strauss it also involved the danger that the end of certainty in philosophy would issue in a practical crisis by spilling over into popular attitudes and by undermining society's faith in itself. Strauss emphasized that the crisis of philosophy, represented by existentialism, and the crisis of politics, represented by liberal democracy, were both parallel and entwined. "The situation to which existentialism belongs can be seen to be liberal democracy, or, more precisely a liberal democracy which has become uncertain of itself or of its future. Existentialism belongs to the decline of Europe."[73]

Strauss maintained that the modern crisis reflected the fact that "all rational liberal political philosophical positions have lost their significance and power," and he personally could not accept "clinging to philosophical positions which have beens hown to be inadequate." But there was no satisfactory philosophical answer to this problem after Heidegger who was "the only great thinker in our time."[74]

A dedicated academic disciple of Strauss once related how after many years he came to realize that Strauss "had no doctrine—or at least a most elusive one." At one intellectual gathering at which Strauss was being discussed, where the participants included H. G. Gadamer and Gershom Scholem, he found himself defending Strauss "against the representatives of Heidegger and God."[75] This anecdote may convey as accurately as any conceptual formulation the meaning of Strauss's work.

---

73. *Ibid.*, p. 39.
74. *Ibid.*, p. 29.
75. Werner J. Dannhauser, "Leo Strauss: Becoming Naive Again," *The American Scholar 44 (1975): 641.*

Philosophy and Law: Leo Strauss as a Student of Medieval Jewish Thought

Hillel Fradkin

Even a casual glance at the list of Leo Strauss's writings devoted in whole or in part to medieval Jewish texts is sufficient to make clear that in any ordinary sense he left a substantial legacy to this field of study. They include two books, *Philosophy and Law*[1] and *Persecution and the Art of Writing*,[2] the monograph length essay which serves as the introduction to the English translation of Maimonides' *Guide of the Perplexed*[3] done by Shlomo Pines and a number of articles.[4] Moreover it is relatively clear that his study of these texts form an important part of his legacy as such. They remained important to his inquiries through his long scholarly career and do not belong only to one phase. Several of the articles devoted to such texts, he chose to republish in subsequent volumes concerned with major themes of his work.[5] More important still, even towards the end of his life when his work was largely devoted to classical Greek texts, medieval Jewish texts continued to play some important role. The last work planned by Strauss, *Studies on Platonic Philosophy*, contains new, albeit short, treatments of Maimonides' *Treatise on Logic* and his *Letter on Astrology* which are the only essays first published in this book.[6]

1. Strauss, *Philosophie und Gesetz: Beitrage zum Verstandnis Maimunis and seiner Vorlaufer* (Berlin: Schocken 1935); English translation: *Philosophy and Law: Essays Toward the Understanding of Maimonides and His Predecessors*, trans. Fred Baumann (Philadelphia, PA: Jewish Publication Society, 1987).
2. Strauss, *Persecution and the Art of Writing* (Glencoe, IL: Free Press, 1952).
3. "How to Begin to Study *The Guide of the Perplexed*," in *Maimonides' Guide of the Perplexed*, trans. Shlomo Pines (Chicago: University of Chicago. 1963). Reprinted in *Liberalism, Ancient and Modern* (New York: Basic Books, 1968).
4. "Quelques remarques sur la science politique de Maimonide et de Farabi," *Revue des Etudes Juives* 100:1–37; "Der ort der vorsehungslehre nach der Ansicht Maimunis," *Monatsschnift fur Geschichte und Wissenschaft des Judentums* 81:93–105; "On Husik's Work in Medieval Jewish Philosophy." Introduction to *I. Husik's Philosophical Essays: Ancient, Medieval and Modern* (Oxford: Basil Blackwell, 1952); "Maimonides' Statement on Political Science," *Proceedings of the American Academy of Jewish Research* 22:115–30; "On the Plan of the *Guide of the Perplexed*," *Harry Austryn Wolfson Jubilee Volume* (Jerusalem: American Academy for Jewish Research), pp. 775–91.
5. *What Is Political Philosophy?* (Glencoe, IL: Free Press, 1956); *Liberalism, Ancient and Modern*.
6. *Studies in Platonic Political Philosophy* (Chicago: University of Chicago, 1983).

It is therefore necessary to try to address not only his contributions to the understanding of medieval Jewish thought but the latter's
role in his general legacy. It is only fair to observe that such a requirement attends the consideration of any portion of Strauss's
scholarship, since the whole of Strauss's scholarship, far-flung and
diverse as it was, was animated by common interests and questions.
But Strauss's researches into medieval Jewish thought were begun
as part of his earliest inquiries and thus appear to have a particularly powerful bearing upon the character of those inquiries.

The immediate purpose of Strauss's work in medieval Jewish
thought is the analysis of the character and perspective of medieval
Jewish rationalism and takes the form of historical research of major
texts belonging to this tradition. Nevertheless, Strauss clearly indicated that the primary inspiration of this work was not historical
curiosity, but derived from concerns more generally philosophic and
Jewish and emphatically contemporary. The origin of this work lay
in concern with the contemporary fate of both rationalism and
Judaism.[7] As these interests were not only primary but lifelong, it
is in these terms that his work in medieval Jewish thought must
ultimately be understood. The present article is offered in the spirit
and service of such an understanding.

Nevertheless, it is useful even to this task to begin with a few remarks about the scholarly context of medieval Jewish studies and
especially of the study of medieval Jewish rationalism. Several considerations recommend this. The first is that the modern study of
medieval Jewish rationalism, beginning in the early nineteenth century, was itself inspired by concern with the fate of Judaism and
rationalism or at least the fate of Judaism and its relationship to
modern rationalism. Moreover, similar concerns are still entailed
in contemporary studies. These concerns, both early and late, and
their effects formed an important part of the initial framework of
Strauss's work or his beginning point.

For Strauss seems to have rather scrupulously adhered to the ancient maxim of Aristotle according to which we must begin our inquiries from what is first for us. At all events his research into medieval Jewish thought texts was expressly intended to clarify the present
as much as the past.[8]

---

7. *Philosophy and Law*, Introduction and chap. 1; "Preface to Spinoza's *Critique
of Religion*," reprinted in *Liberalism, Ancient and Modern*.
   8. *Ibid.*

The second major factor is that however broad Strauss's interests were, they were always pursued through very careful and serious historical research. As such they were partially based upon and have a natural place within the history of research into medieval Jewish thought. Indeed on more than one occasion, Strauss presented his work as a protest against and corrective for the historical deficiencies of other researches.[9]

Let us then briefly consider the course of medieval Jewish studies as this related to Strauss's enterprise. The beginning of modern study of medieval Jewish rationalism belongs to the beginnings of modern Jewish scholarship as such, which arose in Germany in the early part of the nineteenth century. While it shares that distinction with many other fields of Jewish research, it is fair to say that it occupied a particularly prominent place within this endeavor.

This importance was the result of the combination of several factors. To begin with, modern Jewish scholarship was the result of the desire of a portion of German Jewry to integrate itself within contemporary German life. This required by their lights, a form of Judaism which could incorporate contemporary German Enlightenment. The latter defined itself by the twin and intertwined currents of post-Enlightenment rationalism and historical culture. At the same time, however, it was clear that this new form of Judaism would only be Jewish to the extent that its analogs to German culture could be drawn from Jewish roots. While the former circumstances led to the initiation of Jewish historical research, the latter predisposed this research to focus upon a particular period and place within Jewish history, the medieval Jewish community of Spain. The reasons were more or less obvious. Here was a community, whose leading figures had admired and appropriated the prevailing philosophic enlightenment of their day. Moreover, these figures, men like Moses Maimonides and Judah Halevi, were not marginal to Jewish tradition but among its leading authorities, even down to the present. These factors spawned early and extensive researches into the literature of medieval Jewish rationalism, including critical editions of the relevant texts which in many instances stand to the present day or have been revised only very recently. For example, the newest and best edition of Judah Halevi's *Kuzari* is barely ten years old.[10]

9. *Ibid.*

10. See L. Berman, "Medieval Jewish Religious Philosophy" in *Bibliographical Essays in Medieval Jewish Studies, Studies in Judaism*, vol. 2 (New York, NY: Anti-

Contemporary medieval Jewish studies are, of course, built upon this foundation, but it is safe to say that they owe some of their character to a very different context. They still owe a great deal of their energy to hope, but these hopes are radically different from those which animated nineteenth-century German Jewry. They are in fact in part the consequence of the crushing disappointment of the latter's hopes. These hopes are still concerned with finding or preparing a home for the modern Jewish community, but that home is no longer Germany or even Western Europe but Israel. In this context, medieval Jewish studies derive their importance as the study of texts which might inform the construction of a new and distinctively Jewish state and society.

Despite the distance which separates contemporary medieval Jewish studies from its origins, both poles serve to define the context for Strauss's researches. As Strauss made clear in a number of places, including *Philosophy and Law*,[11] his own work began during the initial confrontation between these two forms of modern Jewish hopes and proceeded from concern with those modern Jewish problems, they helped to articulate if not resolve. As a matter of immediate practice, Strauss sided more with the representatives of German Jewish Zionism than those of German Jewish assimilation. But anticipating certain practical as well as theoretical problems of Zionism he turned to the study of the medieval Jewish enlightenment and its rationalism.

In this respect he continued the work of nineteenth-century German Jewish enlightenment and followed a different course than not only contemporary Zionists but German Jewish existentialism.[12] Nevertheless he launched these efforts in *Philosophy and Law* by indicating that his own work was based first on the suspicion and then the conviction, that the preceding and prevailing view of medieval Jewish rationalism was decisively defective.[13] Indeed he suggested

---

Defamation League of B'nai B'rith, 1976); J. Guttman, *Philosophies of Judaism* (New York, NY: Schocken, 1973); G. Vajda, "Les etudes de philosophie juive du Moyen Age depuis La synthese de Julius Guttman," *Hebrew Union College Annual* 43 (1972): 125–47; 45 (1974); C. Sirat, *A History of Jewish Philosophy in the Middle Ages* (Cambridge: University of Cambridge, 1985).

11. *Philosophy and Law*, Introduction and chap. 1; "Preface to Spinoza's Critique of Religion."

12. For a fuller discussion of Strauss's relationship to contemporary Jewish thought see H. Fradkin, "Leo Strauss & Contemporary Jewish Thought," *Contemporary Jewish Thinkers* (B'nai B'rith Books).

13. For this and following, *Philosophy and Law*, Introduction and chap. 1.

that all forms of contemporary Jewish thought had more in common with one another than they had with medieval Jewish thought. They were all, in one way or another, children of the modern enlightenment. His own turn to medieval thought was a reflection of doubt about the status and force of modern thought, as such. As he put it, his work was offered in order to arouse a prejudice in favor of the view that the thought of Moses Maimonides is the classic of rationalism in Judaism and even the classic of rationalism as such, or the truly natural model. Strauss traced the possibility of such a bold endeavor and the distinctive character of his own research into medieval Jewish thought to his discovery or rediscovery of the fact that the subject of law is the guiding theme of the medieval Jewish enlightenment.

In order to understand the character and importance of Strauss's treatment of law and its relationship to medieval Jewish thought, it is helpful to clarify the sense in which this constitutes a rediscovery. Indeed it is practically a necessity. At first glance this might seem no discovery at all. After all, no student of medieval Jewish thought could fail to notice that the theme of law occupies a significant and honored place in medieval Jewish thought. Moreover from time to time scholarly researches were devoted to this and related themes. Nevertheless, Strauss did indeed differ from his predecessors by regarding the theme of law not only as one theme among many but as that one which supplied the fundamental framework of medieval Jewish rationalism. Not only did this distinguish his treatment of law from others devoted to the same subject. It also marked off his treatment from those which put forward other themes as the key to the basic framework of Jewish medieval thought.

To clarify this difference it is necessary to observe that these alternative approaches do at least start from a fundamental agreement. The most obvious theme of medieval Jewish thought or at least that portion known as medieval Jewish Philosophy is the relationship between revelation and reason or more concretely between the Bible and classical or Greek philosophy. More specifically, it seems to be concerned with the actual or potential conflict between the teaching of Biblical revelation and Greek philosophy and devoted to the resolution of that conflict whether this means the reconciliation of the two views or choice between them. Its concern with this conflict and especially those attempts to reconcile the two which it presented were the chief sources of its interest for early Jewish scholarship. For they considered themselves to be faced with an analogous situation or conflict. Strauss's own interest in medieval Jewish thought was no less concerned with this conflict.[14] However, as Strauss understood previous research and presented it, the prevailing view was that the main plane of this conflict, both in principle and methodologically, was theoretical and dogmatic or concerned with the apparent contradiction between the doctrines of the Bible and classical philosophy.[15] In particular, it assigned special importance to the tension between what was understood to be Jewish or biblical theology and classical physics and metaphysics. It therefore understood the discussion of such issues to be both the core of medieval Jewish thought, the key to its interpretation and the criterion of its status and utility.

The circumstances which led them to this orientation are fairly easy to discern. Not only did these questions present themselves as obvious problems for a cultivated medieval Jew, one who had an especially profound grasp of both the Bible and classical philosophy through the medieval enlightenment, but several such Jews appeared to place these questions in the forefront. This appeared especially true of Moses Maimonides who by and large was regarded as the greatest and most brilliant representative of medieval Jewish thought. After all in his *Guide of the Perplexed*, his apparently most important and most philosophic work, he declared that its most important subjects were *Maaseh Bereshit* and *Maaseh Merkavah*, the Account of Creation and the Account of the Chariot, and these were in turn equivalent to physics and metaphysics respectively.[16]

Needless to say, Strauss did not overlook such pronouncements nor disregard the importance of these subjects and issues.[17] But to begin with, he regarded them as profoundly mysterious, and as such the ultimate objects of a satisfactory interpretation rather than its keys. Moreover, in searching for the latter, Strauss came to be impressed or take note of other characteristics of medieval Jewish philosophical literature. Reflection upon them led him eventually to conclude that the theme of law provided the essential beginning point and framework of medieval Jewish rationalism. Neglect of this theme thus led not only to an incomplete view of medieval Jewish rationalism, but also to an abstract and distorted understanding of it.

14. "The Law of Reason in the *Kuzari*," *Persecution and the Art of Writing*, p. 107, note 35.
15. *Philosophy and Law*, Introduction and chap. 1.
16. Moses Maimonides, *Guide of the Perplexed*, Introduction.
17. "How to Begin to Study the Guide of the Perplexed."

Let me briefly enumerate some of these considerations, drawn from the work of Moses Maimonides and Judah Halevi, whom Strauss called the leading figures of medieval Jewish thought and whom he regarded as the most competent judges and analysts of its character and problems. The first among them is the fact that Maimonides presented almost the entirety of his thought within a legal framework. This is most obvious in the case of two of his three major works — the *Commentary on the Mishnah* and the *Mishneh Torah*. The former is a commentary on that text which forms the foundation of the rabbinic legal tradition, that is, the code of Jewish law compiled in the second century A.D. The second is Maimonides' own legal code, compiled in order to present a coherent account of Jewish law as it had developed down to his own time. To be sure these works included discussions of opinions on a variety of topics less obviously legal: ethics, prophecy, providence, eschatology. But their inclusion in such works seemed to confirm rather than deny the primacy of law.

Still, Strauss could not and did not regard this as simply decisive. After all, these were emphatically legal works, and it was not surprising that in such a context, nonlegal subjects should occupy a subordinate role. Nor was it shocking that a medieval Jew, even one as interested in theological or philosophical questions as Maimonides, should devote a great deal of his time and effort to legal exposition and codification. Hence what was most critical was the character and status of Maimonides' third major work, *The Guide of the Perplexed*. For this work seemed to be both his most important work, directed as it was to his most cultivated and thoughtful Jewish contemporaries, and to be emphatically theological in its concerns, devoted in large part to the examination of opinions concerning God, creation, prophecy, etc.

Here Strauss was impressed by the fact that by its own account this work is devoted to what is called a science of the law, to be sure a most unusual science of the law or rather the true science of the law, but nonetheless a science whose theme or basis is somehow law. It is true as indicated before and as Strauss fully recognized that this science proves to be largely concerned with opinion rather than actions. Nevertheless, it remains legal insofar as the subject matter is not opinion as such, or theological or metaphysical opinion in particular, but the "opinions of the law" or "our law" or the "law of Moses our Master," locutions by which Maimonides presents his subject.

It proves to be legal in another sense as well. For in keeping with the legal characteristics of the framework of such opinions, their interpretation, which occupies the greater part of the *Guide*, is viewed as an activity, and as such is subject to legal prescription and even proscription. These conditions are made amply clear by Maimonides in his Introduction to the *Guide*. It is on the basis of such considerations that Strauss could and did propose that the law may be regarded as supplying the essential framework of medieval Jewish rationalism.

Of course, it would not at any time be foolish to wonder whether such formal characteristics, especially legal ones, are not just that, formal, or represent a judicious expression of respect for the authority of law within Judaism. Still less would it be so now, after the work of Leo Strauss who emphasized and devoted so much effort to analyzing the distinction between exoteric and esoteric modes of expressions.[18]

Such questions and considerations, however, do not as such call into question the essentially legal framework of medieval Jewish rationalism, they only complicate its meaning and interpretation. As Strauss noted the "legal" form of medieval Jewish rationalism is a function of its subject matter and task, the interpretation of biblical revelation and its relationship to philosophy.[19] For biblical revelation, like any form of revelation, is a "specific" form of revelation and like some and unlike others, its form is law or *The Law*. To treat it otherwise requires an abstraction from its given character, a proceeding both practically impossible and even more importantly, theoretically undesirable for medieval Jewish rationalists.

To clarify what Strauss means by the primacy of law for medieval Jewish rationalism, it is useful and appropriate to turn at this juncture to certain features of the work of Judah Halevi. He is the other great author from whom Strauss derived his notion of the legal framework of medieval Jewish rationalism. It would be useful because Halevi was much more direct, albeit in his own fashion, in specifying the substantive meaning of this framework and the problem it represents. This no doubt partly derives from the fact that Halevi's purposes, as the greatest critic of philosophy within medieval Judaism, required less reserve than those of Maimonides'

18. *Persecution and the Art of Writing*, chaps. 1 and 2.
19. *Philosophy and Law* and "Preface to Spinoza's *Critique of Religion*."

the greatest defender of philosophy. It would be appropriate since Halevi and Strauss's study of him is often overlooked.

As is well known, Halevi presented his thoughts on the relationship of the Bible and philosophy through the medium of a dialogue conducted almost exclusively between a King of the Khazars and a Jewish scholar. As Strauss showed in his essay on the *Kuzari*, both the circumstances and characters of this dialogue were extremely carefully chosen.[20] In particular, Strauss noted and laid stress on the fact that the dialogue as a whole is set in motion by the desire of the Khazar King to determine with precision what forms of action are pleasing to God. For a variety of reasons the fulfillment of this desire proves to require study of and adherence to the Jewish law, as a result of which the King becomes a convert to Judaism. It is obvious that this context makes especially clear the primacy of Law for the interpretation of the Bible and Judaism. It also solicits, in Halevi's especially gifted hands, a fairly clear account of its implications for the pursuit of philosophy.

Notwithstanding Halevi's criticisms and rejection of philosophy, he or his spokesman have no difficulty in admitting and even goes out of his way to show that the Bible cannot be understood to teach or mean anything which is contrary to a view decisively demonstrated by reason. This includes a fair number of "theological" doctrines.[21] Nevertheless, there is an extremely powerful tension, amounting to an irreconcilable conflict when philosophy is viewed from the perspective of action and the law's concern with it. According to Halevi or the philosopher he briefly presents, philosophy rejects the notion that there is a form of action pleasing to God or indeed that God cares about human action altogether.[22] Hence philosophy is sufficient unto itself to prescribe for itself the way of life it should adhere to.

Indeed as Halevi brings out and stresses by reference to the example of Socrates, inasmuch as philosophy has not actualized its quest for wisdom, it is essentially an activity or way of life rather than a set of doctrines. Thus the principal opposition between the Bible and philosophy concerns the former's claim and the latter's denial that man depends upon divine instruction for the proper ordering of his life. Seen in this way, philosophy requires a defense

20. "The Law of Reason in the *Kuzari*," *Persecution and the Art of Writing*.
21. See especially the beginning of Part II of the *Kuzari*, *Kitab al-Radd wa-'l Dalil fi 'l-Din al Dhalil*, ed. D. H. Banett and H. Ben-Shammai.
22. *Kuzari*, Part I, Par. 1.

not of this or that view but of its activity as such, a defense which by Halevi's lights is unavailable.[23]

Needless to say, Strauss did not regard this as the end of the story or study of medieval Jewish rationalism, but he did regard it as its beginning or the essential meaning of the primacy of law. This was, in his view, as true for Maimonides as it was for Halevi, noting that Maimonides begins his *Guide* with a legal exposition and defense of the activity he is about to undertake and that that activity itself proves in the first instance to be an interpretation of certain biblical verses, an action in general solicited and sanctioned by law.[24]

Strauss was further able to underscore and elaborate this condition of medieval Jewish philosophy by reference to the tradition of Islamic philosophy upon which it depends. In particular he emphasized that work of Averroes, Maimonides' contemporary, which is expressly devoted to a legal examination and defense of philosophy.[25] While this legal grounding of philosophy, as Strauss termed it in *Philosophy and Law,* is the most obvious implication of the primacy of law, there are a number of other more or less immediate consequences. Perhaps the first concerns the categorization of medieval Jewish thinkers. Conventional scholarly practice had for a long time chosen to call men like Halevi and Maimonides philosophers.

Strauss pointed out that the primacy of law and its implications rendered this practice highly questionable and at a minimum inappropriate at the present stage of our knowledge of medieval Jewish thought. Indeed in some cases, like that of Halevi, our present understanding if articulated with sufficient care dictated an entirely different appellation.[26] In the case of Maimonides it might still be an open question but one which would only be resolved on the basis of the most thoroughgoing analysis. In any event, Strauss stressed and showed that the key to the beginning of the study of the *Guide of the Perplexed* required that one regard it as a Jewish rather than philosophic book.[27]

In rejecting conventional terminology and seeking a more ap-

23. For additional treatment see H. Fradkin, "Philosophy or Exegesis: Perennial Problems in the Study of Some Judaeo-Arabic Authors," *Proceedings of the Society for Judaeo-Arabic Studies,* vol. 1 (Forthcoming), and H. Fradkin, "The Dialogic Form of the *Kuzari* and the Interpretation of Judah Halevi's Thought" (Paper delivered at the 14th Annual Conference of the Association for Jewish Studies).
24. "How to Begin to Study the Guide of the Perplexed."
25. *Philosophy and Law,* chap. 2.
26. "Law of Reason in the *Kuzari.*"
27. "How to Begin to Study the Guide of the Perplexed."

propriate one, Strauss turned to the authors and books themselves and their own understanding of the kinds and purposes of literature. This led to the conclusion that works like the *Guide* and *Kuzari* could in a general sense be best defined as works of *Kalaam*, an arabic term used to designate forms of literature whose purpose was to defend the principles of faith from attack. Works such as the *Guide* and *Kuzari* met this description at a minimum by virtue of their announced concern with the doubts engendered by the study of philosophy.[28] It was true, as Strauss pointed out, that this designation required considerable qualification, since both Maimonides and Halevi, were express critics of the *mutakallimoon*, the conventional practitioners of *Kalaam*, but despite this and even because of this he regarded this term as less misleading than philosophy.

This specific consequence of Strauss's research, useful as it is, is connected with and leads to a more general and important one. This is the proposal that the primary framework of medieval Jewish rationalism or its literature is political in character and that political thought provides the primary place and arena for considering the relationship of biblical revelation and philosophy.[29] This is implied in the first place by the designation of these books as works of *Kalaam*. According to Alfarabi, the great teacher of Muslim and Jewish students of philosophy, *Kalaam* is a political art. This classification, however, is derivative from the primacy of law and thus may be more readily articulated from that direction.

The primacy of law as the form of expression of Jewish and also Islamic revelation implies that the primary task of the prophet is to be a lawgiver. Law-giving is emphatically a political action and this fact means that the proper interpretation of revelation requires a political analysis.[30]

As regards the relationship of philosophy and biblical revelation, this means in general that the philosophic discipline most crucial to this consideration is political philosophy or political science. But as Strauss indicated and elaborated, since classical philosophy came in two forms, Platonic and Aristotelian, it means more specifically that it is Platonic political philosophy which supplies the key to understanding the framework of medieval Jewish rationalism. This derives from the fact that the prophet as both legislator and possessor of the highest form of wisdom most nearly resembles a

28. See notes 26 and 27.
29. *Persecution and the Art of Writing*, chaps. 1 and 2.
30. For this and following see *Philosophy and Law*, Introduction and chap. 1.

philosopher-king, the central theme of Platonic political science. This contention helped to explain why despite the "Aristotelianism" of Islamic and Jewish rationalists, Aristotle's *Politics* was unknown to them whereas Plato's *Republic* and *Laws* were not.

The "Platonizing" character of medieval Jewish rationalism was also relevant to the distinction between esoteric and exoteric communication, so important for Maimonidean literature and medieval Jewish literature generally. For this distinction was common to both Platonic and Jewish traditions, and thus one of the most important keys to understanding medieval Jewish thought. As is well known, Strauss investigated this distinction and the problem it presents with great care and therewith provided a solid foundation from which to begin a reconstruction of medieval Jewish thought.

But this and the other characteristics of Strauss's research have an additional impact as well, both contemporary and perennial. The characteristics of medieval Jewish thought just elaborated raise the possibility that it supplies an important and even a decisive key to the clearest understanding of both biblical revelation and philosophy. This is of course partially implied in the subject matter of medieval Jewish thought. But it is strengthened by the fact that, as Strauss showed, medieval Jewish thought considers them from the perspective of their primary and perhaps most radical opposition, the opposition of law and philosophy.

As Strauss indicated in his earliest works, this means among other things, that the discussion presented by medieval Jewish thought reproduces in some measure the circumstances that attended the origins of Socratic or western philosophy, which emerged as an activity in need of justification before the city and its laws. Indeed in some respects the medieval presentation represents an improvement on the original presentation in Platonic literature or can make a decisive contribution to the understanding of Platonic literature.

Platonic literature in its faithfulness to its subject — the activities of Socrates — most evidently presents the tension between philosophy and pagan divine law. But pagan divine law does not exist in the singular but comprises a variety of divine laws. It is not *the* perfect divine law or the Divine Law as such. To examine philosophy's relationship to Divine Law in this sense, Plato would have been obliged to and perhaps did elaborate a hypothetical Divine Law. Medieval rationalism, Jewish and Islamic, was faced with no such necessity. It thus permitted an examination of the Platonic hypothesis and therewith the most radical investigation of the ground of Socratic philosophy. It almost goes without saying that the characteristics of medieval Jewish thought brought to light by Strauss also form the basis of another profound investigation, the radical examination of the Bible and its perspective.[31]

Altogether then, Strauss's study and interpretation of medieval Jewish thought offers a basis for the reexamination of the foundations of Western thought, both philosophic and biblical. The need for such a radical undertaking had been brought to light by the movements of thought contemporary with Strauss's youth and the crisis of the west which they embodied.[32] Strauss shared with some others the intention to undertake such a radical enterprise.

His own efforts were distinctive in a number of ways. Among them was his early and continued focus on medieval Jewish thought. This appears to have led him to the general conclusion that any such endeavor must come to terms with the fact that law presents itself as *the* framework of the original experience of Western man and the civilization to which that experience gave life. Moreover, he appears to have thought that the key to the revitalization of the West, if that were possible, lay in the reappropriation of that experience.[33] His studies of medieval Jewish thought and especially Maimonides seem to have been intended to contribute to that end by making available once again Maimonides understanding and elaboration of the "true science of the Law."[34]

31. "Jerusalem and Athens: Some Preliminary Reflections," *Studies in Platonic Political Philosophy*; "The Mutual Influence of Theology and Philosophy," *Independent Journal of Philosophy*, 3:111-18 (Vienna); "On the Interpretation of *Genesis*" *L'Homme: Revue Francaise d'anthropologie* (Paris) 21, no. 1: 5-36; "Progress or Return? The Contemporary Crisis in Western Civilization," *Modern Judaism* 1:17-45.

32. "Preface to Spinoza's *Critique of Religion*."

33. See "Progress or Return?" *The Rebirth of Classical Political Rationalism, Essays and Lectures by Leo Strauss*, ed. Thomas L. Pangle (Chicago: University of Chicago Press: 1989).

34. It almost goes without saying that Strauss appreciated the fact that medieval Western thought as a whole, which is to say Christian and Muslim thought, have an extremely important bearing upon this inquiry. This is no doubt obvious in the case of Muslim thought. It may be somewhat less obvious in the case of Christian thought insofar as Christianity differs in its understanding of the relationship of revelation and Law. Nevertheless as the Gospels and Letters make clear this difference presupposes the Mosaic Law and this combined with other factors led medieval Christian thought to address itself to questions similar to those addressed by medieval Jewish and Muslim thought. Strauss thus draws attention to the necessity of understanding medieval Christian political theology in the introduction to his essay on Judah Halevi's *Kuzari*. Indeed he presents his research into the *Kuzari* as inspired by questions which have arisen from research of his own into medieval Christian thought already undertaken. The latter research found particular expression in his study of Marsilius of Padua (see "Marsilius of Padua," in *Liberalism, Ancient and Modern*).

Modern Rationalism, Miracles, and Revelation: Strauss's Critique of Spinoza

Walter Soffer

In the 1962 "Preface to the English Translation" of his *Spinoza's Critique of Religion*, Leo Strauss explains that the work was written during the years 1925–28 in response to his need as a young German Jew experiencing the theologico-political predicament. He relates the considerations that "made one wonder whether an unqualified return to Jewish orthodoxy was not both possible and necessary—was not at the same time the solution to the problem of the Jew lost in the non-Jewish world and the only course compatible with sheer consistency or intellectual probity."[1] A return to orthodoxy could occur, Strauss soon realized, only if Spinoza was wrong "in every respect." In the bulk of what follows I present the hermeneutic for the reading of Spinoza employed by Strauss to analyze the motivation and inadequacy of Spinoza's critique of revealed religion, the presupposition of which is the possibility of the miraculous action by a God characterized as inscrutable will, on the basis of modern science and rational metaphysics. Also discussed are Strauss's analyses of the shortcomings of other critiques of revealed religion, on the basis of moral experience and the application of the principle of noncontradiction. In an effort to indicate the direction of Strauss's thought regarding the possible resolution of the quarrel between philosophy and theology, I conclude by briefly discussing the way in which Strauss tried to overcome the *aporia* caused by what he recognized—subsequent to his demonstration of the "self-destruction" of modern rationalism—to be the self-destruction of the argument on behalf of orthodoxy as well.

The research and writing of this paper was made possible by a sabbatical grant from the State University of New York.

1. Leo Strauss, "Preface to the English Translation," in *Spinoza's Critique of Religion* (hereafter = *SCR*), tr. E. M. Sinclair (New York: Schocken Books, 1982), p. 15. On the enduring significance of the theologico-political problem for Strauss's subsequent studies, cf. Leo Strauss, *The City and Man* (Chicago: Rand McNally, 1964), p. 241; Seth Benardete, "Leo Strauss's *The City and Man*," *Political Science Reviewer* 7 (Fall 1978): 1; and Strauss's "Preface to *Hobbes' Politische Wissenschaft*," tr. D. J. Maletz, *Interpretation* 8:1 (January 1979): 2.

The goal of Spinoza's philosophizing was the attainment of human happiness understood as dispassionate contemplation of the whole conceived as a self-contained, nonteleological, completely deterministic system. Spinoza's scientific worldview, according to which everything occurs in accordance with the principle of causal continuity, was necessarily in conflict with the religious-mythical worldview, according to which everything is ultimately dependent on the free actions of divine powers. Two diametrically opposed orientations toward experience of the world thus confront one another. But because it is nonetheless the same world that is responded to by such conflicting orientations, it would appear that the biblical text and the doctrine of miracles could serve as the common (if not neutral) ground on which the truth concerning revealed religion could be contested. But the Bible is denied such a function by Spinoza, says Strauss: "The Bible is a human book—in this one sentence we can sum up all the presuppositions of Spinoza's Bible science."[2] From the perspective of Spinoza's science, the Bible comes into being no differently from any other phenomenon of nature and must be interpreted accordingly. To Spinoza's positivist mentality the Bible cannot be of superhuman origin "unless, indeed, we believe, or rather dream, that the prophets had human bodies but superhuman minds, and therefore that their sensations and consciousness were entirely different from our own."[3] Spinoza's presupposing of the critique of religion as the basis of his biblical hermeneutics has the following two consequences: (1) the debate concerning revealed religion is focused on the theological doctrine of miracles, rather than on the biblical text per se; and (2) Spinoza was obliged to employ a rhetoric of dissimulation regarding his allegiance to biblical teaching. In addition to using traditional theological doctrines for nontraditional purposes, he packs the *Theologico-Political Treatise* with contradictions between orthodox and heterodox statements concerning the possibility of suprarational knowledge; the relationship between philosophy, or reason, and theology, or faith; and the nature of providence. In chapter fifteen, for example, Spinoza supplies us with one of the few instances in which the orthodox statement is immediately followed by its heterodox contrary.

2. *SCR*, p. 263. Cf. pp. 251ff.
3. Benedict de Spinoza, *Theologico-Political Treatise* (hereafter = *TPT*), in *The Chief Works of Benedict de Spinoza*, tr. R. H. M. Elwes, vol. 1 (New York: Dover, 1955), p. 14.

For as we cannot perceive by the natural light of reason that simple obedience is the path of salvation, and are taught by revelation only that it is so by the special grace of God, which our reason cannot attain, it follows that the Bible has brought a very great consolation to mankind. . . .

[However, a]ll are able to obey, whereas there are but very few, compared with the aggregate of humanity, who can acquire the habit of virtue under the unaided guidance of reason.[4]

Spinoza's inclusion of orthodox-heterodox contradictions, along with his use of traditional theology for nontraditional purposes, induced Strauss to formulate the following hermeneutic—a hermeneutic that Spinoza himself makes use of when explaining the contradictions between the statements of Jesus and of Paul[5] and that he acknowledges applies to his own works:

The first of these three "rules of living" which he sets forth in his *Treatise on the improvement of the understanding* reads as follows: "To speak with a view to the capacity of the vulgar and to practice all those things which cannot hinder us from reaching our goal (*sc.* the highest good). For we are able to obtain no small advantage from the vulgar provided we make as many concessions as possible to their capacity. Add to this that in this way they will lend friendly ears to the truth" [*Tr. de int. em.*, para. 7]. . . . If we reduce this procedure to its principle, we arrive at the following rule: if an author who admits, however occasionally that he speaks "after the manner of men." makes contradictory statements on a subject, the statement contradicting the vulgar view has to be considered as his serious view; nay, every statement of such an author which agrees with views vulgarly considered sacred or authoritative must be dismissed as irrelevant, or at least it must be suspected even though it is never contradicted by him.[6]

Spinoza's use of traditional theological doctrines for the purpose of overturning the tradition is nowhere more apparent than in his critique of miracles. In chapter six, "On Miracles," of the *Theologico-Political Treatise*, Spinoza offers—in addition to criticism based

4. Cf. Richard Kennington, "Analytic and Synthetic Methods in Spinoza's *Ethics*," in Richard Kennington, ed., *The Philosophy of Baruch Spinoza* (Washington, DC: Catholic University of America Press, 1980), pp. 307–9.

5. Spinoza explains that Jesus and Paul spoke differently because they addressed different audiences—Jesus, the common people; and Paul, the wise. Cf. *TPT*, chap. 4, pp. 64–65, and chap. 2, pp. 41–42.

6. "How to Study Spinoza's *Theologico-Political Treatise*," in Leo Strauss, *Persecution and the Art of Writing* (hereafter = *PAW*) (Chicago: University of Chicago Press, 1988), p. 177; cf. pp. 169–86.

on biblical exegesis—a twofold critique of miracles. The positive critique challenges the knowability of miracles; the metaphysical critique challenges their possibility. To the extent that revealed religion is positive religion—that is, is anchored in experience—the central theme of the positive critique, whose basis is the methodological or scientific application of empirical reason to the data of experience, concerns the legitimacy of an ascent from the experienced order of the world to theology and to revelation. At issue in the positive critique is the explanatory power of natural science. The metaphysical critique—more radical than the positive critique (and whose basis is the constitution of the system presented in Spinoza's *Ethics*)—begins by doubting the validity of the experienced order of the world as a proper starting point. At issue ultimately in the metaphysical critique is the sufficiency of human reason.

Spinoza begins the dual critique of the theological-traditional doctrine of miracles by reminding his readers of its vulgar-biblical precursor. According to Spinoza's reading of Genesis, the biblical account of miracles rests on the distinction between the mutually exclusive but coeval powers of God and nature. The cause of any phenomenon is attributed to either God or nature, but not both. However, God's power is such that it can override and contravene the lesser power of nature. Accordingly, the only way to prove God's existence and providence on the basis of our experience of nature is by demonstrating that God, if He so wills, providentially contravenes the power of nature—that God performs miracles.[7] It

7. Strauss's explanation of Spinoza's strategy here is instructive:
He starts from the implicit premise that all possibly relevant Jewish and Christian theologies necessarily recognize the authority, i.e., the truth, of the thematic teaching of the Old Testament; he assumes moreover that the true meaning of any Old Testament passage is, as a rule, identical with its literal meaning; he assumes finally that the most fundamental teaching of the Old Testament is the account of creation. Now, Moses does not explicitly teach creation *ex nihilo*; Genesis 1:2 seems rather to show that he believed that God has made the visible universe out of pre-existing "chaos"; his complete silence about the creation of the angels or "the other gods" strongly suggests that he believed that the power of God is, indeed, superior to, but not absolutely different from, the power of other beings. To express Moses' thought in the language of philosophy, the power of nature (which is what he meant by "chaos," and by which he understood a blind "force or impulse") is coeval with the power of God (an intelligent and ordering power), and the power of nature is therefore not dependent on, but merely inferior or subject to, the power of God. Moses taught that uncreated "Chaos" precedes in time the ordered universe which is the work of God, and he conceived

was the earliest Jews, says Spinoza, who originated such a doctrine for the purpose of showing that mankind (but especially the nation of Jews) is the final cause of Creation. Miracles—that alone by which God's existence and providence can be demonstrated—thus became the foundation of revealed religion concludes Spinoza in the *Theological-Political Treatise* (pp. 81–82).

Spinoza's reminder of its biblical origin prepares the metaphysical refutation of the theological doctrine of miracles in the following way. By attributing an initial degree of independence to the power of nature through the denial of Creation *ex nihilo*, Spinoza sets the stage for the complete liberation of the power of nature from the power of God. Spinoza sets out to prove these two contentions:

> I. That nature cannot be contravened, but that she preserves a fixed and immutable order. . . .
> II. That God's nature and existence, and consequently his providence cannot be known from miracles, but that they can all be much better perceived from the fixed and immutable order of nature (p. 82).

---

of God as king. It is therefore reasonable to suppose that he understood the subordination of the power of nature to the power of God as the subjugation of the smaller by the greater power. Accordingly, the power of God will reveal itself clearly and distinctly only in actions in which the power of nature does not cooperate at all. If that only is true which can be clearly and distinctly understood, only the clear and distinct manifestation of God's power will be its true manifestation: natural phenomena do not reveal God's power; when nature acts, God does not act, and *vice versa*. It does not suffice therefore, for the manifestation of God's power, that God has subjugated and reduced to order the primeval chaos; he has to subjugate "the visible gods," the most impressive parts of the visible universe, in order to make his power known to man: God's power and hence God's being can be demonstrated only by miracles. This is the core of the crude and vulgar view which Spinoza sketches before attacking the theological doctrine of miracles. The seemingly nonexistent theologian whom Spinoza has in mind when expounding that view is none other than Moses himself, and the view in question is meant to be implied in Genesis 1, in a text of the highest authority for all Jews and all Christians. Spinoza does then not go beyond reminding his opponents of what he considers "the original" of their position. As is shown by the sequel in the *Treatise*, he does not claim at all that that reminder suffices for refuting the traditional doctrine of miracles. *PAW*, pp. 198–200. Cf. also *SCR*, pp. 127–29; "Jerusalem and Athens," in Thomas L. Pangle, ed., *Leo Strauss: Studies in Platonic Political Philosophy* (Chicago: University of Chicago Press, 1983), pp. 150–52; "Progress or Return?" (hereafter = *POR*), in Leo Strauss, *The Rebirth of Classical Political Rationalism: An Introduction to the Thought of Leo Strauss*, ed. Thomas L. Pangle (Chicago: University of Chicago Press, 1989), pp. 252–53.

Spinoza's intent is to assimilate God to the autonomous and inviolate order of nature. The strategy used for this purpose is a revision of the traditional conception of natural law by means of a reinterpretation of the theological doctrine of the identity of intellect and will in God. This is the theme of chapter four, "Of the Divine Law."

Spinoza offers his identity thesis as the explanation of the relationship between the divine nature and the status of the eternal truths, or laws of nature.

> For instance, if we are only looking to the fact that the nature of a triangle is from eternity contained in the Divine nature as an eternal verity, we say that God possesses the idea of a triangle, or that He understands the nature of a triangle; but if afterwards we look to the fact that the nature of a triangle is thus contained in the Divine nature, solely by the necessity of the Divine nature, and not by the necessity of the nature and essence of a triangle—in fact, that the necessity of a triangle's essence and nature, in so far as they are conceived of as eternal verities, depends solely on the necessity of the Divine nature and intellect, we then style God's will or decree, that which before we styled His intellect. Wherefore we make one and the same affirmation concerning God when we say that He has from eternity decreed that three angles of a triangle are equal to two right angles, as when we say that He has understood it. (pp. 62–63)

By "God's intellect" is meant the understanding of the nature and necessity inherent in Creation's immanent eternal truths. By "God's will or decree" is meant what was traditionally referred to as the "freedom of spontaneity"—as opposed to the "freedom of indifference," whereby the will is constrained by the perception of rational necessity. The result of the identity of intellect and will in God, so understood, is an uncompromising necessitarianism. As Spinoza explains in the *Ethics*, the laws of nature neither contingently depend on God's freedom of indifference, nor do they result from God's perception of an independent criterion of truth or goodness.[8] By "God" is meant the immanent necessity characterizing the

---

8. Against the view that things result from God's liberty of indifference: "If things, therefore, could have been of a different nature, or have been conditioned to act in a different way, so that the order of nature would have been different, God's nature would also have been able to be different from what it now is; and therefore that different nature also would have perforce existed, and consequently there would have been able to be two or more Gods. This is absurd." *Ethics*, pt. I, prop. 33, in *Chief Works of Benedict de Spinoza*, vol.

natural order. And once we recognize that by "God's actions" is meant the unfolding of necessary laws rather than the promulgating of commands or norms, explains Spinoza in the *Theological-Political Treatise*, we must refrain from anthropomorphizing God by conceiving Him "as a lawgiver or prince, and styled just, merciful, etc., merely in concession to popular understanding" (p. 65). All of God's actions—that is to say, all of the events in nature—are characterized by the same necessity, lack of teleology, and moral neutrality as is the communication of motion between bodies (p. 57). Because God is the hypostatization of the principle of natural necessity, Spinoza can say that, to the extent that human reason can fully comprehend the causal connections that constitute nature, human reason is adequate to the task of comprehending God's essence (p. 59). Unlike Descartes' claim in "Meditation IV" that divine inscrutability precludes a teleological physics (such that Cartesian mechanics appears as a consequence of piety, rather than as the product of secular human reason that it is),[9] Spinoza appears to suggest a path from nature to God. But once it is remembered that God has been assimilated to nature, what is stated as the path from nature to God is Spinoza's way of conveying his conviction of the fit between secular human reason and the essential nature of the whole.

In chapter six, the thesis of the identity of intellect and will in God serves as the premise for the metaphysical critique of miracles in the following way. From such a premise, argues Spinoza, it follows not only that natural laws cannot be violated because of their causal necessity, but that, because causal is assimilated to logical necessity, miracles—as violations of natural law—are logical contradictions and thus absolutely impossible. As Spinoza stated in chapter four when explaining the difference between laws based

---

2, pp. 70–71. Against the view that God's intellect perceives an independent standard of truth or goodness: "This is only another name for subjecting God to the dominion of destiny, an utter absurdity in respect to God, whom we have shown to be the first and only free cause of the essence of all things and also of their existence." *Ethics*, pt. I, prop. 33, n. 2, p. 74. For a discussion of the relationship between the voluntarism of Descartes and its repudiation by Spinoza, cf. David R. Lachterman, "Laying Down the Law: The Theological-political Matrix of Spinoza's Physics," in Alan Udoff, ed., *Leo Strauss's Thought: Toward a Critical Engagement* (Boulder, CO: Lynne Rienner, 1991), pp. 127–35. For a somewhat different account of Descartes' voluntarism and its relation to Spinoza, cf. W. Soffer, *From Science to Subjectivity: An Interpretation of Descartes' "Meditations"* (Westport, CT: Greenwood Press, 1987), pp. 102–13.

9. Cf. Soffer, *From Science to Subjectivity*, pp. 99–106.

on natural necessity and those based on human decree, "A law
which depends on natural necessity is one which necessarily follows
from the nature, or from the definition of the thing in question"
(p. 57). Consequently, if God were to perform miracles, by violating
His own eternal decrees, by acting contrary to His own nature, he
would contradict himself (p. 83).[10]

Spinoza's necessitarianism encompasses much more than the
denial of miracles. It also signals the elimination of the ontological
category of possibility or potentiality. The real is the actual. The
merely possible or potential—whether originating by the power of
God or nature—is not. The denial of the possible does not, however, entail a restriction concerning the extent of what can be
brought about by natural causes. Spinoza states that because God's
intellect conceives an infinity of things, and because the power of
God is the power of nature, the power of nature is likewise infinite—"that her laws are broad enough to embrace everything
conceived by the Divine intellect" (p. 83). The only alternative to
the infinite power of nature—one that Spinoza regards as contrary
to reason—is "to assert that God has created nature so weak, and
has ordained for her laws so barren, that He is repeatedly compelled to come afresh to her aid if He wishes that she should be
preserved, and that things should happen as He desires" (pp. 83–
84). Miracles so understood would be evidence of God's providence, whereas what Spinoza implies is that, because God is omnipotent and because He wills the most perfect, He would have
programmed nature so that all such miraculous interventions in
the natural course of things would have been part of the original
Creation and thus brought about through natural causes.[11] Spinoza

10. The rejection of miracles as contrary to reason is anticipated as early as
chapter one, when Spinoza says of the claim that the wisdom of God assumed
human form in the person of Christ, "Those doctrines which certain churches
put forward concerning Christ, I neither affirm nor deny, for I freely confess
that I do not understand them" (*TPT*, p. 19). More candidly to Oldenburg,
Spinoza says of those who assert that God assumed human nature, "To confess
the truth, they seem to me to speak no less absurdly than if some one were to
tell them that a circle assumed the nature of a square." *The Correspondence of
Spinoza*, tr. A. Wolf (New York: Russell and Russell, 1966), letter 63, p. 344.
The assimilation of God to nature is likewise evident in chapter one. Spinoza
states that "prophecy, or revelation, is sure knowledge revealed by God to
man," from which "it is evident . . . that prophecy really includes ordinary
knowledge." *TPT*, p. 13. Cf. Hilail Gildin, "Notes on Spinoza's Critique of
Religion," in Kennington, *Philosophy of Spinoza*, pp. 157–58, 160–61.

11. This would appear to be a critique of Descartes' proof of God in

speaks the language of Creation but precludes the Creator from performing miracles. However, as Strauss observes, the doctrines of Creation and of miracles cannot be so separated because "by the creation of the world the possibility of miracles is posited beyond doubt."[12] (This is so whether God creates the world *ex nihilo* or brings order into original chaos.) Spinoza's metaphysics is consistent on this point. The assimilation of God to the all-encompassing inviolate laws of nature renders both Creation and all subsequent miracles impossible.

Spinoza's purely scientific argument regarding the power of nature marks the transition from the metaphysical to the positive critique of miracles. Because "a miracle being an event under limitations is the expression of a fixed and limited power" (because miracles require natural causes and attendant circumstances), it is not possible, argues Spinoza, to show that the cause of such a limited effect is an omnipotent Being. The most that can be concluded is that there is a cause or concatenation of causes of greater power than the effect (p. 86). Spinoza places the burden of proof on those claiming knowledge of miracles. But such proof is not forthcoming, he claims, because, to repeat, since every particular event is finite and limited, all such limited events may be the result of the cooperation of a potentially infinite number of finite and less powerful causes. Miracles as miracles are thus not demonstrable. It does no good, says Spinoza, to appeal by default to God's inscrutability. Because "it is only phenomena that we clearly and distinctly understand, which heighten our knowledge of God, and most clearly indicate His will and decrees," attributing miracles to God's unfathomable will is "a ridiculous way of expressing ignorance" (p. 86). Miracles are not only nondemonstrable. Because Spinoza grounds the claim of the infinite power of nature in the metaphysical critique, miracles are likewise impossible.

By grounding the positive critique in the metaphysical critique, Spinoza blurs the essential differences between the two kinds of arguments he advances against miracles. The claim at the basis of the metaphysical critique is that nature's power is infinite, and that all events in nature are necessitated by immutable laws. Miracles are therefore impossible. The claim at the basis of the positive

---

"Meditation III" based on the notion of continued existence as constant recreation.

12. *SCR*, p. 190.

critique is that it is unreasonable to limit the capacity of nature. Miracles are therefore nondemonstrable. As Strauss points out, the latter claim as such is independent of Spinoza's (or indeed any) metaphysics. The claim that it is unreasonable to limit nature's power is grounded exclusively in the fact that at present we are ignorant of all of nature's laws, making the claim indifferent to the dogmatic assertion of either nature's infinity or its finitude. Although such an indifference to metaphysics accounts for the claim's appeal to those of differing metaphysical persuasions and to "the more prudent sort" who stood to be released from prejudice to experience the freedom of philosophizing, it also makes visible the failure of the positive critique to prove not only that miracles are impossible, but that miracles are never knowable.[13]

It is when questioned by Henry Oldenburg about the limited capacity of human science that Spinoza moderates his claims for the positive critique. Given our limited knowledge of nature, Spinoza writes to Oldenburg, we will either explain a phenomenon in terms of nature given the available knowledge, or else we should suspend judgment. In the process of conceding that the limits of nature's power have not been established, Spinoza takes the opportunity of accusing the theologians of arrogance when they claim to know that certain phenomena transcend the power of nature.[14] Spinoza recommends suspension of judgment in light of our limited knowledge of nature, but holds out the prospect of perpetual scientific progress. Given such a conception of scientific progress, suspension of judgment is perpetually warranted, and the knowability of miracles forever remains an open question. The resolution of the epistemic paradox contained in the positive critique— namely, the infinity at the heart of nature that makes progress possible precludes its completion—is the completed system of the *Ethics*. The achievement of the positive critique, then, by shifting the burden of proof to the believer in miracles, consists in scoring a rhetorical point against the believer.

One would think that certain reports of miracles could be decided objectively by both believers and nonbelievers because of the perceptual nature of the claimed miracle. This is denied by Spinoza. Because the metaphysical critique has proven that miracles are impossible, reports claiming to have witnessed miracles

13. *SCR*, pp. 130, 177–78.
14. *Correspondence*, letters 74 and 75, pp. 345, 349.

cannot ever be reliable. The occurrence of such reports is explained by asserting that the witnesses were not unbiased scientific observers (pp. 92–93). In addition, skepticism is directed against the claims of biblical miracles when it is recalled that history has recorded miracles also among the pagans. To grant reliability to such reports is to give to the pagan and biblical miracles an equal cognitive status. Consequently, those who are inclined to reject pagan divinities are likewise inclined to reject the biblical divinity (p. 97).

Historically, this kind of intellectual consistency has had the effect of weakening biblical belief, as Strauss observes in *Spinoza's Critique of Religion* (pp. 135–36). Because the positive critique of miracles, when severed from its metaphysical foundation,[15] can refute neither the knowability nor the possibility of miracles, we must locate the impetus for the skeptical and disbelieving attitudes toward Scripture in a certain mind-set or predisposition, rather than in the rigor or success of scientific argument.

> The authority of Scripture was shaken prior to all historical and philosophical criticism, but also prior to all metaphysics, through the establishment of the positive mind, through the disenchantment of the world and through the self-awareness of the disenchanting mind. (p. 135)

Under the predominance of the positive mind in the modern world, it is thought that explanations in terms of miracles have been precluded by scientific observation and analysis of phenomena—by scientific progress, according to which the not presently understood is the not yet understood. But what has been established is only that the unbelieving mind cannot recognize miracles as miracles without faith, that reason without faith is unaffected by claims of miracles because such claims exceed the parameters of scientific cognition. Miracles occur only for the nonscientific consciousness. Because the positive mind sees itself as an advance over the prior form of consciousness—"a finding that first takes the form of the crude antithesis between superstition, prejudice, ignorance, barbarism, benightedness on the one hand, and reason,

15. As Strauss points out, "The complete context of positive criticism is not made fully explicit until Hume's *Enquiry X*, in which he concretizes the claim of necessity in science as understood by Spinoza, into the claim of probability." *SCR*, p. 136 n.173.

freedom, culture, enlightenment on the other" (p. 136)—it occupies a position impervious to proof by miracles. The ahistorical
struggle against appearance, opinion, tradition, and authority that
defined philosophy from its inception assumes a historical dimension with the opposition of the Enlightenment to prejudice. The
necessity that the age of prejudice precede the age of freedom—
that "freedom" means freedom from prejudice—indicates that
"prejudice" denotes a historical category (p. 181).

The self-conscious restriction of the positive mind within the
bounds of unbelieving experience shows that "positive critique is
legitimate only as *defensive* critique, " writes Strauss (p. 145). Is the
self-imposed restriction of the positive mind to the canons of
nonbelieving experience an act of willful defiance of revelation, or
is it to be taken as an admission that the positive mind lacks the
experience of revelation? To be motivated by either willful defiance
of or blindness to the experience of revelation is to concede the
possibility of revelation. For this reason the merely defensive critique of revelation is not sufficient, but must be bolstered by the
metaphysical critique. Only the metaphysical critique—by providing rational justification for the rejection of revelation—can respond to the charge that the positive mind willfully rejects revelation or is blind to the experience of revelation.

On its own, the positive critique is capable of engendering
suspicion of revelation by stressing the difference between the
essential claim of revealed religion and its ancillary claims regarding the verbal inspiration of Scripture, the authorship of the
Pentateuch by Moses, the accuracy of the received text of Scripture,
and the actuality of biblical miracles (p. 145). Despite the reasonable basis for such suspicion, the real prospect for success of the
positive critique, Strauss points out, lay not in the strength of its
argument but rather in the effectiveness of its ridicule. In order to
deny that the scriptural text is corrupt, and in order to explain
hard-to-understand scriptural events, orthodoxy found it necessary to resort to divine inscrutability. Where argument could not
succeed, says Strauss, the doctrine of divine inscrutability became
the object of mockery: "Reason must turn into 'esprit' if reason is
to experience her more than royal freedom, her unshakeable
sovereignty, and to realize it in action" (p. 146). As historically
effective as the Enlightenment's ridicule was, it touches only certain
consequences of—rather than the core of—revealed religion.

For the assertion that God is omnipotent cannot be refuted, but the contrast between divine omnipotence and the use of that omnipotence to inspire Moses with the name of a town or a mountain which that town or mountain will bear only long after the death of Moses is matter for laughter. The assertion that God's wisdom is unfathomable cannot be refuted. But the contrast between the unfathomable wisdom of God and the obscurity of Scriptural texts, which lose their mystery through (humanly speaking) the obvious, unobjectionable, even necessary admission that the text is corrupt, is matter for laughter. The assertion that God can perform miracles cannot be refuted. But the resemblance between the fantastic feats of Samson and the fantastic ascent of Elijah into heaven in a chariot of fire, with the deeds of derring-do of Orlando Furioso or the story of Perseus, as told by Ovid, has a comic effect. (pp. 143–44)[16]

That over the past three centuries the assertion of miracles has progressively been given up (even among believers) is a consequence to a great extent, explains Strauss, of the moral attitude at the basis of Spinoza's critique of revealed religion. Strauss gives us an appreciation of this moral attitude and its significance for Spinoza's critique by comparing it with its polar opposite: the Christian orthodoxy of the Reformation—in particular, the position of Calvin. When one formally evaluates Spinoza's critique of Calvin's position ("the predestined object of the critique"), argues Strauss, the critique "turns out to rest on a *petitio principii*" (p. 192).[17]

For Calvin, biblical revelation rather than reason is essential for coming to know God. The biblical conception of God—knowledge of Whom is implanted in the human heart and is evident from the order and governance of the world—is to be accepted without question. To deny such an access to God merely proves, along with "the shameful multiplicity of philosophies," that the human intellect is incapable of grasping God. Calvin's skepticism concerning human reason is total. What he rejects is both the validity and propriety of theory as such. Accordingly, he does not pursue the question "*Quid sit Deus?*"—not only because it is beyond the power of human reason to answer, but because such "chill speculations" are not salutary for man. What alone is necessary, for Calvin, is the knowledge for the purpose of honoring God, the prerequisite for which is piety.[18] The opposition between Calvin and Spinoza

16. Cf. *TPT*, pp. 111–12.
17. Cf. *SCR*, pp. 193–211.
18. John Calvin, *Institutes of the Christian Religion*, tr. H. Beveridge (Grand Rapids, MI: Wm. B. Erdmans, 1966), bk. 1, chaps. 1–8.

could not be more fundamental. Each challenges what the other accepts as authoritative. Calvin unquestioningly accepts Scripture as guaranteed and made known by the testimony of the Holy Spirit, and sees in the true orthodoxy the resolution of "the shameful multiplicity of philosophies." Spinoza unquestioningly accepts what is manifest to the natural light of reason, on the basis of which can be constructed the true philosophy that remedies the shameful multiplicity of orthodoxies.[19]

The limitation of Spinoza's critique of miracles becomes apparent when confronted with Calvin's notion of the miraculous. As we have seen, Spinoza's critique is directed at the Scholastic (or traditional or theological) doctrine of miracles, which, by radically distinguishing between natural occurrences and miracles, "presupposes the concept of nature that is theoretic in origin," as Strauss puts it (p. 196). Rejecting the theoretic concept of nature, Calvin assimilates the natural to the miraculous. Because God makes use of the entirety of creation for his purposes, the usual is not less miraculous than the rare.[20] Spinoza—assimilating the miraculous to the natural—argues that the rare is not less natural than the usual. For each, the distinction between the ordinary and the exceptional is merely statistical rather than ontological, at the basis of which is the operation of a single power or agency—either nature or God.

The immunity of Calvin's doctrine of miracles to Spinoza's critique is shown by the following. In the first place, because it is

---

19. Spinoza expresses to Blyenberg his confidence in reason and its consequence for the doctrines in the Bible, as follows: "since I openly and unambiguously confess that I do not understand Holy Scripture although I have spent some years in the study of it, and since it has not escaped my notice that when I have a strong proof no such thoughts can occur to me that I can ever entertain any doubt about it, I acquiesce wholly in that which my understanding shows me, without any suspicion that I may be deceived, or that Holy Scripture, although I do not search it, can contradict it: for truth does not conflict with truth." *Correspondence*, letter 21, pp. 172–173. Spinoza is more forthcoming in the *Cogitata Metaphysica*, pt. 2, chap. 8: "For if we find anything in [the Scriptures] contrary to the laws of Reason we should refute that with the same freedom that we refute such statements in the Koran or the Talmud." *The Principles of Descartes' Philosophy*, tr. H. H. Britan (La Salle, IL: Open Court, 1974), p. 158.

20. "When He desired that Jonah should be thrown into the sea, He sent forth a whirlwind. Those who deny that God holds the reins of government will say that this was contrary to ordinary practice, whereas I infer from it that no wind ever rises or rages without His special command." Calvin, *Institutes*, bk. 1, chap. 16, sec. 7.

not a theoretical doctrine, Calvin's all-encompassing doctrine of miracles—which is his doctrine of Providence—does not have to meet theoretical objections. Its necessity and intelligibility derive from a faith that honors God, and also receive from faith "the best and sweetest fruit."[21] From such a perspective it is not possible for a critique from a "carnal" worldview to be meaningful. Spinoza's critique of revelation involved the claim that, for most people, miracles are the foundation of piety. But because for Calvin miracles depend on faith, says Strauss, "the assertion of miracles stands impregnable" (p. 197). Because the separation of the miraculous from the natural—the premise of the seventeenth and eighteenth centuries' debate on miracles—is denied by Calvin, "Spinoza's critique of miracles falls wide of Calvin's conception of miracles." For Calvin, the continuous activity of God is discernible not only in "miracles," but even more so "in every manifest inequality, irregularity, discontinuity that affects the manifest order" (p. 198)—including everything from causing plants to grow prior to the creation of the sun, to the incalculable variations in the sequence of the seasons. What Strauss stresses is that, because Calvin offers an expression of faith rather than a theoretical account, "the issue here is not between a 'rational' and an 'irrational' *philosophy* but between the unbelieving and the believing manner of experiencing the world." Because for Calvin it is the mysterious character of the world that with the guidance by faith allows one to recognize God's activity, it does not count as a refutation of such a view to offer an explanation of the irregular and exceptional in terms of the workings of the regular or lawful.

What induced Spinoza, in the absence of a common ground between him and revealed religion, to believe that positive critique could succeed was his rigorously consistent embracing and thinking through of the consequences of the doctrine of predestination. As Strauss explains it, "Nothing could more strongly confirm him in his belief that he is in harmony with the real teaching of revealed religion than the fact that he, on the strength of his own premises, found himself obligated to adopt the doctrine most abhorrent to all the freer minds—the doctrine of predestination in its harshest and most extreme form" (p. 201). Spinoza sees in the doctrine of predestination, which attributes all things to God, the remedy for

21. Calvin, *Institutes*, bk. 1, chap. 17, sec. 6; cf. also bk. 1, chap. 16, sec. 3.

what he perceived as the inconsistency in Calvin's position—that man is held responsible for his own damnation by his capacity to choose evil, but that such a defective nature had been supplied by God's incomprehensible will. Spinoza's sympathy for predestination, explains Strauss, reveals his deeper opposition to revealed religion. The consciousness of human sinfulness and its concern with the glory of God—essential for Calvin[22]—is rejected by Spinoza, writes Strauss: "The human correlate to the majesty of God is for Spinoza not man's sinfulness, but the fact that he is perishable and only a part. Only with the denial of sin does Spinoza's opposition to revealed religion come to unambiguous expression" (p. 202). The denial of the positive nature of sin exonerates both the human sinner and his divine cause. Because whatever happens is traced to God's power and will (*i.e.*, to nature's necessity), whatever happens is equally perfect and approved by God. Spinoza can thus derive a teaching concerning natural right from his *amor fati*, his love of the necessary. Any being is justified in exercising its power to promote its ends because "every man and every being has a natural right to everything: the state of nature knows no law and knows no sin" (p. 203).

As we have seen, in response to Spinoza's claim to have scientifically demonstrated the nonexistence of sin and the theological premises that substantiate that demonstration, Calvin denies the validity of theory as such. Spinoza and Calvin have come to an impasse, Strauss points out: "Even if all the reasoning adduced by Spinoza were compelling, nothing would have been proven. Only this much would have been proven: that on the basis of unbelieving science one could not but arrive at Spinoza's results" (p. 204).

In addition to the fact that the positive critique is merely a defensive critique, its epistemic shortcomings require that Spinoza attempt a refutation of revealed religion. He must refute the doctrine presupposed by revealed religion: that God is unfathomable will. God's omnipotence requires that God be unfathomable because "to be knowable means to be controllable and therefore He must not be knowable in the strict sense of the term."[23] We have

22. Thus, "our feeling of ignorance, vanity, want, weakness, in short, depravity and corruption, reminds us that in the Lord, and none but He, dwell the true light of wisdom, solid virtue, exuberant goodness. We are accordingly urged by our own evil things to consider the good things of God; and indeed, we cannot aspire to Him in earnest until we have begun to be displeased with ourselves." Calvin, *Institutes*, bk. 1, chap. 1, sec. 1, p. 38.

23. *POR*, p. 256.

seen that, for Spinoza, recourse to the unfathomable will of God is "a ridiculous way of expressing ignorance."[24] Yet positive critique has shown only that the claim that the inscrutable God exists is improbable. Even this modest achievement of positive critique is dubious, according to Strauss, because, concerning the assumption of an inscrutable God, "is not that assumption 'improbable' even in its intention, so that any effort made to prove its improbability is vain?" (p. 205). Positive critique can plausibly accuse those who argue from the experienced order of the world or its *aporiae*, or from miracles, to God of illegitimately closing off the inquiry into nature. Positive critique can also plausibly correlate what it judges to be the anthropomorphic explanation of nonhuman occurrences with the prescientific state of human thought. And positive critique can induce people to appreciate how what revealed religion "primarily and ultimately intends" is inadequately conveyed by reports of miracles. However, so long as recourse to the inscrutable God is not defended on the basis of reason as a theoretic truth, but is held out as a possibility that is admittedly improbable according to the canons of rational or scientific demonstration, the claim of positive critique to establish the improbability of the possibility of the inscrutable God is superfluous.

Spinoza dismissed the notion of an inscrutably free God as a contradiction in terms. According to Strauss, the critique of the intelligiblity of God's nature on the basis of the principle of noncontradiction is

> inapplicable in principle. Is it of any importance whatsoever that men are unable to understand, for instance, how the omniscience of God is compatible with human freedom? If God is unfathomable, is it not necessary that human statements about God contradict each other? Can any statement about God be made except analogically? Does therefore the assertion that two statements about God contradict each other not rest on an unintelligent or unspiritual "understanding" of these statements? (p. 205)

Even if one could prove that God is not unfathomable, adds Strauss, it could be replied that the comprehensible God is the god of Aristotle rather than the God of Abraham.

The meaning of God's inscrutability is clarified in Strauss's discussion (pp. 147–65) of the opposition between Spinoza and

24. *TPT*, p. 86.

Maimonides. The teaching of Maimonides is that God's creation of the world *ex nihilo* is the product of a "creative will as an ordering and rational will," Strauss writes (p. 151). In order to preserve God's unqualified simplicity, the ascription of intellect and will as positive divine attributes is precluded. What we perceive in ourselves as distinct positive faculties cannot be so predicated of God without doing violence to His unity. God's nature as a unity of faculties is therefore ineffable. For Spinoza the identity of intellect and will holds for both man and God, enabling us to base on our self-understanding our understanding of them in God. What is significant in Spinoza's identity thesis, as we have seen, is not his opposition to positive attributes, but his refusal to grant the will any independence from what is understood in the intellect. For this reason Spinoza's God wills and performs the eternally necessary, whereas Maimonides' God wills and creates *ex nihilo*.

Strauss cites one of the "philosophers' " arguments against a Maimonidean conception of God's will.

> If an *agens* acts at one time and at another time fails to act, the cause on the one occasion is that there is a stimulus to action, or hindrances are not present, whereas another time that stimulus is lacking or hindrances are present, which one time cause the will to act, another time to refrain from action—in other words, which change the will. Now God is not moved by stimuli to action, nor by hindrances to refrain from action. Thus it is not possible that on the one occasion He acts, and on another occasion refrains from action. Rather it is the case that He, who is pure actuality, necessarily acts always. (p. 153)

Maimonides' response to the charge that he robs God's will of potentiality and thus of freedom is to claim for God the freedom of indifference whereby the will is not bound by what the intellect understands as the true or the good. Strauss expresses Maimonides' position in terms of the contrast between the spontaneous and the necessitated modes of operation of the will.

> There are in fact no stimuli and no hindrances which at one time determine God to act, and at the other to refrain from acting. His will determines itself spontaneously now in the one way, now in the other. It is peculiar to the will, now to will and another time to refrain from willing. Since the essence of the will is spontaneity, God may on the one occasion will to act and therefore act, and on another occasion will not to act and therefore not act. It is not an imperfection, but the essence of the will that it wills and does not will. (p. 153)

Maimonides does not grant such spontaneity, potentiality, or freedom to God's intellect. Because not knowing—unlike not acting—would be an imperfection in God, it must be that God is perpetually knowing.

Does Maimonides contradict himself by distinguishing between the operations of intellect and will in God while denying that these are positive attributes? Is Spinoza's identity thesis the resolution of such a contradiction? Strauss answers no to both questions.

> In fact no contradiction is present. The denial of positive attributes is to be understood from the assertion that God's essence is incomprehensible. The attribution of will to God—possible only in improper speech, but necessary in such—is the surpassing means of adumbrating the incomprehensibility of God. The very proof that establishes the volitional character of God at the same time establishes the incomprehensibility of God (p. 154).

So long as orthodoxy restricts its claims to the legitimacy of belief (as opposed to the possession of knowledge), its fundamental premise—the possible existence of an omnipotent God whose will is unfathomable—can be refuted neither by human knowledge claims, experience, nor recourse to the principle of noncontradiction. Scientific claims about the age of the solar system, and about the impossibility of knowing the name of the founder of the Persian Empire in the "first" Isaiah, presuppose natural genesis and causation and thus beg the decisive question concerning the omnicompetence of human reason, as Strauss points out in his "Preface" (p. 28).

Regarding the possible refutation of theological claims on the basis of experience, it is instructive to compare Strauss's discussion of the fate of Nikias, the commander of the defeated Athenian forces in Sicily during the Peloponnesian War, with God's command to Abraham to sacrifice Isaac. In the case of Nikias, Strauss is prepared to argue that moral experience can be taken into account when trying to assess whether a theology is true or false. Nikias "had applied himself more than any other of Thucydides' contemporaries to the exercise of that virtue which is praised and held up by the law—as distinguished from another, possibly higher, kind of virtue—but his theology is refuted by his fate."[25]

---

25. "Preliminary Observations on the 'Gods in Thucydides' Work," in Pangle, *Strauss*, p. 101. Cited by David Lowenthal, "Review of Pangle (ed.), *Leo*

162   *Walter Soffer*

The refutation of the theology of Nikias consisted in the contradiction between his fate and his belief that the gods favor those who are just and virtuous as determined by human law. Is such a contradiction possible concerning biblical theology? Can the experience of those whose faith is in the biblical God—a God whose justice *ab initio* is believed to transcend human understanding— ever refute such a faith? Regarding the apparent contradiction inherent in God's command to Abraham to sacrifice Isaac, as Strauss explains, such a "contradiction" can be rendered intelligible once the distinction between human and divine justice is appreciated.

> Abraham's trust in God thus appears to be the trust that God in His righteousness will not do anything incompatible with His righteousness and that while or because nothing is too wondrous for the Lord, there are firm boundaries set to Him by His righteousness, by Him. . . . The fact that the command to sacrifice Isaac contradicted the prohibition against the shedding of innocent blood, must be understood in the light of the difference between human justice and divine justice: God alone is unqualifiedly, if unfathomably, just.[26]

Because God is unfathomably just, it is not possible for there to be a contradiction between human experience—no matter what its character—and divine justice. An experiential refutation of the premise of the inscrutable God is thus not possible.

When Strauss asserts that the possibility of the inscrutable God cannot be refuted on the basis of the principle of noncontradiction, he does not mean that God's omnipotence is not bound by the principle of noncontradiction, but that the conception of God's inscrutable will cannot be charged with exceeding the bounds of intelligiblity by violating the principle of noncontradiction. As he observes in *Spinoza's Critique of Religion*, "This type of critique often disregards the more subtle distinctions made by theologians, and therefore more often asserts contradictions than proves them" (p. 205). Strauss himself points to the fact that God's omnipotence requires His inscrutability, but this is not to say that inscrutability consists in omnipotence carried to the point of contrarationality. The issue is not the epistemic status of the principle of noncontradiction, or the contest between the principle of noncontradiction

---

Strauss: Studies in Platonic Political Philosophy," *Interpretation* 13:3 (September 1985): 317.
    26. "Jerusalem and Athens," pp. 161–62.

and God's omnipotence. Because miracles are not contradictory, the power ascribed to the biblical God—the power to create the world *ex nihilo* and perform all subsequent contraventions of the natural order—is not diminished by precluding the creation of the contradictory. What is defended by Strauss is not the possibility of the irrational, but rather the possibility of the suprarational. By assuming that revelation is suprarational rather than contrarational, "orthodoxy . . . in principle concedes the right of reason" (p. 130). As Strauss has indicated, the spontaneity of God's will, its freedom of indifference, its suprarational inscrutability, is not its defect but rather its essence. In this consists the difference between the God of Abraham and the God of Aristotle.

A genuine refutation of orthodoxy therefore requires, according to Strauss, one of two things: (1) a proof by what Strauss refers to as "natural theology" that the nature of God can be known and shown to be incompatible with the performing of miracles; or (2) a demonstration that the whole can be completely understood, rationally, without recourse to the premise of an inscrutable God, that is, the elaboration of the philosophic system whereby man achieves theoretical and practical mastery over nature and human existence. The argument by natural theology for the refutation of orthodoxy is based on the conception of God as the most perfect Being modeled on the only notion of perfection available to us: human perfection in the person of the wise man. Just as the wise man refrains from silly or purposeless actions, God does not reveal to a prophet the name of a pagan ruler centuries before his rule. However, because God's perfection implies inscrutability, the fact that God's actions seem foolish to man cannot be taken as a proof that such actions are foolish. To refute orthodoxy, natural theology must eliminate God's inscrutability. Because the elimination of God's inscrutability is possible only by means of a complete account of the whole that would make references to the mysterious God superfluous, the refutation of the possibility of revelation depends, in the final analysis, on the devising of the definitive metaphysical system.[27]

Quite apart from the merit of Strauss's charge concerning Spinoza's "incapacity to grasp revealed religion as it presents itself"—a charge made in *Spinoza's Critique of Religion* (p. 207)—the

27. Leo Strauss, "The Mutual Influence of Theology and Philosophy" (hereafter = *MITP*), *Independent Journal of Philosophy* 3 (1979):116–17.

ultimate success or failure of Spinoza's critique of revealed religion depends on the success or failure of the metaphysical system presented in the *Ethics*.[28] If Spinoza can provide a truly comprehensive rational account of the whole, then revealed religion can no longer remain exempt from such a critique on the grounds that its God is other than meant by the systematist; and the stalemate between two irreconcilable orientations toward experience of the world would be broken.

We have seen the necessity of Strauss's hermeneutic in order to translate the exoteric presentation of Spinoza's *Theological-Political Treatise* into its esoteric teaching. An analogous hermeneutic, argues Strauss, is required for a proper reading of the *Ethics*, but with the following difference. By starting from premises conceded by the believer in miracles and in revelation, only to proceed to deduce from such premises doctrines abhorrent to the believer, the aim of the *Theological-Political Treatise* is to liberate the believer from prejudices in order to philosophize. In this sense the *Theological-Political Treatise* serves as Spinoza's introduction to philosophy. The addressee of the *Ethics* is the potential philosopher, freed from prejudices. The *Ethics* accordingly begins with premises that signify the absurdity of orthodoxy. To appreciate the strategy that Spinoza employs in the composition of the *Ethics*, one must realize, as Strauss explains, that " '*ad captum vulgi loqui*' does not mean to present one's thoughts in a popular garb, but to argue *ad hominem* or *ex concessis*, i.e., from a covered position."[29] Illustrated by the fact that Spinoza presented his account of Descartes' *Principles of Philosophy*—a system he judged to be incorrect—in geometric form, the relationship between the truth of the system of the *Ethics* and its geometric format is contingent. Strauss argues not only that the geometric form is not required by the truth of the system of the *Ethics*, but that the geometric order of explication is the cover for the nongeometric order of discovery. In keeping with the require-

28. Although Spinoza intended the *TPT* to be read as a self-sufficient work, in chapter three he indicates that it ultimately depends on the *Ethics*. "By the help of God, I mean the fixed and unchangeable order of nature or the chain of natural events: for I have said before and shown elsewhere that the universal laws of nature, according to which all things exist and are determined, are only another name for the eternal decrees of God, which always involve eternal truth and necessity. So that to say that everything happens according to natural law, and to say that everything is ordained by the decree and ordinance of God1 is the same thing" *TPT*, pp. 44–45.

29. *PAW*, p. 186.

ment that he speak *"ad captum vulgi,"* Spinoza's doctrine of God—seemingly the beginning and foundation of his system—belongs to the exoteric geometric argument that conceals rather than reveals the true beginning of the system. What corresponds to the exoteric/ esoteric distinction in the *Theological-Political Treatise* is the distinction between the methods of "analysis" and "synthesis" in the *Ethics.*[30]

It is in Ludwig Meyer's preface to Spinoza's book *The Principles of Descartes' Philosophy* that the nature of geometric demonstration is explained in terms of the distinction between analysis and synthesis. In stated agreement with Descartes' account in "Response to the Second Objection," Meyer (with Spinoza's approval)[31] describes the two types of apodictic methods in philosophy as well as in mathematics, as follows:

> The one, *Analysis* . . . the true method, by which truth is discovered methodically and as it were *a priori*; the other . . . *Synthesis*, the method in which a long series of definitions, and premises and axioms, and theorems, and problems is used so that if anything is denied in the conclusion, it is immediately shown to have been contained in the premises.[32]

Because analysis is "the method by which such truth is discovered," and synthesis is that "by which it is set in order,"[33] the synthetic method cannot be self-sufficient but must receive the content for its deductions from analysis. But unlike in mathematics where analysis is *a priori*, in the *Ethics* analysis begins empirically in order to produce an account of the existent whole. The method of analysis—which begins with perceived phenomena, learns their causes, and discovers first principles (the method employed in the *Theological-Political Treatise*, chap. 4, p. 59)—is the method presupposed by the synthetic form of the *Ethics.*[34] For this reason, the concept of God as the intelligible first principle from which all else is to be derived is not the true beginning of the *Ethics*, says Strauss.

> According to his [Spinoza's] last word on the subject, the highest form of knowledge, which he calls intuitive knowledge, is knowledge not of

30. *PAW*, p. 189.
31. Cf. *Correspondence*, letter 15, pp. 134–36.
32. In Spinoza, *Principles*, p. 3.
33. *Ibid.*
34. *PAW*, p. 189. In *Correspondence*, letter 37, p. 228, and in the *TPT*, p. 104, Spinoza compares his method to that of Bacon.

the one substance or God, but of individual things or events: God is fully God not qua substance or even in His eternal attributes but in His non-eternal modes understood *sub specie aeternitatis*. The knowledge of God presented in the First Part of the *Ethics* is only universal or abstract; only the knowledge of individual things or rather events qua caused by God is concrete.[35]

The empiricism at the basis of Spinoza's system, in tension with its claim to rational demonstrability, raises the question of the justification or rationale for the definitions and axioms with which the *Ethics* begins. What is at issue is not only the claim to comprehensiveness, demonstrability, and certainty—threatened by the admitted recourse to experienced particulars—but the claim to truth. For even if the order of explication were accepted as the order of discovery, it appears that Spinoza's system is nonetheless guilty of question begging when it comes to its claim to truth. It follows from Spinoza's definition of substance—"That which is in itself, and is conceived through itself: in other words, that of which a conception can be formed independently of any other conception"[36]—that there can be but one substance, called God, from which is derived the entirety of the system. But such a definition, in the absence of a demonstration of its necessity or its self-evidence, would appear to be arbitrary. The need for seemingly arbitrary definitions at the start of the *Ethics*, explains Strauss, arises from the function such definitions are to perform.

> They are not evident in themselves but they are thought to become evident through their alleged result: they and only they are thought

35. "Preface," *SCR*, p. 16. Strauss supports this statement with *Ethics*, pt. V, prop. 25 and prop. 36 scholium, and the *TPT*, chap. 6, sec. 23. Cf. also *Ethics*, pt. II, prop. 17 scholium. The implications, for the understanding of the *Ethics*, of Strauss's conclusion that its synthetic presentation conceals its analytically arrived at premises have been developed by Kennington, "Analytic and Synthetic Methods," pp. 293–318. In the same volume (Kennington, *Philosophy of Spinoza*), see Isaac Franck, "Spinoza's Logic of Inquiry: Rationalist or Experientialist?" pp. 247–72, and Stewart Umphrey, "De Natura," pp. 273–91. See also H. Barker, "Notes on the Second Part of Spinoza's *Ethics*," in S. Kashap, ed., *Studies in Spinoza: Critical and Interpretive Essays* (Berkeley: University of California Press, 1972), pp. 101–67; A. E. Taylor, "Some Incoherences in Spinozism," in Kashap, *Studies in Spinoza*, pp. 189–211, 289–309; D. Lachterman, "The Physics of Spinoza's *Ethics*," in R. Shahan and J. Biro, eds., *Spinoza: New Perspectives* (Norman: University of Oklahoma Press, 1978), pp. 71–111; E. M. Curley, "Experience in Spinoza's Theory of Knowledge," in M. Grene, ed., *Spinoza: A Collection of Critical Essays* (New York: Anchor Books, 1973), pp. 25–59.

36. *Ethics*, pt. I, defn. 3.

to make possible the clear and distinct account of everything; in the light of the clear and distinct account, the Biblical account appears to be confused. The *Ethics* thus begs the decisive question, the question as to whether the clear and distinct account is as such *true*, and not merely a plausible hypothesis.[37]

Citing the account of the emotions as a case in point, Strauss asks concerning Spinoza's system, "Is its clarity and distinctness not due to the fact that Spinoza abstracts from the elements of the whole which are not clear and distinct and which can never be rendered clear and distinct?"[38] Can an abstractive conceptualization of the whole render the truth of the whole? More specifically, can the manifest heterogeneity of the whole be faithfully conceptualized along the model of mathematizable homogeneity? It would appear not. The more comprehensive the axiomatization of experience, the more reason becomes the legislator rather than the discoverer of structure, thereby estranging it from the being of the world. The goal of epistemology is to understand the structure of the world as it is, independently of our knowing; but because human knowledge is necessarily conceptual, to some extent a degree of theoretical alienation from the being of the world cannot be avoided. However, when one's conceptualization reaches the point of translating the objects of experience into clear and distinct ideas, the result is the transformation of the world into the concept of the world. The emancipation of reason from God or nature is one thing. But without either transrational guide, autonomous reason posits (rather than discerns) an ultimate homogeneity at the base of things. If we are to locate principles of intelligibility in the world, either the world itself or God as the cause of the world is their possible source. What makes the Creator God a permanent possibility is that the science of the world—even if completed—would not address the question of the world's origin or eternity because the world, in presenting only itself, discloses neither its eternity nor creation *ex nihilo*.

If the truth claim of modern science is taken in a more restricted sense—namely, that the nature and workings, if not the origin, of the world can be comprehensively explained—the difficulty still remains that the clear and distinct account is arrived at by the imposition of method. What results from such an imposition is a

37. "Preface," p. 28.
38. *MITP*, p. 117.

"metaphysically neutral" account insofar as it is arrived at independently of the knowledge of first principles.[39] Such an approach
makes possible technological control over nature. However, the
result of the replacement of knowledge of first principles by
methodologically defined certainty is an indifference to our ignorance of what is first in the order of being.

What is worse, explains Strauss, the certainty achieved by the
imposition of method proved to be illusory. What united philosophy and religion—quite apart from their fundamental substantive
disagreements—was their attempt to provide a definitive account
of the whole and their conviction that the guidance of human life
required such an account. With the emergence of the pragmatic
approach to knowledge that typified the new scientific project, the
notion of a definitive account of the whole has been increasingly
judged "not only as incapable of realization but as meaningless or
absurd." The contest between philosophy and religion concerning
the discovery of the final account of the whole gave way to the
authorities of science and history. Because science, unlike philosophy, abandons the search for the definitive account of the whole in
favor of progress,[40] it can point to the contrast between the failure
of unscientific philosophy and the success of unphilosophic science.
At the same time, the progressive character of science—its claim to
represent an advance over all earlier human thought and to provide unending future progress—causes science to be superseded
by history. Because of the inability of science to provide a proof
(with any degree of exactness comparable to that attained by its
method, which radically separates facts from values) of the reality
and conditions of progress, and thereby of the possibility of progress in the future, science forsakes philosophy for the history of
human thought. That is to say, "philosophy transforms itself into
history of human thought." The scientific, as opposed to philosophic, study of the history of human thought concludes that all

39. Strauss discusses the meaning and function of "metaphysical neutrality" in Hobbes, Locke, and Rousseau in *Natural Right and History* (hereafter =
NRH) (Chicago: University of Chicago Press, 1965), pp. 173–74, 203–4, 266.
Cf. also Richard Kennington, "Strauss's *Natural Right and History*," in Udoff,
Strauss's Thought, pp. 248–51.
40. As we saw in the case of Spinoza, because the possibility of perpetual
progress depends on nature's inner infinity (the mysteriousness of the whole),
the goal of perpetual progress is perfectly consistent with the rejection of the
search for a definitive account of the whole. Cf. Strauss's "Why We Remain
Jews," Hillel Foundation Lecture, University of Chicago, 1962, in this volume.

human thought is inescapably "historically conditioned." The historicity of human thought means not only that a nonhistorically conditioned account of the whole is impossible, but that modern science must be recognized to be but one among many approaches to the whole offered up by the vicissitudes of history.[41] Spinoza's anticipation of historicism, explains Strauss, is through his adumbration of German idealism. Because for Spinoza complete knowledge of God in Himself is abstract and in order to be made concrete as the cause of all things must be informed by knowledge of the infinite totality of particular phenomena, or effects, "Spinoza thus appears to originate the kind of philosophic system which views the fundamental *processus* as a progress: God in Himself is not the *ens perfectissimum*. In this most important respect he prepares German idealism."[42] Rather than an abiding nature or truth, what is signified by the notion of an infinitely developing totality is the radical historicity of being and its correlative creativist or constructivist epistemologies.

The result of the supersession of science by history is that the nonscientific worldview at the basis of revealed religion is accorded a cognitive status equal to that of the scientific. The decision by Spinoza in favor of the latter and the way of life consistent with it, as we have seen, springs originally from a moral rather than theoretical opposition to revealed religion. The etiology of the unbelief at the core of such a decision is sketched by Strauss as follows. The atheism of Epicureanism, motivated by hedonism, understood its theoretical teachings as the means necessary to be free from natural necessity, the fear of death, and the terrors of religious fear. Modern atheism rejects the religious "delusion" not because of its terrors, but because it is a delusion. Religious belief is the false consciousness that deprives men of the enjoyment of the good things of this world. Once made aware that what the Bible describes as the fallen condition of man is in reality the natural condition, man understands that this-worldly happiness requires that he become the master and possessor of nature. However, the success of the conquest over nonhuman nature is accompanied by a suspicion that such success might be counterproductive. Over time, man becomes less certain that the path to ever-increasing freedom can be attained by mastering nature and imposing his

41. *PAW*, pp. 156–57, for the quotations above in this paragraph.
42. "Preface," p. 16.

laws upon it. This uncertainty engenders the rejection of the religious "delusion" not because of its terrors, but because it is comforting—an escape from the futility of life that cannot be overcome through the technological progress of civilization. The new courage to face existence as it is—the final and most honorable reason for the rejection of revelation—is "intellectual probity," itself a descendant of biblical morality, which can unearth the human roots of the belief in God.

> The last word and ultimate justification of Spinoza's critique is the atheism from intellectual probity which overcomes orthodoxy radically by understanding it radically, i.e., without the polemical bitterness of the Enlightenment and the equivocal reverence of romanticism.[43]

However, because the source of the atheism from intellectual probity is an act of will, an act of belief based on belief, it "is fatal to any philosophy."

The failure of rationalism to refute the possibility of revelation—that is to say, "the self-destruction of rational philosophy"—can be summarized as follows. Because belief in revelation is a prerequisite for persuasion in favor of revelation, and because unbelief is a prerequisite for persuasion by arguments against revelation, one would expect that the contest between philosophy and revealed religion would end in a draw because of the mutual question-begging involved. A genuine debate is precluded from the start because each speaks to the convinced. Yet revelation emerges as the victor because of the following asymmetry at the basis of their debate. Revelation is not only not called upon to refute philosophy, but its inability to do so merely confirms its foundation in faith. The choice of faith on the basis of faith is thereby consistent with itself. Whereas philosophy, which requires that all questions be decided rationally, is called upon to refute revelation but is unable to do so. The choice of philosophy over revelation can only be the result of an "unevident, arbitrary or blind decision." Because grounding the life of rational inquiry on a nonrational commitment is inconsistent, it is philosophy and not revelation that begs the question.[44]

Strauss's early study of Spinoza—by bringing to light the way in

43. *Ibid.*, p. 30.
44. *NRH*, p. 75; *MITP*, p. 116.

which rationalism subverts itself in the attempt to refute revelation—appears to have resolved the question regarding the possibility of a return to Jewish orthodoxy consistent with intellectual probity. Strauss concludes the 1962 "Preface" by indicating why he subsequently came to question such a resolution. The following considerations, which were confirmed by "other observations and experiences," caused Strauss to have doubts regarding the wisdom of abandoning reason. He explains in the "Preface" that—quite apart from the difficulties involved in an actual return to unqualified orthodoxy because of the skepticism and prejudice against orthodox religion that was the legacy of the Enlightenment,[45]— "the victory of orthodoxy through the self-destruction of rational philosophy was not an unmitigated blessing, for it was a victory not of Jewish orthodoxy but of any orthodoxy, and Jewish orthodoxy based its claim to superiority to other religions from the beginning on its superior rationality (Deut. 4:6)" (p. 30). The problem, as Spinoza pointed out to Albert Burgh,[46] is that the various revealed religions contradict each other. Arguments in support of revealed religion must necessarily support a particular revealed religion; but because such arguments support a plurality of revealed religions, they argue in support of no particular revealed religion. The same situation obtains when the ground of revealed religion is faith rather than argument. Each revealed religion claims that its faith is the one true faith; but because each such faith is equally valid, no particular faith can justify its claim to truth. Because revealed religion is essentially particular, each religion regards as fundamental what differentiates it from the others, and thus each refutes the others. The conflict between revealed religions can be resolved neither by argument nor appeal to Scripture. As far as reason is concerned, the mutual refutation of the revealed religions spares reason from having to refute them separately. The irresolvable contradiction between the various revealed religions is orthodoxy's equivalent to the self-destruction of rationalism.[47] In addition to the self-destruction of orthodoxy, there was the fact that the inevitable consequence of the final atheism was the claim that the will to power—the source of all other doctrines—is the one objective truth.

45. On Strauss's approach to the "Jewish Question," cf. Steven B. Smith, "Leo Strauss: Between Athens and Jerusalem," in this volume.
46. *Correspondence*, letter 76.
47. Cf. *SCR*, pp. 139–40.

The "premise, sanctioned by powerful prejudice," of *Spinoza's Critique of Reason* was that the quarrel between philosophy and revelation was a quarrel between modern rationalism and revelation, that premodern philosophy was not a viable alternative. Strauss's resolution of the *aporia* caused by the self-destruction of both rationalism and revealed religion consisted in the realization that, because the self-destruction of reason was the peculiar fate of modern as opposed to premodern rationalism, a return to premodern rationalism was possible. Strauss's return to premodern rationalism culminated in the rediscovery of Socratic philosophizing as the alternative to revelation.[48] In response to the uncertainty regarding the answers to the most important and urgent questions, it is reasonable to engage in reasoned inquiry in an attempt to overcome this uncertainty. Socratic philosophizing as a way of life—as opposed to the dissemination of doctrines—is free of the self-destruction of reason to which modern rationalism succumbed.

Whether one can maintain that Strauss believed Socratic philosophizing would fare better than modern rationalism in its debate with revelation depends on determining the answers he believed could be given to the following kinds of questions. Does its impartiality by postponing judgment until each side presents its case mean that Socratic philosophizing engages in a truly nonpartisan (rather than question-begging) debate with revelation, or does it signify its prior commitment to rational decision? Can Socratic philosophizing do no more than add to the list of fundamental but irresolvable alternatives the multiplicity of conflicting orthodoxies? Can Socrates' admitted inability to overcome the noetic heterogeneity characterizing the whole by providing a rational account— the *sine qua non* of the refutation of the possibility of revelation— be compensated for in some way? Does not the Socratic philosopher merely confirm his lack of comprehension of the either-or nature of the choice between philosophy and revelation when he claims that the biblical God does not condemn and punish the rational pursuit of wisdom? Can unaided human reason come to understand the claim of the suprarationality of the biblical God as anything other than contrarational? Can the Socratic philosopher be genuinely open to the kind of experience at the foundation of

48. Cf. *MITP*; "Jerusalem and Athens."

faith? Can he through self-examination penetrate to the perhaps nonrational source of his own calling? Can a life dedicated to discussions about the nature of virtue and justice promote their understanding and practice better than a life consisting in the obedience to and promulgation of divine law? Can the fact that philosophizing is the way of life open to the few be compensated for by Socrates' claim that the good of the city requires the philosophic gadfly? This essay is not the place for an attempt to answer such questions; however, one point can safely be made. Regarding the fundamental tension between reason and revelation, Strauss advised the following:

> No one can be both a philosopher and a theologian or, for that matter, a third which is beyond the conflict between philosophy and theology, or a synthesis of both. But every one of us can be and ought to be either the one or the other, the philosopher open to the challenge of theology or the theologian open to the challenge of philosophy.[49]

Strauss's discussions of the issues and arguments involved in the conflict between faith and philosophy present a contemporary model of the philosopher open to the challenge of theology. Engaged in with an unrivaled intellectual probity, Strauss's writings do not offer teachings to be inculcated, but rather stimuli to philosophizing.

49. *MITP*, p. 111.

Taking Evil Seriously: Schmitt's "Concept of the Political" and Strauss's "True Politics"

Susan Shell

In the "Preface" to the 1965 edition of *Spinoza's Critique of Religion* (first published in 1930), Leo Strauss notes that the study "was based on the premise, sanctioned by powerful prejudice, that a return to pre-modern philosophy is impossible."[1] "Not entirely by accident," he adds, his subsequent change of orientation found its first expression in his "Comments on Carl Schmitt's *Concept of the Political*" (1932),[2] a translation of which is included at the end of the same volume.

What are we to make of this inclusion, which stands as Strauss's "final word" on his own earlier study? The question seems all the more pressing, given recent suggestions that Strauss's attention to Schmitt compromises Strauss intellectually and morally—suggestions that gain an at least superficial plausibility from the fact that both Strauss and Schmitt criticize liberalism in the name of politics or the political.[3]

What, then, is the significance of Schmitt for Strauss?[4] One clue

---

My thanks to Christopher Bruell for his comments on an earlier version of this essay.

1. Leo Strauss, "Preface," in *Spinoza's Critique of Religion*, tr. E. M. Sinclair (New York: Schocken Books, 1965), p. 31. The original title is *Die Religionskritik Spinozas als Grundlage seiner Bibelwissenschaft Untersuchungen zu Spinozas Theologisch-Politischem Traktat* (Berlin: Akademie-Verlag, 1930).

2. "Anmerkungen zu Carl Schmitt, *Der Begriff des Politischen*." *Archiv für Sozialwissenschaft und Sozialpolitik* 67, no. 6 (August/September): 732–49. Strauss's essay is also reprinted in *Hobbes politische Wissenschaft* (Neuwied am Rhein and Berlin: Hermann Luchterhand Verlag, 1965), German edition of *The Political Philosophy of Hobbes: Its Basis and Its Genesis*, tr. Elsa M. Sinclair (Oxford, England: Clarendon Press, 1936; page numbers cited in this essay are from the later English edition, Chicago: University of Chicago Press, 1963).

3. See John G. Gunnell, "Strauss before Straussianism: Reason, Revelation, and Nature," *Review of Politics* 53 (Winter 1991), 53–74, and now reprinted in this volume; cf. Stephen Holmes, "The Scourge of Liberalism," *New Republic* (August 22, 1988): 36.

4. A recent book by Heinrich Meier—*Carl Schmitt, Leo Strauss, und "Der Begriff des Politischen." Zu einem Dialog unter Abwesenden. Mit Leo Strauss' Aufsatz über den "Begriff des Politischen" und drei unveröffentlichten Briefen an Carl Schmitt aus den Jahren 1932/33* (Stuttgart: J. B. Metzler, 1988)—sheds new and important light on the significance of Strauss for Schmitt. Meier painstakingly reconstructs the unlikely dialogue between the young scholar and the famous

appears at the end of Strauss's "Comments" (p. 351; the final words, so to speak, of his final word), where he identifies as the work's "main concern" a showing of what is "to be learned from Schmitt" for the urgent task of understanding Hobbes and thus criticizing liberalism radically.

Before turning directly to the "Comments" to follow up that clue, it is helpful to look briefly at two flanking works by Strauss that focus on the conflict between enlightenment and orthodoxy as if from two sides of a great divide: *Spinoza's Critique of Religion*, and *Philosophy and Law*.[5]

I

In both of these studies, Maimonides plays a pivotal role—in the first, as the failed champion of enlightened orthodoxy; in the second, as an exemplary expositor of what Strauss calls "medieval rationalism."

Strauss's argument concerning Maimonides in *Spinoza's Critique* proceeds somewhat as follows. Maimonides defines his own position on "two frontiers": before orthodoxy, he defends "the right of reason"; before philosophy, he draws attention to "the bounds of reason" (p. 148). Strauss's peculiarly "Kantian" formulation of the task at hand is striking, calling to mind his youthful study of Friedrich Heinrich Jacobi written nine years earlier, under the direction of Ernst Cassirer.[6]

Against the orthodox, who stand by the authority of the Bible and the Talmud literally understood, Maimonides defends the right of reason to interpret allegorically passages that contradict rational insight. At the same time, however, Maimonides points out the limits of rational insight, which cannot decide between the

---

jurist, a "dialogue in absentia" spanning the time before and after Schmitt's embrace of Nazism. That Schmitt was for reasons both tactical and substantive unwilling to own up to his debt to Strauss makes Meier's analysis all the more indispensable.

5. *Philosophie und Gesetz: Beiträge zum Verständnis Maimunis und seiner Vorläufer* (Berlin: Schocken, 1935), translated as *Philosophy and Law: Essays toward the Understanding of Maimonides and His Predecessors*, tr. Fred Baumann (Philadelphia: Jewish Publication Society, 1987).

Comments appeared in 1932; *Spinoza's Critique* and *Philosophy and Law* in 1930 and 1935, respectively.

6. Leo Strauss, *Das Erkenntnisproblem in der philosophischen Lehre Fr. H. Jacobis* (Hamburg: 1921). Cf. Gunnell, "Strauss before Straussianism," pp. 55f.

doctrine of Creation and the doctrine of the eternity of the world. He nevertheless attempts to use the science of Aristotle, which takes its bearings from the manifest order, to prove the possibility and probability of Creation (p. 151).

The question of the eternity versus the creation of the world is inseparable from that concerning the possibility of miracles: with the eternity of the world, "denial of miracles is given"; with Creation, the "possibility of miracles is admitted" (p. 151). Spinoza's denial of the possibility of miracles is bound up with his claim to understand the identity of God's will and his intellect, so that whatever is is what must be. Maimonides, by way of contrast, takes the more Kantian stance of insisting that the relation of God's will and understanding are beyond human comprehension (p. 152). According to Strauss's view here, both Maimonides and Kant grasp the inadequacy of science to resolve the question of the creation or eternity of the world. Maimonides thus preserves the possibility of moral freedom in something like the Kantian sense: "sin, as sin against God, is impossible according to Spinoza and possible according to Maimonides" (p. 154). More specifically, Maimonides alone holds fast to the assertion that there are "inexcusable rebellions against the Torah" (p. 155). Owing to his conviction as to the incomprehensibility of God, Maimonides also insists on the possibility of selective revelation, that is, on God's choosing to reveal Himself or not reveal Himself, independent of the readiness of someone to receive the revelation.

In addition, however, to establishing the possibility of revelation in general, Maimonides, it seems, also needs to establish our need for revelation, as well as justify historically the particular revelation made to Moses. Concerning the second, Spinoza argues against *all* merely historical knowledge, on the grounds that it fails to live up to the standard of certainty set by mathematics. It would seem, then, that Spinoza succeeds in undermining not only all historical justifications of belief in a particular revelation, but even our very interest in revelation, which can never meet the standard of reliability and certainty set by mathematics.

Against this charge, Strauss wonders if it is not, rather, belief in the revelation that "God is a hidden God" from which interest in revelation springs, that is, whether recognition of the fundamental mysteriousness of God is not prior to any "interest" we might have (again, the Kantian formulation is striking) in turning to revelation.[7] Moral conviction, Strauss suggests, is and must be prior to moral interest. In Maimonides' case on the other hand, insight into the insufficiency of human reason—an insufficiency established on the basis of Aristotelian science, which claims knowledge only of the sublunary world—"motivates recourse to revelation." In other words, concern with revelation out of interest in the question of how to conduct one's life "precedes belief in revelation" (p. 158).[8]

The key question that emerges is thus whether philosophy—that is, "independent human reflection" (p. 157)—suffices as a guide to life. If the latter is the case, as Spinoza insists, then belief in revelation may persist; such belief, however, will lack all interest (p. 160). This insistence, however, proves problematic. As will later become clear, Spinoza's very insistence on the sufficiency of human reason "brings to sight" reason's insufficiency, for much the same reason that Cartesian hubris leads to Kantian modesty.

Maimonides, according to Strauss, views the creation of the world as the indispensable basis of Judaism (p. 160). But this creation, which is not provable on the basis of Aristotelian science, can be vouched for only by miracles. It is precisely here, however, that Spinoza shows his superior strength, for Spinoza provides the unknowability (as distinguished from the impossibility) of miracles (p. 162). It is possible, says Strauss, "for Maimonides to defend against the philosophers of his time a view that can no longer be defended over against Spinoza." On this account, at least, the superiority of modern over ancient science is decisive.

But Strauss does not leave matters here. Were one to do so, he says, one would fail to "do justice to the basis of Maimonides' position, which remains unimpaired by all the changes that have occurred in the time that separates Maimonides from Spinoza." One would thus also fail "to do justice to the problematic character of Spinoza's critique of religion" (p. 163). That crucial basis comes down to this: "knowledge of the truths embodied in faith on the basis of tradition is necessarily prior to proof of those truths, that is, to philosophy." Maimonides does not need nor intend to justify faith before the tribunal of philosophy, but only to "enlighten Judaism where it can be enlightened." Spinoza's insistence that

7. Compare pp. 161, 178.
8. Maimonides' belief in the possibility of "manifest" sublunary knowledge distinguishes him from Kant, whose critique (in both its original and more radical, Jacobian form) of human knowledge applies universally.

Judaism justify itself on grounds external to Judaism—that is, that it divest itself of "prejudice"—is itself predicated on an act of faith, or what could be called "prejudice." For it is no more reasonable to assume, as is the habit of the modern age, that all traditions are to be questioned than it is to suspect, as was the custom of an earlier time, all innovations. Spinoza's doctrine rests on a sheer presupposition: "the free mind becomes free." It "presupposes itself, as faith presupposes itself" (p. 165).

What common ground exists between Spinoza and Maimonides—and it is only by virtue of such common ground that Spinoza's critique of religion is possible—stems from Maimonides' "trespass[ing] on science, i.e., from his effort to *reconcile* reason and revelation by building his theory on the ground of science. It is only here—when, for example, he tries to establish the probability of revelation on the basis of an analysis of the actual order of the world—that Maimonides is vulnerable" (p. 176). But Spinoza overstates his case as soon as he exceeds the "positive" claim that no good reason suggests we should attribute limited power to nature—when he makes the more radical, metaphysical claim that the power of nature is infinite (p. 177). Strauss thus shows himself to be in fundamental agreement with Kant's "non-dogmatic" conception of modern science as "completely open" on the question of whether nature's power is infinite or finite.

The Kantian critique of reason does not, however, go quite far enough. Only when revealed religion is taken into account does the questionable character of enlightenment's struggle against prejudice become evident. For modern science, too, is finally based on an act of will—on a prejudice—prior to all inquiry. Where the positive mind lives in "the present of experience," the hearing of revelation "quenches the will to immediacy, and calls forth the desire for non-presence, for mediacy" (p. 179). All critique of "prejudice" on behalf of experience fails to touch "the seriousness and the depth of the *will*, grounded in immediate hearing, to mediacy."[9] Strauss now asserts what he had earlier only suggested: obedience precedes all inquiry. The revealed commandments are superior to the rational commandments.

> Defection can be spoken of only if fidelity is primary. The perfection of the origin is the condition that makes sin possible. . . .

9. Compare Friedrich Heinrich Jacobi's *Werke*, ed. F. H. Jacobi and F. Köppen (Leipzig: Fleischer, 1812), bk. IV.1, pp. 234–35.

The positive mind, which rebels against revealed religion, is characterized precisely by this: that it looks toward the future, not merely hoping for it, but rather using its own powers to build the future, and that it does not suffer from the past. The positive mind is incapable of suffering from the past, since it has not lost an original perfection by a Fall, but has by its own effort worked itself out of the original imperfection, barbarism and rudeness. What is felt from within as fidelity, as obedience, appears to the positive mind as stupidity, imprisonment in prejudices. To that mind, "rebellion" is "liberation," "to become an apostate" is "liberty." (p. 180)

These words, which apply directly to Spinoza, apply less directly but perhaps more pointedly to Kant. Like Jacobi, Strauss turns Kant's moral faith against his affirmation of human autonomy.[10] Culture in the Kantian sense proves incompatible with the reverential, moral impulse that allegedly inspires it.[11]

The difference between *modern* enlightenment and philosophy as originally conceived, according to Strauss, reduces to the tendency of the former to regard itself not merely as a struggle against appearance and opinion, but as a specifically historical conflict between one age and another. To this positive effort must be added the metaphysical attempt—which both flows from and diverges from the former—to found, on the basis of radical doubt, an absolute foundation from which all doubt has been banished. On the basis of this new beginning comes certain knowledge of

10. Cf. Strauss's treatment—in the "Preface," pp. 23ff—of the neo-Kantian Hermann Cohen, who stressed Kant's cultural optimism at the expense of his appreciation of human evil (p. 21). On this point, see also Strauss's "Introduction" to Hermann Cohen, *Religion of Reason Out of the Sources of Judaism* (New York: Frederick Ungar, 1972), reprinted in Leo Strauss, *Studies in Platonic Political Philosophy*, with an introduction by Thomas Pangle (Chicago: University of Chicago Press, 1983), pp. 241, 244. In *Political Philosophy of Hobbes*, p. viii, n, Strauss suggests that Kant's difficulty arises at least in part from the "conditional" character of modern as opposed to ancient natural law.

11. In the "Preface," Strauss credits Jacobi's revelation of Lessing's secret adherence to philosophy of Spinoza for the fact that "the philosophy of Kant's great successors was consciously a synthesis of Spinoza's and Kant's philosophies" (pp. 16–17). Strauss adds that Spinoza's characteristic contribution to this synthesis was a novel conception of God (a conception that, as we have seen, avoids the traditional notion of sin). That Kant, who was himself given a "decisive impulse" by Spinoza (p. 16), preserves a vestige of the old sternness seems to result from his continuing attachment to the idea of a creator God. See Leo Strauss "On a New Interpretation of Plato's Political Philosophy," *Social Research* 13, no. 6 (1946): 358n. Kant's philosophy, for Strauss, rests on an uneasy compromise between the old notion of sin and the new notion of autonomy.

God not as originator or creator, but as what preserves me at present. The foundation of (modern) metaphysics is "to be what is present, what is available as present." By virtue of this foundation, any reasoning based on the actual order of the world is "in principle impossible against Spinoza" (p. 182).

But Maimonides does not, finally, rest his position on "any reasoning based on the actual order of the world." He relies on the latter only as a means of defending his "pre-given Jewish position" (p. 191). If Spinoza's critique touches Maimonides, it is only where he and Maimonides share a common ground, that is, only where Maimonides argues, or claims to argue, scientifically. "It was our belief," Strauss significantly adds, "that we could justifiably assume that the pre-givenness had a more radical significance, but Maimonides himself casts no light on this more radical significance" (pp. 191–92).

That significance is to be sought not in the accommodations of Maimonides, but in the orthodoxy of the Reformation, which understands the "pre-givenness of its position as already vouched for by the doctrine of the 'inner witness of the Holy Spirit.'" The questionableness of Spinoza's position thus first becomes manifest in the orthodoxy of the Reformation—for example, in the doctrines of Calvin, which Strauss characterizes as "immune" to the critique of Spinoza. By blurring the distinction between natural events and miracles—by treating every event as a miracle—Calvin parries the thrust of Spinoza's argument concerning the unknowability of miracles (p. 196).

Both the basis of Spinoza's illusion, and his peculiar *pathos*, lie in his severing of the *gloria Dei* (which he might think himself to serve to an exceptional degree) with consciousness of human sinfulness.[12] For Spinoza, the correlate of divine glory is not man's sinfulness, but his perishability or partiality (p. 202). Spinoza's "most potent hold" on religion stems from his "resolute derivation of all human phenomena from egoism" (p. 203). Thought through to its final conclusion, self-love yields to the most selfless love of God—a love, in other words, that does not aspire to be loved in turn. The purest love of God is one that denies the fact of sin.

12. Even Franz Rosenzweig—to whom Strauss's book is dedicated—falls prey, in part, to this illusion. By making the "Jewish nation" rather than "the Law" the key to the Jewish experience, he reveals not only a reflexive concern with Christianity, but also, and more importantly, an insufficient appreciation of "the power of evil in man." "Preface," pp. 13–14.

Divorced from the acknowledgment of sin, Spinoza's "radical" understanding of man's dependence on God is both unbiblical and, as Jacobi showed, unjustifiable.[13]

The essential difference between Maimonides and Calvin lies in the former's failure to illuminate the "positive meaning inhering in the pre-given character of revelation." Strauss's preference in this respect for Calvin over Maimonides ought not, however, be taken as a criticism of Judaism as such. By contrasting carnal fear and spiritual love, Spinoza fails to understand as it understands itself that revelation which distinguishes between slavish fear and fear of the Lord. Like certain strains of Christianity, in other words, Spinoza fails to understand that fear of God which is the essential precondition of love of God. The basis of this lack of understanding is a revulsion on Spinoza's part against "the jealous God of Wrath shown in Scripture, in favor of the God of Love." Spinoza's critique of religion "not by chance" converges with the truly world-historical opposition within and on the borders of Christianity to Judaism—despite, or even because, it is directed primarily against Christian orthodoxy (p. 209). In this sense, at least, Hermann Cohen's charge[14] that Spinoza's thought represents a betrayal of Judaism meets with agreement in Strauss (p. 208; cf. p. 21).

Spinoza's conflation of the slavish fear that lies at the basis of superstition and the genuinely religious attitude arises from his own ungrounded attitude of unbelief. Hence he interprets the "will to mediated hearing" as slavish and fearful susceptibility to clever deception. In his simple opposition of carnal fear and spiritual love—and hence in his failure to address the difference, to which all revealed religions subscribe, between slavish fear and fear of the Lord—Spinoza shows his peculiar hostility to the spirit of Judaism or the Law (p. 208).[15]

---

13. See "Preface," p. 204:
Spinoza is convinced that denial of sin . . . [is] capable of being demonstrated by strictly scientific means. . . . Even if all the reasoning adduced by Spinoza were compelling . . . only this much would have been proven: that on the basis of unbelieving science one could not but arrive at Spinoza's results. But would this basis itself thus be justified? It was Friedrich Heinrich Jacobi who posed this question, and by so doing lifted the interpretation of Spinoza—or what amounts to the same thing, the critique of Spinoza—on to its proper plane.
14. See Cohen, *Religion of Reason.*
15. Strauss connects the political impetus of modern Epicureanism with this very failure, through which "the will to mediated hearing of the message"

In summary, *Spinoza's Critique* is, by its own account, "Jacobian" in orientation. It draws its strength from defects of enlightenment that first come fully to light in the opposition between the claims of orthodoxy and the limits of reason as laid bare by Kant. Spinoza's criticism of Maimonides is valid to the extent that Maimonides defends religion on the basis of reason—an attempt that presupposes a pre-Kantian if not premodern confidence concerning what can be rationally known. Against Calvin, on the other hand, Spinoza fails to find the shared ground in "what is common to all men," without which, he believes, criticism is not possible (p. 195). Thus his position and that of Calvin "stand opposed to each other, without being able to arrive at agreement or even mutual toleration." The plane of eternal truth they share is not one of "criticism," but of "life and death combat" (p. 196).

Strauss's critical examination of Spinoza can, however, be faulted—and indeed seems to fault itself—for failing to provide any other clear basis by which the gulf between science and orthodoxy might be bridged, or by which criticism might otherwise be grounded. Enlightenment finds its limit in the self-contradictory (Nietzschean) realization that its opposition to prejudice is itself a prejudice[16]—a fact that may explain the peculiar inconclusiveness of Strauss's argument.

II

Spinoza's Critique of Religion suffers from what Strauss later calls the "powerful prejudice" that a "return to pre-modern philosophy is impossible." His early critique of enlightenment culminates in an opposition between science and religion—an opposition that calls into question (in principle, if not in practice) the possibility of their mutual accommodation.

Philosophy and Law, by way of contrast, joins in its very title what that earlier work opposes. This conjunction is not, however, to be confused with the sort of synthesis between science and religion with which modern thought is peculiarly burdened.[17] Rather,

---

appears as the result of "fear implanted in the minds of the people by clever deception" *Spinoza's Critique*, p. 207; Benedict de Spinoza, *Theologico-Political Treatise*, in *The Chief Works of Benedict de Spinoza*, tr. R. H. W. Elwes, Vol. 1 (New York: Dover, 1955), pp. 218–21.

16. On Nietzsche, see "Preface," p. 30; and *Philosophy and Law*, p. 18.

17. See, *e.g.*, *Philosophy and Law*, pp. 113–14n; and "New Interpretation of Plato," pp. 338–39.

Strauss wishes to arouse a suspicion in favor of the possibility of a philosophic orientation toward the Law—an orientation that differs both from the traditional Epicurean attack on religion, and from the "atheism out of probity" in which modern enlightenment culminates (pp. 16, 18).

What such an orientation means becomes clearer at the end of the first chapter in *Philosophy and Law*. In contrast to modern assumptions, medieval philosophy does not regard religion as a "domain of culture," but as Law (p. 40). Moreover, philosophical grounding of the Law "is the place in the structure of teachings of medieval philosophy in which the presuppositions of (medieval) philosophizing becomes the theme of philosophy." In grounding the Law, in other words, philosophy justifies itself philosophically, and this despite the fact that the "first and fundamental" task of medieval philosophizing is the legal grounding of philosophy (pp. 40–41). Strauss thus answers *in concreto* the question raised by Maimonides concerning the adequacy of reason as a guide to human life.[18]

In *Philosophy and Law*, then, Strauss moves beyond the "domain of culture" (in which his earlier criticism of Spinoza's criticism remained trapped) through a new understanding of the significance of Law for philosophic inquiry. He examines Julius Guttmann's treatment of Maimonides as a "Revelation-believing" rationalist[19] and finds that it falls short, like Strauss's own earlier analysis, because it fails to account for the *interest* of a rationalist in revelation—an interest that presupposes *need*. The conviction of the inadequacy of human understanding to know the decisively important truth is the condition of the possibility of a philosopher's having an interest in revelation as a philosopher. Maimonides, Strauss goes on to say, is "imbued with this conviction" (p. 44). But what is the decisively important truth or teaching? The decisively important teaching for a Jew is the createdness of the world—a teaching that is not finally subject to rational proof. Whether,

18. On the problem of the concrete as it relates to the political, see *Philosophy and Law*, p. 51.

19. Strauss focuses on Guttmann's *Die Philosophie des Judentums* (Munich: 1933) which was subsequently translated into English by David W. Silverman, *Philosophies of Judaism* (New York: Schocken Books, 1973). Attention is also given to Guttmann's *Religion und Wissenschaft im Mitteralterlichen und im Modennen Denken* (Berlin: 1922) subsequently reprinted in *Selected Writings of Julius Guttmann*, ed. Stephen Katz (New York: Arno Press, 1980).

however, this is the decisive teaching for man as such, or for the philosopher, may be questionable (cf. p. 70). The philosopher's interest in the Law might then be based on need or needs of another sort.

What then—apart from or in addition to the need for revelation, stemming from the inadequacy of human understanding—leads the philosopher to be interested in the Law? Strauss takes up this question in the third chapter, "The Philosophic Grounding of the Law." Here Strauss directly confronts the question of politics and thus sheds immediate light on the significance of his encounter with Schmitt. The general subject of the third chapter is prophetology. The prophet is to be understood as philosopher-statesman-seer (miracle worker) in one (p. 99), that is, as the culmination of what is highest for reason and what can be had only via revelation. But prophecy can be distinguished from "vulgar" divination of all grades only by its *political* mission: "prophecy proper can only be radically understood from the context of politics." But here, Strauss emphatically adds, " 'politics' and 'political' are to be understood in Plato's sense." That is, "Alfarabi is not concerned with the state in general but with the state directed to the proper perfection of man, with the 'excellent state,' the ideal state" (pp. 103–4). Politics or the Law—for Plato no less than for Maimonides—proves to be the guiding theme of philosophy, the forum before which it justifies itself, both out of obligation and in freedom (pp. 20, 110).

Both Schmitt and Strauss see in the idea of the "political" an answer to the deficiencies of liberalism, or the cultural worldview. They differ fundamentally, however, in their understanding of what politics is.[20] That difference is brought out clearly in Strauss's discussion of Rabbi Levi ben Gerson, the first genuine "revelation-believing rationalist" who, by virtue of that very fact, presupposes the "disintegration" of genuine Platonism. The key to this disintegration is the emergence of an "abstract" providentialism also characteristic of a later deism. By virtue of that providentialism, which "overlooks the power of evil," one forgets the necessity of human care for human things; that is, one forgets that the ideal state must be effected by human beings, even if they are prophets (pp. 56–57). (One can here say in anticipation that Strauss's fundamental criticism of Schmitt grows out of the latter's failure to

20. See Strauss's letter to Schmitt, 4 September 1932, published in Meier, *Schmitt, Strauss, und "Begriff des Politischen,"* pp. 132–33.

reflect adequately on the distinction between human evil and guiltless or animal dangerousness.)

The difference between a still essentially Platonic Maimonides and a no longer genuinely Platonic Levi lies in the latter's forgetfulness of human evil. At precisely this point in the argument—at what he calls the "crux of interpretation"—Strauss refers to the "necessary connection between politics and theology (metaphysics), which we stumbled on by chance" (pp. 56–57). In referring to this lucky stumble, does Strauss have Schmitt—author of his own *Political Theology*[21]—specifically in mind?

III

We turn finally to the 1932 "Comments," whose main concern is to show what may be learned from Schmitt for the urgent task of understanding Hobbes and thereby criticizing liberalism radically (see "Comments," in *Spinoza's Critique*, p. 351). Showing what is to be learned does not necessarily mean adhering to what Schmitt meant to teach.[22] Strauss begins by pointing out a discrepancy

21. Carl Schmitt, *Politische Theologie: Vier Kapitel zur Lehre von der Souveränität* (Munich and Leipzig: 1922). The English translation—*Political Theology: Four Chapters on the Concept of Sovereignty*, tr. George Schwab (Cambridge, MA: MIT Press, 1985)—is based on the 1934 edition. See also Strauss, *Spinoza's Critique*, p. 345.

22. Schmitt published a book on Hobbes in 1938: *Der Leviathan in der Staatslehre des Thomas Hobbes: Sinn und Fehlschlag eines politisches Symbols* (Hamburg-Wandsbek: Hanseatischen Verlagsanstalt; 2nd ed. Köln-Lövenich: "Hohenheim" Verlag, 1982). In that work Schmitt criticizes the "Jewish scholar" Leo Strauss for his treatment of Hobbes in *Spinoza's Critique of Religion*; he does not mention Strauss's book-length study of 1935, *Political Philosophy of Hobbes* (first published 1936).

Schmitt reads the symbol of Leviathan as a mixture of Jewish/Kaballistic abhorrence and Germanic celebration. Schmitt's somewhat daring citation of a Jew at *Leviathan in Staatslehre*, p. 38n, is offset by passages such as the following: "[While Behemoth and Leviathan (who stand for the great land and sea powers) destroy each other] the Jews stand apart and watch as the peoples of the world kill one another; for them this mutual 'slaughter and carnage' [*Schächten und Schlachten*] is lawful and 'kosher.' Thus they eat the flesh of the slaughtered peoples and live upon it" (p. 18). Much of the work is devoted to attributing the "death" of Leviathan to such "Jewish" thinkers as Spinoza, Mendelssohn, and Friedrich Julius Stahl-Jolson; the effect of the last—a convert to Christianity and a political conservative—being especially insidious (pp. 106ff). That Hobbes believed in the divinity of Christ is both crucial to Schmitt's interpretation and a major point of disagreement between Strauss and him (pp. 20–21 n).

On Schmitt's continuing interest in Strauss, see Meier, *Schmitt, Strauss, und "Begriff des Politischen,"* pp. 51, 70–71.

between Schmitt's intention—inquiry into the "order of human things," that is, the state—and his general principles, which preclude all truth other than "present" truths. This tension, if not contradiction, places Schmitt's thesis—that the state is founded in the political—in an immediately ambiguous light. Schmitt's fundamental thesis, which can only be understood "polemically" or from the "concrete political existence," is "altogether determined" by his fight against liberalism, writes Strauss (p. 332). Schmitt's task is thus determined by his enemy, that is, by the fact that liberalism's effort to negate the political has failed to do more than cover it over or disguise it.

This polemical quality is in part a strength. Unlike other opponents of liberalism, Schmitt does not come with a ready-made illiberal theory in his pocket. He alone seems to grasp the astounding power of liberal thought—a fact that "suffices in itself to characterize the significance of his attempt" (pp. 332–33). But this fact also points to a fundamental limitation: unable fully to escape the systematics of liberal thought, his position remains provisional (p. 333). The polemical meaning of Schmitt's concept of the political—its essential dependence on his critique of "culture"— dooms both concept and critique to be less than exhaustive (p. 335).

This polemical meaning is connected, according to Strauss, "in the closest possible way" with Schmitt's critique of the prevailing concept of culture. According to this concept—based in the presupposition that man is essentially autonomous—human activities divide up into separate, mutually autonomous realms. Against this view, Schmitt affirms the political as the source of authoritative decisions about life and death. So understood, the political is not merely one realm among others (which include the moral, the legal, the economic, and so on) but that which defends the *seriousness* (*Ernst*) of human life.

By returning to Hobbes's state of nature, Schmitt not only counters modern forgetfulness of the natural foundations of culture;[23] he also provides his concept of the political with a genus (i.e., a state or status) under which the specific difference of the political may be placed. The political is the *natural* status of man,

23. Leo Strauss, "Comments on Carl Schmitt's *Concept of the Political*," in *Spinoza's Critique*, p. 335; see also "New Interpretation of Plato," pp. 355f: "The historical root of our concept of 'culture' is the fundamental change in the meaning of 'nature' which became visible in the seventeenth century, and particularly in Hobbes' concept of 'the state of nature.' "

in the sense of his fundamental or extreme status. To this extent, at least, Schmitt's definition loses its merely polemical character. But Schmitt also alters Hobbes's conception of the state of nature: what Hobbes defines "polemically" as a state of war among individuals, Schmitt defines "unpolemically" as a state of war among groups of men divided into friend and foe. Where Hobbes would negate the state "either of nature or the political," Schmitt affirms it. By restoring "to a state of honor" (p. 336) what Hobbes presents as a defect to be removed, Schmitt fails to acknowledge the latter's central contribution to the worldview against which Schmitt struggles.

This difficulty is disguised by Schmitt's "explicit" view, according to which the desirability or abhorence of the political is irrelevant (p. 339). He resists *evaluating* the political because he holds all such evaluations to be mere "normativities," or "fictions," in contradistinction to the political, which deals with life and death—hence with what is real. Schmitt, one could say, retains a view of morality as merely "subjective"—not publicly binding—that is characteristic of liberalism. In place of such evaluation, Schmitt insists that the political simply is—in other words, is man's inescapable destiny.

This is not Schmitt's "final word," however, as Strauss is at pains to show (p. 341). Despite Schmitt's repeated assertions to the contrary, the political for him is not simply inescapable. Schmitt promotes the political because the political—that is, man's "dangerousness"—is actually threatened. At bottom, Schmitt defends the political out of *disgust* (*Eckel*) before the prospect of a world of entertainment, a world devoted to production and consumption and in which men have forgotten what really counts (p. 346). Precisely in this, however, Schmitt himself forgets "the political" as ordinary citizens understand it.[24] A totality of men engaged in war will not wish for more dangerous foes (p. 342). Where Schmitt understands the political in terms of the exception or the extreme, Strauss looks to the typical case.[25]

24. As Strauss states in a private letter (4 September 1932), Schmitt (rightly) recognizes that men are naturally evil and must therefore be governed. Men can be ruled, however, only if they are organized against other men. The tendency to form exclusive groupings is in this sense "given with human nature." But the political so understood is only a condition of the state, not the state's constituent principle. Schmitt's failure to recognize this hierarchy unambiguously opens him to the charge of "sociologism," *i.e.*, of losing sight of the political in the decisive sense. Meier, *Schmitt, Strauss, und "Begriff des Politischen*," p. 133; cf. *Political Philosophy of Hobbes*, p. 5.

25. See *Philosophy and Law*, pp. 111–12n: "In contrast to ancient and

Schmitt's affirmation of man's dangerousness supports the "authoritarian" conviction that man is evil in the sense of needing to be governed (p. 343). Schmitt fails, however, to take the decisive step necessary to the "radical critique of liberalism he has in mind"—a step that would require him to "work his way back to conception of evil as moral depravity (*Schlechtigkeit*)" (p. 345).

Instead, Schmitt's "correction" of the Hobbesian understanding of evil as "guiltless" (*unschuldigen*) is not only inadequate to Schmitt's purpose, but actually contradicts it: where Hobbes, in the end, lifts up (*hervorheben*) the naturalness and hence the guiltlessness of evil in order to combat it, Schmitt "speaks of evil not to be understood morally with unmistakable *sympathy*" (p. 345, my translation).[26]

It is true that, according to Schmitt's own proper opinion, "affirmation (*Position*) of the political leads back to affirmation of the moral" (p. 349), in the sense of raising the question of what is right rather than accepting agreement at any price (p. 348).[27] His affirmation is inconsistent, however, because he continues to accept the liberal-individualistic opinion that relegates the moral to the "private" realm of "mere normativities" (p. 349). As Strauss puts it, "If it is presupposed that all ideals are private, and therefore not binding, then obligation cannot be understood as duty, but only as a kind of inescapable necessity." This assumption leads Schmitt to appeal to natural necessity—which thus takes the place of duty in his analysis of the political—and, when this fails, to "conceal his moral judgment."

One's suspicion concerning the decisive importance of this failure of understanding with regard to obligation is confirmed by a reading of Strauss's later (1935) study of Hobbes. According to that study, Hobbes too conceals behind an appeal to "natural necessity" a moral judgment that replaces obligation or the Law

---

medieval philosophy, which understand the extreme on the basis of the typical, modern philosophy . . . understands the typical on the basis of the extreme. In that way the 'trivial' questions of the essence of virtue and whether it can be taught are ignored, and the extreme ('theological') virtue of love becomes the 'natural' ('philosophical') virtue." It remains the case, however, that the "traditional" critique of the natural ideal of courage—a critique that modern thought radicalized—is itself based on an "extreme ideal of knowledge." Cf. *Spinoza's Critique*, p. 37.

26. To this extent, Schmitt is guilty of the very "aestheticism" that he condemns. "Comments," pp. 344, 335.

27. *Political Philosophy of Hobbes*, p. 152.

with individual right—a concealment upon which hinges the "epoch-making significance of Hobbes' philosophy."[28] Schmitt's concealment, one could say, reveals—albeit in a way of which he is not himself explicitly aware—the "moral" and therefore questionable basis of Hobbes's thought.[29]

Because Schmitt accepts the claim of "humanitarian-pacifist" morality "to be morality," he remains under the spell of the opinion he combats, says Strauss in his "Comments" (p. 349). For this reason above all, Schmitt's "illiberal tendencies are arrested by the 'undefeated systematics of liberal thinking' " (p. 351).

To defeat those systematics, the preliberal moral horizon within which Hobbes founded liberalism must be recovered. The main concern of the "Comments"—to show what is to be learned from Schmitt for understanding Hobbes—would seem to consist in just this excavation.

IV

Strauss's final (public) word on Schmitt, which appears in the new preface to the German edition of Strauss's study of Hobbes, draws attention to these same systematics.

> The first time I heard about Hobbes in a way that caused me to take notice was in the lectures of Julius Ebbinghaus . . . [who] already believed that the significant part of Hobbes' teaching had been "sublated in" the Kantian philosophy. Carl Schmitt, in quite unconscious opposition to Ebbinghaus, asserted in his essay *The Concept of the Political* . . . [1927], that Hobbes is "by far the greatest and perhaps the only truly systematic thinker."[30]

This judgment—which corresponded, Strauss says, to his taste or feeling at the time—strengthened, "understandably," his interest in Hobbes. That interest did not, however, make him a Hobbesian:

28. *Ibid.*, p. 155.
29. *Ibid.*, pp. 29, 152. See also Christopher Bruell, "A Return to Classical Political Philosophy and an Understanding of the American Founding," *Review of Politics* 53 (Winter 1991): 172n, and now reprinted in this volume.
30. Donald Maletz, tr., "Strauss's New Preface to *Hobbes politische Wissenschaft*," *Interpretation* 8 (January 1979): 1.
The weaker 1932 version of Schmitt's statement speaks of Hobbes as "a great and truly systematic thinker." On the importance of this fact for the interchange between Schmitt and Strauss, see Meier, *Schmitt, Strauss, und "Begriff des Politischen,"* p. 43.

philosophic interest in theology linked him—*not* with the author of *Political Theology*—with the Kant scholar Gerhard Krüger.

> The final sentence of [Krüger's] Kant book [1931], which corresponded completely to my view at the time, and with which I would still today, with certain reservations, agree, explains why I directed myself wholly to the "true politics."[31]

In the end, Strauss's understanding of politics owes more to the "true politics" of Kant—a politics that cannot "take a single step without paying homage to the moral law"—than to Schmitt's equivocally Hobbesian polemics.[32] At the same time, Strauss is also no Kantian: freedom and obedience for him find reconciliation not in human "autonomy" (nor in the "will to mediation"), but in the justification of philosophy.

What then, for Strauss, is the significance of Schmitt? Let me tentatively suggest the beginning of an answer. Schmitt argues in the face of and against a prevailing concept of culture that is itself a decayed Kantianism—a Kantianism, in other words, that has lost (as Jacobi foresaw it would) its "objective" moral bearings. Schmitt goes partway toward returning to the state of nature that underlies all culture, but is prevented from taking what Strauss regards as the decisive step. The sign of that failure is Schmitt's peculiar—and ultimately self-contradictory—treatment of human evil. On the one hand, Schmitt affirms the political because man is dangerous and needs to be governed. On such an understanding, dangerousness is a defect. On the other hand, he admires or "sympathizes" with this dangerousness, out of a deeper moral worry that the seriousness of life is itself threatened by the prevailing concept of culture.

31. Maletz, "Strauss's New Preface," p. 2. The phrase *true politics* appears in Immanual Kant's *Zum ewigen Frieden, Werke*, vol. 8 (Berlin: Walter de Gruyter, 1968), p. 380; translated as *Perpetual Peace*, in *On History*, ed. Lewis White Beck (Indianapolis: Bobbs-Merrill Company, 1963), p. 128.
The last sentence of Krüger's book is as follows: "That the decisive question remains *true*, even if it finds *no* answer, can be taught him who questions thus by the example of *Socrates*." Gerhard Krüger, *Philosophie und Moral in der Kantischen Kritik* (Tübingen: Verlag J. C. B. Mohr, 1931); see Maletz, "Strauss's New Preface," p. 3n.
32. See here Strauss's ironic reference to the "fate that was in a way kind" that "drove him to England." Both Schmitt and Ernst Cassirer recommended Strauss for the Rockefeller Foundation support that enabled him to leave Germany. Strauss's letter of thanks to Schmitt (13 March 1932) is in Meier, *Schmitt, Strauss, und "Begriff des Politischen,"* p. 131.

In order to recover the state of nature underlying all culture, Schmitt would have to take evil seriously in the sense in which ordinary citizens understand it, that is, as moral depravity. In fact, the prevailing concept of culture represents just such an evil to Schmitt, although he is loath to admit it. What prevents him from taking this necessary step is his acceptance of his opponents' understanding of the moral as merely private and hence not genuinely binding.[33]

By furnishing concrete and authoritatively binding decisions concerning the *Ernstfall* (the emergency or "earnest case"), Schmitt's concept of the political opposes itself to the subjective moralism and the abstract universalism characteristic of the liberal worldview.

But why does Schmitt accept his opponents' understanding of morality against his own deeper insights or instincts? Part of the answer may lie with his acceptance—as a believer—in the skepticism of the modern enlightenment concerning the "knowability" of the fundamental teachings of the tradition. One is reminded here of Strauss's suggestion that as a consequence of the Enlightenment it became "clearer and better known" that the presuppositions of faith "lack the peculiarly obligatory character of the known." Hence, perhaps, one can understand the peculiar relation between Schmitt's faith and his attitude toward the obligatory as something fundamentally threatened.[34]

According to Strauss, what must be recovered in order for the horizon of liberalism to be transcended is, above all, a recognition of the primacy of duty for political life, and hence an understanding of the significance of Law in its original premodern sense.

---

33. In an earlier work (*Politische Theologie* of 1922), he similarly defines "sovereignty" as the power to decide the exception—hence, as the power to override merely legal norms. Schmitt, *Political Theology*, pp. 4–5.

34. So understood, Schmitt exemplifies the tendency of the "defensive critique" of religion to obscure the common ground that lies in the "problem of divine law." See Strauss, *Philosophy and Law*, p. 12:

> The formation of the new science . . . led to the result that fundamental teachings of the tradition, which had also been counted as knowable under the presuppositions of the older science, came more and more to be viewed as merely believed. The destruction of natural theology and natural law, which, to say the least, was prepared in the age of Enlightenment, is the most important example and indeed the peculiar mark of this formation. Its final result is that unbelieving science and belief no longer have, as they did in the Middle Ages, a common basis in natural knowledge upon which a meaningful quarrel between belief and unbelief is possible.

Because Schmitt adopts the neo-Kantian view of law as an abstract universal norm, just as he adopts the prevailing liberal view of morality as a matter of private and hence nonbinding ideals, he finds himself impelled to discover or create a political domain in which the concretely obligatory can reappear. But Law in the original sense requires no such "political" correction: it is, after all, only with Hobbes—who denies (for reasons of his own) the connection between reason and the claim to rule—that "sovereignty" and "concreteness" become problematic.[35]

In order for the "common ground" between orthodoxy and "free inquiry" to be recovered (and hence in order for "criticism" genuinely to occur), this denial must be questioned.[36] Schmitt's "difficulty" points the way out of (without allowing him to transcend) the cave beneath the cave from which, for Strauss, the philosopher's ascent begins in earnest.

35. Strauss, *Political Philosophy of Hobbes*, pp. 158, 164.

36. See, *e.g.*, Leo Strauss, "Progress or Return?" published in *The Rebirth of Classical Political Rationalism*, selected and introduced by Thomas L. Pangle (Chicago: University of Chicago Press, 1989), p. 248: "the common ground between the Bible and Greek philosophy is the problem of divine law." I must therefore disagree with Pierre Manent's suggestion, in his generally luminous introduction to the French translation of Meier's study, that the *fundamental* reason for Schmitt's failure lies with his religiosity as such. In Heinrich Meier, *Carl Schmitt, Leo Strauss, et la Notion de Politique: Un Dialogue entre Absents*, tr. Francoise Manent (Paris: Julliard, 1990), pp. 11–12. Cf. Meier, *Schmitt, Strauss, und "Begriff des Politischen,"* pp. 117–18.

Leo Strauss, the Bible, and Political Philosophy

Harry V. Jaffa

What follows is my response to a remarkable letter that I received in January 1988 from two younger scholars, Larry Arnhart of Northern Illinois University and Leonard Sorenson of Assumption College in Massachusetts.[1] The questions they addressed to me about God and man, the Bible and philosophy, were more direct and comprehensive than any that had been asked me in a teaching career of some forty-five years. Their questions were prompted by an article of mine entitled "Crisis of the Strauss Divided," which had been published in late 1987.[2] That article was the revised text of a lecture I had given at the New School for Social Research earlier in the year, as part of a symposium on the contributions of foreign-born scholars to the understanding of the American Constitution, whose bicentennial was being celebrated. I was asked to speak on the contributions of Leo Strauss.[3]

In my lecture I had taken my bearings in part from Strauss's assertions concerning the insolubility of the opposition between revelation and reason—Jerusalem and Athens—as to the highest principle of human life. I had also taken my bearings from Strauss's assertion that, according to Aristotle, the ends of the city—that is, of political life as such—are the ends of the moral virtues. And I had noted Strauss's pronouncement that, notwithstanding their theoretical disagreement as to the end or ends served by the moral virtues, revelation and reason had agreed substantially on what in practice morality was. And I had taken my bearings further from Strauss's assertion that the very life of Western civilization depended on the continuing dialogue—the eternal dialogue—between revelation and reason. But both the continuity and the beneficence of this dialogue depended on its

1. My response was dated 13 February 1989. In the following version I have made a few revisions, and added formal scholarly references and a few notes for the sake of readers who may not share the background of the correspondents.

2. Harry V. Jaffa, "Crisis of the Strauss Divided," *Social Research* 54:3 (Autumn 1987): 579–603.

3. George Kateb of Amherst spoke on Hannah Arendt, and Dante Germino of the University of Virginia spoke on Eric Voegelin.

remaining theoretical, with neither side demanding, or being entrusted with, political power with respect to the conduct of the dialogue between them. In the postclassical world, government by sectarian religious authority—or by sectarian philosophic authority (as in the case of Marxist-Leninist regimes)—were equally tyrannical and equally abhorrent. From this perspective, the intention of the American Founding, with its unprecedented separation of church and state—its guarantee of the free exercise of religion, and of freedom of speech and of the press—could be seen, as not a lowering of the goals of political life, but an emancipation of man's highest aspirations for truth from the tyranny of the political passions. In this sense it could be seen as the best regime of Western civilization. However, this regime was endangered from the outset (notably in the slavery controversy), and continues to be ever more endangered, by the moral relativism—culminating in nihilism—of modern philosophy. Strauss's critique of modern philosophy, as it seemed to me, was directed above all toward overcoming what he often called the "self-destruction of reason," so that the authority equally of classical philosophy and the Bible, with respect to virtue and morality, might be restored. This restoration, I am convinced, is also nothing less than the restoration of the perspective of the American Founding.

I should mention finally that, although I cite Leo Strauss repeatedly as the ground of my assertions, I do not claim Strauss's authority for the conclusions I draw from them. Other students of Leo Strauss draw very different conclusions—indeed, in some cases, opposite conclusions—from his writings than I have done. I only say here (as elsewhere) what I believe to be true, and what in Strauss's writings has led me to think as I do. Others must judge whether, in thinking as I do, I think truly.

Gentlemen:

In yours of January 27, 1988, you propounded a number of interrogatories (as Lincoln would call them), to which I will now respond. You flattered me greatly by addressing me as you did, but I am not so lost to all decency, not to say modesty, as to think that my responses will constitute answers. I can only hope that I may contribute something to your continuing discussion.

You ask "two general questions to which all our other questions are subordinated."

(1) What is the specific, substantive teaching that is novel or unique to biblical revelation?

I reply first that it is the idea of the One God Who is separate from the universe, of which He is the Creator. As both separate and unique, God is unknowable. We can properly be said to know only those things that have class characteristics that identify them as members of species or genera. That is, if I say "This is a chair," I imply that there is an infinite number of possible chairs, each different from this, but each equally a chair. Reason means recognizing the idea of the chair in the chair, and understanding thereby why the particular is different from the universal. Once I understand what a chair is, I understand why there can be many chairs besides this one. Moreover, any particular which we experience by sense perception—however unique it may be understood to be— immediately implies the possibility of the existence of other particular objects of its class. This would be true, for example, of the first electric light bulb, the first airplane, the first of anything. It would be true also of any object that can be conceived by the imagination: for example, a centaur, which is half man, half horse. I may never have experienced a centaur; but by imagining one, I know I can also imagine others that resemble this one and yet are different. But the God of the Bible is not only one, but the only possible One. As such, He cannot become an object of knowledge. And He cannot be imagined. A god that can be imagined would be a pagan deity (of which there always can be many), but not the One of the Bible. This is why the second of the Ten Commandments forbids the making of images; that is to say, it forbids any suggestion that God can become an object of knowledge by being an object of sense perception. It is *because* He cannot become an object of knowledge that He can, and indeed must, be an object of faith. There is therefore a clear and distinct epistemological reason why faith—and not reason—has primacy. To summarize: I cannot know anything of which there is and can be only one. If God is One, and if there can be no other God, there can be no idea of God. God is unique in that in Him no distinction can be drawn between the universal and the particular, which is the ground of all intelligiblity within the dispensation of unassisted human reason. God is therefore unknowable. This is the fundamental premise of the Bible.

Since internal reflection, or reasoning, about human experience can never lead men to the idea of the God of the Bible—since the

God of the Bible is not an idea, and He is not a cause within the order of nature—revelation as the form of communication between God and man becomes "reasonable." Revelation is marked by miracles, although Creation itself is the primary miracle. This is shown by the first sentence of Genesis, which reports something that only God could have known or witnessed. All other miracles are lesser miracles, but their reason for being is already implied in the story of Creation. God's reasons for communicating with man must be subsumed under His reason for communicating to him His account of His creation of the world—and man. If the highest things (God and the story of Creation) are unknowable, then the highest capacity or virtue of man cannot be theoretical wisdom. In Aristotle, for example, practical wisdom is in the service of theoretical wisdom. In the Bible, theoretical wisdom is replaced by—or perhaps is constituted by—the study of God's speeches and deeds, of which the Bible (or Torah, or Law) is a record.

> Blessed is the man who walks not in the counsel of the wicked,
> Nor stands in the way of sinners,
> Nor sits in the seat of scoffers;
> But his delight is in the law of the Lord,
> And on his law he meditates day and night. (Psalms 1:1–2)

Your second general question was as follows:

(2) If biblical revelation poses an unanswerable challenge to philosophy and therefore is—in Strauss's words—"The refutation of philosophy by revelation,"[4] *then why should one not reject philosophy?*

The "refutation of philosophy by revelation" has some of the same ambiguity as "I know that I know nothing." Strauss has placed this

---

4. The words quoted from Strauss are taken from *Natural Right and History* (Chicago: University of Chicago Press, 1953), p. 75. They emerge at the end of a long passage, and are the latter part of a sentence, not its beginning, as may be seen in the following:

> Philosophy has to grant that revelation is possible. But to grant that revelation is possible means to grant that philosophy is perhaps something infinitely unimportant. To grant that revelation is possible means to grant that the philosophic life is not necessarily, not evidently, *the* right life. Philosophy, the life devoted to the quest for evident knowledge available to man as man, would itself rest on an unevident, arbitrary, or blind decision. This would merely confirm the thesis of faith, that there is no possibility of consistency, of a consistent and thoroughly sincere life, without belief in revelation. The mere fact that philosophy and revelation cannot refute each other would constitute the refutation of philosophy by revelation.

"refutation" in the mouth (so to speak) of revelation in much the same way that Socrates put the argument of the laws (the Torah of Athens!) into the mouth of the laws of Athens in the *Crito*.

There is an Aristotelian maxim that goes: "When we have refuted all the errors, what remains is the truth." Refutation is the method of philosophy, rather than of revelation. (The "method" of the Bible is found in such expressions as "Thou shalt . . ." or "I am. . . .") Strauss's refutation of philosophy by revelation is a Socratic elenchus. This, however, does not mean that it is not serious, or that it is meant to subvert the argument for revelation by making it depend on philosophy. God did not create man without reason, or without making it obligatory upon him to obey reason, in all these matters with respect to which reason can be a sufficient guide. Philosophy—insofar as it is the perfection of human reason—is the perfection of a God-given gift. Only the function of philosophy is differently conceived, depending on whether that function is understood as ultimately ministerial to the teachings of divine revelation, or as identical with an intrinsic rationality that is itself the most divine thing in human life.

The context of your quote from *Natural Right and History* is important. Strauss shows how in Max Weber revelation has been transformed into "value judgments"—the sublime into the ridiculous! In restoring the dignity of revelation, Strauss shows why the conflict between reason and revelation is *not* a ground for declaring reason impotent. Because we may not be able to say which of two mountains whose peaks are covered by clouds is higher does not mean we cannot tell a mountain from a mole hill![5]

The argument for revelation becomes in Strauss a defense of the common ground on which Socratic political philosophy and the Bible both stand. "I know that I know nothing"—awareness of ignorance, of the need to know—itself leaves open the question of whether satisfying this need depends primarily on reason or on faith. Socratic progress in wisdom—such progress as may be said to result from every Socratic conversation—always is accompanied by an increased awareness of what we do not know. The mystery of the universe, the mystery of being, grows—rather than diminishes—as a result of Socratic progress in wisdom. How can a Socratic know that his "progress" is in "wisdom" if the goal of

5. I have used this familiar saying of Strauss without quotation marks.

philosophy recedes with every supposed advance? Does not philosophy—confidence in the ultimate significance of reason—depend on an act of faith as much as belief in the God of the Bible? Hence, reason itself points to, and cannot reasonably deny, the possibility that the mystery of being is impenetrable, because the Author of the universe is a mysterious God who, being separated from the universe He created, is beyond being.

Modern rationalism comes to sight as the attempt to dispel the mystery of being by so radicalizing skepticism as to abolish skepticism from philosophy. It attempted (notably in Descartes, but also in Spinoza) to discover premises that could not be doubted, and to proceed therefrom both inductively and deductively to conclusions that could not be doubted and that did not require any "faith in reason." In so doing, it believes in the possibility of the ultimate transformation of philosophy into wisdom. The consummation and transformation of philosophy—love of wisdom—into wisdom itself, were it to succeed, would put an end to both Socratic skepticism and biblical faith. For in such a case, there would be nothing left either for inquiry or for faith. Strauss's critique of modern philosophy showed the impossibility of this enterprise more than any intellectual event of our times. His demonstration that the self-destruction of reason ends in nihilism proved the superiority both of Socratic skepticism and of biblical faith to the modern attempts to supersede them. Whatever opposition may be intrinsic to the difference between biblical faith and Socratic skepticism, they stand as one in their dissimilarity to modern rationalism. Both employ reason, whether as autonomous reason or as the handmaiden of revelation, to make authoritative moral judgments. And while differing as to the ultimate purpose of morality, they yet agree substantially as to what morality is. In his autobiographical preface, Strauss cites Deuteronomy 4:6.

> Keep them and do them; for that will be your wisdom and your understanding in the sight of the peoples, who, when they hear all these statutes, will say "Surely this great nation is a wise and understanding people."[6]

Why were the "peoples"—namely, the Gentiles—expected to say of the Israelites, that they were a "wise and understanding people"?

6. "Preface to the English Translation," in *Spinoza's Critique of Religion* (New York: Schocken Books, 1965), p. 30.

What in them enabled them to recognize wisdom and understanding (remember Meno's dilemma!), if no direct revelation had been vouchsafed to them? And why did God expect that a comparison of the laws of different nations would disclose—presumably to a wise and understanding judge—the superior righteousness of the laws of Moses? Does not the Bible then presuppose that the recognition of wisdom is a human potentiality, and that righteousness is an object of all law, and not only of the Torah? Does it not thereby presuppose that the teachings of reason and of revelation will not contradict each other, since both reason and revelation are God's gifts to mankind? Nothing in the proposition of the One Unknowable God forbids our believing that among His deeds was creating us as reasonable beings, with access by our reason to everything implied in the idea of "the laws of nature and of nature's God." While Strauss is careful to say that the Old Testament does not have in it any word for nature, he does emphasize (in part by the epigraphs chosen from the Old Testament for *Natural Right and History*)[7] that the experience of justice and of injustice underlies all human experience. St. Paul declares,

> When Gentiles who have not the law do by nature what the law requires, they are a law to themselves. . . . They show that what the law requires is written on their hearts. (Romans 2:14–15)

This passage parallels Deuteronomy 4, which implies something like natural law, although that concept is not yet explicitly formulated.

From the point of view of the Bible, God's revealed Word and not autonomous human reason is the source of the highest wisdom. But the role of reason—hence of political philosophy or natural right, as distinct from metaphysics—is not thereby negated or even diminished. Consider the following from Strauss's introduction to *The City and Man*:

> It is not sufficient for everyone to obey and to listen to the Divine message of the City of Righteousness, the Faithful City. In order to propagate that message among the heathen, nay, in order to under-

7. The story of Nathan and David (2 Samuel 12) is an example of the human ability to recognize (*contra* Meno) even our own acts of injustice, if our own persons are disguised, and we are able to look upon those acts as a neutral observer. Strauss is telling us that the recognition of natural right does not even depend on the prior discovery of nature.

stand it as clearly and as fully as is humanly possible, one must also consider to what extent man could discern the outlines of that City if left to himself, to the proper exercise of his own powers. But in our age it is much less urgent to show that political philosophy is the indispensable handmaid of theology than to show that political philosophy is the rightful queen of the social sciences . . . : even the highest lawcourt in the land is more likely to defer to the contentions of social science than to the Ten Commandments as the words of the living God.[8]

Strauss here speaks of political philosophy as "the indispensable handmaid of theology." But it is much more urgent, he says, to show that it is "the rightful queen of the social sciences." I would argue that establishing political philosophy as the ruler of the social sciences has become a necessary condition for the very survival in our times of biblical religion and morality.[9] Within the framework of historical modernity, the authority of revelation cannot and ought not to be the ground of political authority. Since the moral teachings of revelation are in great measure (as the Bible itself attests) also the teachings of reason, political philosophy provides authority, within a nonsectarian political constitution, for a moral teaching in agreement with revelation. In our time, revelation has become—as Strauss's chapter on Max Weber makes clear—confounded and confused with "value judgments." In the wake of the transformation of modern philosophy not into wisdom but into nihilism, the Bible itself has been interpreted to mean whatever is in accordance with anyone's strongest passions. The homosexual rights movement, for example, has made great strides in persuading the mainstream churches that the injunction to "love your neighbor" is a divine justification of sodomy and lesbianism. Passionate commitment has become identified—or confused—with revelation. The irrefutability of revelation has been confounded with the alleged undemonstrability of all "value judgments" and

8. *The City of Man* (Chicago: Rand McNally, 1964), p. 1.
9. See Harry V. Jaffa, "Political Philosophy and Honor: The Leo Strauss Dissertation Award," originally published in *Modern Age* 21:4 (Fall 1977): 387–94, and reprinted as the appendix to *How to Think about the American Revolution* (Durham, NC: Carolina Academic Press, 1978). This annual award by the American Political Science Association—ostensibly in honor of Leo Strauss—was established on the initiative of a number of his students. It celebrated the "recognition of political philosophy as one of the important traditions within the discipline"—not as "the rightful queen of the social sciences," but as the equal (perhaps) of public administration, urban government, empirical theory, methodology, etc.

hence is held to be another justification for rejecting all authoritative moral teaching. But deference to the authority of revelation, from the Bible's point of view, is not arbitrary. It is because God is, to repeat, both One and separate that revelation is the necessary means for communicating to man his true place in the universe and his relationship to God. Revelation, although miraculous in its origin and essence, is not subjective; God is an objective reality, and He does not authorize subjective moralities inconsistent with the teachings of unassisted human reason. The idea of authoritative traditions as the ground of human well-being is an idea flexible enough to take into account the defects of fallible human minds as the light of revelation is filtered through them. But the differences among genuine traditions—and traditions based on the Bible often do differ—must not be regarded as a justification for regarding all traditions as merely arbitrary. The idea of natural right and natural law can be seen as the means by which genuine traditions can be distinguished from the many false pretenders to that claim. We cannot suppose that revelation would authorize moralities incompatible with what we know to be naturally right.

It is clear from the foregoing, I believe, that Socratic skepticism and biblical faith stand on the same epistemological foundation. It is impossible to restore the claims of the one without restoring the claims of the other. The transformation of modern philosophy into modern rationalism, and modern rationalism into nihilism, leads to the rejection of all rational standards for human thought or human action. This it does in part because of a spurious resemblance of nihilism to the doctrine of *creatio ex nihilo*, which the Bible itself genuinely and necessarily teaches. Modern nihilism culminates in each person's being invited to create his own moral universe. Nothing inhibits man, seen in the light of the nihilistic dispensation, from himself laying claim to the attributes of God. Faith becomes then the justification equally of anything—or nothing. In this situation, only the refutation of modern rationalism and its mutation into nihilism can restore the possibility of biblical faith in its genuine bearing on human life.

Let me conclude this part of the discussion by observing that the attack on reason and rationalism (and the natural law tradition) that is the hallmark of a certain modern political conservatism is—no less than modern political liberalism—in the service of nihilism. On the surface, this conservatism appears only as a rejection of modern rationalism. It is in fact a vehicle of modern romanticism,

of a preference of the heart over the head. Its preference for the
heart, however, is vindicated by no systematic thought such as has
informed all the great religious traditions of the West, whether it
be the Talmud or the Canon Law, whether it be the *Summa
Theologiae* or the *Guide of the Perplexed*. However decent these conservative Christians or Jews may be, they have no inner defense
against, for example, the demand for recognition of the rightful-
ness of homosexuality and other forms of sexual freedom (so
called). Having rejected the authority of reason, they have literally
no reasons by which to object to whatever the passions may demand
in the name of freedom.

I turn to what in the House of Commons would be called your
"supplementary questions." They are in six paragraphs—the first
being as follows, in your words:

> *You link biblical revelation to faith, law, monotheism, and divine omnipotence.
> Is it the combination (or some combination) of these that is unique to biblical
> revelation? Or is one of them more crucial than others? You emphasize faith,
> but it is not yet clear to us what you mean by the content of faith. To speak of
> the content of faith as the Bible as a whole, as obedient love of God, or as in
> God as the source of the resolution of the very doubts that sustain the philosophic
> way of life, leaves us in the dark about the unique content of biblical faith as
> opposed to pagan religion.*

I believe I have already answered the foregoing. I think it is clear
not only that—but why—faith (accompanied by the "obedient love
of God") can be "the source of the resolution of the very doubts
that sustain the philosophic way of life." Of course, as Strauss says,
it is also true that "man is so built that he can find his satisfaction,
his bliss, in free investigation, in articulating the riddle of being."[10]
Whether one *should* live one's life "articulating the riddle of being"—rather than "resolving" it by faith—remains a question.
While biblical faith may be said to offer an alternative to "free
investigation," human freedom requires only that one recognize
either alternative as consistent with that freedom. Modern rationalism, or the nihilism into which it self-destructs, represents an
abandonment or denial of human freedom.

You speak of "biblical faith as opposed to pagan religion." I
think that in Plato's *Euthyphro* we find a definitive confrontation
between pagan religion and philosophy. The issue is reduced to

10. *Natural Right and History*, p. 75.

either fighting gods or the ideas. (The modern equivalent would be fighting, more commonly, "contending values.") The gods can be made to stop fighting—that is, to provide noncontradictory guidance to human life—only if they are reduced to a role ministerial to the ideas. In Plato (and still more in Aristotle), one can see the philosophers replacing the poets (and/or the Sophists) and the gods of the poets (and/or the Sophists) as the source of a noncontradictory moral instruction. Of course, the philosophers will not rule directly, but through the new breed of Sophists and poets that results from the philosophers' influence on education—or, as in the case of Aristotle, through the gentlemen whose education they will supervise. But the God of the Bible is immune to Plato's critique of paganism, for reasons I have already, I think, made sufficiently clear.

Your second set of "supplementaries" begins as follows:

> You define and distinguish revelation as Jewish law and revelation as Christian faith. Is the uniqueness of biblical revelation found in Christian faith as opposed to Judaic law? If so, does this mean that Judaic law is fundamentally closer to pagan revelation and the ancient city?

What you call "Judaic law" was certainly originally the law of an ancient city. Since all ancient cities (as represented by the beginning of Plato's *Laws*) claimed their laws to be of divine origin, ancient Judaism may be said in that respect to resemble other ancient cities. However, faith in God was the principle underlying and informing every aspect of the laws of Moses; hence, faith as such was never less fundamental to Judaism than to Christianity. In Judaism, however, obedience to the law was always regarded as the basic test of fidelity. Absent this legalistic orientation, Christianity placed more reliance or emphasis on tenets of faith, apart from their consequences for conduct. In its monotheism, ancient Israel was unlike any other ancient city. One effect of this unlikeness was that the Jews did not cease to have God as their God when Israel ceased to be an ancient city, when the Torah was no longer their civil as well as their divine law.

You continue:

> You claim that the theme of Strauss's lifework was the reason/revelation issue, which you seem to distinguish from the theological-political problem, the latter of which you proceed to call the "absolutely novel" problem which was caused by Christianity. You then identify this problem as at the center of Strauss's life

and work, as "the theme of his investigations." Could you clarify what you take
to be the difference of these two issues and how both, if different, could be at
the core of one's work?

I have long thought that two sentences from Strauss's autobiographical preface characterize better than anything else the thrust
and purpose of his lifework.

> It is safer to try to understand the low in the light of the high than
> the high in the light of the low. In doing the latter one necessarily
> distorts the high, whereas in doing the former one does not deprive
> the low of the freedom to reveal itself fully as what it is.[11]

This is writing of classic beauty and simplicity. It embodies Strauss's
quiet rejection of Machiavelli, while admitting—or rather insisting—that the full revelation of the low is something that political
philosophy and especially statesmanship cannot afford to neglect.
As we cannot too often repeat, Strauss never forgot the claims of
revelation, no less than of reason, to be the "high." But a judgment
with respect to these claims was ultimately dependent on speculative reason, which he did not think could in fact render any final
decision. While human freedom requires recognition of the philosophical and biblical alternatives, there is nothing to compel acqui-
escence in one more than the other. Strauss wrote as much at the
end of "Progress or Return?":

> The very life of Western civilization is the life between two codes, a
> fundamental tension. There is therefore no reason inherent in West-
> ern civilization itself, in its fundamental constitution, why it should
> give up life.[12]

I believe that Strauss devoted his life, above all else, to keep Western
civilization from "giving up life." The self-destruction of reason in
the ultimate "wave" of modernity meant abandoning both philosophy and revelation, and affirming the human will as the sole
authority for what had been attributed either to autonomous
reason or to God.

Strauss's articulation of the differences between ancients and

11. "Preface to the English Translation," p. 2.
12. "Progress or Return?" in *The Rebirth of Classical Political Rationalism: An*
Introduction to the Thought of Leo Strauss, ed. Thomas L. Pangle (Chicago:
University of Chicago Press, 1989), p. 270.

moderns I called "practical," rather than "theoretical." The heart of the modern experiment, which had its origins in Machiavelli, was to transcend the differences between the two competing views of the high. "Transcend" may be the wrong word, however, since the human problem was now to be addressed by lowering—not elevating further—the ends of human life. The human problem was to be solved by the conquest of fortune. This conquest, as it turned out, was to be accomplished by science. Science would supply the goods that men wanted most—health, wealth, freedom—without any requirement of virtue, either in their acquisition or in their enjoyment. Science would give men here on earth what most men had hitherto expected only in heaven: the effortless enjoyment of boundless pleasure. Science would replace God. This new God would in the truest sense be a *Demiourgos*, a slave of the people, and not their master. The high would be in the service of the low.

Strauss's rejection of modern principles rested not primarily on the folly of the optimistic assumption that the boundless power promised by science would be man's servant and not his master. Machiavelli's quarrel was seen to be equally with classical political philosophy and with Christianity. He accused them both of "utopianism." What he meant by this, however, was not the difficulty inherent in the achievement of the best regime. This was essentially a straw man in Machiavelli's argument. What Machiavelli really objected to was the tyranny of moral virtue. The subordination of the passions to reason in the economy of human well-being was a doctrine common to both Athens and Jerusalem. Certainly in Aristotle, moral virtue is always subject to prudential reason. As such, it is anything but utopian. Strauss thought that Machiavelli's turning away from moral virtue, as a necessary ingredient of human well-being, was mistaken. The emancipation of the passions of the body from the restraints of reason by the conquest of nature (and fortune) was not a project that could succeed. Taking one's bearings not by what men ought to be but by what they are—or lowering the goals of political life in order to guarantee their actualization—was doomed to fail. It was doomed to failure because of its insufficient attention to, or its ignorance or forgetting of, the ineluctable character of the human soul. The project of subordinating the higher elements of the soul to the lower could only lead to a tyranny greater than anything that had existed hitherto. Machiavellian modernity meant reversing the classics by establishing the primacy of practical over theoretical reason. Science would be in the service of man's estate—but not of man himself. The idea that the passions could furnish more rational goals for human life than reason itself was essentially absurd. What Strauss meant by devoting his "investigations" to the "theological-political problem" was restoring the authority of the moral order common to philosophy and the Bible, and restoring with it the conviction that human life could be well lived only by devotion to the "high." Recognition of what was truly the "high," moreover, would engender modesty and humility, and therewith moderation.

As has been said, the authority of revelation rests on the proposition that the universe is the creation of the One God Who is separate from the universe He created. Because God is separate, reasoning about the universe (going from effects to causes) will not lead to the first cause. The authority of philosophy, or of reason, arises from the perception (as, *e.g.*, affirmed in the first and tenth books of the *Nicomachean Ethics*) that reason is the best or most divine thing in us, and that the way of life devoted to its cultivation is the best way of life for man.

The establishment of Christianity as state religion in the fifth century is understandable in light of the fact that every ancient city had attributed its law to its God. When Rome became the universal city, it was consistent with previous human experience that men should now transfer their loyalty to a universal God. But experience revealed that the universal city was not a city in the sense in which previous cities had been cities. A city *qua* city has to be particular, not universal. Different peoples require different laws adapted to their different characters and circumstances. The homogenization of the different regimes into a single regime can take place only by means of despotism, against which human nature—a God-given human nature—must of necessity rebel. The universal city may, however, be understood in a way that does not contradict nature; it may be understood as the City of God—the city that is the eternal home of man, but not his mortal or terrestrial one. All the citizens of the different mortal or terrestrial cities may become fellow citizens of the City of God without ceasing to be good—and thus different—citizens of their particular regimes in this world. Moreover, the City of God may be understood, within the dispensation of philosophy, as the best regime—the regime that, in speech, is always and everywhere best, although it may not exist in actuality or in deed, anywhere or ever.

Although the establishment of Christianity in the fifth century was understandable, it was nevertheless inconsistent with both reason and revelation. The vitality of Western civilization, of which Strauss spoke, was the vitality arising from "arguments advanced by theologians on behalf of the biblical point of view and by philosophers on behalf of the philosophic point of view."[13] The very idea of religious establishment meant an attempt by political means—that is to say, by practical reason—to resolve theoretical questions on the nature of faith and its relationship to reason. The result was theological despotism.

The essence of modernity, on the other hand, is the parallel attempt to resolve theory on the basis of practice, by asserting that philosophy has been transformed into wisdom—as in the persons of Hitler or Stalin. The earlier attempt led to theological despotism, and the modern effort has led to ideological despotism. Political moderation is rooted in the refusal to resolve the mystery of human life by political means. It is rooted in the recognition of human freedom as grounded in the openness of the human soul to that mystery. It is rooted, as well, in the recognition of a moral order—which understands human freedom not as the mere absence of restraint, but as directed to living a human life in the light of its transcendent ends, whether these are defined by reason or by revelation.

You ask later whether the possibility of revelation is something that can be proved. I believe—with, I think, both Leo Strauss and Thomas Aquinas—that it cannot. Suppose someone had argued once upon a time that airplanes, for example, were impossible. Now, if someone had genuinely proved this to be true, then flying would be a miracle. On the other hand, since we now know that flying is indeed possible, we know that no such proof was ever possible. But at least since Leonardo, men have known that flying is possible. This is to say that, long before they knew how to fly, human beings understood what causes could bring it about that men would actually fly. By this fact, they knew that flying, when it happened, would not be miraculous. The essence of revealed

13. "Progress or Return?" p. 270.

truth—*qua* revealed—is that it comes from a God who, faith tells us, is outside the order of nature, within which unassisted reason alone can overcome ignorance. If we could prove that revelation is possible, then revelation would be like anything else that we might believe we can someday understand even if we have not yet understood it.

A Latitude for Statesmanship?
Strauss on St. Thomas

James V. Schall, S. J.

> A work like Montesquieu's *Spirit of the Laws* is misunderstood if
> one disregards the fact that it is directed against the Thomistic view
> of natural right. Montesquieu tried to recover for statesmanship a lati-
> tude which had been considerably restricted by the Thomistic teaching.
> — Leo Strauss, *Natural Right and History.*[1]

Leo Strauss often spoke of Jerusalem and Athens.[2] He never spoke
of Rome in the same context, never of Jerusalem, Athens, and Rome.
Western civilization, in his view, was fertilized by the dynamic tension between only two, not three, cities. This theoretically unresolvable stress between Jerusalem and Athens was what made this culture unique. Western civilization stood between reason and
revelation. For Strauss, it seemed self-evident that this tension, which
initially arose when the pious Jews encountered the philosophers
Plato and Aristotle, was incapable of intellectual reconciliation but
still it remained the font of its cultural vitality.

The implication of this position, therefore, was that to save this
civilization, the universal civilization, as Strauss rightly called it in
The City and Man,[3] it was necessary to return to the initial contrast
between Jerusalem and Athens. This diversity of approach between
these two cities could not be adulterated by any third strand which
might maintain their mutual insufficiency but therefore their mutual
compatibility. Strauss often spoke eloquently by his silence. Strauss
spent his life opposing that modernity which was characterized by
relativist presuppositions. This relativist modernity had, paradoxically in Strauss's view, medieval roots because medieval theory
claimed, wrongly as it turned out in his view, that the higher tensions could be harmoniously mitigated. This possibility of resolution was what Strauss rejected when he wrote that Montesquieu
was "nearer in spirit to the classics than to Thomas."[4]

---

1. Leo Strauss, *Natural Right and History* (Chicago: University of Chicago Press,
1953), p. 164.
2. Leo Strauss, "Jerusalem and Athens: Some Introductory Reflections," *Commentary* 43 (1967): 43–57.
3. Leo Strauss, *The City and Man* (Chicago: University of Chicago Press, 1964),
p. 3.
4. Strauss *Natural Right and History*, p. 164.

Recently, it has been suggested that perhaps Strauss was a kind of covert atheist or agnostic. All sorts of people, of course, have been suspected of atheism, from Socrates himself to the early Christians. Nietzsche even suggested that God is in fact dead in the hearts of all of us, believers and moderns alike. Speaking in the name of St. Thomas, Father Fortin has argued, to the contrary in the case of Strauss, claiming that Strauss was merely insisting on the same kind of strict logic characteristic of the Angelic Doctor.

> [Shadia B. Drury, *The Political Ideas of Leo Strauss*] objects to Strauss' characterization of philosophy as the embodiment of what *Genesis* calls the knowledge of good and evil, and she is less than comfortable with the view that emphasizes the total suprarationality of the assent of faith. . . . The least that can be said by way of cursory reply is that . . . Strauss's views are close to, if not actually identical with, those of any number of orthodox theologians, beginning with Thomas Aquinas, who insists that the unaided human reason is powerless to establish the possibility, let along the truth, of divine revelation. Thomas will go no further than to say that the highest achievement of natural reason is to prove, not that divine revelation is possible – to administer such a proof would be to deny implicitly the supernatural character of revelation – but that the arguments leveled against it on rational grounds are never such as to compel our assent.[5]

Reason is thus required to protect the mystery of faith. Spirits, even good spirits, therefore, must be tested by the only tool with which we have to test them, with our reason. But reason is not itself a god or, though grounded in the principle of contradiction, an absolute but only an instrument with which to inquire whether such things as gods and absolutes might be possible. Strauss was the first to acknowledge, however, that Christian seminarians were legitimately required, because of the nature of the Christian faith, which included doctrine not just law, to study philosophy in a way not required of the Muslim or Jewish cleric.[6] "Nothing is more revealing," Strauss wrote in what is itself a most revealing observation,

> than the difference between the beginnings of these two most representative works. The first article of Thomas' great *Summa* deals with the question as to whether theology is necessary apart from, and in addition to, the philosophic disciplines: Thomas defends theology be-

5. Ernest Fortin, "Between Lines: Was Leo Strauss a Secret Enemy of Truth?" *Crisis* 7 (December 1989): 25.

6. Leo Strauss, *Persecution and the Art of Writing* (Westport, CT.: Greenwood, 1973), p. 19.

fore the tribunal of philosophy. Maimonides' *Guide*, on the other hand, is especially devoted to the science of the law. . . .[7]

In a sense, as Strauss implicitly admitted, St. Thomas was also a philosopher who could bring theology before the court of philosophy, whereas law, in the Muslim and Jewish sense, cannot ironically stand before this same court. Yet, it seems, that nothing of that which theology can stimulate philosophy to consider is valid as philosophy because of the inciting source in revelation. When philosophy proves that something in revelation is not "contrary to reason," the Thomistic proposition, what philosophy learned by this exercise, in Strauss's view, is not "philosophy." Just why it is not is not quite clear unless of course revelation is not something, even when challenged in its own domain, that must be considered by reason. Strauss's own position wanted to uphold but not rule revelation out of consideration.

In classic times, when the city killed the philosopher, philosophy, at least in Plato's view, fled to the academy. The modern academy seems sometimes rather less hospitable. I myself have argued that Strauss, along with Eric Voegelin, has been the primary reason in the modern academy, at least in political philosophy, why the question of reason and revelation again had to be taken seriously in that forum which had often succumbed to ideology.[8] No doubt, Strauss took this question of reason and revelation more soberly than the modern academy. This concern merely confirms the charges of the followers of Strauss like Allan Bloom about the sorry condition of the contemporary university in which such ultimate questions that concerned Strauss are never really asked.[9] Modern universities do not kill classic philosophers; they just do not let their students know about them.

Strauss's middle name, if it can be so put, almost seems to be "caution." He writes nearly as cryptically as he finds to be the case with the great thinkers, who had to hide their real thoughts for fear

---

7. Leo Strauss, "How to Begin to Study Medieval Philosophy," *The Rebirth of Classical Political Rationalism: An Introduction to the Thought of Leo Strauss*, ed. Thomas L. Pangle (Chicago: University of Chicago Press, 1989), p. 222.

8. James V. Schall, "Revelation, Reason, and Politics: Catholic Reflections on Strauss," *Gregorianum* 62 (1981): #2, 349–66; #3, 467–98; *Reason, Revelation, and the Foundations of Political Philosophy* (Baton Rouge: Louisiana State University Press, 1987).

9. Allan Bloom, *The Closing of the American Mind* (New York: Simon & Schuster, 1987).

of repression or public opinion.[10] Academics and politicians evidently must be tricked or lured or charmed into confronting the highest things. If there is anywhere this caution is most manifest, it is in Strauss's unwillingness, in the light of the academy's contrary hostility, altogether to exclude revelation, at least Jewish revelation, from the issues about which even the philosopher must consider.[11]

Philosophy claims to be a search for a clear knowledge of the whole so that, *a priori*, to exclude the claims of revelation in behalf of the whole would be to exclude a knowledge untested by that discipline, philosophy itself, which claims to be open to *all that is*. Paradoxically, however, as I shall suggest, Strauss's claim for the credibility of Jewish revelation is strangely philosophic, even perhaps covertly Thomistic. One cannot apparently, in Strauss's view, be a philosopher and a theologian. One must choose one vocation or the other. One does not ascend from philosophy to theology, but both remain enclosed in their own worlds which yet are aware of one another. The Thomist notion that a number of positions in revelation, such as the argument for the existence of God, are first and primarily philosophical (so that there is some grounds for a linkage between reason and revelation) finds little sympathy in Strauss.[12]

Strauss thus spoke of the "mutual influence of theology and philosophy" in the sense that one could not, on its own principles, exclude or include the other.[13] Strauss, like St. Thomas, was not an Averroist who held "two truths," one of reason and one of revelation, which could be mutually true and mutually contradictory. Were that possible, there would be two worlds and not one. For St. Thomas, however, grace built on nature, which meant that revelation had something to do with reason. Some writers will, in discussing religion, no doubt argue that the nature of revelation is as such "unreasonable." "Religion" is said to be the substitute for reason in the minds of the ordinary masses who cannot philosophize. Religion

10. Strauss, "Persecution and the Art of Writing," *Persecution*, pp. 22–37.

11. See Thomas L. Pangle, "The Theological-Political Problem," in his Introduction to Leo Strauss, *Studies in Platonic Political Philosophy* (Chicago: University of Chicago Press, 1983), pp. 18–23.

12. See Ralph McInerny, *St. Thomas Aquinas* (Notre Dame: University of Notre Dame Press, 1982), pp. 157–58; James V. Schall, "Aristotle on Friendship," *The Classical Bulletin* 65 (1989): 83–88.

13. Leo Strauss, "On the Mutual Influence of Theology and Philosophy," *Independent Journal of Philosophy* (Vienna) 3 (1979): 111–18.

thus has a political, not a philosophic, origin. Its purpose is not the worship of God but the indirect control of the masses.

An "unreasonable" revelation, however, could not, at least for St. Thomas, be a "revelation" at all, however much God's ways were not our ways. For St. Thomas, the philosopher existed and existed legitimately not in opposition to the ordinary people and their religion but to show that the intelligibility of even faith was in fact intellectually defensible in reason. The philosopher, in other words, had a place precisely as philosopher and not solely as politician. Human intellect is not divine intellect, but both are "intellects" nonetheless. For Strauss, however, there was not any constructive relationship between revelation and reason in the same edifice or any mutual clarification. There were two impregnable fortresses. If revelation had any validity, it could only be to confirm, not confound and stimulate, the philosopher in his ways. The philosopher could be delighted that something in revelation agreed with him, but he could not be cajoled or stimulated to become a better philosopher because of the effect of revelation's propositions on his own thinking. Nothing philosophically "new" or more true could arise from the encounter or if it did, the philosopher could not admit its truth.

Strauss himself did choose to be a philosopher in the sense that his philosophy had to be kept pure from untoward influence of theology, however legitimate it was for rabbis and clerics. The idea that one could be a better philosopher *qua* philosopher because of revelation was apparently alien to him. Strauss certainly did not consider St. Thomas a "better" philosopher because he was a theologian, which is precisely how St. Thomas would have described himself were he asked. In what is perhaps his most well-known treatment of St. Thomas, in *Natural Right and History*, Strauss carefully and persistently excluded any possible "improvement" on Aristotle found in St. Thomas.[14] Strauss did not exclude any more adequate philosophic understanding on the grounds that what St. Thomas said was somehow "unreasonable." Rather, he excluded it on the grounds that St. Thomas was incited in arriving at his philosophic improvements through the exercise of reason on doctrine by biblical revelation. Thomas himself judged that probably only the "wise"

---

14. E. B. F. Midgley at the University of Aberdeen is in the process of completing an important manuscript upon the philosophic integrity of St. Thomas's treatment of Aristotle.

would understand these improvements or more profound conclusions of reason driven by revelation to comprehend their possibility.

Strauss chose to remain within a system that allowed no mutual relation of theology and philosophy. This system was only doubtfully the same one in which Aristotle himself lived.[15] Aristotle of course did not have to deal with revelation as St. Thomas or Strauss himself did. It is by no means certain that Aristotle's system is not one of open progression.[16] It is clear that Strauss's position is, in this sense, closed: "Thomas solves this difficulty by virtually contending that, according to natural reason, the natural end of man is insufficient, or points beyond itself. . . . Thus natural reason itself creates a presumption in favor of the divine law. . . ."[17] Strauss in the name of his philosophy denied any such "presumption."

In his lovely eulogy for Strauss, Harry Jaffa remarked that Strauss had great esteem for St. Thomas particularly because St. Thomas saved Aristotle for posterity.

> Strauss did not believe that the principles of reason and revelation could ever be reduced, one to the other. Nor did he believe in the possibility of a synthesis, since any synthesis would require a higher principle than either, a principle which regulated the combination. Catholic Christianity, which found its highest expression in Thomas Aquinas, attempted such a synthesis. Strauss admired the magnificence of Thomas' efforts, and he saw in them a great humanizing and moderating of Catholic theology. Perhaps the greatest gain from the Thomistic synthesis was that Aristotle, after being a forbidden author, eventually became a recommended one. But only in traditional Judaism did the idea of revelation, and of a tradition undivided and uncompromised by syncretism, find its full expression. And Western civilization at its highest expressed the tension between Greek rationalism and Jewish revelation.[18]

---

15. See on this matter, Frederick D. Wilhelmsen, *Christianity and Political Philosophy* (Athens: University of Georgia Press, 1980), pp. 194–216; Charles N. R. McCoy, "On the Revival of Classical Political Philosophy," *On the Intelligibility of Political Philosophy: Essays of Charles N. R. McCoy*, ed. James V. Schall and John J. Schrems (Washington: The Catholic University of America Press, 1989), pp. 131–49; E. B. F. Midgley, "Concerning the Modernist Subversion of Political Philosophy," *The New Scholasticism* 53 (Spring 1979): 168–90.

16. See E. F. Schumacher, *A Guide for the Perplexed* (New York: Harper Colophon, 1977), pp. 27–39; also James V. Schall, "The Natural Law—Aristotle," *Vera Lex* 7 (1987): 11–12, 26; "Nature and Finality in Aristotle," *Laval théologique et philosophique* 45 (1989): 73–85.

17. Strauss, *Natural Right and History*, p. 164.

18. Harry V. Jaffa, "Leo Strauss: 1899–1973)," *The Conditions of Freedom: Essays in Political Philosophy* (Baltimore: The Johns Hopkins University Press, 1975), p. 6.

That is, in this view, St. Thomas did not contribute anything of himself, but he did make it possible to return to the Greek classics. Catholic theology needed to be moderated and humanized. Philosophy did not need prodding to know what it was about in its own order.

In this sense, no doubt, St. Thomas was of service in the rejection of modernity which is so dear to the heart of the Straussian mind. Yet, to recall the words of Strauss used at the beginning of this essay, St. Thomas himself contributed to this same modernity by depriving statesmanship of a certain needed "latitude," or breadth of option not limited, presumably, by natural law, in dealing with human morals and politics. Indeed, Strauss suggested that modernity was justified in its rejection of the sort of natural law for which St. Thomas stood. St. Thomas's natural law did have "universally obligatory" moral laws binding on all men.[19] Without identifying himself with Machiavelli, Strauss wanted a return to what he felt to be the Aristotelian flexibility due to the undefinability of "extreme actions" which might sometimes, though apparently evil, be in fact "just."[20]

What Strauss had in mind here, of course, was the difficulty of good men in dealing with a scientific, political, or philosophic mind devoted to the pursuit of evil. "Natural right must be mutable," Strauss reflected, "in order to be able to cope with the inventiveness of wickedness."[21] This position was not, I think, an "end-justifies-the-means" view, however much it looks like it. Strauss wanted to return to Aristotle's latitude in order to allow statesmen the freedom to deal with evil without themselves becoming corrupted through their own actions and the policies apt to stem it. Strauss's dance with Machiavelli here is, admittedly, almost too close. This closeness is doubly dangerous if the philosophic positions derived through the stimulus of revelation are in fact correct in their more precise formulations of evil itself. In this case, the Aristotelian "latitude" would in fact open up, albeit tacitly, a kind of Machiavellian "liberty to do evil," which Strauss was at pains to avoid. Strauss never hesitated to acknowledge that Machiavelli was a teacher of evil.[22] But it is also true that the evil results of objectively evil actions continue even

19. Strauss, *Natural Right and History*, p. 163. See Charles N. R. McCoy, *The Structure of Political Thought* (New York: McGraw-Hill, 1963), chaps. 2, 4, and 5.
20. Strauss, *Natural Right and History*, p. 161.
21. *Ibid.*
22. Leo Strauss, *Thoughts on Machiavelli* (Glencoe, IL.: The Free Press, 1958), pp. 11-14.

if the philosopher thinks them good. Such is the danger of Strauss's own latitude.

The mere fact that Strauss, as an apparently self-evident confirmation of his own thesis, cited as an example of extreme influences of theology in philosophy "birth control and divorce" suggests an agreement with modernity on the supposed unreasonableness of such activities. Or at least if their intelligibility is ignored, there is here an appeal to the position of modernity as to the apparent principles of civil peace, which principles would not attend to the validity of the issues as such.[23] What is of interest in both of these instances, however, is the growing evidence of the effects of their practice, evidence itself open to understanding, evidence of where in terms of human life these practices leave individuals, families, and societies. The natural law position would argue with Strauss not on the basis of revelation but of reason. It would not agree with the terms of Strauss's discourse that these positions are due solely to revelation or that their consideration, even if inspired by revelation, makes them thereby irrational.

Indeed, birth control and divorce, whatever their revelational status, have been argued essentially on the grounds of reason. They are not examples of revelation's undue influence on philosophy but of its stimulation on philosophy to define the truth more precisely. While it is perhaps most difficult, as St. Thomas recognized, to accumulate the evidence on such matters so that even the wise could properly consider it, the fact is that there is such evidence, and it is on this, not faith, that the argument is really based. The evidence cannot be thrown out of court simply on the basis of some presumed connection with revelation. Whatever one may make of Strauss's rejection of St. Thomas on these grounds, they are grounds on which Strauss himself could today with some irony point to many Christians as standing with him, but this is an agreement based on modernity, not on a Christian philosophy or on Aristotle for that matter. The fact is, however, that there is evidence for the philosophically reasonable position of the church on both of these issues. Whatever role the faith may have had as a stimulus for thought in arriving at this position, it does not justify excluding the evidence and the argument on which it is based. The point here is not to chide Strauss for citing these two issues for which he would have massive support from even believers, but to suggest that there is an argument, open to debate, which is philosophical and also claims evidence for its validity.

23. Strauss, *Natural Right and History*, p. 164.

Though one can appreciate Strauss's sensitivity to the nature of evil, it remains almost chilling to hear him deny that there are any moral absolutes. In saying this, of course, he is consciously *not* identifying himself with Machiavelli or Hobbes but with Aristotle by proposing a moral way to deal with wickedness, a way that is not bound by merely abstract definitions of evil.[24] Strauss claimed that his position was based on Aristotle, while he thought that St. Thomas went beyond Aristotle and deprived him of his "flexibility" in dealing with wickedness. The counterargument would be that St. Thomas did not go against or contradict Aristotle but drew the more correct conclusions of arguments that were already in the Philosopher. Neither Strauss, nor Aristotle, nor St. Thomas would hold that a clearly evil act ought to be done in any circumstances. They all would agree with Socrates who, given a choice between death and doing evil, chose death because he did not know whether death was evil.

Strauss held this position on moral absolutes also because of a certain understanding of the relation of practical and speculative intellect. Strauss did not intend to deny metaphysics in his emphasis on the priority of political philosophy.[25] Nevertheless, there is something curious about Strauss's discussion that led him to reject St. Thomas and find his way back to Aristotle through Montesquieu via the modernity of Machiavelli, which Strauss saw to be a rejection of something exaggerated in St. Thomas.[26] Strauss separated what in Aristotle seemed to belong to a whole. If there is more of a link between speculative and practical intellect than Strauss would acknowledge, then the position of St. Thomas must be taken more seriously.

Referring obviously to book 10 of Aristotle's *Ethics*, Strauss considered St. Thomas's position that the natural law was "a law knowable to the unassisted human mind, to the human mind which is not assisted by divine revelation."[27] Strauss wanted to reject any hint

24. See Strauss, *Thoughts*, pp. 254–56. See also the discussion of this same point in Jacques Maritain, "The Problem of Means in a Regressive or Barbarous Society," *Man and the State* (Chicago: University of Chicago Press, 1951), pp. 71–79. For a comment on Strauss's view of statesmanship in extreme situations, see James V. Schall, "Christians and War: Playing God," *Hillsdale Review* 7 (Fall 1985): 29–34.
25. See James V. Schall, "The Recovery of Metaphysics," *Divinitas* 23 (1979): 200–219.
26. Strauss, *Natural Right and History*, p. 164.
27. *Ibid*, p. 163.

of natural law in favor of what he called rather natural right, which did not embrace any moral absolutes and thereby restrict unduly the politician in his dealing with "wickedness." Again, it is important to recognize that Strauss probably had no intention in this discussion of defining "liberty" as the freedom to do good or evil for the ends of the state, the worry of Shadia Drury and the teaching of Machiavelli. The effect of Strauss's position may sometimes have been the same in practice, but this result is certainly not what he thought he was bringing about. What he thought he was doing was to explain and to recover Aristotle.

But it is a rather strange Aristotle that is retrieved. Strauss suggested that for Aristotle

> the natural end of man . . . is twofold: moral perfection and intellectual perfection; intellectual perfection is higher in dignity than moral perfection; but intellectual perfection or wisdom, as unassisted wisdom knows it, does not require moral virtue.[28]

Strauss was concerned to emphasize this dimension of Aristotle's thought because he felt that St. Thomas had undermined the notion that "the end of man cannot consist in philosophical investigation, to say nothing of political activity."[29] Strauss saw himself to be by option a philosopher — devoted to "the natural end of man"— so the import of St. Thomas position, in his view, would militate against the integrity of his own choice.

Strauss saw Thomistic natural law as inseparable both from natural theology, which Strauss saw also as unduly influenced by "biblical revelation," but also from "revealed theology." This latter position justified, for Strauss, modernity's reaction to a natural law absorbed by theology.[30] The origin of the fanaticism which Strauss found in modernity, something that particularly concerned Strauss as a Jew, had much to do with this presumed Thomistic overexpectation about what was possible. The secular ideologue, in this view, was an offshoot not so much of Plato but of a natural law claiming more accurate information about human action than was warranted by Aristotle.

This worry about the origins of ideology was the import, I think,

28. *Ibid.*, pp. 163–64.
29. *Ibid.*, p. 164.
30. *Ibid.*, p. 164.

of Strauss's most perceptive remark in *Thoughts on Machiavelli* about the difference between Aristotle and modernity.

> The peculiar difficulty to which Machiavelli's criticism of the Bible is exposed is concentrated in his attempt to replace humility by humanity. He rejects humility because he believes that it lowers the stature of man. But humanity as he understands it implies the desire to prevent man from transcending humanity or to lower man's goal. As for the other elements of his critique of the Bible it would be useless to deny that they were implicit in the teaching of Aristotle and developed by those intransigent Aristotelians who knew the Bible. The Aristotelian God cannot be called just; he does not rule by commanding but only by being the end; his rule consists in knowing, in his knowing himself. Aristotle tacitly denies cognitive value to what is nowadays called religious experience. There is no place for piety in his ethics. According to him, humility is a vice. On the other hand, he identifies the virtue opposed to humility not as humanity but as magnanimity.[31]

Strauss went on to point out that Machiavelli differed from Aristotle. Machiavelli replaced any order of nature or man with chance, a chance that still allowed a kind of practical shrewdness or "prudence," which enabled politics to take full advantage of the fact that no distinction between good and evil existed by nature. As Strauss remarked, "there is no place in (Machiavelli's) cosmology for a ruling mind."[32] It was to this ruling mind that Strauss wanted to return as a philosopher, a position in itself with which St. Thomas would have agreed.

What are we to make of these trenchant observations? First of all, we might wonder whether Aristotle's ethics and politics are as independent from his metaphysics as Strauss seemed to suggest. Certainly, in Aristotle's view, the ethics and the politics were preparatory for leisure, for the activities that required the proper dispositions of the passions before the true end of man might philosophically be seen. It is true that in most existing cities, the order of polity would interfere with the order of philosophy in most living souls. But that was not the purpose or intent of ethics or politics. The discussion of leisure had a proper place in the *Politics*. And when it is suggested that intellectual perfection does not require moral virtue, as Strauss intimated to be the view of Aristotle, certain cautions must be put in place.

One reason we might argue that intellectual excellence does not

---

31. Strauss, *Thoughts*, pp. 207–208.
32. *Ibid.*, p. 221.

depend on prior moral virtue, or that a moral man need not be an intelligent man, or that an intelligent man may be morally vicious, would be the example of Socrates himself. Socrates though nurtured there did not appear in Athens solely as a product of its education, of its ethics and politics. He appeared as guided by his voice, as if to say that philosophical intelligence could, indeed must appear from outside the ordinary paths of moral training. Of course, Socrates maintained that he would have been crushed sooner by the disordered passions of his own city had he allowed himself to be subject to its authority. He remained a private citizen. And certainly Socrates taught the intimate relation of virtue and knowledge.

Aristotle also held in book 10 of *The Ethics*, immediately after he distinguished political happiness and contemplative happiness, that we should not listen to those who tell us to concentrate on human (political) things. But even though the difficulty in dealing with them is great and the rewards are scant, Aristotle held, we should pursue the highest things because they are more worthy. Now, apparently, Strauss wanted to defend the position of the philosopher without endangering the philosopher's concern for "divine" things, which is his proper object. Strauss did not want to so lower our sights that we saw only the less than human, the bestial, as Machiavelli and Hobbes seemed to, as the basis of our ethical and political conduct. But Strauss did not want to incite the philosopher into expecting that perhaps there is something more than philosophy. This possibility was what Strauss rejected in St. Thomas.

In a recent essay on Strauss, Hillel Fradkin assessed Strauss's interest in and relation to the modern Jewish problem, to the question of the place and security of Jews, granted their unhappy experiences with modernity. What is of interest in this analysis for my purposes here is Fradkin's explanation that Strauss sought to find, in his understanding of the modern situation, a way to secure a basis for Judaism that would be protected from the danger implicit both in Zionism, for which Strauss had much sympathy, and in modern liberalism. This liberalism, Strauss held, had lost its grounding in reason and now was a mere "will" philosophy that could not be relied upon in principle. Behind all of this thought was a certain unease with all "orthodoxies" which were subject to irrational movements dangerous to Jewish interests.

> Strauss observed . . . that even to the extent that contemporary circumstances marked the "victory of orthodoxy," the accomplishment of that victory "through the self-destruction of rational philosophy was

not an unmitigated blessing, for it was a victory, not of Jewish orthodoxy, but of any orthodoxy, and Jewish orthodoxy based its claim
to superiority to other religions from the beginning on its superior
rationality (*Deut.* 4:6).[33]

It was this latter remark from *Deuteronomy* that made me wonder
earlier whether Strauss's ultimate defence of Judaism would almost
seem Thomistic, for here we have not the mutual "disinterest" of
theology and philosophy but an effort to show how revelation, on
its own apparent grounds, can appeal to reason.

The text from *Deuteronomy* is as follows: "I have taught you statutes and laws, as the Lord my God commanded me; these you must
duly keep when you enter the land and occupy it. You must observe
them carefully *and thereby you will display your wisdom and understanding
to other peoples.*"[34] Thus, if other peoples who are not Israelites can
learn from this wisdom and understanding, it must be on the basis
of rational thought not of revelation. In a sense, the best regime,
so elusive in political philosophy, and which admittedly has no actual existence, seems to be grounded in revelation but as philosophy. Athens and Jerusalem, in an obscure way, do meet.

Fradkin's summary of Strauss's position is as follows:

> The investigation of the thought of the past permits the emergence
> and elaboration of the view shared by both classical philosophy and
> Biblical revelation that the strictly knowable God will be impersonal
> and the distinctly personal God will be mysterious. It is this agree-
> ment that was the original grounds of the pursuit and fulfillment of
> Western man's religious longings no less than his philosophic eros,
> the plane that is to say of the Torah's claim to be wisdom in the sight
> of the nations, no less than Socrates' claim to have a certain kind of
> human wisdom. Perhaps then it is in this sense that the thought of
> the past may offer some immediate prospect of an alternative Jewish
> response to the contemporary crisis as well as the prospect of the fu-
> ture of the West.[35]

What is to be remarked here is that Aristotle did in fact, though
he did not think it possible, wonder about whether there is friendship in God, whether God was alone and whether we could be

33. Hillel Fradkin, "Leo Strauss and Contemporary Jewish Thought," in *Contemporary Jewish Writers*, 1989, manuscript p. 22, forthcoming, B'nai B'rith. The
citation in text is from Leo Strauss, *Liberalism: Ancient and Modern* (New York: Basic
Books, 1968), p. 256.
34. *Deuteronomy*, 4:6 (italics added).
35. Fradkin, "Leo Strauss and Contemporary Jewish Thought," p. 39.

friends with Him. Likewise, it is well to note that St. Thomas, in dealing with the question Strauss brought up in his discussion of Machiavelli and Aristotle, maintains that God does know all else in knowing Himself. That is to say, it is at least philosophically possible to draw other conclusions about Strauss's understanding of Aristotle's God. These other conclusions would not necessitate that the tensions between the mysterious God and the impersonal God, however defensible in their own way, be drawn from a principle "higher" than both theology and philosophy. They would rather be drawn from a principle deriving from theology or divine wisdom but addressed to philosophy, to a philosophy which has asked its own proper questions and remained perplexed.

In his Introduction to *The City and Man*, there is a remarkable phrase of Strauss's that perhaps serves as a link between the fear of an "orthodoxy" that is not also grounded in reason and the fanaticism that is seen endemic to all orthodoxies. Strauss seems to have held that all orthodoxies, except classical philosophy and Jewish revelation, were irrational. Strauss here wrote in the context of the most successful of modern political philosophies, that this philosophy aspired

> to build on the foundation laid by classical political philosophy but in opposition to the structure erected by classical political philosophy, a society superior in truth and justice to the society toward which the classics aspired. According to the modern project, philosophy or science was no longer to be understood as essentially contemplative and proud but as active and charitable; it was to be of service of man's estate; it was to be cultivated for the sake of human power; it was to enable man to become the master and owner of nature through the intellectual conquest of nature.[36]

Strauss recognized that this latter intellectual conquest, in absence of any grounding of human nature in some non-hypothetical reason which would guarantee its not being otherwise, would turn on man himself and propose to alter man in the name of science. This consequence caused Strauss to realize the importance of refounding modern thought again in the classics.[37]

But the two words that are of especial interest in Strauss's remarks are "charitable and active." These words were to characterize

36. Strauss, *The City and Man*, pp. 3–4.
37. See the conclusion to "What Is Political Philosophy?" in Leo Strauss, *What Is Political Philosophy and Other Studies* (Glencoe, IL.: The Free Press, 1959), p. 55.

not human action as Aristotle understood it or charitable deeds as
the Christians understood them, but precisely a science that had
no moorings in anything other than a liberty presupposed to nothing
but itself, to pure will. The highest of the practical sciences was politics.[38] And politics too was now through Hobbes "scientific" in the
modern sense. This theoretical background would mean that man
could be formed into not what the classical authors meant by virtue
but what the politician meant by his purpose.[39] Speaking of Rousseau, Strauss wrote:

> What you need is not so much formation of character and moral ap-
> peal, as the right kind of institutions, institutions with teeth in them.
> The shift from formation of character to the trust in institutions is
> the characteristic corollary of the belief in the almost infinite mallea-
> bility of man.[40]

This "malleability" not only undermines any stable human nature
or principle of its good, but it leaves the state the freedom to decide
what this good might be once the classical considerations are elimi-
nated. This thesis is the theoretic origin of the fanaticism that Strauss
most worried about.

But the word that is most instructive is the word *charitable*. Both
classic virtue and Christian charity were thought to be habits rooted
in the soul either from natural or supernatural sources. In St.
Thomas, charity was the supernatural virtue that corresponded to
and built upon the Aristotelian virtue of friendship. It implied that
man and God could be friends and that men could love one another
with a divine love. Both of these possibilities were in response to
Aristotle's two penetrating reservations that men could not be friends
with God and that God had no concern for men, that there was,
in other words, no basis for piety in Aristotle's God.

The doctrines of the Trinity and the Incarnation were in fact what
caused Christians to include philosophy in the curriculum of their
clerical and academic studies. Strauss noted that this philosophy
was included.[41] He did not, however, emphasize that the reason for
this inclusion was because of these two doctrines that urged further

38. Strauss, *The City and Man*, p. 1.
39. See Leo Strauss, *The Political Philosophy of Hobbes* (Chicago: University of
Chicago Press, 1963).
40. Strauss, *What Is Political Philosophy?* p. 43.
41. Strauss, *Persecution*, p. 19.

consideration of the Aristotelian God who knew by knowing itself, who moved by love and desire. St. Thomas's "presumption" that theoretical questions did in fact also deal with moral questions was justified if we allow the revelational questions to be really considered by the philosopher.

Strauss implied that the elevation of human expectations due to charity "caused," indirectly at least, a sort of fanaticism in modernity. This fanaticism arose, however, only when the supernatural grounds for this charity were eroded. Replacement was located in the scientific state itself no longer energized by "charity" but by the theory of human malleability with no stable nature. In this analysis, Strauss seemed to imply a remote Christian, not ideologically anti-Christian, origin for modernity in the worst sense of that term as Strauss used it. I would not disagree with the facts of this case as argued.[42] Those Christians and post-Christians who lost their faith or transferred it into this-worldly movements to establish the Kingdom of God on earth, the Enlightenment project, did in fact need a replacement for faith, a replacement generally now known as ideology in various forms. What I would not so easily admit is that the premises of St. Thomas, as he himself argued them, gave rise to this phenomenon. As St. Thomas argued them, in fact, revelation addressed precisely the unsettled questions of classical thought, which would, in themselves without the prod of revelation, remain philosophically unanswered. Merely "returning" to the questions is where Strauss, the philosopher, leaves us. It is a noble place, no doubt, though as incomplete as when originally argued.

Strauss, as I remarked, understood himself to be a philosopher in the tradition of Socrates. "Men are constantly attracted and deluded by two opposite charms," he wrote:

> the charm of competence which is engendered by mathematics and everything akin to mathematics, and the charm of humble awe, which is engendered by meditation on the human soul and its experiences. Philosophy is characterized by the gentle, if firm, refusal to succumb to either charm. It is the highest form of the mating of courage and moderation. In spite of its highness or nobility, it could appear as Sisyphean or ugly, when one contrasts its achievement with its goal. Yet it is necessarily *accompanied, sustained and elevated* by *eros*. It is graced by nature's grace.[43]

42. Eric Voegelin made a similar argument, *Science, Politics, and Gnosticism* (Chicago: Regnery-Gateway, 1968), pp. 99–114.

43. Strauss, *What Is Political Philosophy?* p. 40 (italics added).

Strauss had said that, for Aristotle, there was no necessary connection between moral and intellectual virtue. If philosophy is the "highest form" of courage and moderation, both moral virtues, however, such philosophy is as such still "practical" intellect. If this mating leads to philosophy as such, to metaphysics, then moral virtue seems at least to contribute to its success.

The words "accompany, sustain, and elevate" were the words usually used by St. Thomas to describe how supernatural grace and nature were related. Here Strauss used them rather of philosophic *eros*. He concluded that philosophy is "graced" by nature's grace in order to prevent us either from seeing it as ugly or from being too easily charmed. Yet we can wonder if the charm of supernatural grace needs to be so mightily resisted and whether philosophic *eros*, in all its nobility, does not present questions that at least might legitimately feel such charm.

In *Natural Right and History*, Strauss referred to St. Thomas's use of "the Second Table of the Decalogue."[44] Strauss here, wanting to retain his latitude and flexibility, was worried that the "principles of the moral law," summed up in the Second Table, "suffer no exceptions, unless possibly by divine intervention." Obviously, here, Strauss was referring to Question 100 of the *Prima Secundae* of the *Summa Theologiae* among other places, where St. Thomas discussed this Second Table. And while it is true that St. Thomas "suffers no exceptions" in principles, he seems much more cautious about our understanding of these principles than Strauss would lead us to believe. Indeed, St. Thomas seems rather in agreement with Strauss about the essentials of the matter with this difference that St. Thomas is open enough to allow himself to be instructed in those areas where the philosopher admittedly does not know the answers.

> Certain issues in human acts are so clear that immediately, with a little consideration they are accepted or rejected through common and first principles. Certain ones, however, require much consideration of diverse circumstances, the diligent consideration of which is not for everyone but for the wise, such as to consider the particular conclusions of science does not pertain to all but to only philosophers. Certain other ones however man needs to be assisted by divine instruction (I-II, 100, 1).[45]

---

44. Strauss, *Natural Right and History*, p. 163.
45. Translations from St. Thomas are the author's.

In principle and in light of his rejection of Machiavellianism, I see nothing in Strauss's concern for latitude to deal with particular complexities of action that would prevent him from agreeing with St. Thomas here. Strauss would simply not consider the "divine instruction," so that he would be left with Aristotle, whereas St. Thomas, quite aware of Aristotle, would want to know, in addition, if it was "unreasonable"—a philosophic act — to do what was laid down in revelation.

In conclusion, let me remark that the last footnote in *Thoughts on Machiavelli* cited, among others, St. Thomas, or at least a section of a book attributed to St. Thomas, namely, to Lectio IX of book 7 of the *Commentary on the Politics.* The subject matter footnoted had to do with Machiavelli's use of natural "cataclysms" to mitigate the fear of scientific technology. Strauss bluntly remarked that experience of the "last centuries" has made this hope of Machiavelli "incredible." It is not exactly clear why Strauss referred to this *Commentary* in this context. The text deals with the proper physical location and the proper arrangement, including the defenses, of parts of a city. This may have been the only point.

Strauss, of course, was concerned in his careful treatise to reject the influence of Machiavelli as an "unarmed prophet" about how to teach us how to live. The return to the classics was designed to do this:

> It would seem that the notion of the beneficence of nature or of the primacy of the Good must be restored by being rethought through a return to the fundamental experiences from which it is derived. For while "philosophy must beware of wishing to be edifying," it is of necessity edifying.[46]

This "edification," however, must proceed from the "lowering of sights" attributed to Machiavelli to the elevation of philosophy in Plato and Aristotle. It must not proceed to the further "edification" of St. Thomas, however much the whole, even Strauss's whole, might seem to warrant it.

Marsilius of Padua, one of those "intransigent Aristotelians who knew the Bible," as Strauss called them,[47] was said to have noticed that the one thing Aristotle did not have to deal with was priests,

---

46. Strauss, *Thoughts*, p. 299.
47. *Ibid.*, p. 208.

who were the causes of civil turmoil in modernity due to their alien interests.[48] It is curious that in Lectio IX of book 7 of this *Commentary on the Politics*, to which Strauss referred in his last footnote, there is a treatment of the place of priests in the Aristotelian city, specifically their habitations. The *Commentary* reads:

> Since the multitude of parts of a city is distinguished into priests who are ordained to divine cult, and rulers who care for the order of the city, it is opportune that the habitations of priests and the place of their living together be situated near the sacred temples ordained to the divine cult, in order that the place of their habitation be not remote from the place of the cult to which it is ordained; and because it is expedient for them to have a place of quiet for that contemplation according to which they ought in the highest degree to live with one another.[49]

The politicians need a place near the activity where they also can perform their proper tasks.

"In asserting that man transcends the city, Aristotle agrees with the liberalism of the modern age," Strauss wrote. "Yet he differs from that liberalism in limiting this transcendence only to the highest in man. Man transcends the city only by pursuing true happiness, not by pursuing happiness however understood."[50] St. Thomas, no doubt, would have had little difficulty with such an observation. The only thing he might have asked further would be the latitude to consider, even as a philosopher, all the proposals addressed to man about the nature of this happiness. Aristotle's priests sounded very much like St. Thomas's philosophers. Again in I-II, 100, St. Thomas wrote:

> The community to which the divine law is ordained is that of men to God, either in the present or in the future life. Therefore the divine law proposes precepts of all those things through which man is well ordered in his communication with God. Man, however, is joined to God by his reason, or his mind, in which he is the image of God. And therefore the divine law proposes as precepts all those things through which the reason of man is well ordained. This ordering takes place through the acts of all the virtues; for the intellectual virtues properly ordain the acts of reason in themselves; the moral virtues, on the other

48. See Leo Strauss, "Marsilius of Padua," *History of Political Philosophy*, ed. Leo Strauss and Joseph Cropsey, 2nd ed. (New York: Rand-McNally, 1972), pp. 251–70.
49. Sancti Thomae Aquinatis, *In Octo Libros Politicorum Aristotelis* (Quebeci: Tremblay & Dion, 1940), Lectio IX, Liber VII, p. 378.
50. Strauss, *The City and Man*, p. 49.

hand, properly order the acts of reason concerning the interior passions and external deeds (Art. 2).

The contemplation in a quiet place according to which priests in Aristotle's view ought to live together, the transcendence that comes in the pursuit of true happiness, the precepts according to which man is well ordered in all things—such are the ingredients of a philosophic latitude for a statesmanship needed to "display wisdom and understanding to other peoples," even those for whom divine law addresses questions raised by the political philosophers. St. Thomas has sufficient latitude for the whole of Leo Strauss's political philosophy, a philosophy which allows ultimate questions again to be asked, questions formulated not by modern writers in political philosophy but by Plato and Aristotle.

On The Epistolary Dialogue Between Leo Strauss and Eric Voegelin

Thomas L. Pangle

The philosophic correspondence between Leo Strauss and Eric Voegelin, stretching over thirty years, sheds some helpful light on each of the thinkers' philosophic positions.[1] To be sure, only a few of the letters seem truly significant, and it would of course be a mistake to allow the rather informal and ad hoc remarks in any of the letters to eclipse either theorist's considered and matured published reflections. Moreover, the correspondence peters out in the mid-fifties, after which each thinker arguably made important modifications in his respective outlook. But the letters, or at least the most significant, do not seem careless; the principal issues addressed go to the very heart of things; and if the letters are interpreted with careful attention to the contemporary published, as well as some unpublished, writings, then, it seems to me, the engagement between the two theorists does indeed clarify some of the more obscure but weighty premises and implications of the two philosophic positions.

I take my initial bearings from the most superficial surface. The title of Voegelin's great work is *Order and History*. Strauss for his part produced no single great work, but I believe that remarks in the correspondence (especially Strauss's letter of 25 February 1951) support the view that the book whose title most clearly captures Strauss's overarching theme is *Philosophy and Law*. A comparison of the two titles seems to adumbrate the two thinkers' common ground (concern for order or law), and their decisive parting of the ways: over the estimation of the rank and relation, and hence the very definition, of history and philosophy, especially as correlated to law or lawful order.

THE COMMON GROUND

Both Strauss and Voegelin were abidingly preoccupied with the problematic character of the lawful ordering of human society, un-

---

1. The correspondence has been assembled, transcribed, and translated from the original German by Peter Emberley of Carleton University and Barry Cooper of the University of Calgary in *Faith and Political Philosophy: The Correspondence Between Leo Strauss and Eric Voegelin 1934–1964* (University Park, PA: Penn State Press, 1993), which will contain the complete correspondence in translation along with comments, including a slightly different version of the following essay.

derstood not merely as the effective regulation, but above all as the moral direction and the spiritual ennobling of humanity's necessarily social or political existence. Both theorists were convinced that the modern West, especially in the twentieth century, suffered from an obscuring or distortion of the elemental moral and religious experiences (for example, the full demand of justice linked to divine law and the ordering of the soul, the at once undiminished and unexaggerated confrontation with death, the higher reaches of the bewitchment of love) which lie at the root of humanity's restless quest for truly satisfactory lawful order.

The cause of this obscuring or distortion Strauss and Voegelin both traced, to a large extent, to modern science and philosophy. They saw the minds of the inhabitants of the modern West to be deeply and thoroughly shaped from earliest youth by certain basic presuppositions shared by the various warring versions of modern thought. These presuppositions, regarding morality, divinity, nature, and human nature, are not simply or totally wrong but, insofar as they are correct, they are drastically incomplete, or in need of being integrated into a higher and fuller kind of self-knowledge. Yet these presuppositions are held in such a way as to mask their incompleteness. They thus constitute a veil between the mind and a clear view of itself and its own experiences. Modern science and philosophy permeate and structure the consciousness of contemporary humanity with such uncontested power as to make necessary enormous efforts of liberation if one is to achieve a view of life freed from, that is, freed to question radically, these unquestioned ultimate presuppositions of modernity.

Both Strauss and Voegelin responded to their diagnoses of the moral and philosophic self-estrangement of modern man by turning to amazingly extensive, painstakingly meticulous, and radically unconventional or challengingly unorthodox reinterpretations of past thinkers and texts. They did so in order to disinter the authentic, lost or forgotten or misunderstood, spiritual wellsprings of the West.[2]

2. See Strauss's letter of 13 February 1943: "I share the enthusiasm about your essay [referring to a manuscript submitted to, but eventually not accepted for publication by, *Social Research*—a chapter entitled "The People of God," from Voegelin's unfinished history of ideas]. Above all, I completely agree, that the radical doubt about the dogmas of the last three or four centuries is the beginning of every pursuit of wisdom. The frankness with which you address this preliminary question is praiseworthy in the highest degree. Only I am not sure if you proceed far enough: . . .."; and Voegelin's letter of 12 March 1949, reacting to Strauss's essay "Political

VOEGELIN'S PHILOSOPHY OF HISTORY

We can begin to circumscribe the region of divergence between Strauss and Voegelin when we observe that for Voegelin, the study of history becomes or constitutes a philosophy of history. The history of order reveals the order of history: human experience is given its most important shaping by what is historically changing in humanity's consciousness, and in particular by the changing "myths" or "symbols" by which mankind orders and apprehends and thereby undergoes its most important (moral-religious) experience differently at different epochs. The doctrines and especially the "systems" of the "great" thinkers are misleading in their pretention to permanent or universal validity: "the motivation of ideas through sentiment is covered by the exigencies of immanent logical consistency." In fact, even the greatest thinkers achieve at best only "the approximately rational expression" of "the matrix of sentiments in which they are rooted." Even the very greatest thinkers of a very great era (*e.g.*, Plato and Aristotle) were literally unable to think *decisive* insights or symbolic mediations of a later era (*e.g.*, the Middle Ages); and this is *not* due simply or even chiefly to intervening, miraculous revelations (as thinkers like Maimonides and Thomas Aquinas, who were insufficient, from Voegelin's viewpoint, in their historical consciousness, have claimed). For Voegelin, this is due to the historical process: to the human condition as such, as the condition of a being whose conscious essence unfolds in history.[3]

Philosophy and History," in *Journal of the History of Ideas* 10 (1949), 30–50, and republished in *What Is Political Philosophy?* (Glencoe, IL: The Free Press, 1959): "I have the impression, that we are in very much greater agreement than I first supposed in the direction of our work. Your main thesis—based on Hegel—that historical reflection is a peculiar requirement of modern philosophy seems completely right to me; and I view this motive also as the *raison d'être* of my own historical studies. As I have only engaged myself with these questions in English, allow me my English formulation of the problem: To restore the experiences which have led to the creation of certain concepts and symbols; or: Symbols have become opaque; they must be made luminous again by penetrating to the experiences which they express.—Very fine too is your critique of the attitude that would understand the thinker better than he understood himself; and your insistence that the purpose of historical analysis is the production of meaning, as it was intended by the author."

3. The quotations are from *From Enlightenment to Revolution*, ed. John H. Hallowell (Durham, NC: Duke University Press, 1975), p. 68: as Voegelin makes clear on pp. 116–17, his philosophy of history draws heavily on Schelling (especially *The Philosophy of Mythology and of Revelation*); and, for the political implications of this posture toward history, Bergson (especially *The Two Sources of Morality and Religion*)—who writes "strongly under the influence of Schelling." Yet in *The New Science of*

Voegelin's philosophy of history is not in its intention relativistic. Reflecting upon our experience in the twentieth-century West, viewed in the comparative light of historical research, we can pronounce some epochs, such as our own, to be spiritually more impoverished or threatened than others, such as that of ancient Israel or Greece, or above all, the Augustinian Christian period. An epoch such as ours has lost or is in danger of losing, on account of a pathological historical evolution, the ability to be guided by myths or symbols that play a soberly inspiring rather than a fanatically destructive or spiritually stultifying cultural and personal role. More specifically, historical epochs and epochal transformations may be judged and evaluated by the degree to which they preserve, in a "differentiated" experience, the awareness of the distance between mundane human existence and the realm of the divine, the realm of the ultimate end and purpose of all existence — to which Voegelin refers by using the Greek term *"eschaton."* When correctly experienced and symbolized, the *eschaton* is not immanent in but is instead transcendent of, and thus limiting and humbling of, human action and nonsymbolic thinking. When pathologically or "gnostically" experienced and symbolized, the *eschaton* is falsely believed to be "knowable," and, in the extreme cases, even attainable by human action in history.[4]

Politics: An Introduction (Chicago: University of Chicago Press, 1952), p. 124, Voegelin classifies Schelling along with Hegel as attempting an illegitimate "contemplative gnosis" in "the form of speculative penetration of the mystery of creation and existence"; Voegelin must therefore be confident that his own philosophy of history avoids the overwhelming gravitational pull toward "gnostic" thinking that has tainted the historical philosophies of even his closest predecessors. For the importance, but also an indication of the gravely problematic character, of Bergson, see *The New Science of Politics*, pp. 60–61 on the one hand, and p. 79 on the other. In the correspondence, see especially Voegelin's letter of 9 December 1942, and Strauss's letters of 14 March 1950 and 10 April 1950. For the principles of Voegelin's philosophy of history, see also *The New Science of Politics*, pp. 1 (first sentence), 78–79, 87–89, and especially the statement of principle on p. 125: "the substance of history is to be found on the level of experiences, not on the level of ideas" (in Strauss's annotated copy, this sentence is highlighted in the margin, with cross-references to the discussion of Augustine on pp. 87 and 89).

4. See *The New Science of Politics*, chap. 4, "Gnosticism—The Nature of Modernity," on "the fallacious construction of history which characterizes modernity" (p. 126); and also p. 79: "Theory is bound by history in the sense of differentiating experiences. Since the maximum of differentiation was achieved through Greek philosophy and Christianity, this means concretely that theory is bound to move within the historical horizon of classic and Christian experiences. To recede from the maximum differentiation is theoretical regression . . . ." (Strauss highlights the quoted passages in the margin of his annotated copy.) Cf. Voegelin's letters to Strauss of 2 January 1950, and 4 December 1950; and his letter to Alfred Schuetz

THE CHALLENGE FOR VOEGELIN

For Voegelin, then, philosophy in the highest sense is absorbed by historical philosophizing, guided and limited by faith or faithful intimation through symbolization of moral-religious experience. Now the great question or difficulty this raises is one that may be addressed to all positions resting on faith — but in the case of Voegelin, as we shall see, the question becomes especially pointed because of the unorthodox character of Voegelin's historicized faith. The question is this: what is the precise nature and foundation of the normative standpoint from which Voegelin issues evaluations and judgements — the standpoint from which, indeed, he takes the bearings for his whole existence? The superiority of the Christian conception or symbolization of the soul and its experiences, in general but even more in the specific, historicized, way in which the Christian conception is understood by Voegelin, does not seem to be *demonstrated* by Voegelin. It does not seem to be arrived at by reasoning from premises that are necessary, that are compelling, for all of us, or for all thinking human beings in all times and places. If Voegelin's Christian conception is an undemonstrated or indemonstrable presupposition of faith, what, if anything, makes it persuasive to those who do not share this faith? What ranks it above, or gives it more validity than, other faiths or interpretations of faith, Christian and non-Christian — with their often diametrically opposed moral and political commands? How does this faith provide an answer to the person who takes with utter seriousness the moral duty to do what is right in truth, and not merely what one feels or believes to be right, or what some authority commands as right (without explaining why, or without justifying the right to issue such commands)? This question, and the moral need to answer this question, is manifestly imbedded in what we all call duty. Surely Voegelin intends his Christian conception to be something more than a subjective presupposition of personal faith. But precisely how does Voegelin escape what Strauss refers to (in his letter of 4 June 1951) as "the desert of Kierkegaard's subjectivism"?

---

of 17 September 1943. See also Voegelin's critique of Hannah Arendt's historicism, or loss of a normative conception of nature, in his review of *The Origins of Totalitarianism: Review of Politics* 15 (1953): 68–76, together with Arendt's response, *ibid.*, pp. 76–85.

The Dispute Over the Status of Revelation

These challenges emerge most clearly in the correspondence when Voegelin responds to Strauss's having "quite rightly identified" the "problem of revelation" (along with "that of the Platonic dialogue") as "the cardinal points at which our views probably differ."[5] Strauss had insisted that "there is an essential distinction between the thinking of the Middle Ages based on revelation and the thinking of classical antiquity not based on revelation," and had furthermore insisted on the dual importance of "not obscuring this essential difference in any way":

> First, it is in the interest of revelation, which is by no means merely natural knowledge. Secondly, for the sake of human knowledge, *epistēmē*. You yourself have said that science matters very much to you. For me, it matters a great deal to understand it as such. Its classics are the Greeks, and not the Bible. The classics demonstrated that truly human life is a life dedicated to science, knowledge, and the search for it. Coming from the Bible the *hen anagkaion* [one thing necessary] is something completely different. No justifiable end is served by obscuring this contradiction. . . . You speak of the religious foundation of classical philosophy. I would not do so. . . . One would have to elucidate further which *experiences* of the divine the philosophers recognized as genuine. Plato and Aristotle attained, after all, *demonstrated proof* (*Beweis*: Strauss's italics) of the existence of gods not from experiences and customs but rather from the analysis of motion.

In his response, Voegelin seems to wish to soften somewhat this sharp dichotomy between scientifically demonstrative philosophic knowledge, and knowledge based on revelation; he seems to wish thereby to remove the challenge to faith-based thinking from scientific thinking. He tries to argue that *all* coherent thinking *must* be based in "revelation." He appeals to a revised Augustinian view, according to which "revealed knowledge [*das Offenbarungswissen*]" is "the knowledge of the pre-givens of perception [*das Wissen um die Vorgegebenheiten der Erkenntnis*]." This is what Augustine calls "*sapientia*, closely related to the Aristotelian *nous* as distinguished from *epistēmē*." To these "pre-givens" belong, Voegelin says, the experience of man himself as a being with will. But, "to these pre-givens belongs further the being of God beyond time," in the dimension of "creation" as well as "order and dynamics," and in addition "the human knowledge of this being through 'revelation.'" "Within this knowledge pre-

5. Voegelin's letter of 22 April 1951, responding to Strauss's letter of 25 February 1951.

given by *sapientia* stirs the philosophic *epistēmē*," Voegelin concludes (para. 7). Voegelin can consequently dismiss as "pseudo-problems" (*Scheinproblemen*) all the agonizing issues concerning the ground of valid human consciousness over which Husserl struggled in the *Cartesian Meditations*: "materialism and idealism disappear as philosophical problems when the order of being and its recognition belong to the pre-givens" (para. 8).

Now this is doubtless true — all philosophizing is either rooted in acceptance of God the creator or it becomes otiose or delusionary — *if* the "pre-givens" are indeed as rich as Voegelin claims. For then to deny the creator God is to deny the presuppositions manifestly underlying all human perception. But is there not an enormous difference between the status of the first sort of "pre-given" (man's awareness of himself as knowing and willing), and the rest (knowledge of God the Creator existing beyond time)? The first sort of "pre-given" is indeed given or available to all self-conscious human beings in all times and places; it is manifestly present in every self-conscious thought. Similarly, awareness that our duty to do what is right entails a duty to distinguish between what is truly right and what is merely commanded is present in or can be made intelligible to every reflective moral sense.[6] Knowledge of God the Creator existing beyond time is, to say the least, rather more restricted in its availability and potentially compelling power. A few pages earlier in his letter of 22 April 1951, Voegelin had noted that Hesiod and Homer — two human beings whom no one would characterize as mentally defective or lacking in piety — quite lacked a notion of a transcendent God beyond time (not to mention God the Creator, who was unrecognized by Aristotle as well): "revelation in the Jewish and Christian sense seems possible only when man historically developed a consciousness of his humanness, which clearly separates him from transcendence. Such consciousness is, for example, not yet given in Homer's polytheism or Hesiod's" (para. 6). Furthermore, Voegelin had also earlier in this letter declared that "the essential contents of revealed knowledge [*der wesentliche Inhalt des Offenbarungswissens*]" include not only a self-understanding of man as in contrast to a transcendental being who is understood as the highest reality, but also a knowledge of this transcendental being as one

---

6. Consider Sophocles, *Antigone*, and Genesis 18:23–33; see Strauss's *Natural Right and History* (Chicago: University of Chicago Press, 1953), pp. 79–80 and chap. 3, "The Origin of the Idea of Natural Right."

Thomas L. Pangle
238

"who addresses, and therefore is a person, namely God [*ein Sein, das 'anspricht,' also Person ist, Gott*]" (para. 5). Such a God is of course not the *nous* or the heavenly beings whose existence is acknowledged, because it has been scientifically demonstrated, by Aristotle and Plato's Athenian Stranger. As Voegelin himself puts it (para. 6):

> in Plato and even more clearly in Aristotle, the maximum closure of the soul [*das Maximum der Seelenschliessung*] seems to have been reached, in which the maximally concentrated soul comes to an understanding of transcendent Being, and orients itself "erotically" to such being, *but without finding a response* [my italics]. . . . Decisively in contrast to the Aristotelian *philia*, which is excluded between god and man, is the Thomistic *amicitia* between god and man (para. 6; cf. *The New Science of Politics*, pp. 77–78).

Voegelin here admits that the most important so-called "pre-given knowledge within which the philosophic *epistēmē* stirs" was in fact not given, pre- or post-, to even the wisest and noblest among the Greek philosophers, whose philosophic *epistēmē* or science, and scientific conviction regarding the divine, was therefore completely independent of any such presuppositions.

Only that minority of human beings who share Voegelin's faith will share what he calls "the pre-givens." This minority shrinks, the danger of subjectivism in Voegelin's position becomes greater, when one notes, as Strauss insists on doing in his renewed challenge in a letter of 4 June 1951, that Voegelin does not himself seem to follow faithfully Augustine and Thomas Aquinas, that is, the twin pillars of the Christian tradition. In crucial respects, Strauss insists, his own philosophic position is closer to those pillars.

In the first place, Strauss observes, the conception of the order of historical experiences of the soul that Voegelin sketches in his letter and elaborates in his great work, the conception leading from Homeric polytheism through Platonic "maximum closure of the soul" to Christianity, is drawn not from Augustine or any other traditional Christian authority but is strictly "Voegelinian." This modern historical philosophy does not supplement but in fact supplants the Augustinian historical teaching, which was a teaching about the history of the *cosmos*. "Now is there no problem," Strauss writes in his letter of 4 June, "in your quietly replacing this teaching on the cosmos with a modern view of history (ascent from polytheism to monotheism and the like)?"

In the second place, while appeal to faith means an appeal to divine guidance, this divine guidance is known only through the formulations uttered or written by men, who *believe* they have such guidance. How do we judge which of them really do, and, of these, which have formulated their experiences properly? Which formulations of the divine commandments are valid and legitimate, which distorted, or delusionary, and hence invalid? Either one is unable to judge between claims, "and then," Strauss warns, "one winds up in the desert of Kierkegaard's subjectivism," or

> the human formulation is *not* radically problematic — that is to say there are *criteria* that permit a distinction *between* illegitimate (heretical) and legitimate formulations. If I understand you correctly, the latter is your view. On the basis of the same you accept Christian dogma. I do not know, however, if you do this in the Catholic sense. In case you did this, we would easily come to an understanding. Because my distinction between revelation and human knowledge to which you object is in harmony with the Catholic teaching. But I do not believe that you accept the Catholic teaching. Here a considerable difficulty could result, from your getting rid of the principle of tradition (in distinction from the principle of scripture), and Catholicism is most consistent in this respect.[7]

But the deepest and broadest question, Strauss goes on to indicate in his letter of 4 June, is not how Voegelin legitimates his version of Christianity over and against others, and particularly traditional Catholicism. The deepest and broadest question is one that Strauss, on behalf of philosophy, addresses to Jew and Christian alike:

> It is with some reluctance that I as a non-Christian venture on this intra-Christian problem. But I can do so precisely because I can make it plain to myself that the problem, and the whole problem area, is, exactly, a Christian one, and, through an appropriate extension, also a Jewish one; but then precisely it is not a "universal-human" one.

---

7. See *From Enlightenment to Revolution*, p. 23: "man in search of authority cannot find it in the Church"; in the context, esp. pp. 24–25, Voegelin shows his clear awareness of the traditional, Thomistic dichotomy between "natural reason" and "faith" or revelation. See also the characterization of "the essence of Christianity" as "uncertainty," in *The New Science of Politics*, p. 122. For a striking illustration of the distance between Voegelin's perspective on the problems and the perspective of St. Ambrose and St. Augustine — which in this crucial respect seems closer to that of Strauss, see the following remark in *The New Science of Politics*, p. 87: "It is curious that both St. Ambrose and St. Augustine, while bitterly engaged in the struggle for the existential representation of Christianity, should have been almost completely blind to the nature of the issue. [to them] Nothing seemed to be at stake but the truth of Christianity versus the untruth of paganism." (This passage is highlighted in the margin of Strauss's annotated copy.)

240 *Thomas L. Pangle*

That means that it presupposes a *specific* faith, which philosophy as philosophy does not and cannot do. Here and here alone it seems to me lies the divergence between us. . . .

The real issue is how any faith-grounded position establishes its *morally* as well as intellectually binding necessity in the face of philosophy which does not rest on faith or revelation but grounds all its beliefs, including its beliefs in justice and nobility or virtue, *and* its beliefs in divinity, on demonstrative knowledge that starts from truly self-evident premises that must be granted by all thinking men (*e.g.*, the existence of oneself as thinking and willing, the duty to do what is truly right, the visible motions, causality). The supreme version of such a philosophic position, Strauss never tires of insisting, is the Platonic-Socratic-Aristotelian.

THE DISPUTE OVER THE MEANING, AND VALIDITY, OF PLATONIC RATIONALIST PHILOSOPHY

In the same few letters on which we have just been focusing, Voegelin and Strauss join issue also over the interpretation of Platonic-Socratic-Aristotelian philosophy. They begin from a very considerable range of agreement, often in opposition to all conventionally respectable contemporary approaches to the Platonic dialogues. Above all, both see a necessity for distinguishing between a public, "exoteric," political purpose or intention of the dialogues. and a partly hidden, private, "erotic," and "esoteric" intention. In Voegelin's words, which I believe Strauss largely endorses,

the dialogue is no longer a political cult like the Aeschylean tragedy, but instead becomes an exoteric work of literature [*exoterisches Literaturwerke*] intended for every private person who may wish to listen. . . . When the conversation is carried on with success — in the Socratic-Platonic circle — then a further motive comes to light: the formation of the community through eros. This is the point that the members of the Stefan Georg Circle saw clearly. To see the image of the beautiful-good man (the *kalosk'agathos*) in the other, to awaken it and draw it out (complicated by the mystery, that the image in the other is one's own image) is possible only through the eroticism of conversation. . . . what is involved in his philosophizing is not a "doctrine," but instead a dialogic awakening through the living word. (on the esoteric details of this awakening [*zur Esoterik dieser Erweckung*], it would be necessary to draw from the less-known *Theages*). When this process is extended over the community of the spoken word, then the literary form of the dialogue (particularly, the factually resultless dialogue) seems to be again appropriate.[8]

Strauss responds (in his letter of 4 June 1951): "You are quite right: Georg understood more of Plato than did Wilamowitz, Jaeger, and the whole gang." But, Strauss asks, "was this not a consequence of the fact that he did not think in Biblical or secularized-Biblical concepts?" Strauss goes on to put the disagreement in a nutshell:

> Said in one sentence — I believe that philosophy in the Platonic sense is possible and necessary — you believe that philosophy understood in this sense was made obsolete by revelation. God knows who is right. But: insofar as it concerns the interpretation of *Plato*, it appears one must, before criticizing Plato, understand Plato in the sense in which *he* wanted. And this was, from the first and to the last, philosophy. Only here can the key to the dialogue be found.
>
> Naturally, I do not say that someone who thinks in biblical concepts cannot understand Plato. I only say that one cannot understand Plato, if, in the undertaking of Platonic studies, one thinks in biblical concepts. In this sense the biblical question is to be separated from the philosophic one.

What Strauss is objecting to here is the tendency he finds in Voegelin to try to disarm and hence avoid the challenge from Plato by interpreting Plato as fundamentally a "religious" thinker who, because he lived in a pre-Christian epoch, could find no satisfactory response to his "religious" longings or experiences. As Strauss had stressed in his letter of 25 February 1951, there is not even a word in ancient Greek for "religion" or "religious experience."

Voegelin's critical posture toward Plato and Aristotle, and the problem in that posture, emerges most clearly in his letter of 9 De-

---

8. Voegelin's letter of 22 April 1951, secs. 3 and 7 of Plato discussion. It is especially striking to observe that Voegelin and Strauss agree on the importance of the *Theages* (and its indications about the "esoteric" dimensions of the "erotic" in Plato), since the *Theages* is a dialogue which contemporary, conventionally respectable scholarship rejects as spurious (the dialogue was never questioned in antiquity, and was in fact regarded as perhaps the best introduction to the Platonic corpus as a whole: see Albinus's *Isagogē* [*Introduction to Plato*], sec. 6, and Diogenes Laertius, *Lives of the Eminent Philosophers*, III 62). For Strauss's understanding of the importance of the *Theages*, see his *Studies in Platonic Political Philosophy* (Chicago: University of Chicago Press), pp. 46–47. For Voegelin's praise of *Persecution and the Art of Writing* (Glencoe, IL: The Free Press, 1952) see his letter of 5 August 1952; for his approval of Strauss's interpretation of Locke, ascribing to Locke a covert teaching, see letter of 15 April 1953; for Voegelin's ascription of "esotericism" to Voltaire, see *From Enlightenment to Revolution*, pp. 29–30.

cember 1942. "At the center of Platonic *political* thinking," Voegelin finds "the fundamental experiences, which are tied together with the person and death of Socrates—catharsis through consciousness of death and the enthusiasm of eros both pave the way for the right ordering of the soul (*Dikē* [Justice])." Voegelin then adds that "the *theoretical* political-ethical achievement seems secondary to these fundamental experiences." But is this how it seems to *Plato*, or his *Socrates*? Does not Plato or his Socrates argue that the theoretical achievement in fact completes experience, or makes it truly human? That prior to this achievement life and life-experience is cave-like? "The unexamined life is not worth living for a human being" (*Apology* 38a). Voegelin goes on to indicate that his perspective on Plato decisively breaks with Plato's own self-understanding: I understand the theoretical-scientific achievement of Plato as founded in myth"; but "Plato orients his idea of science to the non-mythical, person-peripheral sphere of logic, mathematics, and dialectic." According to Voegelin, Plato thereby involves himself in "the problem of scientism"; Plato is at best guilty of a "neglect" that taints his whole theory of ideas; Plato surely sets in motion the scientistic distortion of the fundamental experiences, which can only properly be apprehended by the personal, the historically subjective, the mythic and symbolic:

> The problem of scientism in the science of man as spiritual being appears to me to have its roots in the fact that the idea of science that is oriented to the model of person-peripheral areas is transferred to the subject fields that have to substantiate their scientific meaning in the mythical order of the soul (in the case of Plato it has less to do with a transfer than with a neglect of differentiation; out of this problem then arises the difficulty, that the "idea" of a triangle can be a biological genus or that of the Good).

Aristotle's situation seems even worse, for he has lost "existential participation in the myth." As a result, he falls into the delusion that "the completely scientific-theoretical treatment of the political [is] possible." Yet Voegelin seems to retract or qualify this on the next page, where he suggests that it is a "misunderstanding," born of the Renaissance, to suppose that the Greek thinkers ever intended a universal political science: "precisely from the Hellenic position a universal political science is radically impossible." Instead, it is "Christianity and historical consciousness" that lead to the "universalization of the image of man," and "that is the decisive reason for the superiority of the Christian anthropology over the Hellenic."

If I understand Voegelin aright, he suggests that Christianity achieves a "universal" image of man which is undistorting because it is a "differentiated" image of all men as distinct and unique individuals, with diverse sorts of symbolic access to the divine. The political reflection of this image would be some version of Bergson's mystically inspired "open society." I cannot help wondering how this interpretation of Christianity avoids becoming so open-ended or indiscriminating and formal as to lose all decisive content. In any case, it would appear that Plato and Aristotle are charged with profound confusion: on the one hand, they introduced the methods of logic, mathematics, and dialectic into the study of the fundamental human experiences, thereby beginning the obscuring of those experiences — which can be apprehended only through historically changing myths and symbols, interpreted by various individuals in more or less kindred but always distinct ways; and, at the same time, they failed to grasp the true, if rather formalistic or vague, spiritual universality of mankind.

Strauss's criticism of Voegelin's interpretation of Plato is more than a dispute over the meaning of the dialogues. It is at the same time Strauss's intransigent defense of the propriety, consistency, and absolute moral necessity of the Platonic-Aristotelian use of universalizable logic and dialectic, inspired in some crucial degree by the model of mathematical knowledge, as *the* key to the fundamental human experiences. To see the implications, or what is at stake, we need to recognize that the return to the fundamental experiences which Strauss seeks is of a different kind from the return sought by Voegelin, since Strauss sees those experiences differently. The difference is due ultimately to the fact that Strauss insists on the sovereign importance of one specific experience which he contends that Voegelin fails to make room for or admit. Voegelin does not do justice to the experience of doubt: not the "feeling" or "sentiment" of doubt; not guilty doubt ("doubting Thomas"); but the erotic doubt of the scientist or philosopher such as that young Socrates who knew something about the criteria of validity or clarity, and whose soul was electrified by the recognition or admission of his overwhelming *certainty* that he did *not* know the answer to certain specific moral and human questions on which his whole life depended.[9]

9. On p. 122 of *The New Science of Politics*, Voegelin asserts that "uncertainty is the essence of Christianity." The impressively eloquent description of the "uncertainty" he has in mind indicates how far it is from Socratic doubt, or how much

It is this experience, in its compelling, if forgotten and obscured, necessity—it is this experience and all the wonderful consequences that follow in its train—to which Strauss returns and seeks to help others return. Strauss does seek a return to the experiences Voegelin mentions—but in their full, that is, problematic, troubling, questionable character: "the question concerns the *beginning*; clarity about the fundamental questions and how they should be approached" (letter of 9 May 1943). For the fundamental experiences Voegelin speaks of (justice, love, mortality) are not only ambiguous but *contradictory*. Their contradictoriness arises above all from the recognition that the *opinions* which are inseparable from—indeed lie at the heart of—the *meaning* of the experiences, the opinions reflected in the myths and symbols and commandments that loom as authoritative, *contradict* one another. The experience of justice, for example, as an experience of contradictory commands or laws, and, behind those commands or laws, of contradictory conceptions of the right society and ordering of the soul, compels the question, "What is Justice?"—"What is the best regime?"

One might go so far as to say that Strauss seeks to return to precisely that Socratic moment in experience which Voegelin seems to wish to avoid or blur: the moment where one must *finally justify* to one's conscience or heart a fundamental choice between two contradictory, authoritative or compelling, interpretations and two contradictory moral laws or commandments entailed in those interpretations (the moment when, for example, one must take a stand toward the commandment that prohibits one from asking, "*quid sit deus?*").[10]

---

the uncertainty presupposes faith: "The life of the soul in openness toward God, the waiting, the periods of aridity and dullness, guilt and despondency, contrition and repentance, forsakenness and hope against hope, the silent stirrings of love and grace, trembling on the verge of a certainty which if gained is lost." There is no word for "doubt" in the Old Testament; as for the New Testament, see especially Matthew 14:31, 21:21, and 28:17; Mark 11:23; Acts 10:20 and 11:12; Romans 4:20 and 14:23. It is illuminating to juxtapose these passages with the exhortation of Plato's Athenian Stranger, speaking as lawgiver, to the young atheist (Plato *Laws* 888a-d): "Lad, you are young, ... If you should be persuaded by me, you'll wait until after you have a doctrine about these matters that is as clear as it can be, and meanwhile you'll investigate (*anaskopeō*) whether things are as we say or are otherwise, and you will inquire from others, and especially from the lawgiver. During this time you would not dare to do anything impious . . .." Consider in this light Strauss's description of the "younger ones'" reaction to his Walgreen lectures on natural right: letter of 10 December 1950.

10. Compare Strauss's *Spinoza's Critique of Religion* (New York: Schocken Books, 1965), pp. 193ff.

This experience, of the contradictory character of reality as it manifests itself in our speech or opinion, that is, in our only intelligible beginning point for the comprehension of reality, at the morally and humanly most serious moment of our existence, is what compels the beginning of rigorously logical, dialectical analysis of this and all fundamental opinions or experiences. This rigorously logical analysis, as a dialectical analysis, as an analysis that proceeds through Socratic dialogue or conversation, cannot of course copy, but it is surely inspired in part by, the procedure of the undialectical arts and especially of mathematics.[11] For it is in mathematics that we find the most undeniable and readily available experience of clarity and universalizability; it is there that we find or experience what is, for Plato and Strauss at least, a priceless model of clarity and universalizability—a model of what *epistēmē* can and ought to be. If or insofar as our knowledge falls short of this model, we have matter for grave reflection. This, I believe, is why Strauss states in his letter of 11 October 1943 that he assigns a "much more serious and crucial meaning" than does Voegelin to "demonstrations of the existence of God."

Strauss is well aware that the life of most, perhaps all, men who are not truly philosophic in some degree is a life that tries to avoid or seek refuge from the initially painful confrontation with the fundamental problems. But he addresses Voegelin as one who can be brought to recognize the inescapability of the questions. In the course of a striking criticism of Voegelin's employment of the term "existential," Strauss writes (letter of 17 December 1949):

> *If* one wants to use Kierkegaardian expression, one has to say that
> for Socrates-Plato, "existential" and "theoretical" are the same: insofar

11. Cf. Strauss's "Mutual Influence of Theology and Philosophy," *Independent Journal of Philosophy* 3 (1979): 112: "[The classical philosophers'] quest for the beginnings proceeds through sense perception, reasoning, and what they called *noesis*, which is literally translated by "understanding" or "intellect," and which we can perhaps translate a little bit more cautiously by "awareness," an awareness with the mind's eye as distinguished from sensible awareness. But while this awareness has certainly its biblical equivalent and even its mystical equivalent, this equivalent in the philosophic context is never divorced from sense perception and reasoning based on sense perception. In other words, philosophy never becomes oblivious of its kinship with the arts and crafts, with the knowledge used by the artisan and with this humble but solid kind of knowledge." For a most illuminating treatment of Strauss's understanding of the meaning of Socratic "dialectic," see Christopher Bruell, "Strauss on Xenophon's Socrates," *Political Science Reviewer* 14 (Fall 1984): 263–318.

as I am serious and there are questions, I look for *the* "objective" truth. The sophist is a man to whom the truth does not matter — but in this sense all men except for the *gnēsios philosophountes* [the ones genuinely philosophizing — see *Republic* 473d, and cf. *Phaedo* 66b] are sophists, especially the *polis* as *polis* (and not only the decadent ones). The passion for *knowledge* [*Erkenntnis*] that moves the Platonic dialogue, this highest *mania*, cannot be understood within Kierkegaard's concept of "*Existenz*," and [the attempt to do so] must be discarded as a radical illusion. This *mania*, from which Faust himself turns away: [is] in opposition to the creature in Paradise, on the Islands of Blessed, or to the painstaking researches of Goethe himself.

The "passion for knowledge" of how we *ought* to live, and hence of who or what we are as moral beings, seems to be understood by Strauss not only as a kind of burning, inescapable thirst, but also as a reaching out for what is intrinsically attractive or lovable. Philosophy, he says in his letter of 11 November 1947, must be distinguished from art or poetry, "philosophy meaning *the* quest for *the* truth (a quest that, for everyone who understands what that means, is an erotic affair), and poetry meaning something else, that is, at best the quest for a particular kind of truth." This may be the crucial difference between Platonic philosophizing as Strauss understands it and the form of philosophy he finds so beautifully expressed in Lucretius.[12] At the very least, I suspect Strauss would say, we find in Plato to a greater or more successful degree than we find in Lucretius an argument that demonstrates, *dialectically* and hence conclusively, the *naturalness* of the ascent from love or eros, as we experience it primarily, to love or eros for the truth as such: we find in the conversations presented in dialogues like the *Phaedrus*, *Lysis*, and *Symposium* the irresistible charm or appeal (for those who will listen to and follow Socrates' dialectical arguments) of that ascent, and hence the irresistible charm or appeal of the love of truth seen not merely as the consolation, but as a kind of completion of our primary natural longings. Despite all the towering barriers to the attainment of happiness, that attainment is possible and natural: the theoretical life is the life toward which our soul is naturally, essentially directed. As Strauss puts it in his letter of 25 February 1951: "the classics *demonstrated* that truly human life is a life dedicated to science, knowledge, and the search for it" (my italics). One small but significant sign of the naturalness of philosophy is the natural-

---

12. Discussed in Strauss's letter of 15 April 1949.

ness of laughter. Voegelin characteristically stresses the link between the Platonic dialogues and tragedy, even Aeschylean tragedy; he goes so far as to interpret the *Apology* as "the tragedy of Socrates."[13] Strauss responds (letter of 4 June 1951) by noting, "you are silent about comedy, even though the dialogue just spoken about [Strauss had just spoken about the *Laws*] is a synthesis of tragedy and comedy;" Strauss proceeds to clarify the link between the Platonic dialogue and comedy: "On the basis of known statements of Plato one might say that tragedy and *polis* belong together — correspondingly comedy and doubt about the *polis* belong together. From the standpoint of the philosophers the decay of the *polis* is not simply the worst thing." Laughter may be crude, but it may also be very fine; at its finest, laughter is the explosion of our natural pleasure at the sudden insight that liberates. Laughter of course marks only the starting points, not the core, of the philosophic experience, which moves beyond the moments of liberation, and comes to be animated by a more serene kind of passion. But tears, or a "tragic sense of life," is certainly alien to the philosophic experience as portrayed in the life of Socrates.

This is not to say that tragedy, tears, and a tragic sense of life are unnatural. In Strauss's understanding of Plato and Aristotle, tragedy belongs to the city or to political life, and man is by nature a political animal. In other words, man is not by nature simply or immediately or easily philosophic, because man's nature is dual, and the duality is to some extent a tension. The duality is traceable ultimately to the body, without which we could not think (sense perception) but which is not inclined to thinking: see above all Aristotle *Nicomachean Ethics* 1154b22-35. The city or political society attempts to mediate between the two poles of human nature, body and *nous* — animal and divine. But this mediation is of only limited success at best: the regime in the *Republic* demonstrates the limits by trying to force them. Voegelin, in Strauss's view, takes too unambiguously the proposition on which the conversation in the *Republic* is based, namely that there is a strict correlation between types of soul and types of society.[14] The true teaching at the heart of the *Republic* is

13. Voegelin's letter of 22 April 1951, sec. 1 of Plato discussion; see also *The New Science of Politics*, pp. 76-77.
14. Voegelin's letter of 22 April 1951, sec. 2 of Plato discussion; see also *The New Science of Politics*, pp. 61-66.

an analysis of this proposition, and more broadly an analysis of the meaning of justice, which demonstrates dialectically that there is no empirical or possible political order that correlates with the philosophic soul. This same teaching is presented in a different way, on the basis of a more direct analysis of law, in the *Laws*, to which Strauss appeals for a vivid indication of the problem in Voegelin's thesis:

> You say that the order of the soul is a properly functioning conversational community. . . . [and] the proper order of the soul corresponds to the proper order of the *polis*. Can one call the proper order of the *Polis* (in Plato's *Laws*) a *conversation*? Here [in the *polis* established in the *Laws*] exist domination by command and legend, but precisely no conversation, which as such is based on the fiction or the reality of *equality*. There is no Socratic dialogue in the Platonic sense [in the city established in the *Laws*]. (Letter of 4 June 1951)

This teaching entails very large consequences. To begin with, it means that the philosopher is never at home in any political order. But therefore he is far more independent than he would otherwise be of every political order, and in particular of his own "historical situation," or the political order that surrounds him (hence Plato and Aristotle were far more independent of the *polis* than Voegelin perceives). What is more, it follows that Voegelin, in Strauss's view, exaggerates the degree to which Plato and Socrates are concerned with "the restoration of public order"; he exaggerates the degree to which they are hopeful about such restoration, and hence the degree to which they are disappointed and saddened or filled with a tragic sense at the spectacle of the decay of the *polis*. The political hopes and goals of Platonic philosophizing as Strauss conceives that philosophizing are much more sober and modest than appears in Voegelin's interpretation. By the same token, in Strauss's view Voegelin exaggerates the degree to which the Socratic dialogue, as a "weapon for the restoration of public order," depends, if it is to avoid becoming "a meaningless undertaking," on "the judgment of the dead" by an "otherworldly leader of the dialogue" who "has healing and punishing sanctions at his disposal." Strauss certainly does agree with Voegelin when the latter says that "the problem of the Platonic myth" has "a close connection to the question of revelation." To the degree to which the Platonic enterprise were a political enterprise, which depended on an otherworldly judgment in order to avoid becoming "meaningless," Voegelin would be right in his claim that Plato needs what he has not yet found, "the experience of a prophetic address from God."[15]

But for Plato and Aristotle as Strauss reads them, there is a fundamental disjunction between theory or the theoretical life and practice or the political life. The moral virtues, which enrich and adorn the life of action, are not the same as the intellectual virtues of the philosophic life; they are not even, strictly speaking, deducible from the philosophic virtues. Still, they are dependent on those philosophic virtues, and most obviously in the following way. The moral virtues are a product of common sense, which is rooted in the habits instilled by a decent upbringing. The practice of these moral virtues does not require knowledge of their foundations. But moral virtue, precisely because it is a matter of action and habit and practical wisdom rather than speculative inquiry, is threatened by challenges or questions that arise from such inquiry. Philosophy, which necessarily traffics in this kind of inquiry, is therefore under an obligation to protect the moral sphere from the possible, erroneously disturbing consequences of theorizing: philosophy does this by providing a quasi-theoretical defense of the moral virtues, such as will to some extent calm the waters philosophy inevitably has a hand in troubling. At the same time, the political philosopher, having listened with painstaking care to the most thoughtful opinions of the "most serious" practical men, brings an order, clarity, and awareness to the moral life that it would otherwise lack. The political philosopher even opens the moral man to the higher philosophic virtues — but in such a way as will do the least damage to the integrity of the moral virtues as they are known to and experienced by men of action. The supreme example of this activity of the political philosopher is Aristotle's *Nicomachean Ethics*, which is explicitly indebted to Plato's *Laws*.

From this perspective, the modern attempt — from which Voegelin does not seem entirely to depart — to break down the distinction between theory and practice, to provide a philosophical ethics for the direct guidance of moral and political life, or to make practice an autonomous realm without any dependence whatsoever on theoretical defense, is a fundamental misstep. Strauss indicates that he suspects this to be the fundamental mistake of modernity altogether. To quote again from Strauss's criticism of Voegelin's employment of the concept "existential" (letter of 14 March 1950):

15. Voegelin's letter of 22 April 1951, secs 4–6 and 10 of Plato discussion.

The closest classical equivalent of "existential" is "practical" insofar as one understands "practical" in contradistinction to "theoretical." Existentialist philosophy will perhaps appear at some time in the future as the paradoxical effort to lead the thought of the praxis of the practical to its, in my mind, absurd last consequences. Under these conditions praxis ceases indeed to be actually praxis and transforms itself into "existence." If I am not totally mistaken, the root of all modern darkness from the 17th century on is obscuring of the difference between theory and praxis, an obscuring that first leads to a reduction of praxis to theory (this is the meaning of so-called rationalism) and then, in retaliation, to the rejection of theory in the name of a praxis that is no longer intelligible as praxis.

The Challenge for Strauss

In contrast to Voegelin's faith-inspired historical philosophizing or philosophy of history, we find Strauss taking an intransigent stand for philosophy as rigorous science. Strauss does recognize the need, in our peculiarly alienated epoch, for the blazing of a new trail up to this original level of philosophizing. For Strauss, the study of the history of the West, and especially the study of the history of Western thought, is a temporary means — "a desperate remedy for a desperate situation"— to the recovery of a standpoint from which can be renewed an "ahistorical" philosophizing, in the sense intended but not entirely achieved by Husserl and achieved, at least in the decisive foundational sense, by Plato and Aristotle and their greatest medieval students (the *falasifa*, especially Farabi and Maimonides).[16] Despite

16. See Strauss's *Persecution and the Art of Writing*, p. 154; see also the context, for a remarkable statement of Strauss's understanding of the "historical situation" of thought in our epoch. Cf. Strauss's letter of 10 December 1950. As Strauss repeatedly stresses, when these thinkers (Plato, Aristotle, Maimonides, or for that matter Thomas Aquinas) interpreted—as they constantly did—past thinkers, or when they discussed and analyzed historical events, persons, and societies, they did *not* do so as part of an enterprise that can be called "the history of philosophy," or that can be classified under the modern historical sciences and disciplines. To interpret old texts philosophically—*i.e.*, to confront and argue with them dialectically, in pursuit of *the* truth—is not to engage in a "historical" study. One could also say: dialectics in the Socratic sense does not presuppose essentially, but only "accidentally" (in our time and for the time being), historical dialectics (*e.g.*, dialectics in the Hegelian sense). Strauss's own studies of past thinkers weave together, I believe, the historically dialectical (*i.e.*, the preliminary or temporarily necessary) and the nonhistorically dialectical (*i.e.*, the truly philosophic) modes of analysis of past philosophers. In some works, most notably *Natural Right and History*, the historical or preliminary mode tends to bulk large; in others, for example, *Thoughts on Machiavelli*, and to an even greater degree the late works on Socrates, the philosophic mode predominates.

"the inadequacy of certain aspects or views which deform the surface of Husserl's thesis," which are largely "due to the situation in which Husserl started," Strauss holds that one should not, as does Voegelin in Strauss's opinion, lose sight of the heart of the Husserlian achievement.

> Husserl's phenomenological analysis ended in the radical analysis of the whole development of modern science (the essay in *Philosophia*, and the essay on geometric evidence, as well as the great fragment on space consciousness in the Husserl Memorial Volume)—I know nothing in the literature of our century that would be comparable to this analysis in rigor, depth, and breadth. Husserl has seen with incomparable clarity, that the restoration of philosophy or science—because he denies that that which today passes as science is genuine science—*presupposes* the restoration of the Platonic-Aristotelian level of questioning. His egology can be understood only as an answer to the Platonic-Aristotelian question regarding the *Nous*—and only on the level of this question is that answer to be discussed adequately. (Letter of 9 May 1943)

> The decisive point in Husserl is the critique of modern science in the light of genuine science, that is to say, Platonic-Aristotelian. His work can only be understood in the light of the enormous difficulties in which Platonic-Aristotelian science culminated: the problem of the *nous*. Considering the enormous difficulties of understanding *De Anima* III, 5ff., Husserl's egological foundation of the ontologies is at least excusable.[17]

Strauss admits, then, that Platonic-Aristotelian science "culminated in enormous difficulties"—the problem of "the *nous*." These difficulties "excuse" Husserl's decisive departure from the highest doctrine or conclusion or proposition of the Platonic-Aristotelian science, whose "level of questioning" Husserl and Husserl alone sensed the need to return to. Husserl's departure from Plato and Aristotle, his "transcendental phenomenology" centered on the "egological analysis," apparently does *not*, then, *remedy* the "enormous

17. Strauss's letter of 11 October 1943; the importance of the writings of Husserl to which Strauss refers had been signalled by Strauss's close friend Jacob Klein, in "Phenomenology and the History of Science," in *Philosophical Essays in Memory of Edmund Husserl*, ed. Marvin Faber (Cambridge, MA: Harvard University Press, 1940); reprinted in Jacob Klein, *Lectures and Essays*, ed. Robert B. Williamson and Elliott Zuckerman (Annapolis: St. John's College Press, 1985); see esp. note 24. The "essay on geometric evidence" to which Strauss refers is the posthumously published "Die Frage nach dem Ursprung der geometrie als intentional-historisches Problem," ed. E. Fink, *Revue internationale de Philosophie* 1:2; the "essay in *Philosophia*" has been translated by David Carr as Parts I and II of *The Crisis of European Sciences and Transcendental Phenomenology* (Evanston: Northwestern University Press, 1970).

difficulties" which one encounters when one attains the Platonic-Aristotelian "level of questioning."

Elsewhere Strauss, following Farabi's lead, suggests that the classics were fully aware of these enormous difficulties — that they regarded their metaphysics or theology as tentative or incomplete, and, what is more, uncompletable: "Classical philosophy understands itself as the uncompletable ascent from *proteron pros hēmas* [what is first for us] to *proteron physei* [what is first by nature]." "Classical philosophy denies" that "the *hylē* [basic stuff or matter of the universe]" can "be resolved into intelligible relations or the like." "Classical philosophy is" the "*search* [my italics] for the *aie on* [that which exists always]." But "the decisive questions," the "fundamental questions — 1) the question of the *archē* or the *archai* [the fundamental cause or causes], 2) the question of the right life or the *aristē politeia* [best regime]"— "necessarily relate to the aie on."[18]

If knowledge of the first principles of the universe and of the relation between them and intelligence (*nous*) remains forever tentative or incomplete in critical respects, how can knowledge of the right way of life not remain in a similar condition? At first sight, the answer would seem to be, that one may understand human nature without necessarily understanding the nature of the whole of which human nature is a part or a derivative. Strauss sometimes gives this answer. But even as he gives it, he tends to note its provisional or soberly practical character. And in highly visible places — for example at the outset of *Natural Right and History*—Strauss draws attention to the inadequacy, in the final analysis, of this answer.[19] This answer neglects, above all, the challenge posed by faith-inspired theology. The answer to the question how one ought to live depends on the answer to the question about the first causes. For while classical moral teaching and the biblical teaching on justice agree on almost all points, they disagree on certain crucial points. Again Strauss speaks of this fact in very prominent places — for example, at the dramatic beginning of the chapter on Machiavelli he wrote for the introductory textbook in the history of political philosophy

18. Strauss's letter of 10 December 1950; see also *Xenophon's Socratic Discourse* (Ithaca: Cornell University Press, 1970), pp. 147–50. The penultimate sentence of Farabi's most philosophic work, *The Philosophy of Plato and Aristotle*, includes the assertion that "we do not possess metaphysical science."

19. *Natural Right and History*, pp. 7–8; cf. "Social Science and Humanism," in *The Rebirth of Classical Political Rationalism: An Introduction to the Thought of Leo Strauss*, ed. T.L. Pangle (Chicago: University of Chicago Press, 1989), pp. 7–8.

he edited with Joseph Cropsey. There Strauss did not hesitate to draw the conclusion that is so problematic for philosophy as he understands philosophy

> Who is right, the Greeks or the Jews? Athens or Jerusalem? And how to proceed in order to find out who is right? Must we not admit that human wisdom is unable to settle this question and that every answer is based on an act of faith? But does this not constitute the complete and final defeat of Athens? *For a philosophy based on faith is no longer philosophy* [my italics]. Perhaps it was this unresolved conflict which has prevented Western thought from ever coming to rest.[20]

According to Strauss, philosophy, in the sense that was discovered and defended by the Greek thinkers and their students, and partially resuscitated by Husserl, represents not only the ultimate or richest source for humanity's understanding of the principles of just and noble lawful ordering of society; philosophy as a way of life consumed by the unfinished quest for scientific or rational knowledge and self-knowledge (*epistēmē*) is demonstrably the summit of human existence and the highest, though of course by no means the only high, rationally demonstrable purpose of society. Insofar as a higher notion of contemplation and action than that known to the Greeks claims to make itself manifest in other climes and later times, that higher notion originates not from history or historical experience as such but only from the shattering interruption into history of the altogether unexpected and unprepared claim to divine revelation, as delivered in the scriptures. How does philosophy meet this claim? Certainly not by any sort of psychological reduction; certainly not by any claim to explain away revelation on the basis of some philosophic psychology—however subtle and comprehensive. Strauss joins Voegelin in rejecting any attempt to meet the issue on a psychological level (in the manner, for example, of Heidegger):

> You are completely right when you say that a "psychologizing," that is to say, atheistic interpretation of revelation leads to confusion. It is sufficient to remember the example of Heidegger, whose interpretation of conscience ends in the calling being grasped as *Dasein* calling itself—here guilt, conscience, action lose their meaning.[21]

---

20. Leo Strauss and Joseph Cropsey, eds., *History of Political Philosophy*, 3rd. ed. (Chicago: University of Chicago Press, 1987), pp. 296–97.
21. Strauss's letter of 4 June 1951; cf. Voegelin's letter of 22 April 1951.

The reflection on the mutual challenge or debate between nonhistorical philosophy as rigorous science, and nonhistorical theology as spokesman for the divine call, is for Strauss the highest theme of essentially nonhistorical *political* philosophy. In our peculiar age, this highest theme must be prepared by a preliminary reflection on the mutual challenge or debate between nonhistorical and historical philosophizing; here again, Husserl at the end of his life took the first steps. *Political* philosophy understood in terms of these tasks is thus necessarily the first or most fundamental philosophy, the true or adequate fulfillment of that to which Husserl's phenomenology aspired, the philosophy that is essentially prior to and more fundamental than metaphysics or philosophic theology as well as psychology and physics.

But with what right does Strauss assign to *political* philosophy the supreme task? What makes political philosophy, and political philosophy alone, capable of this gravest responsibility? Political philosophy for Strauss means above all Socratic philosophy; and Socratic philosophy means above all dialectics, the art of friendly disputation. According to Aristotle, this art is used "in the philosophic sciences"

> with a view to the first premises in each science. For from its own first principles any given science is incapable of saying anything about them, since the first principles are the first of all; it is instead necessary to proceed by way of the generally accepted opinions concerning them. But this task is either uniquely or especially the province of dialectic. For to it, as the art capable of thorough scrutiny, belongs the path to the ultimate first principles of all paths of knowledge [*exetastikē gar ousa pros tas hapasōn tōn methodōn archas hodon echei*].[22]

What does Aristotle mean? Dialectics is the method exemplified in Socratic political philosophy. The theme of Socratic dialectics is justice, or the "ethical virtues," or the just and noble things (*Metaphysics* 1078b18–30). How can a dialectical inquiry into this theme ground all the sciences? How can this dialectical inquiry dispose of the debate between the competing claims of reason and revelation? What is the relation between these two momentous tasks? How does Socratic political philosophy proceed in these tasks, according to Strauss? What, for Strauss, is political philosophy?

---

22. *Topics* 101a37-b4. I am indebted to David Bolotin for drawing my attention to this passage and its importance.

No one can say that Strauss failed to bring this question before his readers. But I at least have had some trouble finding, among his readers friend or foe, people who can give me a satisfactory account of what Strauss's answer is. The Straussian answer one finds most frequently cited or referred to is a two-page answer that Strauss characterizes, in the midst of developing the answer, as "even the most provisional explanation of what political philosophy is." The book which includes this "most provisional explanation," the book whose title trumpets the question, takes its title from its opening chapter, a lecture on the question delivered in Jerusalem. The lecture, and hence the book, begins with a section entitled "The Problem of Political Philosophy," and opens with the following words:

> It is a great honor, and at the same time a challenge to accept a task of peculiar difficulty, to be asked to speak about political philosophy in Jerusalem. In this city, and in this land, the theme of political philosophy—"the city of righteousness, the faithful city"—has been taken more seriously than anywhere else on earth. Nowhere else has the longing for justice and the just city filled the purest hearts and the loftiest souls with such zeal as on this sacred soil. . . . I shall not for a moment forget what Jerusalem stands for.

The taking seriously of justice is obviously a most important common ground between the Bible and Plato, especially Plato's *Republic*. In the same lecture however, Strauss says that "the character of classical political philosophy appears with the greatest clarity from Plato's *Laws*, which is his political work *par excellence*."[23]

This characterization of Plato's *Laws* is repeated at the beginning of the last book Strauss completed before he died, a commentary on Plato's *Laws*. For the epigraph to this commentary, Strauss made a literal translation from Arabic of a statement of Avicenna's to which Strauss had often referred previously, and which (as I understand) hit him, the first time he read it (when he was a young man in his thirties), as a bombshell: " . . . the treatment of prophecy and the Divine Law is contained in . . . the *Laws*." The commentary is marked, as are all Strauss's commentaries, by a meticulousness as regards terminology: Strauss almost never expresses a thought of Plato's in language that is not capable of literal translation into Platonic Greek. There is one striking exception. Early on we find him characterizing a crucial step of Plato's Athenian Stranger as

23. *What Is Political Philosophy?* pp. 9–12, 29.

follows: "He appeals as it were from the accepted interpretation of revelation to revelation itself, which discloses its true meaning only to those who never forget that, being divine, it is supremely reasonable." If this sentence is not Maimonidean, it surely reminds one of Maimonides. The sentence would seem to describe the start, though only the start, of the dialectic that is exemplified in the *Laws*. That dialectic, Strauss repeatedly indicates, is "sub-Socratic," even though the Athenian Stranger is himself Socratic. The dialectic of the *Laws* needs to be complemented or completed by the dialectic of the *Republic*. But it has this key advantage over that of the *Republic*: certain essential first principles which are taken for granted in the *Republic* are not taken for granted but are instead demonstrated dialectically in the *Laws*: "in the *Republic*, reason or intellect guides the foundation of the city from the beginning."[24] The *Laws*, it would seem, is understood by Strauss to exemplify the art of conversational examination by which one can ascend from the quarrel between reason and revelation to its resolution.

24. *The Argument and the Action of Plato's "Laws"* (Chicago: University of Chicago Press, 1975), pp. 1, 7, 27 and 38; see also the comparisons between the *Republic* and the *Laws* drawn at pp. 14, 31, 75, 113, and 128.

Part Two

Strauss: Classical Political Philosophy, Modernity, and the American Regime

On a Certain Critique of "Straussianism"

Nathan Tarcov

This article examines a certain critique of what I will take the liberty of calling "Straussianism," a critique which raises questions I believe are worth discussing, especially by all those interested in the work of Leo Strauss. This particular critique appeared in a review of a book on Platonic political philosophy, a review by a young scholar who had published only a couple of articles on classical political philosophy himself.

This reviewer aptly characterizes the author as one who, "thoroughly dissatisfied with modern philosophy in all its forms, and unwilling to take refuge in Thomism . . . turns back to classical philosophy, to the teaching of Plato and Aristotle, as the true teaching" (p. 326).[1] According to this perceptive critic, the author considered the quarrel of the ancients and the moderns "definitely settled in favor of the classics. After having disposed of this fundamental question, which as such is a theoretical question, he can pursue a practical or political intention on the foundation of the classical teaching."[2] The skeptical reviewer insists, however, that "the teaching of the classics can have no immediate practical effect, because present-day society is not a *polis*" (p. 332). He cautions that "Since there are essential differences between modern society and the society envisaged by the classics, the classical teaching cannot be immediately applicable to modern society, but has to be *made* applicable to it, that is, must be modernized or distorted" (p. 333). He therefore rejects the author's assumption "that we can find in the classical teaching the solution to our modern problem. . . . [that] the classics must be presumed to supply us with an analysis, diagnosis and therapy of the modern disease" (pp. 334–35).

The alarmed reviewer warns that this false assumption "leads to

This article derives from a lecture prepared for a symposium of the Institute for the Study of Religion and Politics at Boston College directed by Ernest Fortin and Christopher Bruell, and it has profited from the responses of the symposium's directors and participants.
1. Cf. Leo Strauss, *The City and Man* (Chicago: Rand McNally, 1964), pp. 10–12.
2. Cf. John Gunnell, "The Myth of the Tradition," *American Political Science Review* 72 (March 1978): 127.

dangerous consequences" (p. 332). In contrast to the author's suggestion that liberal democracy is based on the classical view of human
nature and his attempt to reconcile democracy and Platonism,[3] this
critic demands that "anyone who wishes to restore Plato's teaching
in accordance with 'the living aspirations of our time'" must squarely
face the fact that classical political philosophy does not supply a
philosophic basis for aspirations toward liberal democracy. On the
contrary, he argues, "The political significance of the 'realistic' political philosophy of the modern era, which refuses to take its bearings
by 'transcendent' standards [for which it is so much decried by the
author], consists in the fact that it raises the status of man, that
is, of every man, and thus for the first time supplies a philosophic
basis for aspirations toward democracy, more precisely toward liberal
democracy," whereas for Plato "democracy is against natural right"
(pp. 357, 359). Indeed, the reviewer accuses the author of not adhering consistently to his impossible effort to make Plato a political
liberal who will save democracy from totalitarianism and of instead
lapsing into the emphatic demand that democracy be abandoned
for authoritarianism (pp. 358, 366).

Aside from this biting critique of the practical intention and consequences of this attempted restoration of classical political philosophy, the reviewer raises some other serious theoretical questions.
He charges this return to the classics with failure to do justice to
modern political philosophy owing to its "failure to give serious consideration to the question why modern philosophy revolted against
the classical tradition, in other words, to the difficulties to which
classical philosophy was and is still exposed" (p. 338). In particular,
such a restoration must recognize that, for the classics, science presupposes the intelligibility of the world or perhaps even the possibility
of natural theology, and that "It was especially due to the influence
of the Bible that the classical view became questionable, even for
many of its adherents." The reviewer suggests that "a case could be
made for the view that it was reflection guided by the Biblical notion of creation which ultimately led to the . . . assertion [of modern
philosophy] that the world as far as we can understand it, that is,
the world as studied by human science, must be the 'work' of the
human mind" (p. 339). The failures of this attempted restoration
of classical philosophy to do justice to modern philosophy or to consider the difficulties or defects of classical philosophy seem to be

3. Cf. Leo Strauss, *An Introduction to Political Philosophy: Ten Essays by Leo Strauss,*
ed. Hilail Gildin (Detroit: Wayne State University Press, 1989), p. 98.

connected to its barely alluding to the Reformation when speaking of the origins of the modern break with classical philosophy. In contrast, this critic compares the idea of popular enlightenment of Hobbes and other modern philosophers to Luther's view (p. 360 n.44). Similarly, he raises the question whether the idea of the freedom of the individual is not derived from the Christian doctrine of the infinite value of the individual (p. 358). Conversely, he argues that the attempt to make Plato relevant to contemporary politics rests on an "extremely questionable" "attempt to interpret Platonic philosophy in Biblical terms" (p. 344, 362).

According to this critique, a genuine confrontation of classical and modern philosophy, let alone a decision in favor of the classics, must seriously consider the difficulties or defects of classical philosophy not only through recognition of the biblical influence on modern philosophy, but also through facing the supposedly "well-known fact" that the difficulties to which classical philosophy is exposed find today their most massive expression in the success of modern natural science" (p. 339). That "obvious" success "has brought about a situation in which the possibility of natural theology [on which classical philosophy can be said ultimately to depend] has lost all the evidence it formerly possessed."

This critic further objects that the "contention that we can find in classical teaching the solution to our problem is exposed to a further difficulty, caused by what one may well call 'the fundamental opposition of Plato and Aristotle.'" "To justify this enterprise," the critic points out, one "has to assert that there is a fundamental harmony between the two philosophies" (p. 345). Any such harmonization is false insofar as it rests on understanding the answers of one philosopher as answers not to his own questions but to those of the other, or on inserting the answers of one into the arguments of the other about his most important questions. One must consider, first of all and with the utmost care, Aristotle's reports about Plato's teaching, which the author only "barely alludes to" (p. 346). The most important thing, the critic demands, in order to prove a basic agreement between Plato and Aristotle, would seem to be to reconcile their manifestly different views of the ranking or relation of practice and theory (pp. 347–48).

Finally I will point out the reviewer's emphasis on the paradox that the very effort to restore classical philosophy is far from "Plato's sovereign disregard for historical truth." Writing about Plato's political philosophy is itself an "un-Platonic venture" (p. 334). The critic plausibly reminds us that "Certainly, Plato considered the philosophic question of the best political order infinitely more important than the historical question of what this or that individual thought of the best political order; hence he never wrote a book on other people's 'theories'" (p. 333). The critic tellingly points out that even and precisely the effort to restore classical philosophy through historical interpretation seems to depart from classical philosophy through admitting that the classical distinction between philosophy and history is "misleading" and "dangerous" in "the present situation," which requires instead a kind of fusion of philosophy and history (p. 332). The critic therefore complains that the author "would have come nearer to the spirit of Plato's unconcern with, or even contempt for, the merely historical truth if he had expounded his own 'philosophy . . .' in his own name, or if, following the example of Sir Thomas More, he had written a free imitation of the *Republic*, that is, if he had taken the responsibility for a teaching which is actually his own teaching and not sought refuge behind the shield of Plato's dazzling authority" (p. 333). The failure either to do so or to write according to the modern standards of historical exactness despised by Plato "exposes him to the danger of substituting for proof of the historical contention that Plato held certain views some sort of philosophic reasoning showing that the views in question are sound, and of substituting for the demonstration of philosophic theses references to Platonic passages where those theses are asserted" (p. 334).[4] The question raised is whether the paradoxical effort to philosophize through historical inquiry into a philosophy that despised historical inquiry is necessarily self-contradictory or self-defeating and a threat to both sound philosophy and sound history.

In summary, this trenchant critique of what I have taken the liberty of calling "Straussianism" stresses the following:

(1) the falsehood and danger of applying classical political philosophy directly to modern political problems;
(2) the failure of this approach to do justice to modern philosophy or to consider the difficulties in classical philosophy : (a) that modern philosophy discerned under the influence of the Bible and especially of the Reformation and (b) that are expressed in the success of modern natural science;
(3) the fundamental opposition between Plato and Aristotle and the

---

4. Cf. M. F. Burnyeat, "Sphinx without a Secret," *New York Review of Books* (30 May 1985): 32.

difficulty it causes for any attempt to find *the* solution in classical philosophy as such;

(4) the paradoxical character of a philosophical historical inquiry into a philosophy that despised historical inquiry and that distinguished philosophy from history.

Whether or not one regards this critique as respectfully and sympathetically as I do, those readers who have only a casual familiarity with Leo Strauss's work, not to say a detailed familiarity with his entire corpus, will, of course, have recognized major features of "Straussianism" in the work being criticized here and will naturally have assumed that I have been discussing a recent critique of his work. Those readers, however, who know his work thoroughly or recognize his style, will have realized that the author of the work being criticized was not Leo Strauss but John Wild, and that the young critic was Leo Strauss himself, writing in *Social Research* in 1946 (all parenthetical page numbers in this article refer to that review)![5] (They will need no reminder that one can write so that most of one's readers misunderstand in a way that one intends.) But yet this possible misunderstanding of my article so far would not be simply a misunderstanding — I do believe that that review was after all a critique of Straussianism. I can therefore now reveal that the alternative title of this article is "Leo Strauss's Critique of Straussianism."

Whatever can I mean by that? First of all, I mean to some extent to distinguish Strauss's own work from "Straussianism," that complex of writings, teachings, and other practices belonging to those students, students of students, followers and imitators of Strauss, such as myself. I believe that in this article Strauss meant to warn against some of the errors and dangers involved in the project that he had begun to launch, perhaps errors or dangers that he himself might be exposed to but certainly ones that his students might fall into. It is an extraordinary piece of self-reflection by an extraordinary man at an extraordinary moment. He had published on classical political philosophy only "The Spirit of Sparta or the Taste of Xenophon"[6] and "On Classical Political Philosophy,"[7] not yet *On Tyranny*, let alone *Natural Right and History*, *The City and Man*, *Xenophon's Socratic Discourse*, *Xenophon's Socrates*, *The Argument and the Action*

5. Leo Strauss, "On a New Interpretation of Plato's Political Philosophy," *Social Research* 13 (September 1946): 326–67.

6. *Social Research* 6 (November 1939): 502–36.

7. *Social Research* 12 (February 1945): 98–117.

of Plato's Laws, and *Studies in Platonic Political Philosophy.* But he knew
what he was doing and the need to consider for himself and to warn
students about the errors and dangers that it might give rise to. I
do not mean, of course, that he was not also writing a review of
Wild's book. That work seemed to exemplify for Strauss practically
everything false or dangerous that might beset the attempt to restore classical political philosophy (p. 367). And in this devastating
critique he tried to protect that attempt from the consequences of
what he regarded as Wild's incompetence and irresponsibility. But
I do mean that Strauss was doing more than criticizing Wild as such.
This review was his equivalent of Marx's famous statement that he
was not a Marxist.

But precisely because Strauss's project was hardly launched and
practically unknown, this review had to be much more than a critique of the errors and danger his project was exposed to. It was
also a statement of his project especially as a new interpretation
of Plato's political philosophy. In other words, the title of Strauss's
article ("On A New Interpretation of Plato's Political Philosophy")
also was ironical or ambiguous: the article was at least as seriously
concerned with setting forth Strauss's new interpretation of Plato
as with refuting Wild's. It contains some of Strauss's best and most
elaborate statements on how to interpret Plato and also a succinct
treatment of the central question of Plato's political philosophy, the
relation of philosophy and politics or the meaning of the image of
the cave (pp. 348–55, 360–62).

I had already come to suspect that Strauss had his own project
in mind in writing his review of Wild's book when I came upon
what I took to be authoritative confirmation of this conclusion. In
the first paragraph of the review Strauss wrote: "At present very few
will be prepared to accept his [Wild's] basic premise [that classical
philosophy is the true teaching]. But it is safe to predict that the
movement which his book may be said to launch in this country
will become increasingly influential and weighty as the years go by"
(p. 326). The meaning of this amazing prediction about a book which
the review ends by suggesting richly deserves to be at best forgotten
(p. 367) was clarified when the *Independent Journal of Philosophy* published in 1983 the extant correspondence from 1946 between Strauss
and Karl Lowith.[8] In a letter apparently not extant Lowith seems

8. "Correspondence Concerning Modernity," trans. Susanne Klein and George
Eliott Tucker, *Independent Journal of Philosophy* 4 (1983): 105–19.

to have objected in some way to this strange prediction. Strauss replied in a letter of 15 August 1946 as follows: "But assume I knew
of two or three people, who are striving for the restoration of classical philosophy and whose works will appear and distinguish themselves in the course of the next ten years, and who understand something about the matter. Then however the thesis represented publicly
in *America* for the first time, *accidentally* by Wild, would gain greater
influence and greater weight than it has at the moment. For I do
not prophesy a *fashion*. In short," Strauss concluded, "you underes-
timate my irony."[9] This seems to me as clear an admission as we
have a right to expect that Strauss had himself (and perhaps his
friend Jacob Klein and a third man?) and his plans in mind in writing
this review. Since he had himself rather than Wild in mind in making
the strange prediction at the start of the review, then we may suspect that he had his own project more in mind also in the criticisms
in the rest of the review. At the end of this response to Lowith, Strauss
wrote: "If I may come back once more to my article, I wrote it really
for *students* [his emphasis]. I wanted to show them with an exemplary case *what* sort of rubbish is praised by idiots in *The New York
Times*, *Tribune*, etc., in order to make them a little bit more wary.
The only thing I did not write only for students is the interpretation of the, in a certain sense decisive, passage of the *Seventh Letter*."
Given Strauss's irony, underestimated by Lowith, this may not have
been the only respect in which Strauss hoped to make students "a
little bit more wary."

Let us briefly reconsider the main points of this critique now understood as Strauss's "critique of Straussianism." The warning against
the error and danger of applying classical political philosophy as
the solution to modern political problems might seem to the casual
reader of Strauss to be directed squarely against his own work. Strauss
certainly used our sense of the problems of modern politics, the crisis
of the West as he called it, to interest his readers in the possible
truth and utility of classical political philosophy. But precisely in
doing so Strauss later repeated the objection he had made against
Wild. In the introduction to *The City and Man*, he wrote:

> We cannot reasonably expect that a fresh understanding of classical
> political philosophy will supply us with recipes for today's use. For
> the relative success of modern political philosophy has brought into

9. *Ibid.*, p. 106.

being a kind of society wholly unknown to the classics, a kind of society to which the classical principles as stated and elaborated by the
classics are not immediately applicable. Only we living today can possibly find a solution to the problems of today. But an adequate understanding of the principles as elaborated by the classics may be the indispensable starting point for an adequate analysis, to be achieved
by us, of present-day society in its peculiar character, and for the wise
application, to be achieved by us, of these principles to our tasks.[10]

Strauss thus recognized the danger that the return to classical
political philosophy he proposed might be turned into a search for
classical recipes for contemporary political concoctions. But Strauss
was concerned not merely with the dangerous political consequences
of such a project, but with the intellectually distorting effect on the
return to classical political philosophy if it were not to be "carried
out seriously, *i.e.* without squinting at our present predicament."[11]
He differed from Wild only secondarily in recognizing that we could
not find a practical solution to modern political problems in classical political philosophy; he differed primarily in not being moved
ultimately by the intention to find a practical solution to modern
political problems, a point both some of his critics and some of his
followers seem to have difficulty in grasping.

In this respect Strauss acted in agreement with his interpretation of Plato, whose inability to solve modern political problems
or provide a philosophical basis for liberal democracy is only in-
cidental to his ultimate purpose, which was not the solution of any
political problems or the provision of a philosophical basis for any
particular regime. Strauss wrote in this review: "Plato composed
his writings in such a way as to prevent for all time their use as
authoritative texts. . . . In the last analysis his writings cannot be
used for any purpose other than philosophizing. In particular, no
social order and no party which ever existed or which ever will exist
can rightfully claim Plato as its patron" (p. 351). More precisely or
more vaguely, Strauss admits that the political utopia of Plato's
Republic "cannot guide political action (except in the vague sense
of 'inspiring' it)" (p. 362 n.49).

This fact, together with the fact emphasized in Strauss's review
that it is modern political philosophy that for the first time supplies
a philosophic basis for aspirations toward liberal democracy, must

10. *The City and Man*, p. 11.
11. *Ibid.*

be borne in mind when interpreting such later statements of Strauss's as that "liberal democracy, in contradistinction to communism and fascism, derives powerful support from a way of thinking which cannot be called modern at all: the premodern thought of our western tradition."[12]

Strauss's critique of Wild also compels us to ask whether Strauss's own works did justice to modern philosophy and seriously considered the difficulties in classical philosophy suggested by the biblical influence on modern philosophy and by the success of modern natural science. The biblical influence on modern philosophy and the success of modern science are not, however, manifestly topics emphasized or elaborated at length by Strauss in his confrontation of classical and modern political philosophy.

Strauss tended to discuss less the biblical influence on modern philosophy's rejection of classical philosophy than the relation between the Bible and philosophy as such, the modern philosophic critique of the Bible, and the secular, moral, political, or philosophic origins of modernity. It could be said of Strauss that he, like Wild, only "barely alludes to the Reformation when speaking of the origins of the modern break with classical philosophy" (p. 338).[13] Strauss preferred to emphasize the manifest common ground between classical philosophy and the Bible in opposition to modern philosophy. He certainly did not always conduct his confrontation of classical with modern political philosophy in such a way as to make the influence of the teaching of the Bible on modern political philosophy come "immediately to the center of attention" (p. 328). In the light of his critique of Wild, however, we recognize that Strauss's emphasis on the quarrel of the ancients and the moderns may imply alternatively that, as he wrote in explaining the review to Löwith, "modern philosophy has much in common with Christian medieval philosophy" (cf. p. 328).[14] His correspondence with Löwith at this time also makes clear that he did not mean by this to adhere to the convenient fable of the nineteenth century that the Enlightenment was "Christianly motivated."[15] His suggestion seems to be rather that

12. *Introduction to Political Philosophy*, p. 98.
13. Cf. Leo Strauss, *Natural Right and History* (Chicago: University of Chicago Press, 1953), pp. 60–61 n.22. On this issue see Ralph C. Hancock, *Calvin and the Foundations of Modern Politics* (Ithaca: Cornell University Press, 1989), pp. 164–77, 185–94.
14. "Correspondence," p. 106.
15. *Ibid.*, p. 112.

the biblical doctrine of creation of the world by an omnipotent, om-
niscient, and mysterious God may have led modern philosophers
to doubt the possibility of human knowledge of things as they really
are and to seek a new basis on which to secure the possibility of
knowledge against that doubt. In the light of Strauss's critique of
Wild, we are also directed to pay serious attention to such matters
as Strauss's later interpretation of what he called Machiavelli's "imitation of Jesus," the understanding of Christian propaganda as the
model of modern enlightenment.[16]

As to the difficulties in classical philosophy expressed by the success
of modern natural science, we must consider not merely Strauss's
occasional references to modern natural science but his whole interpretation of classical philosophy as an effort to explore whether
classical philosophy strictly depends on premises, above all natural
theology, called into question by the success of that science. His review of Wild, after all, left open two possibilities in response to the
obvious success of modern natural science: the attempt to restore
natural theology as a genuine science (the requirements for which
Strauss explicitly "said nothing" about) or alternatively (and only
implicitly) the investigation into whether it is a misleading
simplification to say that classical philosophy ultimately depends
on the possibility of natural theology as a science (pp. 338–39). Strauss
indeed says there that "It goes without saying that there is no place
in Plato's teaching for a theology that 'lays down certain specifica-
tions which determine the general form of philosophy,' and that Wild
is somewhat nearer to Plato when he designates as mythology what
in his own language would be theology" (p. 363).

As to "the fundamental opposition of Plato and Aristotle," it can
be said that Strauss, like Wild, only "barely alludes to" (p. 346)
Aristotle's reports about Plato's teaching. One can see, however, from
Strauss's review itself that his attempt to establish a fundamental
harmony between the two philosophies was the opposite of Wild's
unsuccessful attempt. Whereas Wild tried and failed to show that
Aristotle as well as Plato regards the philosophic life as intrinsically
practical or moral, Strauss tried to show that Plato as well as Aristotle
regarded the theoretical or philosophic way of life as fundamentally

---

16. Leo Strauss, *Thoughts on Machiavelli* (Glencoe, IL: Free Press, 1958), p. 173
and *What Is Political Philosophy?* (New York: Free Press, 1959), p. 45. Note the triple
statement in the latter passage.

different from and absolutely superior to the practical way of life (pp. 347–48, 354–55). At any rate, the Wild review alerts us to the extent to which Strauss had to regard his attempted restoration of classical political philosophy as an attempt to establish "a fundamental harmony between the two philosophies" (p. 345; the phrase "harmony between the two philosophies" points to Strauss's predecessor in this attempt, Farabi, and to the relation not merely between Plato and Aristotle, but between theoretical and practical philosophy and between exoteric and esoteric philosophic teachings).[17]

The last point raised in the Wild review I will consider is the paradoxical character of a philosophical historical inquiry into a philosophy that despised historical inquiry and distinguished philosophy from history.[18] It is the problem, in other words, of the relation between the manifestly historical character of Strauss's own work and what he called historicism. Is the historical philosophical character of Strauss's own work closer in spirit to the fusion of history and philosophy of the historicism he criticized than to the distinction between philosophy and history of the classical philosophy he attempted to restore?

Strauss's discussion of interpretation of Plato in the Wild review itself does suggest that philosophy and history, however theoretically distinct, are practically inseparable. On the one hand, the review argued that the philosophic necessity for a free reexamination of the modern principles necessarily requires an adequate historical understanding of classical philosophy, so that "insistence on the fundamental difference between philosophy and history—a difference by which philosophy stands or falls—may very well, in the present situation, be misleading, not to say dangerous to philosophy itself" (p. 332). One cannot philosophize today without historical inquiry. On the other hand, the review reminds us that Plato compels us in interpreting his writings to depend not merely on historical interpretation but on our own philosophizing (p. 351). One cannot engage in that kind of historical inquiry without philosophizing. Besides, in one sense it is obviously absurd or ironical of Strauss to assert in the review that Plato was not interested in what

17. See Leo Strauss, "Farabi's *Plato*," in *Louis Ginzberg Jubilee Volume* (New York: American Academy for Jewish Research, 1945), pp. 357–93.

18. See my "Philosophy and History: Tradition and Interpretation in the Work of Leo Strauss," *Polity* 16:1 (Fall 1983): 5–29, pp. 20–29.

this or that individual thought or that he never wrote a book on other people's theories (p. 333)—in one sense that is *all* Plato did in his dialogues (pp. 348-53).

For Strauss the pursuit of historical truth required philosophical activity. It first of all had to begin with a philosophic recognition of ignorance. He remarked in the Wild review that before the historian can recover "the signposts" that guided earlier philosophers, he must be "in a condition of utter bewilderment: he finds himself in a darkness that is illumined only by his knowledge that he knows, that is, understands, nothing" (p. 331). Strauss viewed this experience of ignorance or wonder as dependent on the prior philosophic effort to become aware of and to free oneself from conventional or traditional assumptions. An "antiquarian" or "historical" interest is not sufficient; one needs, according to the Wild review, "philosophic passion," "a philosophic incentive," "a philosophic motive for the genuinely historical effort" to understand the philosophic thought of the past (pp. 329, 332, 331).

This does not imply that the historian necessarily criticizes the thought of the past from the point of view of present day thought.[19] Indeed, "he embarks on a journey whose end is completely hidden from him. He is not likely to return to the shores of our time as exactly the same man who departed from them" (p. 331). Dogmatism prevents either genuine philosophizing or genuine historical interpretation. The belief in progress is probably the most disastrous form of dogmatism for historical interpretation, but the historicist dogma that the (nonhistoricist) thought of the past was mistaken is also disabling, as is the dogma of the superiority of the ancients to the moderns, as we see in the case of Wild (pp. 329-32).[20]

Historical interpretation requires a very special incentive. Only men living in an age of intellectual decline, or at least those who regard it as possible that they live in such an age, have a sufficient incentive for interpretation of the thought of the past.[21] The philosophic incentive required for an adequate interpretation of classical philosophy is present "for the first time in a number of generations" in the demand for a philosophic reexamination of the modern principles (p. 332).

19. Leo Strauss, "On Collingwood's Philosophy of History," *Review of Metaphysics* 5 (June 1952): 559-86, p. 583.

20. Strauss, *What Is Political Philosophy?* pp. 66-68, 71, 266; "On Collingwood's Philosophy of History," pp. 574-75.

21. Strauss, "On Collingwood's Philosophy of History," pp. 576, 585.

Philosophical concern with the text's claim to truth is necessary not only as an incentive for, but as part of, the activity of historical interpretation. Strauss wrote, "Plato's thought claims to be an imitation of the whole. It is impossible to understand the imitation without looking at the original." Philosophical concern with the objects of the text, guided by the text, is required for interpretation. Strauss argued that it is "impossible to understand what Plato thought without thinking, i.e., without articulating the subjects about which Plato thought."[22]

The necessity of philosophical activity is increased by the literary character of the Platonic dialogues, shared to different degrees and purposes by most of the writings Strauss interpreted. He explains in his review of Wild that Plato's dialogues "have the function not of communicating but of intimating the most important truths to 'some,' while they have at the same time the much more obvious function of producing a salutary (civilizing, humanizing and cathartic) effect on all" (p. 350). Therefore, according to Strauss, "No interpretation of Plato's teaching can be proved fully by historical evidence. For the crucial part of his interpretation the interpreter has to fall back on his own resources: Plato does not relieve him of the responsibility for discovering the decisive part of the argument by himself" (p. 351). Adequate historical interpretation of such works requires philosophizing.

Not only may historical interpretation require philosophizing for Strauss, but so may philosophy require historical inquiry. Strauss can say that "insistence on the fundamental difference between philosophy and history—a difference by which philosophy stands or falls—may very well, in the present situation, be misleading, not to say dangerous to philosophy itself" (p. 332) because insistence on their theoretical difference may be but should not be taken to imply the necessity of their practical separation. Political philosophy always depends on some history for "the experience of the variety of political institutions and convictions." Such history, however, is "only preliminary and auxiliary to political philosophy; it does not form an integral part of it." But in our time the dependence of political philosophy on history is far more fundamental. Political philosophy today needs its own history "as an integral part of its own efforts."[23]

22. *Ibid.*, pp. 582–84.
23. Strauss, *What Is Political Philosophy?* pp. 56–57, 77.

The increasingly insistent theoretical attack on the principles of modern civilization requires a free and impartial reexamination of the modern principles. But the modern principles were "evolved in opposition to, and by way of transformation of, the principles of classical philosophy" (p. 327). The modern principles are peculiarly traditional in their character and cannot be reexamined, either understood or judged, without being confronted with classical principles (p. 328). And that confrontation must be not with a peculiarly modern understanding of classical principles but with their original understanding (pp. 328–29).

Strauss argued that the dominance of historicism makes philosophy appear impossible so that "the original meaning of philosophy is accessible only through recollection of what philosophy meant in the past," through history. Philosophy is no longer in its "natural situation" confronting nonphilosophic accounts of the whole but in an artificial situation confronting the denial of the possibility of an account of the whole by what appears to be philosophy. This means primarily that instead of confronting revelation, philosophy confronts historicism, which perhaps surprisingly Strauss suggested can be understood as a transformation of revelation. Strauss expressed this situation in a Platonic image: philosophy instead of starting in "the natural cave" that Plato confronted now begins from an artificial cave "beneath the cave." To go from there merely to the natural cave requires an elaborate artificial historical investigation.[24]

That investigation is in part the application of historicism to itself.[25] This requires ultimately a nonhistoricist account of the genesis of historicism out of previous nonhistoricist thought. Historical understanding of nonhistoricist thought frees one from historicism, at least to the extent of enabling one to see its problematic character, all that is required for the possibility of philosophy.[26] This is "the self-destruction of historicism."[27]

The escape from historicism Strauss sketches is doubly historical, requiring historical investigations made necessary by this historical situation. But the recognition that "the fusion of philosophic and historical questions" is in a limited way "inevitable" for us, is

24. Leo Strauss, *Persecution and the Art of Writing* (Glencoe, IL: Free Press, 1952), pp. 155–57.
25. *What Is Political Philosophy?* pp. 72–73, 77; *Natural Right and History*, p. 26.
26. *Natural Right and History*, pp. 32–33.
27. *Persecution and the Art of Writing*, p. 158.

not identical with historicism itself. Strauss not only denied emphatically that his enormous historical achievement renders him superior to the classical philosophers who had no need of it, or even to the "ancestral cave dwellers," but affirms that philosophy has not changed; only the introduction to it has.[28]

This point is clarified in the correspondence with Lowith. Lowith apparently objected to the sentence in the Wild review in which Strauss wrote that "insistence on the fundamental difference between philosophy and history—a difference by which philosophy stands or falls—may very well, in the present situation, be misleading." Strauss wrote in reply:

> We agree that today we need historical reflection—only I assert that it is neither a progress nor a fate to submit to with resignation, but it is an unavoidable means for the overcoming of modernity. One cannot overcome modernity with modern means, but only insofar as we are still natural beings with natural understanding; but the way of thought of natural understanding has been lost to us, and simple people such as myself and those like me are not able to regain it through their own resources: we attempt to *learn* from the ancients.

When Lowith objected that "not only historical *consciousness* has changed but our historical *being*," Strauss replied, "Of course! But if this change rests on erroneous presuppositions, then we cannot sit idly by, but must do our best to undo it—not socially or politically but *privatissime*."[29] Thus Strauss attempted to offer not a historical substitute but a historical preparation for the natural experience of philosophy.

The last section of the Wild review begins and ends with formulations that suggest authors other than Wild. It begins: "One can imagine a man writing a book on the political problem of our time in the guise of a book on Plato's political philosophy. While it would be a very bad book if regarded as an interpretation of Plato, it might be excellent as a guide amidst the perplexities of our age."[30] Did Leo Strauss himself go on to write such a guide for the perplexed? He insisted, on the contrary, that he adhered to the standards of historical exactness. Did he instead write studies in Platonic political philosophy that ascended from the political problem of our time?

---

28. *What Is Political Philosophy?* p. 77; *Persecution and the Art of Writing*, pp. 155–56.
29. "Correspondence," pp. 106–107, 109, 114.
30. Cf. *What Is Political Philosophy?* pp. 263–64.

At the end of the review Strauss wrote: "A man who claims to be a Platonist, and who publishes in this country at this time a book on Plato's political philosophy, bears more than the ordinary responsibility that is borne by every writer" and went on to condemn Wild for not meeting that responsibility (p. 367). Strauss himself later took on that responsibility and tried to fulfill his duties both to Plato and to his country at his time.

Natural Right and Philosophy

Stewart Umphrey

"The problem inherent in the surface of things, and only in the surface of things, is the heart of things." So wrote Leo Strauss in his *Thoughts on Machiavelli*.[1] The sentence may seem to be a passing remark, and yet it states his main hermeneutical principle. On the one hand it articulates the abiding hypothesis that what is first for us, the very looks of things, is somehow first in itself. On the other hand it guides his commentaries on great books, ancient as well as modern. What if we let this principle guide our commentaries on Strauss's own books? Then the heart of *Natural Right and History*, for example, is arguably the disproportion between what first appears to be his teaching about natural right and what first appears to be his skepticism about the knowability of natural right.

In the course of *Natural Right and History* Strauss considers three views according to which there can be no natural right: radical historicism, Weberian positivism, and classical conventionalism. He refutes all three, and when refuting the third he seems to conclude that there is natural right.[2] But there is natural right, he maintains, only if it is in principle knowable.[3] He thus presents himself as one who takes natural right to be in principle knowable. Furthermore, when surveying "classic" and "modern" natural right, he takes the side of classical philosophers; he strongly suggests that at least one classical philosopher succeeded in the attempt to replace opinions about what right is with knowledge of natural right. But surely Strauss would not have adjudicated this dispute with such confidence had not he too attained knowledge of natural right. He thus presents himself as one endeavoring to renew an old teaching which he knows

1. L. Strauss, *Thoughts on Machiavelli* (Seattle: Washington University Press, 1969), p. 13.
2. L. Strauss, *Natural Right and History* [hereafter *NRH*] (Chicago: Chicago University Press, 1953), pp. 9–80, 93–127. The argument on pp. 93–108 is not against the thesis of classic conventionalism itself but against its reason for rejecting natural right. And the account on pp. 108–113 is explanatory, not justificatory; had it been offered as an argument against the thesis of conventionalism itself, it would have instantiated the genetic fallacy.
3. *NRH*, pp. 3, 24, 35, also pp. 28, 203. I find in Strauss's writings no argument for this verificationalist premiss, nor any explication of what "knowing" means in these contexts.

to be true. With respect to natural right itself his thought is finally at rest.

In the course of *Natural Right and History* Strauss no less strongly suggests that there are certain fundamental problems whose resolution one must discover if one is to become wise in the full sense of the term. Of every such problem there may be many putative solutions, but of these putative solutions only a few are "fundamental." Between these fundamental alternatives the unaided reason cannot decide. Every such problem is thus irresolvable; we cannot become wise. We may in time ascend from opinions to awareness of the fundamental problems, and therewith the fundamental alternatives, but we will never ascend any higher. Strauss also speaks repeatedly of "the problem of natural right," and he seems to regard it as fundamental. The implication is that, while there are maybe only a few major teachings about natural right, none is evidentially superior to its major alternatives, none is final. He thus presents himself as one who holds natural right itself to be in principle unknowable. With respect to it his thought remains in motion.[4]

The problem apparent in the surface of *Natural Right and History* can be put in two ways. First, it seems to teach that no final natural right teaching is available even as it makes available (in outline) the final natural right teaching. Alternatively, it seems to teach that there is no natural right, since it is strictly unknowable, even as it supposes that natural right is strictly knowable, since there is natural right. On either formulation *Natural Right and History* seems incoherent. One may well claim that it is not absolutely self-refuting, on the ground that Strauss neither says nor strictly implies that anyone has attained knowledge of natural right. It seems however to be pragmatically self-refuting, for Strauss does seem to give an account of natural right while implying that no one is in a position to give such an account; what he does arguably discords with what he says. He puts one in mind of the man who says, "Virtue is some sort of knowledge, but I don't know what virtue is, I'm still trying to find out."

To conclude that Strauss's work is incoherent would be too hasty. My inchoate formulation of the problem in its surface is very likely inadequate. Yet I think this problem, as it first appears, in our main clue to his teaching in *Natural Right and History*. It is like those onto-

---

4. *NRH*, pp.32, 35 (cf. 74, 78, 92, 125); 7, 8, 24 (cf. 100, 141, 145, 150).

logical problems which Aristotle likened to fetters and signs: it both straitens and directs our thought about Strauss's thought. And just as one can become wise, Aristotle held, only by going through those problems in a fine way, so too can we achieve full understanding of *Natural Right and History*, I suggest, only by investigating thoroughly this problem in its surface. Let us undertake such an investigation.

I

If two things *a* and *b* appear incommensurable, there are roughly two ways in which one might try to explain away the appearance. One is to show that *a*, more precisely understood, is commensurate with *b*. The other is to show that *b*, more precisely understood, is commensurate with *a*. Let us now suppose that Strauss presents the natural right teaching I have ascribed to him, and look to see whether his alleged skepticism is really incompatible with the presentation of that teaching.

First, is Strauss a skeptic at all? He does strictly distinguish skepticism from historicism. He does imply that skepticism, like philosophy in the full sense of the term, is superior to historicism.[5] But he also asserts that "for the skeptic, all assertions are uncertain and therefore essentially arbitrary," and for Strauss not all assertions are uncertain or essentially arbitrary. He maintains, for example, that there is a transhistorical horizon to which human beings can aspire in thought, and a way of life to which we should now aspire in deed. And he holds, apparently without reservation, that the way toward wisdom is investigation of historical or political phenomena, not Cartesian skepticism.[6]

Furthermore, the transhistorical horizon to which philosophers look is not identical, on Strauss's account, with the fundamental problems. For that transhistorical order is said to be "the whole" and to be "eternal," whereas the fundamental problems are spoken of as many, but never as parts, and they are said to be "coeval with human thought."[7] What is coeval with human thought would be eternal only if human thought were eternal, and Strauss nowhere

---

5. *NRH*, pp. 20, 29, 30, 32, 35.
6. *NRH*, p. 20 with pp. 124, 171, 196, 320.
7. *NRH*, *e.g.*, pp. 20, 32, 35, 89, 90, 116, 122–23, 125, 151, 176.

suggests that human thought is even sempiternal. He barely alludes to the Aristotelian speculation that humankind is as old as the cosmos, or to the Kantian speculation that any horizon to which we can successfully aspire in thought is relative to subjective conditions of thought. Indeed, his very use of the word "coeval" in this context leads one to believe that he would reject the former speculation; and his refusal to follow those who reduce the eternal to the temporal, or the knowable to the constructible, leads one to believe that he would reject the latter speculation as well. On Strauss's account, then, there is a transhistorical order beyond even the transhistorical problems with which philosophers become involved in their pursuit of wisdom. Consequently Strauss himself is neither a Pyrrhonian skeptic, who would make no such judgment, nor an Academic skeptic, for whom every such judgment is objectively uncertain.

Furthermore, Strauss introduces his account of the fundamental problems in chapter one, where his chief purpose is to refute radical historicism. How does his account serve that purpose? It delineates, I believe, the only plausible position which is clearly anti-historicistic and which clearly avoids historicism's objection to anti-historicism. It is clearly anti-historicistic because the fundamental problems are not themselves relative to any given historical situation. And it clearly avoids historicism's critique of the philosophical tradition because the admission of fundamental problems does not itself presuppose that to be is to be intelligible, or to be always, and it is just these traditional presuppositions to which historicists object.[8] Indeed, Strauss could consistently assert not only that the fundamental problems are transhistorical without being thought-independent, but also that they come to light differently in different epochs, just as one and the same form may look different from different points of view. If this interpretation should be correct, however, then his inchoate theory of problems is a device for revealing the limits of historicism, not necessarily an expression of skepticism on his part.

From such considerations one might infer that Strauss is neither modern nor a classic skeptic. And if he is not a skeptic of either sort, then the problem apparent in the surface of *Natural Right and History* is merely apparent.

8. *NRH*, esp. pp. 23–24, 30–33. On the Kantian background here, see V. Gourevitch, "Philosophy and Politics, I-II," *Review of Metaphysics* 22 (1968): 300. In being coeval with what partakes of them, "Straussian" problems are unlike "Platonic" ideas but perhaps not unlike "Socratic" ideas.

But this inference should be resisted. First, although he is not an Academic or Pyrrhonian skeptic, and he rejects the Cartesian way of doubt, he is nevertheless skeptical in the original, Socratic sense of the term. To philosophize, he maintains, is to proceed toward or within human wisdom, and human wisdom consists in "knowledge of what one does not know, or awareness of the fundamental problems and, therewith, the fundamental alternatives." Such knowledge is not to be conceived as Rousseau conceived it. Yet it and not more-than-human wisdom is the peak of philosophical or "theoretical" inquiry.[9]

Secondly, it is true that Strauss's account of the transhistorical is tantalizingly brief and obscure. Like Plato's accounts of what is beyond the cave, it leaves much to be desired. But it is not true that on his account all uncertainty is subjective, intersubjective or historical. For each fundamental problem admits of various so-called solutions, two (or a few) of which are fundamental. A "solution" is said to be fundamental when philosophy is incapable of deciding between it and its principal competitor. Therefore, while the philosopher may be able to ascertain which alternatives are fundamental, which are not, he remains in a state of perplexity regarding the fundamental alternatives themselves. And he remains in such perplexity because the fundamental problems are themselves somewhat indeterminate or cloudy. They determine which alternative is fundamental, but not which side of a fundamental alternative is final. Consequently they underdetermine a philosopher's suggested resolution of them. They are such that neither side of an alternative is certain, even if the alternative should be certainly fundamental.[10]

9. *NRH*, pp. 32, 34, 35, 42, 79. Compare pp. 258, 262–63, 312, 320. See also L. Strauss, *On Tyranny* (Ithaca: Cornell U.P., 1963), pp. 209–210, and *What is Political Philosophy?* (Westport: Greenwood Press, 1973), p. 38.

10. *NRH*, esp. pp. 32, 35. One may usefully compare Sextus Empiricus on *isostheneia*. Some readers will be reminded of W. v. O. Quine's Hobbesian thesis that the world, or the flux of experience, underdetermines our theories about the world. On Quine's account, however, though the flux of experience puts some constraints on our theory-making, it nevertheless admits of indefinitely many theories none of which is evidentially superior to any other, whereas on Strauss's account the number of fundamental options is quite small. Some readers will also be reminded of R. Nozick's claim that there are several true but mutually incompatible theories of the world. On Nozick's account, however, all these theories are indeed true, whereas on Strauss's account none of the fundamental options is indeed final. Some readers might insist that the problematic character of every fundamental alternative is due not to the problems themselves but to the unprova-

Finally, it is true that as Socrates' inchoate theory of forms serves in the *Republic* to reveal the limits of the political, so Strauss's theory of problems serves in chapter one to reveal the limits of the historical. It is also true that Strauss makes no further use of this theory in *Natural Right and History*. Nor does he pause to elaborate it. Yet he does reiterate it in the beginning of chapter two, and evidently it is for him an abiding hypothesis.[11] We should then view his theory of problems not only as an elenctic device, but also as involving a kind of skepticism which he shares.

I conclude that the problem apparent in the surface of *Natural Right and History* cannot be dissolved by denying what first appears to be Strauss's Socratic skepticism about the attainability of more than human wisdom. Socratic skepticism is questionable, to be sure. For one thing, is knowledge of ignorance without perplexity? If so, how can it be knowledge of such *problems*? And if not, how can it be *knowledge* of such problems? But to pose these questions is only to note that part of the problem inherent in Strauss's work is itself problematic.

II

One can accept Socratic skepticism, however, and still deny that it entails the irresolvability of the problem of natural right. There are two ways in which one might argue that Strauss denied this entailment.

First, consider *The City and Man*. There too Strauss (following Plato) takes wisdom to be of the whole. One part of the whole he calls "the political sphere." Like every other part it is partial; it is, like a cave, both partly closed and partly open to the whole. The parts are in various ways closed not only to the whole but also to one another. They are mutually discriminable. They can be counted. Each can be isolated in thought and investigated. Political philos-

---

bility even of those options which are final. This, however, is nowhere stated or implied in Strauss's account. In the relevant contexts he does not even mention the problem of persuading others to accept a statement one knows to be true. And probably he would agree that no fundamental option could be demonstrated even if it were final, on the ground that arguments to first principles can be deictic but not apodeictic.

11. *NRH*, pp. 35, 125, and, *e.g.*, *Thoughts on Machiavelli*, p. 14; *What Is Political Philosophy?* pp. 11, 26, 33, 39, 116; *The City and Man* (Chicago: University of Chicago Press, 1977), p. 21.

ophy is about the political sphere in particular. It is the sustained attempt to gain precise and comprehensive knowledge of this sphere. Such knowledge is attainable because the political community is "completely intelligible," and it is completely intelligible "because its limits can be made perfectly manifest" without having attained knowledge of the other parts, and without having answered "the question regarding the whole; it is sufficient to have raised the question regarding the whole."[12]

Might not Strauss have handled the problem of natural right in a similar way? There are the problems. These problems are inter-related and yet, unlike clouds on a cloudy day, they can be counted. Each can be picked out and figured out. One can pose and answer the question of natural right, for example, without answering "the cosmological question." More precisely and generally, one can ascend from philosophical perplexity to knowledge about natural right while remaining in philosophical perplexity about the other problems. Per-haps one must be aware of other problems as problems if one has resolved the problem of natural right alone. The question of nat-ural right could then be answered once and for all within a context of questions pursued but never answered. In this way, at least, po-litical science would be metaphysically neutral.

Natural Right and History does seem to be neutral in some such sense, and yet I find in it no evidence that Strauss tried to reconcile his skepticism with his natural right teaching in the way just now described, and some evidence that he would have rejected the at-tempt. For on his account, while Plato or Socrates took the whole to be heterogeneous in a way that allows for a variety of discrete what-is questions about its various parts, he nevertheless maintained that "the meaning of a part depends on the meaning of the whole," consequently no what-is question can be answered once and for all apart from a good understanding of the whole. With some such metaphysical holism Strauss evidently agrees.[13] Consequently his distinction between the subject matter of cosmology or physics and the subject matter of political science or ethics must ultimately differ from what the Scholastics called *distinctio realis*. In this respect, too,

---

12. *The City and Man*, pp. 21, 62, 138; cf. *What Is Political Philosophy?*, p.38; and *NRH*, pp. 123, 145–46. One should ask whether one can make "the cave" a part in the way that the cosmos or universe is a part, without obfuscating the distinc-tion between *nomos* and *physis*; consider *NRH*, p. 137.
13. Cf. *NRH*, pp. 126–27 with pp. 7–8, and p. 36 with p. 74.

it must differ from Kant's distinction between nature and freedom and Weber's distinction between facts and values. When he says "natural right" Strauss means *natural* right as well as natural *right*. His investigation of political affairs, like Socrates', only seems to be independent of the all-important question, "*Quid sit natura?*" When he says "political philosophy" he means political *philosophy* as well as *political* philosophy.[14]

There is, however, a second way in which Strauss might have reconciled his skepticism with his natural rightism. *Ex hypothesi* there are certain fundamental problems. Each is an irremovable mover of our thought; we are able to understand it and yet unable to ascertain which side of the fundamental alternative pertaining to it is true. Philosophy, then, cannot resolve the problem of natural right in a more than provisional manner, if indeed this problem should be fundamental. Is it? Did Strauss believe that it is?

Nowhere in *Natural Right and History* is it clearly said to be fundamental. There is mention of "the fundamental political problem," and no political problem is more fundamental than the problem of natural right.[15] But while it may be fundamental in relation to citizens everywhere and always, and to everyone in our historical situation who apprehends "the crisis of the West," the fundamental political problem may not be fundamental absolutely or in relation to human thought.

Furthermore, if Strauss did take the problem of natural right to be fundamental, he would presumably have set out the fundamental alternative pertaining to it. But the alternative he sets out in *Natural Right and History* is that between "classic" and "modern" natural right, and this alternative does not appear fundamental. Modern political philosophers turned from nature as man's transpolitical end to the state of nature as man's subpolitical condition, from men as radically social to men as radically individual (persons), from pursuit of the good to flight from the bad, from virtue to comfortable, institutionalized freedom, and from reason to passion, the general to the local, the eternal to custom or fate. In making this turn they inverted the traditional ranking of theory and practice, and subordinated philosophy to wholly political ends. One result has been that, unlike the classical teaching in opposition to which it emerged, modern natural right is inherently subject to "crisis." Another result

---

14. Cf. *NRH*, pp. 121–22, and *The City and Man*, p. 241.
15. *NRH*, p. 36 with p. 35 (compare pp. 193–94; also p. 141 with p. 198).

has been that, unlike classical philosophy, modern philosophy is almost bound to degenerate into historicism and nihilism. Now, is it the case that philosophy cannot decide between these two disparate views? No; *Natural Right and History* is a sustained philosophical critique of modern natural right together with modern (political) philosophy, and a sustained philosophical defense of classic natural right together with classic (political) philosophy.[16] But if philosophy can decide between these two views, the alternative they articulate is not fundamental. And if the alternative they articulate is not fundamental, the problem for which it is the principal alternative is itself not fundamental. That problem is evidently the problem of natural right. Therefore, the problem of natural right is not fundamental. Therefore, Strauss's skepticism about the fundamental problems is compatible with his teaching about natural right.

But this interpretation, too, is unacceptable. First, nowhere in *Natural Right and History* is the problem of natural right said not to be fundamental, so there is at least an argument from silence on both sides. The silence, moreover, is only partial. For Strauss plainly asserts that "the problem of justice" is fundamental, and that "no alternative is more fundamental than this: human guidance or divine guidance."[17] This alternative evidently represents the two fundamental answers to the question of how man ought to live. The question of how man ought to live thus addresses a fundamental problem. It is also a human problem, hence broadly political. Now, are the problem of justice, the problem of how one ought to live, and the problem of natural right one, two, or three? Let us reconsider *The City and Man*. There Strauss (following Plato) says that the city is completely intelligible insofar as it is limited, "closed." But he does not say that justice is likewise limited. Instead he implies that it is not. He implies that a complete answer to the question of justice will come only if one looks to the soul as well as to the city: justice in the full sense of the term is both political and human.[18] Strauss, I suggest, thought that natural right must be un-

16. Consider esp. *NRH*, pp. 18, 22, 33. Also *Thoughts on Machiavelli*, pp. 290, 293, 295.
17. *NRH*, pp. 32, 74, also pp. 35, 36.
18. *The City and Man*, p. 138; also p. 1 and *NRH*, pp. 144–45, 151, and Plato, *Apology of Socrates* 20b4–5 and context. Strauss says that man's natural sociality provides the basis of natural right "in the narrow or strict sense" of the term (*NRH*, p. 129). Is it man's natural orientation to the good, or the hierarchy within his nature, which provides the basis of natural right in the full or comprehensive sense of the term?

derstood both in terms of the city and in terms of the soul or of what is highest in our soul. And he thought that the problem of natural right is irresolvable because the political and the human constitute an indeterminate dyad: the city is both "closed" and "open" to the soul or to what is highest in our soul.[19] The problematic structure of right he described in several ways: in terms of the theologico-political question, the philosophico-political question, the theologico-philosophical question; in terms of the city and man, persecution and the art of writing, natural right and history, *Philosophie* and *Gesetz.* But I don't see that he regarded any of these descriptions as final in the sense that it adumbrates a resolution of the problem.

Secondly, classic and modern natural right do in a way represent the fundamental alternative. For natural right must be understood in terms of city and soul; and while city and soul cannot be comprehended apart from one another, there is a natural inclination on our part to take them apart in thought and to conceive natural right in terms of soul rather than city, or vice versa. This, I suggest, is the fundamental alternative for the problem of natural right: civic right or psychic right. To early modern political philosophers it appeared (erroneously) that their predecessors opted for psychic right or philosophy, and denigrated civic right or individuality. Ancient political philosophy appeared to have aimed too high. In reaction to this apparent error the first modern political philosophers opted for civic right and neglected psychic right. More pointedly, they personalized right and politicized philosophy. In so doing they lost sight of the transpolitical principle of right. Consequently they lost sight of the dyadic structure of right and therewith the problem of natural right.[20] By comparing modern with classic natural right, however, we can become clearer about what the classic political philosophers supposedly overlooked, we can become aware of what the modern political philosophers under-looked, and we can thus begin to understand the problem of natural right as a problem. It is in the disparity between modern and classic natural right that the fundamental alternative first becomes evident to us.[21]

19. Cf. S. Benardete, "Leo Strauss' *The City and Man,*" *Political Science Reviewer* 8 (1981): 1–11. It is pertinent here to ask how the problem of natural right is related to that problem regarding homogeneity and heterogeneity which Strauss mentions in *What is Political Philosophy?* pp. 39–40. Their relation will become evident, perhaps, on investigation of the fact that justice appears to be both a measure of more-and-less and a measure of fittingness. Cf. Plato, *Statesman.*

20. That they lost sight of the political as well is understandable, given the "openness" of the political to the soul.

21. Consider *Thoughts on Machiavelli,* p. 295 with p. 14. (Strauss took the state-

For Strauss, then, the problem of natural right is fundamental. Therefore his skepticism extends to it. This explains why his refutation of radical historicism (chapter 1) is stronger than his refutation of Weberian positivism (chapter 2): he is more positive about the possibility of philosophy than he is about the possibility of natural right, and more certain, therefore, about the possibility of political philosophy than he is about its practical value.[22] Is it then the case that Straussian skepticism, like Weberian positivism, leads to nihilism? No, for Weberian positivism is dogmatic and clearly pertains to the unknowability and (alleged) mutual incompatibility of all ultimate values, whereas Straussian skepticism is hypothetical and clearly pertains to natural right in particular.[23] One wonders, however, whether such skepticism does not extend to the (hypothetical) goodness of political philosophy as well. One wonders, moreover, whether Strauss is no more than Socrates gripped by the alternative between a philosophical and a religious way of life.[24]

III

Again, the problem apparent in the surface of Strauss's *Natural Right and History* is the disparity between what first appears to be

---

ments on these two pages to be consistent, and presumptively they are.) The dyadic structure of natural right, as I have described it, is arguably too simple. According to Strauss, at any rate, Aristotle held natural right to be mutable on the ground that otherwise it would be unable to cope with the inventiveness of evil; more generally, perhaps, it would not be applicable in extreme as well as normal situations. Plato, too, avoided the Skylla of absolutism and the Charybdis of relativism; he too held that there is a universally valid hierarchy of ends but no indefeasible rules of action. (*NRH*, pp. 160–63. Notice the absence of footnotes to his account here.) This, according to Strauss, is an explication of the mutability of natural right, or mutability of its instantiation in practice, and not an explication of its dilution by conventional right. (Compare *NRH*, pp. 152–53.) Perhaps, then, we should explicate the dyadic structure of natural right in terms of the contrast not only between civic and psychic, but also between normal and extreme. I would regard this as an elaboration of my proposal, however, not as an alternative to it.

22. *NRH*, p. 35. In this respect Strauss may be more Socratic than Platonic (p. 36).

23. *NRH*, p. 42 (not inconsistent with p. 5). It is the contemporary rejection of natural right which entails nihilism. Classic philosophical conventionalism, which also rejects natural right, does not. And Socratic human wisdom does not reject natural right, but rather acknowledges it as a problem.

24. Compare *NRH*, pp. 36, 74, 86–87, 97, et passim with Plato's *Meno* 80b6, 81d3-el, 86b6-c2. Strauss nowhere asserts, with Weber, that ultimate values are mutually incompatible. Weber did not realize that he was in no position to make such an assertion (*NRH*, pp. 64–71).

his skepticism about natural right and what first appears to be his positive teaching about natural right. This problem I have tried and failed to resolve by arguing that the former, more precisely understood, accords with the latter. So let us now make the contrary attempt. Let us suppose that Strauss is a skeptic of the kind I have described, and look to see whether his alleged natural right teaching is really incompatible with such skepticism.

First, does Strauss offer any positive natural right teaching in *Natural Right and History*? Beyond chapter two there is little "philosophic analysis" or dialectic in the original sense of the term, and much history of ideas. In this history the "idea" of natural right is not only regulative, it also has an origin and a career. There are not only various conceptions of natural right, there are also "classic natural right" and "modern natural right." Having defeated historicism Strauss adopts the language of historicism. His account takes on the look of Nietzsche's *Twilight of the Idols*.[25]

Notice, moreover, that Strauss fails to show which (if any) of the three classic natural right teachings is most adequate. Is it the Socratic-Platonic, the Aristotelian, or the Thomistic? He seems to regard the third as quite inadequate. Suppose he does. There remain the Socratic-Platonic and the Aristotelian teachings, and about this important alternative he offers very little critical discussion.[26]

Notice, thirdly, that Strauss does not even establish the existence of natural right. In particular, he fails to show that classic "philosophical conventionalism" is false: his critique is at most a refutation of hedonism, and one could accept conventionalism with regard to justice while rejecting hedonism with regard to goodness; one could, for example, maintain that our natural end is a life in philosophy rather than pleasure, and that justice like political society is an indispensable albeit conventional means to this end.[27] He fails, moreover, to proceed openly in accordance with his own proposed method. For he claims near the end of chapter two that

25. See especially the section entitled " 'Reason' in Philosophy" in *Twilight of the Idols*. In Nietzsche's account the intrahistorical concepts are those of unity, thinghood, substance, permanence, the true, the good, the perfect, the ego. In Strauss's account they are the ideas of philosophy, nature, natural right, the best regime, science, the city and virtue, and History (*NRH*, pp. 3, 11, 12, 31, 38, 80, 81, 82, 84, 93, 167, 180, 191, 253, 261, 316).

26. *NRH*, pp. 146ff. When Strauss remarks the noble simplicity of the Thomistic doctrine, he seems to be speaking politely; see p. 163 with p. 262.

27. *NRH*, pp. 107–109, 126–27, 151.

the search for natural right must involve a thoroughgoing investigation of the relevant "phenomena," but he does not then undertake any such investigation. There is little examination of those prephilosophical "experiences" of right and wrong articulated, for example, in the epigraphs to his whole account, and no explicit examination of the democratic and oligarchic conceptions of right operative in, for example, our own country: his rehearsal of the gigantomachy between ancient and modern political theories (not regimes) appears quite removed from the conflicts inherent in political life.[28] Above all, he fails even to pose the fundamental question: what is right? His account is thus like Plato's *Gorgias*. And when it turns instead to the generation and corruption of authoritative teachings about right, it takes on the look of a likely story or a myth of the kind found in Plato's *Republic* VII-IX.[29]

So Strauss has failed, apparently, if indeed he intended to give a positive natural right teaching. But was that his intention? Consider the following alternative. Strauss wants to know what natural right is. He realizes that in order to know as much, one must begin from the proper starting point. He realizes, moreover, that insofar as we are children of our historical situation, we are removed from that starting point. We must make a preliminary ascent in order to undertake the properly philosophical ascent toward natural right. Strauss's intention in *Natural Right and History* is to represent this preliminary ascent, to indicate the way to the beginning or surface. It is then propaedeutic. The goal is retrieval or renewal (*Wiederholung*) of the fundamental question of right (*Rechtsfrage*, not *Seinsfrage*), and the way to that goal is a gradual disclosure of the real relationship between natural right and history (not *Sein* and *Zeit*). Such disclosure requires first a philosophical critique of radical historicism and positivistic social science or nihilism, then a genetic account of the kind given in chapters three and following. This account is indeed like Nietzsche's *Twilight of the Idols*, and a tame dog is like a wolf. But whereas Nietzsche historicizes in the guise of an unrelenting demythologizer, Strauss dehistoricizes in the familiar guise of an historian of ideas. He also demotes the idea of progress: the new and strange possibilities he articulates are in fact possibilities articulated by the first philosophers in "the West." Readers are thus led

28. *NRH*, pp. x, 31–32, 78–80, 105, 125, 137–38, 144. Compare Aristotle's *Politics*, bk. 3.
29. Cf. Plato *Republic* 545d8 with 369a5–6, 376d9, 378c4.

to recall, as it were, the distinction between *nomos* and *physis*, recognition of which is coeval with philosophy in the full sense of the term.[30] They recall, too, the idea of natural right and begin to grasp the problem of natural right as a problem, recognition of which is coeval with political philosophy in the full sense of the term.

If this interpretation be correct, Strauss's intention in *Natural Right and History* was not to give a natural right teaching; rather, it was on the one hand to revive political philosophy, and on the other hand to counter its ongoing politicization. And he succeeded, as much as one can, notwithstanding the fact that his chosen means (historical studies) are not without some crucial, acknowledged deficiencies.[31] Certainly he exposed the distortions wrought by the image-making of contemporary social scientists and historicists. Certainly he has shown us how to break out of the downward spiral of attempts to overcome modern natural right, whose outcomes have been yet more extreme versions of modern natural right ending in Weberian positivism and existentialism. Alternatively, he has shown us how to break out of the downward spiral of attempts to overcome classic natural right, whose successive outcomes have been progressive deformations of classic natural right and eventually waves of fanaticism in the image of philosophy.

We must, however, ask whether this interpretation is entirely correct. There is much evidence that Strauss sought to revive political philosophy in the original, full sense of the term. But there is also evidence of a strong inclination, on his part, toward a positive natural right teaching. The evidence is soft because Strauss rarely speaks in his own voice. Yet all readers of *Natural Right and History* are aware of the inclination. Many, I dare say, would agree that Strauss tends to accept as true the Socratic answer to the question of what is most needful or important for us, and to side with those natural rightists who taught that political societies should be ordered with a view to this most important thing. Some would agree, moreover, that he tends to understand natural right apart from natural law, to side with the Socratic-Platonic over against the Aristotelian alternative, and consequently, to stress the tension between natural and conventional right. Strauss does not say what justice is, nor does he preach justice or cry out for a spiritual renewal, but he does give signs. His book is thus like one of Plato's aporetic dialogues: it is

---

30. *NRH*, pp. 11, 31, 83, 95.
31. *NRH*, pp. 13, 57, 120. On the need for historical studies of a certain sort: pp. 33–34, 95.

plainly incomplete in that it clarifies without finally answering the question "What is right?" and yet, while clearing the way for discovery of that answer, it is not altogether silent about what that answer is likely to be. Strauss evidently intends to renew the question of natural right and to answer it. His suggested answer is not a doctrine, if by "doctrine" one means an expression of knowledge or of dogma. It is rather a carefully considered hypothesis couched in further questions—like Socrates' hypothesis that virtue is knowledge—and hypotheses of this kind are doctrines in a sense; they tell us where to keep looking.

Those of us seeking to complete the foregoing sketch of Strauss's positive natural right teaching do encounter a few little questions. *Ex hypothesi*, in "the basic controversy in political philosophy," he sides with the naturalists against the conventionalists.[32] But what, then, is his full argument against classic philosophical conventionalism? Does he too hold that man's nature is hierarchically ordered? If so, what exactly does he take its order to be, how does he justify this conception, and how does he deal with the content (as distinguished from the origin) of nonteleological modern science?[33] Does he agree with Plato that natural right is immutable, or with Aristotle that it is mutable? Does he too hold that man is naturally political, or does he hold that "the cave" is itself only by convention? If the latter, how does he avoid the conclusion that all political right is conventional? And how does he then avoid the reduction of natural right to what I have called "psychic right"? Or would he, contrary to what I have said, advocate such a reduction? If so, would he not also hold that political and human virtue constitute a determinate dyad?

In any event, Strauss's natural right teaching is more than a declaration of natural right as a problem. It is not correct, therefore, to claim that the problem apparent in the surface of *Natural Right and History* is merely apparent, on the ground that what appears to be his positive natural right teaching is no teaching at all.

IV

It is difficult to square Strauss's natural right teaching with his skepticism about natural right if they are on a par, or if they are

32. *NRH*, pp. 93ff. See above, note 2.
33. Cf. V. Gourevitch, op. cit., pp. 289–293, and R. Kennington, "Strauss's Natural Right and History," *Review of Metaphysics* 35 (1981): 61, 74, 80–86. Strauss himself speaks of the difficulty with which every teleological physics is beset (*NRH*, p. 172).

in the same dimension or element. Let us consider the possibility that they are not.

On the one hand, Strauss's skepticism about natural right is theoretical or philosophical; it belongs to his human wisdom. On the other hand, his positive teaching about natural right is practical or political; it evinces his good sense. Human wisdom and good sense are heterogeneous. At any rate, while the latter is subordinate to the former, it cannot depend on the former for all of its fundamentals. This all classical and some modern political philosophers have granted.[34] Good sense is then either partially or wholly independent of philosophy. Let us suppose that Strauss's positive natural right teaching is wholly independent of his awareness of the problem of natural right, that it is a thoroughly practical and not properly philosophical teaching. It is then difficult to see how one could be inconsistent with the other. Just as Pyrrho's ordinary behavior cannot have contradicted his suspension of judgment, or as Socrates' unrelenting decency cannot be incompatible with his perplexity about goodness itself, so too the moral suggestions made in *Natural Right and History* cannot be incompatible with the skeptical attitude revealed in *Natural Right and History*.

This alternative is plausible. Strauss's works all have a high moral tone, a seriousness that is foreign to skepticism as such. This seriousness is due principally to his concern with our political or historical predicament. Is it not such concern, rather than wonder before the eternal order or perennial problems, that initiates his philosophical investigations and determines their direction if not their manner? If so, Strauss belongs to that tradition of political philosophy which Hobbes identified as public-spirited, and which Strauss (following Hobbes) appears willing to call "idealistic."[35]

Furthermore, he is acquainted with a tradition of exoteric speaking and writing. He observes, for instance, that one of the characters in Cicero's *Laws* is his friend Atticus, "who assents to the Stoic natural law doctrine but who, being an Epicurean, cannot have assented to it because he regarded it as true or in his capacity as a thinker; he rather assented to it in his capacity as a Roman citizen and more particularly as an adherent of aristocracy, because he regarded it as politically salutary." Strauss moreover observes that "Cicero's seem-

---

34. *NRH*, pp. 192, 295ff.
35. *NRH*, 167–68. This is not the only passage in which Strauss notes the connection between such spiritedness and idealism; cf. pp. 142, 177–78.

ingly unqualified acceptance of the Stoic natural law teaching has the same motivation as Atticus'. Cicero himself says that he wrote dialogues in order not to present his real views too openly. After all, he was an Academic skeptic and not a Stoic. And the thinker whom he claims to follow, and whom he admires most, is Plato himself, the founder of the Academy. The least that must be said is that Cicero did not regard the Stoic natural law teaching, in so far as it goes beyond Plato's teaching of natural right, as evidently true."[36] Might not Strauss's seemingly unqualified acceptance of *some* classic natural right doctrine have much the same motivation as Cicero's? His overarching duty in *Natural Right and History* was to promote political philosophy in the original sense of the term, to make this very high activity appear very urgent or needful.[37] But he was also a concerned citizen who saw vividly and diagnosed accurately the crisis of the West. He realized that whereas in philosophy one can well proceed in perplexity, in moral and political life we must take a stand. He realized, moreover, that acceptance of modern natural right is not only philosophically deleterious insofar as it entails a denigration of *theoria*, it is also politically deleterious inasmuch as it involves political atheism, hedonism, and individualism, and inasmuch as it evinces an idealism or spirit of dogmatism willing to lower its sights in order to secure for mankind a comfortable home on earth.[38] Acceptance of classic natural right, on the other hand, is politically as well as philosophically salutary.[39] Accordingly, Strauss played up the theoretical weaknesses in all modern natural right teachings, and played down the theoretical weaknesses in classic natural right teachings. He thus gave the impression of being partisan: ancient Greek political theory is a sort of golden age from which there has been only decline into our benighted era; the good for us is something ancestral. Indeed, would not Strauss's stand seem reactionary were it not for the indirect, tentative way in which he

36. *NRH*, pp. 154–55; see also pp. 3, 6, 206–207. Strauss takes the Stoic natural law doctrine to be Socratic-Platonic in principle.

37. *NRH*, p. 163 with pp. 3, 36.

38. *NRH*, pp. 18, 155, 162, 169, 175, 192, 196f n 39, 303, 313, 320.

39. The crucial difference can be summarized thus: (i) classic natural right provides something like divine support for citizen-morality, whereas modern natural right does not; (ii) classic natural right ranks both nobility and justice above pleasure or comfort, whereas modern natural right does not. It is true that some if not all classic natural right teachings point to a disproportion between political life and philosophy, or between a decent regime in fact and the best possible regime. But acceptance of some such teaching need not be unsalutary.

presented it? Be that as it may, his published adherence to this stand is rather practical or prudential than theoretical or philosophical. His positive natural right teaching is a well-deliberated political opinion, not an expression of wisdom or philosophical awareness. And it might be correct.

So this alternative, too, is plausible. Yet it, too, is not quite acceptable. For Strauss seems inclined to a Socratic-Platonic more than an Aristotelian understanding of the relationship between theory and practice.[40] He repeatedly starts from the observation that we conduct ourselves politically in accordance with thoughts about the political good. Most of these thoughts are opinion not knowledge. Suppose all are opinions. It is nonetheless possible, and likely, that some of these opinions are correct, others incorrect, and that some are more adequate than others. The opinions about the complete political good held by men of good sense are generally more adequate than those held by men without good sense. What accounts for this difference? Nothing can account for it if, in principle, there can be no true definition of the complete political good. And there can be no such statement, in principle, if there be a fundamental, undecidable alternative regarding the complete political good. There is such an alternative, however, if the fundamental political problem is transhistorically fundamental, irresolvable. Therefore, Strauss should not and presumably would not separate practice from theory in the way lately proposed. More precisely, he would not and does not claim that political philosophy ends properly in human wisdom apart from statesmanship or good sense. It is because he accepts no such dualism, perhaps, that he repeatedly speaks of the need to *know* what right is, even when one might deem right opinion to be good enough.[41] Even right opinion cannot be good enough when it is of utmost importance to be sure which opinion is right.

So the alternative lately proposed is not quite acceptable; one cannot square Strauss's natural right teaching with his philosophical skepticism by denying that the former is in the least philosophical. Yet this proposal serves to draw attention to Strauss's near silence, in *Natural Right and History*, about the relation between political philosophy and political wisdom or statesmanship. The former must involve awareness of natural right as a problem. Must the latter as

40. *NRH*, pp. 6–7, 35, 36, 78, 127, 144, 164. He evidently rejects the Rousseauean and Burkean conceptions of this relation: pp. 288, 302, 309, 311.
41. *NRH*, pp. 3, 24, 48, 74, 98, 100, and perhaps pp. 35, 203, 274.

well? The latter must be a source of correct (if not effectual) judgments about actual political affairs. Must the former as well? This proposal also draws attention to an important ambiguity: political philosophy is political in manner of presentation as well as in subject matter.[42] This ambiguity reminds us of the compromise between the good and the necessary, or between wisdom and consent, which arguably is essential to political life. It reminds me also of the problem inherent in Strauss's own published work: the two ways in which political philosophy is political appear to be at once internally related and hardly relatable.

V

I have tried to resolve the problem which appears in the surface of *Natural Right and History*, first by showing that the skepticism it exhibits really accords with what seems to be its natural right teaching, then by showing that its positive natural right teaching really accords with the skepticism it evidently exhibits. My attempt has ended in failure. The problem may now be clearer, but surely it remains a problem.

It is tempting to "forget" a problem of this kind by ignoring one of its two sides. This temptation, however understandable, we should resist. For it was in some such way that Socratic philosophy fathered both Stoicism and Academic skepticism. The incoherence apparent in the surface of Socrates' public work was thus refracted into two opposed sects, each of which lacked the completeness as well as the complexity of its original. Straussian political philosophy is liable to suffer a similar doubling. Whereas its more theoretical offspring would be friends of natural right as a problem, and criticize any stand taken in the cave, the other more practical offspring would engage decisively in political affairs and vilify any open-mindedness in the face of natural right as a problem. Both parties would be truncated versions of the original. The former "Straussians" would be unduly playful, having lost touch with their own groundings in practical affairs; they would lack self-knowledge of the kind Strauss himself had. And the latter "Straussians," having lost sight of first principles, would be doctrinaire; they would lack Strauss's moderation.[43]

42. I investigate this ambiguity in "What Is Politike Philosophia?" *Man and World* 17 (1984): 431–52, reprinted in *Phenomenology and the Human Sciences*, ed. J. N. Mohanty (Boston: Nijhoff, 1985), pp. 191–212.
43. *NRH*, pp. 6, 59–62, 114–15, 206–207.

Another reason for resisting this temptation is the plain fact that, by trying and failing to show that it is really coherent, I have not shown that Strauss's political philosophy is after all really incoherent. The problem inherent in *Natural Right and History* remains perplexing. It seems fitting, therefore, that we go on investigating it. I've noted in passing several ways in which we might do so. My main suggestion, obviously, is that we compare this problem with one inherent in the surface of Plato's Socratic dialogues. In the *Republic*, for instance, Socrates admits that he doesn't at all know what justice is, asserts that even the best of mere opinions are blind, and yet proceeds to answer the question, "What is justice?" In the *Gorgias* he admits that he does not speak as one who knows what he is talking about, and yet he proceeds to make severe claims about right and wrong, good and bad, and to refute those who make strong counterclaims. He alone puts his hand to the political art, he says, and yet his elenctic ability is evidently a new variety of punitive rhetoric, not an art. And in the *Apology of Socrates* he presents himself in ways seemingly incommensurate. On the one hand he knows that he is quite unwise. In service to the god he has displayed this human wisdom, not by exhorting and rebuking others but simply by refuting them. He is a paradigm of human worthlessness. On the other hand he is a new Achilles who maintains that the soul is superior to honor and wealth, that the greatest good for a human being is philosophy, and that the unexamined life is for a human being not worth living. In adherence to god or nature he acts on these beliefs, by examining himself and others and by rebuking and exhorting his fellow Athenians most of all. He is a paradigm of human and political excellence or concern.[44] In sum, there is in Plato's Socrates a disproportion between what first appears to be his skepticism about the attainability of wisdom and what first appears to be his dogmatism about the good for man: the sustained pursuit of wisdom is both the greatest good for us and utterly in vain.

This disproportion, laid up by Plato in the surface of his more openly Socratic writings, I call "the problem of Socrates." The disproportion in the surface of Strauss's *Natural Right and History* I call "the problem of Strauss." The problem of Socrates and the problem of Strauss are plainly similar. Maybe they are two manifestations

---

44. *Republic*, esp. 354b1-c3, 506c2-9. *Gorgias* 509a4-7 with 458a2-b1, 521d6-7 with 464b2-466a3, and 465a6 with *Symposium* 202a6, 204a1-7. *Apology of Socrates* 20d8, 21b4 (cf. *Symposium* 175e3); 23b1, 28a2ff., 38a2-6.

of the same fundamental problem, one that we encounter while trying to answer the question, "What is philosophy?" But maybe there is an essential difference. Whereas Socrates wrote little or nothing, Strauss wrote and published a great deal. Whereas Socrates was wholly free of the Enlightenment, Strauss was not. Where Socrates speaks of the good, or the first principle of the all, Strauss speaks simply of the whole.[45] While there is no tradition of political philosophy for Socrates, for Strauss there is. And, most obviously, Strauss's work has a historical dimension which Socrates' lacks. This difference probably encompasses the others. Perhaps it is accidental; historical studies may now be necessary as a propaedeutic or as an academic cover.[46] Perhaps it is not accidental; Strauss's thinking may be in the grip of the historical school, or its radical legacy, to a greater extent than Socrates' dialectic could be. The difficulty can be put in the following way. Natural right and history are conjoined as well as distinguished in Strauss's account. What is the nature of that conjunction?

In any case, the problem of Socrates and the problem of Strauss are alike. By considering them synoptically, by rubbing them together like sticks, we may well achieve the illumination we need.[47]

45. Compare *Thoughts on Machiavelli*, p. 299.
46. Strauss himself recommends the former interpretation: *NRH*, pp. 7, 33, 34, also pp. 16, 56. I do not find that he has justified his assertion that our most urgent need can be satisfied *only* by means of historical studies, or his suggestion that the problem of natural right must today be a matter of historical (non-Socratic) recollection.
47. An earlier version of this essay was presented at the 79th annual meeting of the American Political Science Association. I benefited from questions and comments directed to me on that occasion, particularly those by L. Berns, F. Canavan, V. Gourevitch, H. Jaffa, and T. G. West.

Blasphemy and Leo Strauss's Machiavelli

Dante Germino

In 1966, I published a review article hailing Leo Strauss's *Thoughts on Machiavelli* as an instant classic. I also expressed some reservations or "second thoughts" about its conclusions.[1] In the intervening years my appreciation for the profundity and originality of Strauss's interpretation has only increased, but many of my doubts have also remained. Here I wish to restate both my admiration and reservations with particular attention to parts of Strauss's chapter on Machiavelli published in the 1972 edition of his *History of Political Philosophy*, co-edited with Joseph Cropsey.[2]

Let me at the outset state the obvious: Strauss's interpretation of Machiavelli is well — indeed overwhelmingly — supported by textual evidence, given Strauss's manner of reading between the lines. No interpreter, therefore, is entitled to dismiss it out of hand, even if he or she disagrees with Strauss's methodology, in whole or in part. In this respect, Claude Lefort has provided a model for scholars whose philosophical orientation differs widely from that of Strauss.[3] Strauss has given us a truly fresh look at the great Florentine.

I do not choose here to enter into a debate with what might be called Strauss's strict constructionist interpretation of the great texts in political theory. For a variety of reasons, I do not agree with Strauss that it is possible to understand a thinker "as he understood himself," any more than I agree with Ranke that history can be written *wie sie eigentlich gewesen ist.* "Nevertheless" (as Machiavelli would say), I agree that the attempt to grasp and portray a great political theorist's achievement empathetically from the inside is entirely laud-

---

1. "Second Thoughts on Leo Strauss's Machiavelli," *Journal of Politics* 37 (1966): 794–817. Without in any way implying his assent to my arguments, I would like to express my gratitude to my friend Prof. Harvey Mansfield for his comments on an earlier version of this article.
2. Leo Strauss and Joseph Cropsey, eds., *History of Political Philosophy*, 2nd ed. (Chicago: Rand McNally, 1972), pp. 271–92.
3. Claude Lefort, *Le travail de l'oeuvre: Machiavel* (Paris: Gallimard, 1972), pp. 259–309. By contrast, Gennaro Sasso, one of Italy's premier Machiavelli scholars, refused even to discuss Strauss's conclusions because he did not want to spend the time necessary to understand Strauss's teaching. *Machiavelli e gli antichi*, 2 vols. (Milan - Naples: Riccardo Ricciardi, 1987), 1: 4–5.

able. With respect to Machiavelli, Strauss has made one of the great
attempts at such a portrayal.

I wish here also to look at Strauss himself empathetically and
from the inside, especially as it concerns his conclusion that Machiavelli was a deliberate (religious) blasphemer, whose blasphemy
is all the more serious because it was covert. This matter is of crucial importance to Strauss's understanding of Machiavelli's entire
teaching and its relationship to modernity. Only the uncritical acceptance of a convention of modernity itself, that is, that religion
is a "private affair" and should have nothing to do with politics, can
prevent a scholar in political theory from taking the blasphemy question with the utmost seriousness.[4]

Strauss identifies Machiavelli as a blasphemer on the basis of an
apparent mistake in *Discourses* I, 26, where David rather than God
appears to be the referent and author of certain words in the *Magnificat*
(*Luke* 1:53). For Strauss, every blunder by Machiavelli — and especially every "manifest blunder"— is deliberate and hides a deception.
Inasmuch as the passage in question is the only New Testament quotation in the *Discourses*, and inasmuch as it occurs in the twenty-
sixth chapter, Machiavelli's "mistake" with regard to it conceals a
deception of mammoth proportions, Strauss alleges.

Strauss's reason for attributing crucial importance to *Discourses*
I, 26 deserves to be quoted at some length:

> We have seen [because the *Discourses* has 142 chapters to correspond
> to Livy's 142 books] that the number of chapters of the *Discourses* is
> meaningful and has been deliberately chosen. We may thus . . . wonder
> whether the number of chapters of the *Prince* is not also meaningful.
> The *Prince* consist of 26 chapters. Twenty-six is the numerical value
> of the sacred name of God in Hebrew, of the Tetragrammaton. But
> did Machiavelli know of this? I do not know. Twenty-six equals 2 times
> 13. Thirteen . . . for quite sometime has been considered an unlucky
> number, but in former times it was also and even primarily consid-
> ered a lucky number. So "twice thirteen" might mean both good luck
> and bad luck, and hence altogether: luck, *fortuna*. A case can be made
> for the view that [for Machiavelli] . . . God is fortuna [and] . . . sub-
> ject to human influence (imprecation).[5]

Having established, to his satisfaction, the importance of the
number 26 for Machiavelli's theology, Strauss turns to consider the
26th chapter of the *Discourses*, whose heading declares that "a new

4. See Leo Strauss, *Thoughts on Machiavelli* (Glencoe, IL: The Free Press, 1958),
p. 231.
5. Strauss and Cropsey, *Political Philosophy*, p. 286.

prince . . . must make everything new." This means that the subject of the chapter is tyranny, he says, because at the end of chapter 25 Machiavelli had written that he who wants absolute power must make everything new (offices, names, authorities, leaders).[6] Although Machiavelli avoids using the term tyranny in both the *Prince* and in *Discourses* I, 26, tyranny is the actual subject of the one and the other, Strauss concludes.

According to Strauss, Machiavelli's inference that the *New Testament* verse "He hath filled the hungry with good things and the rich he hath sent empty away" applies to King David must be interpreted as follows:

> The quotation forms part of the Magnificat, the Virgin Mary's prayer of thanks after she heard from the angel Gabriel that she would bring forth a son called Jesus; he that "hath filled the hungry with good things and sent the rich empty away" is none other than God himself. In the context of this chapter [*Discourses* I, 26] this means that God is a tyrant, and that King David, who made the rich poor and the poor rich, was a Godly king, a king who walked in the ways of the Lord because he proceeded in a tyrannical way. We must note that this is the sole *New Testament* quotation occurring in the *Discourses* or in the *Prince*. And that sole New Testament quotation is used for expressing a most horrible blasphemy. Someone might say . . . that the blasphemy is not expressly uttered but only implied. But this defense, far from helping Machiavelli, make his case worse, and for this reason: when a man openly utters or vomits a blasphemy, all good men shudder and turn away from him, or punish him according to his just deserts; the sin is entirely his. But a concealed blasphemy is so insidious . . . because it . . . compels the hearer or reader to think the blasphemy by himself and so to become an accomplice of the blasphemer. Machiavelli thus establishes a kind of intimacy with his readers . . . whom he calls "young," by inducing them to think forbidden or criminal thoughts. . . . This is an important part of his education of the young, or to use a time honored expression, of the corruption of the young.[7]

The most striking phrase in the above passage is "vomits a blasphemy." By using it, Strauss clearly means to align himself on the side of the phrase's author, the sixteenth-century French Calvinist Innocent Gentillet, one of the principal founders of the tradi-

6. Niccolo's Machiavelli, *Tutte le opere* (Florence: Sansoni, 1971), pp.25–26. The conclusion of *Discourses* I, 25 reads: "ma quello che vuole fare una potestà assoluta, la quale dagli autori è chiamata tirannide, debbe rinnovare ogni cosa, come nel seguente capitolo si dirà" (but he who desires an absolute power, which the authors call tyranny, must make everything new, as is explained in the following chapter).
7. Strauss and Cropsey, *Political Philosophy*, pp. 287–88.

tion which associates Machiavelli's name with scandalous and immoral "Machiavellianism."[8] Although Strauss thinks that the traditional version of Machiavelli as a diabolical figure forgets that the devil himself was a fallen angel, he thinks that one can "ascend" from that version to a more adequate understanding. On the other hand, the revised version (Machiavelli as humanist, republican, friend of the people, politically secular but not antireligious) represents the triumph of Machiavellianism itself. Those scholars who hail the "good," "progressive," "democratic" Machiavelli have been unknowingly corrupted by Machiavelli's evil message, hidden under a cover of good thoughts and good works.[9]

Let me now begin my criticism of Strauss on Machiavelli as blasphemer by comparing what Machiavelli has to say about David and about blasphemy in his "Exhortation to Penitence." (The Exhortation is a sermon believed to have been delivered by Machiavelli to a religious confraternity of which he was a member. Some scholars of note now place the date of the composition between 1525 and 1527, that is, during the last two years of Machiavelli's life.) I shall next proceed to a critique of Strauss's interpretation of *Discourses* I, 26. In conclusion, I will consider Strauss's closing words to his 1972 textbook chapter on Machiavelli as they appear to me to bear on the question of philosophy versus revelation, or Athens versus Jerusalem.

Regrettably, Strauss himself referred only fleetingly (once in the text and twice in the footnotes) to Machiavelli's lay sermon on penitence, so that it will be necessary to flesh out his view as to why this seemingly pious work does not challenge his interpretation of *Discourses* I, 26 and in general of Machiavelli as arch-atheist and blasphemer.[10]

---

8. See Le A. Burd, *Il Principe* (Oxford: Oxford University Press, 1895), p. 55, which is Strauss's source for the following remark by Gentillet. "C'est atheiste . . . a bien osè vomir ce blasphéme . . ." (Strauss, *Thoughts on Machiavelli*, p. 334, n. 72).
9. Strauss, *Thoughts on Machiavelli*, p. 13.
10. *Ibid.*, pp. 322, n. 133 and 332, n. 47. Strauss's first footnote refers to the Exhortation as comparable to the three "sermons"– or discourses on a Latin text – found in the *Discourses* (*ibid.*, p. 138) The second footnote begins with a reference to *Discourses* I, 30, which demonstrates that the vice of ingratitude (in a prince, toward his victorious general, for example) is "the effect of a natural necessity" (*ibid.*, p. 194). Strauss continues: "As for the significance of the subject of gratitude, see Machiavelli's *Esortazione alla penitenza*" (*ibid*, p. 332). These cryptic remarks seem to me to suggest that Machiavelli views any profession of gratitude, especially toward one's "Lord" (*signore*), as feigned, and that therefore his counsel

In the "Exhortation," Machiavelli refers to David as the author of the *Psalms*, as "reader [*lectore*] of the Holy Spirit" and as "prophet."[11] Inasmuch as the *Magnificat* itself is redolent with phrases from the *Psalms*, it would appear that an obvious justification for Machiavelli's linkage in *Discourses* I, 26 of the words "He filled the poor with good things and the rich he sent empty away" to David was that he believed him to have been author of the Psalms, interpreter of the Holy Spirit, and prophet. Indeed, Machiavelli begins the "Exhortation" by quoting the opening verse to Psalm 130 in the Vulgate: "Out of the depths have I cried unto thee, O Lord. Lord hear my prayer." He could have proceeded to quote the next verse: "If Thou, Lord, shouldest mark our iniquities . . . who shall stand?"

As defined by the *Oxford English Dictionary*, blasphemy is the "profane speaking of God or sacred things" as well as "impious irreverence." Another dictionary gives this definition of blasphemy: "In Jewish law, cursing or reviling God or the king, who is God's representative; in later usage, pronouncing the forbidden name of God, the Tetragrammaton" (or the four Hebrew letters, written without vowel points, and transliterated YHVH).[12] If in *Discourses* I, 26 Machiavelli in fact declared or even implied God to be a tyrant, he would certainly have been guilty of blasphemy. But did he? My own reading of the chapter reveals only that Machiavelli says of David

---

of contrition for ingratitude toward God and one's neighbor in the Exhortation is also feigned. Strauss's only textual reference to the Exhortation — and his only direct quotation from it — occurs in *Thoughts on Machiavelli*, p. 201, toward the end of his discussion of *Discourses III*, 6 on conspiracies. Noting Machiavelli's observation that the dangers of conspiracies "surpass by far every other kind of danger," Strauss interprets this phrase as intended to include "the danger of damnation." He continues with the following qualification: "Or did Machiavelli believe that the danger of damnation can be averted by repentance, and perhaps even repentance on the death bed? 'Penitence,' he says in his *Exhortation to Penitence*, 'is the sole remedy which can wipe out all evils, all errors of men.'" Neither David nor Saints Peter, Jerome, or Francis (all mentioned in the *Exhortation*) repented on their deathbeds.

11. All references to the "Exhortation to Penitence" — entitled "Exortatione alla penitenza" — rather than "Esortazione alla penitenza" as used by Strauss and many others — are from Mario Martelli, ed., *Nicclό Machiavelli: Tutte le opere* (Florence: Sansoni, 1971), pp. 932–34. The title was not Machiavelli's own; his autograph manuscript left it untitled. An English translation is in Alan Gilbert, *Machiavelli: The Chief Works*, 3 vols. (Durham, NC: Duke University Press, 1965), 1: 170–75. I have used my own translation, however.

12. *The Shorter Oxford English Dictionary*, 2 vols. (Oxford: Clarendon Press, 1985), 1: 200; *Webster's Dictionary of the English Language* (New York, 1952), pp. 90, 879.

that "when he became King he made the rich poor and the poor rich." He does not say that David was the addressee of the precise words of the *Magnificat*. Nor does he say of David that he made everything new with new governments, new names, new authorities and new men. It was Philip of Macedonia, not King David, who "built new cities, destroyed buildings, and transferred inhabitants from place to place." These "very cruel means, inimical to every way of living, not only Christian but human" were employed by Philip, father of Alexander the Great, and not by David.[13]

What Machiavelli says about David in the "Exhortation to Penitence" is that he deeply repented of having committed adultery and indirect murder in the affair with Bathsheba. In this one grievous instance, David abused his power as king by taking Bathsheba for his mistress and arranging to have her soldier husband killed on the front line of battle. This one instance, growing out of his lust of the flesh, hardly makes David a tyrant. Furthermore, wrote Machiavelli, in David "no greater penitence can be found in a man, nor in God can there be discovered any greater generosity to forgive."[14]

Is there "profane speaking of God" or "impious irreverence" to be found in this? It is true that Machiavelli's sermon presents God as most merciful, "as mindful of human weakness," and as opposed to "the rigors of the *vendetta*." How is this "profane speaking of God," however? How is Machiavelli guilty of "impious irreverence" when in the "Exhortation" he declares God to have devised "the most pious remedy for human weakness," namely penitence? How do these words square with an alleged vomiter of blasphemies?

In his recent intellectual biography of Machiavelli, Sebastian de Grazia has sifted through every scrap of writing left by the great Florentine. De Grazia concludes, somewhat surprisingly, that Machiavelli "discourses about God always in the conventional reverent attitude." Far from being an atheist or a blasphemer, Machiavelli emerges in de Grazia's reconstruction as a man with a sincere belief in God. Here is de Grazia's summation:

> Scattered about his writings . . . like poppies in a field of chick peas, are many references to God. Together they form an unmistakable likeness. Niccolo's God is the creator, master deity, providential, real,

13. Machiavelli, *Discorsi sopra la prima deca di Tito Livio*, in Martelli, *Machiavelli: Tutte le opere*, p. 109.

14. Machiavelli, [Exortatione alla penitenza] in Martelli, *Tutte le opere*, 933.

universal, one of many names, personal, invocable, thankable, to be revered, a judge, just and forgiving, rewarding and punishing, awesome, a force transcendent, separate from but operative in the world.[15]

In the "Exhortation to Penitence" Machiavelli appears to take sin — defined ultimately as ingratitude to God and enmity toward one's neighbor — seriously. Yet it is not sin "but the perseverance in sin" which God judges to be punishable with "eternal hellfire." God opens up "the way of penitence" as the path to eternal salvation, human beings having lost "the other way" of a sinless life, as a result of the Fall.

"Everything is created [by God] for the honor and good of man, and only man is created for the good and honor of God," declares Machiavelli in the "Exhortation." Man is given speech with which to praise God, hands with which to build temples and make sacrifices in His honor, and "reason and intellect with which he is able to speculate about and understand" His greatness. See, however, continues Machiavelli, with what ingratitude man rebels against God's gifts! The tongue, given for speech so that man might honor God, is used "to blaspheme" Him.

Surely it is noteworthy that in the "Exhortation" Machiavelli the alleged blasphemer explicitly condemns blasphemy. He also condemns converting our intellect from an instrument for understanding God's greatness into a means for speculating about the world. Not insignificantly, Machiavelli the alleged philosopher of supreme worldliness concludes the Exhortation with these lines from Petrarch:

> to repent and to know clearly
> that everything which pleases the world is
> but a brief dream.[16]

Strauss's case against Machiavelli for blasphemy in *Discourses* I, 26 relies heavily on the conviction that the number twenty-six had a special theological significance for Machiavelli.[17] Yet Strauss himself

---

15. *Machiavelli in Hell* (Princeton: Princeton University Press, 1989), p. 58.
16. Machiavelli, [Exortatione alla penitenza], p. 934.
17. Cf. *Thoughts on Machiavelli*, pp. 48–53. After observing that "in taking seriously the number 26, we are on the right path" to understanding Machiavelli's intention, Strauss compares *Prince* 26, *Discourses* I, 26, and *Discourses* II, 26. (*Discourses* III, 26 is not mentioned, however). He then notes that Machiavelli "speaks of twenty-six emperors from Caesar to Maximinus, and adds: "This is not the place to give further examples of Machiavelli's use of the number 26 or, more precisely of 13 and multiples of 13" (p. 52). Apparently the proper "place" for Strauss to

admits that he "does not know" whether Machiavelli was aware that 26 is the numerical value of the Tetragrammaton.[18] Could not Machiavelli also have been ignorant that thirteen was both a lucky and an unlucky number and hence stood for *fortuna*, a blasphemous substitute for the God of revelation? There is no more evidence for the latter supposition than the former.

The difference between Sebastian de Grazia's and Strauss's attempts at empathetically grasping Machiavelli's teaching from within is that de Grazia allows that teaching to emerge from its author's own words — and from *all* of those words — placed in biographical context. By comparison, and despite his intention, Strauss gives the appearance of forcing Machiavelli to conform to a pattern imposed by him from without. Machiavelli to de Grazia is very much the citizen-activist and master of irony that one encounters in the letters. Strauss's Machiavelli, on the other hand, resembles a reclusive philosopher or perhaps a gnostic sage who pores over ancient texts — especially Plato, Aristotle, Xenophon, and the Bible — and who with truly diabolical cleverness hides a subversive message between the lines, a message that by the nineteenth century had succeeded in turning two thousand years of western philosophy and religion upside down, almost single-handedly.

To such criticisms as I have offered, Leo Strauss might well have responded regretfully that I am just one more modern scholar who has been corrupted in his thinking by the very success of the Machiavellian doctrine.[19] We moderns are said no longer to know what blasphemy is because our "enlightened" minds are closed to revealed truth.[20] Strauss would presumably have responded to de

---

mention these further examples is in his chapter in Strauss and Cropsey. See footnote 5 above. This is not to say that Strauss did not give numerous examples of multiples of 13 in *Thoughts on Machiavelli*. None of these places seems to qualify as "*the* place" when he discusses the significance of the number 26, however.

18. Strauss and Cropsey, *Political Philosophy*, p. 286. So far as I know, in *Thoughts on Machiavelli* Strauss does not mention that the numerical value of the Tetragrammaton in Jewish law is 26.

19. "To do justice to Machiavelli requires one to look forward from a pre-modern point of view toward an altogether unexpected and surprising Machiavelli who is new and strange, rather than to look backward from today towards Machiavelli who has become old and our own, and therewith almost good" (*Thoughts on Machiavelli*, p. 12).

20. *Ibid.*, pp. 49–52, Strauss defends his use of the term blasphemy not only with regard to *Discourses* I, 26 but to Machiavelli's entire teaching. The blasphemy of I, 26 is said to be "only the spearhead of a large column" (p. 49). Indeed, Machiavelli of necessity, so to speak, had to commit blasphemies and had to commit them covertly, because in his time the authority of the Bible was "generally recog-

Grazia's reconstruction of a Machiavellian theology with the observation that, under fear of persecution, Machiavelli of course masked his atheism in conventional references to the deity. In order to be effective, Machiavelli's blasphemy had to be subtle, so as not to bring the wrath of the authorities, including the papacy which had commissioned him to write the *History of Florence*, down on his head, or to frighten and anger his readers, who were to be brought little by little to consider worldly humanism as a substitute for biblical revelation.

My response to such a conceivable rejoinder by Strauss is as follows. For all his brilliance, ingenuity, and formidable knowledge, Strauss has imposed on Machiavelli the consistency of a system-builder. My own sense of Machiavelli is that he was a man in love with the tangible, the concrete, and the comical. The Florentine Secretary was a man who dismissed his book the *Prince* as a "whim" or "fantasy."[21] The *Discourses* on Livy seem to have only the most general kind of plan, and it is not clear to me that he ever finished the work.

In effect, Strauss argues that anyone who dissents from his overall interpretation of Machiavelli has to be, even if unknowingly, in the service of Machiavelli's antireligious modernism.[22] Strauss contends that each wave of modernity has been more radical than the last, so that to the extent that we ourselves are moderns, Machiavelli has to seem "moderate" in comparison with Hobbes, Hegel, and Nietzsche.[23]

---

nized and supported by law." To bring forth what moderns call his innerworldly humanism, he had to challenge that authority by impugning its alleged source — *i.e.*, God — and for fear of persecution he had to do it covertly (p. 52).

21. Machiavelli, letter to Francesco Vettori, 10 December 1513 in *Tutte le opere*, p. 1160. "Et se vi piacque mai alcuno mio ghiribizoy. . . ."

22. "The kinds of unbelief with which we are most familiar today are respectful indifference and such a nostalgia for lost faith as goes with an inability to distinguish between theological truth and myth" (*Thoughts on Machiavelli*, p. 51). This is not one of Strauss's better "thoughts." See Dante Germino, *Political Philosophy and the Open Society* (Baton Rouge: Louisiana State University Press, 1982), for a discussion of myth, philosophy, revelation, and mysticism as modes of openness toward transcendent Being, the Being that revealed itself to Moses in *Exodus* 3 as "I AM THAT I AM." I shall reserve exploration of this complicated matter for another place. See *Faith and Philosophy: The Correspondence Between Leo Strauss and Eric Voegelin 1934–64*, eds. and trans. P. Emberley and B. Cooper (University Park, PA: Penn State Press, 1993), for Eric Voegelin's alternative understanding of philosophy and revelation.

23. Given Strauss's splendid mastery of Italian, it is appropriate that the best book I have read on Strauss on modernity is in Italian: Raimondo Cubeddu, *Leo*

I do not think that there exists a Rosetta stone to decipher the Machiavellian hieroglyph, and therefore, I do not think that Strauss has found it. I do not think that I personally am under the spell of modernity, against whose premises I have argued in print over the years. I do think that Strauss is a great interpreter of Machiavelli, precisely because he is greater than either his method (counting words, numbers of chapters, sentences, noting first and last words, etc.) or his conclusions about Machiavelli as a philosopher with a metaphysical system. Where Strauss is greatest is in his eye for textual detail, his insistence on taking seriously every apparently idle word.

Let me conclude with a consideration of Strauss's notion of what it means to philosophize. Not accidentally, he refers to Machiavelli as a "corrupter of the young"— for these words of course were originally part of the indictment returned by the jury against Socrates, as reported in Plato's *Apology*. Socrates was said to have corrupted the youth because he did not worship the gods worshipped by the *polis* and because he introduced "new divinities." In other words, Socrates corrupted the young because he was allegedly blasphemous.

The last words of Strauss's 1972 chapter on Machiavelli are: " . . . Machiavelli and Socrates make a common front against the Sophists."[24] Is Strauss deliberately silent about the "common front" Machiavelli and Socrates also make against revelation?

In his famous Jerusalem lecture, Leo Strauss refused to decide

---

Strauss e la filosofia politica moderna (Naples: Edizioni Scientifiche Italiane, 1983). See the whole part II: "La modernità: Storia di una decadenza," pp. 165–315.

24. Strauss and Cropsey, *Political Philosophy*, p. 292. See also *Thoughts on Machiavelli*: "Machiavelli's claim that he has taken a road not yet trodden by anyone implied that in breaking with the Socratic tradition he did not return to an anti-Socratic position. . ." (p. 291).

25. See Strauss's Jerusalem lecture on "The Mutual Influence of Theology and Philosophy," in V *Ivyun — Hebrew Political Quarterly*, no. 1 (Jerusalem. 1954) and "Jerusalem and Athens" in *The City College*, no. 6 (New York, 1967). In "Mutual Influence" he declares the Bible and philosophy to be "alternatives and antagonists in the drama of the human soul" (pp. 113–14). Strauss's overall conclusion is that philosophy can never refute revelation nor can revelation ever refute philosophy. Philosophy as the *search* for the just way of life is incompatible with the biblical teaching which claims to *possess* the truth about the just way of life. "Strauss's teaching does not lead to a subordination of philosophy to revelation. As a Jew, although distanced from the Synagogue, he does not refuse to speak of faith in an atheist world" or as a philosopher "to indicate to the believer those rational conclusions of philosophy which are antithetical to the faith. The *tertium non datur* . . . remains his secret position" (Cubeddu, *Leo Strauss*, pp. 44–45).

whether philosophy or biblical revelation has the ultimate hold on our allegiance.[25] Does this refusal bring him closer to Machiavelli and suggest that Strauss himself recognized that there was something to be said in favor of Machiavelli, thereby mitigating the charge of blasphemy? Was the charge of blasphemy a deliberate exaggeration by Strauss to bring the entire dilemma of Athens versus Jerusalem back into public view? However one answers these questions, one should never lose sight of the fact that the title of Strauss's Machiavellian masterpiece is *Thoughts on* [and not *Certainties about*] *Machiavelli*. In the end, we are indeed left with the thoughts of Leo Strauss as inspired by an original reading of the Florentine Secretary with the enigmatic smile.

Leo Strauss and the American Founding

Thomas G. West

I

Strauss devoted his life to the recovery of classical political philosophy. The incentive for this enterprise was what Strauss called "the crisis of the West." That crisis "consists in the West's having become uncertain of its purpose," which was to establish the good society on the basis of reason and science. Twentieth-century history revealed that the progressive spread of democracy throughout the world was hardly assured. Moreover, the "good society" of Western liberalism no longer looked unquestionably good. Modern philosophy eventually concluded that reason itself was to blame: not only could reason not establish the good society; it could not even say what the good society is.[1]

The crisis of the West is visible in America in the educated classes' abandonment of the principles of the Declaration of Independence. In 1953 Strauss said,

> Does this nation in its maturity still cherish the faith in which it was conceived and raised? Does it still hold those "truths to be self-evident"? About a generation ago, an American diplomat could still say that "the natural and the divine foundation of the rights of man . . . is self-evident to all Americans."[2]

Today the very notion of self-evident truths discovered by reason is equated by sophisticates with belief in ghosts. An eminent historian has denounced as "fundamentalist" the view, held by some of Strauss's students, that the American Founders might actually have been right about the principles of justice.[3]

Strauss refused to join Nietzsche and Heidegger's farewell to

---

1. *The City and Man* (Chicago: Rand-McNally, 1964), pp. 1, 3.
2. Strauss, *Natural Right and History* (Chicago: University of Chicago Press, 1953), pp. 1-2.
3. On ghosts: Mark Tushnet, "The Relevance of the Framers' Natural Law Views," in *Constitutionalism in Perspective*, ed. Sarah B. Thurow (Lanham, MD: University Press of America, 1988), p. 182. Gordon Wood, "The Fundamentalists and the Constitution," *New York Review of Books*, 18 February 1988, pp. 33-40.

reason. Instead, he wondered whether the disillusionment with reason did not rather stem from the specifically modern understanding of reason. The thinkers who originated the modern project to solve the human problem had rejected the classical understanding of reason. The classics had taught that justice exists, that it is discoverable by reason, and that it can be a guide for political life. What if the classics were right?

Strauss turned to classical political philosophy tentatively but conscientiously. He did not expect the classics to "supply us with recipes for today's use." But he believed that "an adequate understanding of the principles as elaborated by the classics may be the indispensable starting point for an adequate analysis, to be achieved by us, of present-day society in its peculiar character, and for the wise application, to be achieved by us, of these principles to our tasks."[4] Strauss pointed to, but did not supply, this "adequate analysis" of "present-day society," including American society.

II

Those who have been persuaded by Strauss of the need for a return to the classics have disagreed in their assessment of America. Some have argued that American politics is grounded on a modern (Hobbesian) understanding of human nature. According to this understanding God and nature give man no guidance as to how he should live. Consequently American government is indifferent to the moral character of the citizens. Statecraft renounces soulcraft. This article, on the contrary, will argue that American government, through most of its history, was based on Locke's practical political principles but not on Locke's (and Hobbes's) hedonistic view of human nature.

THE FOUNDING PRINCIPLES AS THE HEART OF AMERICA

To orient ourselves to the classical approach, these five summary statements by Strauss on Aristotelian political science will help:

1. "Political science is identical with political philosophy."
2. "Human action has principles of its own which are known independently of theoretical science (physics and metaphysics). . . . The prin-

---

4. *The City and Man*, p. 11.

ciples of action are the natural ends toward which man is by nature inclined and of which he has by nature some awareness."

3. "The awareness of the principles of action shows itself primarily to a higher degree in public or authoritative speech, particularly in law and legislation, rather than in merely private speech. Hence Aristotelian political science views political things in the perspective of the citizen."

4. "Aristotelian political science necessarily evaluates political things."

5. "Man is a being *sui generis*, with a dignity of its own: man is the rational and political animal." His dignity is based "on his awareness of what he ought to be or how he should live."[5]

What defines a political community, then, is not sheer sovereignty or force, but rather the conviction about justice and happiness that lies behind the authority of government. This conviction, being an opinion about what is right, contains within it an implicit view of "the natural ends toward which man is by nature inclined." The political scientist will want to know what that ruling opinion is; how it is embodied in the laws and institutions of government, the speeches and deeds of politicians, and the private lives of citizens; and how sensible the opinion is. Is it worthy of the community's wholehearted devotion? Is it true?

Lincoln said, "Public opinion, on any subject, always has a 'central idea' from which all its minor thoughts radiate. That 'central idea' in our political public opinion, at the beginning was, and until recently has continued to be, 'the equality of men.'"[6] The equality idea was the centerpiece of the Declaration, the first official document of the independent United States. Its fundamental law, the Constitution, was framed by men who understood themselves to be struggling to make that idea the practical basis of a republic that really did protect the equal rights of individuals while operating by the consent of the governed. Americans still live under the Declaration and Constitution. Their principles were reaffirmed, and their implementation strengthened, through the Civil War and its aftermath. A classical political scientist will therefore turn especially to these documents to understand the heart of American politics.

I leave aside in this article the recent departure in our politics from the founding principles. Since 1965 opponents of the traditional constitutional order have greatly changed the character of

5. *Liberalism Ancient and Modern* (New York: Basic Books, 1968), pp. 205–207.
6. *Collected Works of Abraham Lincoln*, ed. Roy P. Basler (New Brunswick: Rutgers University Press, 1953), 2: 385.

Thomas West

government. But before trying to understand what America has become, we must first understand what it was through most of its history, what principles it adhered or aspired to.

But here is an embarrassment. For when the Founders spoke of their political principles, the man they deferred to above all was the philosopher John Locke. And Strauss himself exposed most forcefully the dubious pedigree of Locke's ideas in the originators of modern political philosophy, Hobbes and Machiavelli. Could the only country that is founded "in explicit opposition to Machiavellian principles" turn out to be based on a variant of those same principles?[7]

The Radical Locke

Obviously America is Lockean in the sense that the leading Founders, from Samuel Adams and James Wilson to Jefferson and Madison, warmly endorsed Locke's formulations on the rights of man and government by consent. Those formulations found their way into the most authoritative political documents, notably several state constitutions and the Declaration. But did the Founders understand that Lockean language as Locke himself did? And if they did not, do we not owe it to the Founders, and to the truth, to understand them as they understood themselves? Strauss justly criticized historians who try "to understand the thought of the past better than it understood itself before [they have] understood it exactly as it understood itself."[8]

To approach these questions, it is helpful to glimpse how radical the thought of John Locke really is. Strauss argues persuasively that Locke was secretly a Hobbesian, although a democratic Hobbesian. Following Hobbes, Locke broke with both orthodox Christianity and the natural law tradition stemming from the classics. Man according to Locke is a poor, needy creature who creates value and meaning by his efforts alone, against the indifference or even hostility of God and nature. This, Strauss suggests, is the ultimate meaning of the modern doctrine of rights: God and nature give man nothing, no positive guidance about how to live, no means by which to live. The state of nature is a state of misery and death. Man is endowed

7. The quotation is from Strauss, *Thoughts on Machiavelli* (Glencoe, IL: Free Press, 1958), p. 13.
8. *On Tyranny* (Glencoe, IL: Free Press, 1963), p. 24.

by nature only with unease about the future, which expresses itself in endless striving for comfortable self-preservation. Everything of value in man's life, be it reason or security, comes from man's own laborious efforts to escape the poverty and terror of his natural state. On this basis, natural right is the license (indistinguishable from a necessity of man's nature) to do whatever man judges to be necessary to preserve himself.[9]

Strauss distinguished between the modern and the classical doctrine of natural right in this way: Either one views man as Hobbes and Locke did, as a being who is himself the source of meaning for life, or one views man, as Aristotle and Plato did, as guided by his nature toward ends that he does not make up for himself. "Through the shift of emphasis from natural duties or obligations to natural rights, the individual, the ego, had become the center and origin of the moral world, since man—as distinguished from man's end—had become that center or origin."[10] In other words, the alternative, Strauss argued, is *freedom* or *virtue*.

To say that man is the source of all value seems to exalt him above the condition of enslavement to nature or God against which post-Machiavellian philosophers declared war. But exalting man on this foundation cannot help degrading him. If everything of value is created by man, then nothing of value exists in nature or by nature, including human nature. Man's creativity is godlike, but his nature is shallow or rather vacuous. Any way of life, however frivolous, self-indulgent, or vicious, is equal in rank to any other. Nothing but a narrow calculus of the usefulness of virtue can restrain man from exploding in world-ravaging cruelty or from deflating into a silly cipher. Without a moral order inherent in human nature, the dignity of man fades into nothing.

If this is the American understanding of natural rights, the country would care nothing about the moral and intellectual character of its citizens. The only possible exception would be to promote virtue for the sake of liberty. Public virtue would then be solely instrumental. Virtue would be fostered, if at all, for the sake of securing everyone's right to sink to whatever depth of degradation happened to be to his taste. Public restraint serves private vice. In this view, the country is and always has been spiritually empty at its core. This disheartening heart of American politics would then have been responsible

9. *Natural Right and History*, pp. 202–251.
10. *Ibid.*, p. 248.

for the gradual decay of the conditions of public order and public-spirited community, conditions which in this view we owed to a lucky inheritance, destined to wither away, from a premodern age.

LOCKE AND AMERICA I: CONSENT AND VIRTUE

On the other hand, a case can be made that Locke's ultimate conception of man does not matter for understanding America. That is because it was not John Locke who founded the United States, but men who admired Locke only to the extent that they agreed with him.

The key question is: in what respect did the Founders understand all men to be "created equal"? The short answer is: equal with respect to the inalienable rights to life, liberty, and the pursuit of happiness. The Declaration speaks of two implications of this equality. First, governments are instituted to secure these rights of human nature. Second, the just powers of government derive from the consent of the governed.

The consent principle follows from the right to liberty: no one has a right to rule another without that other's consent. No one is born a natural master or natural slave. But why should this be so? There are two possibilities. One is that all men are born free because there is no principle in human nature by which men can reasonably be ranked. If there is no high or low in man's nature, if reason and passions hold the same rank, then there can be no natural superiority of one man to another. If instead of looking to what is highest in man, we look to what is strongest, we find a passion: the fear of violent death or desire for comfortable preservation. In this respect all men are alike.

The Founders did believe that the most urgent, overriding natural right was that of self-preservation. But they did not infer that reason thereby lost its authority in man or in government. They admitted in principle the right of the wise and virtuous to rule in human affairs — if only they be truly wise and virtuous!

> Supreme or unlimited authority can with fitness belong only to the sovereign of the universe: And that fitness is derived from the perfection of his nature.—To such authority, directed by infinite wisdom and infinite goodness, is due both active and passive obedience: which, as it constitutes the happiness of rational creatures, should with cheer-

fulness and from choice be unlimitedly paid by them.— But with truth this can be said of no other authority whatever.[11]

God's monarchical government of the universe does not and should not rest on the consent of the governed. "If angels were to govern men, neither external nor internal controls on government would be necessary" (*Federalist*, No. 51). But men are not gods or angels. No man is so superior to another as to deserve to rule him without his consent. However reasonable a human being may be, he shares in the passionate, bestial part of human nature.

Conversely, however passionate a human being may be, he shares in the rational part of human nature. No man is godlike, but all are touched by the divine spark. Reason distinguishes men from beasts. Madison says it is not by nature but by the unnatural force of the slavery laws that blacks have been "*degraded* from the human rank, and classed with those *irrational* animals which fall under the legal denomination of property."[12] Human beings have "one common original: they participate in one common nature, and consequently have one common right."[13]

Although the Founders distrusted the reason of any one man, they placed considerable confidence in the reason of the people. The people's reason, to be sure, was easily overcome by their passions. But democracy would prove to be a curse, not a blessing, if the passions of the people rather than their reason controlled the government. The right constitutional structures, embodying and eliciting the people's enduring reason and capable of resisting their momentary passions, would help. But finally the people themselves had to possess knowledge — of their rights and their duties, and of the government. "The spirit of liberty," said John Adams, "without knowledge, would be little better than a brutal rage." He praised the New England policy of making "the education of all ranks of people . . . the care and expense of the public, in a manner that I believe has been unknown to any other people ancient or modern." To this ex-

11. Answer of the Council, 1774, in *The Briefs of the American Revolution: Constitutional Arguments between Thomas Hutchinson, Governor of Massachusetts Bay, and James Bowdoin for the Council and John Adams for the House of Representatives*, ed. John P. Reid (New York: New York University Press, 1981), p. 35.
12. *Federalist*, No. 54, emphasis added.
13. Alexander Hamilton, *A Full Vindication of the Measures of the Congress*, 1774, in *Papers of Hamilton*, ed. Harold C. Syrett (New York: Columbia University Press, 1961), 1: 47.

tent, democracy, in Strauss's words, "is meant to be an aristocracy which has broadened into a universal aristocracy."[14]

Plato and Aristotle began from the frankly antidemocratic principle that the most virtuous ought to rule, with or without consent. But they acknowledged that perfect wisdom and perfect virtue was unavailable to mortals. Besides, wisdom is by its nature invisible to the unwise, who are ever the majority. In practice, therefore, wisdom's claim to rule must be qualified by consent. Political offices must therefore be hemmed in by institutional devices to prevent abuse. These qualifications of the rule of virtue are a major theme of Plato's *Laws* and Aristotle's *Politics*.

America's Founders, in the language of Locke, proclaimed the equal right to liberty, but unlike Locke, they did not deny the rightful supremacy of moral and intellectual excellence. Strauss endorses this point in the following remark:

> [According to the classical philosophers,] "aristocracy" (rule of the best) presented itself as the natural answer of all good men to the natural question of the best political order. As Thomas Jefferson put it, "That form of government is the best, which provides the most effectually for a pure selection of [the] natural *aristoi* into offices of the government."[15]

The classics proclaimed the absolute right of virtue to rule, but they did not believe that the political institutionalization of such virtue is possible. Both perspectives lead to the sensible blending of wisdom, virtue, and consent in the construction of good government.

The classics were willing to maintain that virtue was *the* title to rule because they thought they had found a politically reliable substitute for real virtue, namely, the leisured wealth and education of gentlemen. Whatever may have been the case in antiquity, in the Christian era the claims of virtue were advanced by monarchs and priests grasping for worldly power. The actual result was an unholy alliance of the Roman Catholic Church with hereditary monarchy and aristocracy: "ecclesiastical and civil tyranny."[16] Far better to assert publicly what was always true for the classics, namely, that using

14. *Federalist*, No. 49; Adams, "Dissertation on the Canon and Feudal Law," *Works*, ed. C. F. Adams (Boston: Little, Brown, 1865), 3: 456, 462; Strauss, *Liberalism*, p. 4.

15. Strauss, *What Is Political Philosophy?* (New York: Free Press, 1959), p. 86.

16. Adams, "Dissertation," p. 451.

virtue as a title to rule enthrones not genuine excellence but a pale imitation at best and vicious self-seeking at worst. The right to liberty—no rule without consent of the governed—follows.

LOCKE AND AMERICA II: RIGHTS AND VIRTUE

Besides consent, the right to liberty has another consequence in the Declaration, already mentioned: the purpose of government is to secure that right (besides securing the more urgent right to life). Men are to be free not only in the sense of being governed by rulers and under laws consented to by themselves. They are also to be free from government intrusiveness. Politics must be not only *democratic* but *liberal*. Government must leave men alone in their private lives, above all in that area of private life which is the source of the deepest convictions and greatest controversy: religion. For the most part a liberal government will limit itself to protecting men's bodies, leaving the care of their souls to families, churches, and other private institutions.

Here too, as with the consent principle, there are two foundations of the protection of private liberty. One is the view that man is free not only of the despotism of other men but free also of any natural or divine standards of how he should live. Religion is a delusion; there is no such thing as the highest good for man, and there is no answer to man's longing for eternity: man's restless ego is the only source of value. That is the heart of Hobbes' conception of man, and of Locke's, if Strauss is right. But the surface of Locke certainly denies this, since Locke takes pains to insist that even natural man is obliged by the law of nature. And the Founders seem to have understood Locke's law of nature in light of the traditional, ultimately classical, natural law doctrine. In short, here too Locke's radicalism may have been housebroken by American common sense.

The other foundation of private liberty would be a prudential or common-sense judgment that government is not likely to do a good job dictating men's convictions about the greatest things, especially in times of universal religions that claim authority over politics.

The politics recommended by Plato and Aristotle was in principle illiberal. The political order was supposed to foster virtue in its citizens, by the laws and through education. Politics is the "art whose task is tendance of souls" (Plato *Laws* 650b). We have just seen that the classics' antidemocratic premise has to be qualified because of the rarity of real virtue. The same is true for their antiliberal premise. Since the rulers themselves are imperfect, the conception of virtue that they promote through law will also be defective or even perverse (Plato *Republic* book 8).

This fact raises special problems in Christian times. When doctrinal purity is demanded by the political authority, religious warfare and persecution have often followed. Under such circumstances it makes sense to limit the scope of politics to minimal moral standards and protection of the body. Liberalism with respect to private life — the establishment of a realm of privacy by the separation of state and society — follows as a *prudential* conclusion. The Christian writers Thomas Aquinas, Marsilius of Padua, and John of Paris, all adherents of the classical approach to politics, made arguments that could provide the ground for this sort of liberalism. These men tried to protect political life from the inappropriate intrusion of priestly authority by lowering the goal of political life. Aquinas said that although the purpose of politics in principle is to make men virtuous, in practice law must limit itself to forbidding only the "more grave vices, from which it is possible for the greater part of the multitude to abstain," such as murder and theft. Otherwise, disorder will ensue: "He that violently bloweth his nose, bringeth out blood."[17]

The teachings of these Christian Aristotelians failed to solve the religious problem in politics. Only the modern doctrine of individual rights achieved that goal. In order to exclude priestly doctrinalism from politics, an anti-ecclesiastical doctrinalism had to be developed. Paradoxically, latitude for prudence in political affairs was bought by setting a principled limit on government control of private life. The degree of that control had been previously left to the prudent judgment of statesmen. Now it was set forth in the ringing phrases of the rights of human nature.

The American Founders adhered to a common-sense understanding of those ringing phrases. For example, although Locke opposed in principle any governmental role in the formation of citizen character, the Founders endorsed it. Several state constitutions contained provisions for the moral education of citizens. Laws everywhere regulated relations between the sexes and standards of public decency. Institutions of government were frequently evaluated by their effect on public morals. John Adams praised local self-government because through it Americans acquire "the habit of dis-

17. *Summa Theologiae*, I-II, Q. 96, Art. 2.

cussing, of deliberating, and of judging of public affairs," confirming them in the disposition of spirited but responsible self-assertion.[18] A leading concern of the Framers of the Constitution was "an almost universal prostration of morals" which state government policies had occasioned.[19] Jefferson devoted considerable effort to promoting public education in Virginia, as did Washington toward the establishment of a national university.

The Founders regarded virtue as an indispensable condition of freedom, for without self-restraint in their private lives men would be unable to govern themselves in public. This is the instrumental conception we have already spoken of. But virtue was also judged intrinsically worthy, a necessary ingredient of human happiness. These two concerns, private and public, were often joined in important public documents. The best example is the well-known provision of the 1787 Northwest Ordinance:

> Religion, morality, and knowledge, being necessary to *good government* and the *happiness of mankind*, schools and the means of education shall forever be encouraged." (emphasis added)

There is another reason for liberalism on a classical basis, a positive reason. It is indicated in book 8 of Plato's *Republic* in the discussion of democracy. That is the only actual political order in which the philosophic life can be freely lived. There Socrates finds a home. By giving up the claim to be the be-all for its citizens, liberal politics acknowledges the freedom of the mind. Politics cannot satisfy the deepest longings of the soul. Religious liberty is an inalienable right, as Madison said, "because the opinions of men, depending only on the evidence contemplated by their own minds, cannot follow the dictates of other men." The right to liberty is the community's bow to the dignity of the human mind, which strives to see things as they are.[20] George Washington displays the gentleman's appreciation for the Socratic life, as the life most fully in accord with our rational estate, in these words:

> The science of figures, to a certain degree, is not only indispensably requisite in every walk of civilized life; but the investigation of mathe-

18. Adams, *Works*, 5: 495.
19. *Federalist*, No. 85.
20. Quoted from "Memorial and Remonstrance against Religious Assessments," in *American Political Writing during the Founding Era*, ed. Charles S. Hyneman and Donald S. Lutz (Indianapolis: Liberty Press, 1983), p. 631.

matical truths accustoms the mind to method and correctness in reasoning, and is an employment peculiarly worthy of rational beings. In a clouded state of existence, where so many things appear precarious to the bewildered research, it is here that the rational faculties find a firm foundation to rest upon. From the high ground of mathematical and philosophical demonstration, we are insensibly led to far nobler speculations and sublimer meditations.[21]

Whether these sentiments were echoed from another, or were just an expression of Washington's native good sense, we see that the most respected of the Founders knew and endorsed this high theme of the great tradition.

In sum, liberalism may be chosen on the basis of Aristotle (be sensible about how much can be expected from politics) or Hobbes (there is no human good).

More Evidence

That the Founders would not have agreed with the radical Locke is shown by Hamilton and James Wilson, both of whom explicitly attacked Hobbes. In a 1775 pamphlet Hamilton denounced Hobbes's doctrine that "Moral obligation . . . is derived from the introduction of civil society" and that "there is no virtue, but what is purely artificial." James Wilson, a leader at the Constitutional Convention, rejected Hobbes's claim "that nothing draws us to the love of what is without or beyond ourselves." Wilson thought that there *is* a natural order of human inclinations that directs us toward what is good. Hobbes's views, said Wilson, are "totally repugnant to all human sentiment, and all human experience." Jefferson expressed a similar view when he said that the people "are inherently free of all but moral law." (The moral law is not the creation of the ego.) John Adams grounded man's natural liberty not in his having been abandoned by God and nature, but in "the dignity of his nature, and the noble rank he holds among the works of God."[22]

21. Letter to Nicholas Pike, 20 June 1788, in *Writings of George Washington*, ed. John C. Fitzpatrick (Washington: Government Printing Office, 1931–44), 30: 2–3, quoted in Eugene F. Miller, "Washington's Discourses on Education," mimeographed, prepared for a Liberty Fund Symposium, October 1986.
22. Hamilton, "The Farmer Refuted," *Papers*, ed. Syrett, 1: 87; Wilson, *Works*, ed. James D. Andrews (Chicago: Callaghan, 1896), 1: 255–56; Jefferson, letter to Spencer Roane, 6 September 1819, in *Writings* (New York: Library of America, 1984), p. 1426; Adams, "Dissertation," p. 462.

The suggestions I have put forward here do not demonstrate that the Founders' understood Locke in a "classical" spirit. That would require a much fuller discussion of their thought in the whole context of the founding.[23] Above all, on the basis of classical political science, we should beware of trying to understand the prudence of political men in light of the philosophers' private understanding of the doctrines they teach. "The Fathers weren't Straussians."[24] The logic of political life has only a remote connection with the thought of philosophers. The consistency of statesmen must be sought in a sympathetic overview of their speeches and deeds. As Strauss suggested, Aristotle's virtue of prudence, the virtue of the statesman, stands largely independently of wisdom, the virtue of the thinker.

On the other hand, even if I am right about the Founders' conception of politics, that does not settle the question. The later history of America must also be considered. For the question would still remain whether the radical premise that may have been at the heart of Locke was responsible for those aspects of American life that seem to bear the stamp of radical modernity.

I cannot answer that question here, but one piece of evidence impresses me greatly. Those writers who have done the most to open America to the view that liberty means complete moral autonomy — the right to privacy, in today's judicial language — those writers have also consistently opposed the Lockean language of natural rights and limited government. I believe the pedigree of their thought can be shown to be Continental European, in fact German. The critique of the Founding was promoted in this country, as best I can tell, not by people following out the logic of the Declaration, but by intellectuals disaffected for various reasons from democracy and individual rights. New England Transcendentalists disgruntled with the vulgarity of democratic politics, Southern apologists for slavery, progressive intellectuals impatient to bring socialism to America, liberals disgusted with the banality of middle class comforts, con-

---

23. I plan to do so in a book in progress. In the meantime, see my "The Classical Spirit of the Founding"; both Charles R. Kesler, "The Classics and the Founding," in *The American Founding*, ed. J. Jackson Barlow et al. (New York: Greenwood Press, 1988), pp. 1–90; and Harry V. Jaffa (to whom the present article owes an obvious debt), "Equality, Liberty, Wisdom, Morality, and Consent in the Idea of Political Freedom," *Interpretation* 15 (January 1987): 3–28.

24. Joseph Sobran, summarizing Harry V. Jaffa, quoted in Jaffa, *American Conservatism and the American Founding* (Durham, NC: Carolina Academic Press, 1984), p. 24.

servatives longing for the intense communities and beautiful aspirations of aristocracy— these and others have been quick to attack the Founders' doctrines in order to indulge their tastes or advance their agendas.

Whatever may have been Locke's private intentions, the language of Locke proved to be well suited to the traditionalist framework in which the Americans understood it. Calvin Coolidge was an outstanding example of the many American politicians who understood the rights of men to be inseparable from their duties:

> It is along the path of reverence and obedience that the race has reached the goal of freedom, of self-government, of a higher morality, and a more abundant spiritual life. . . . The worst evil that could be inflicted upon the youth of the land would be to leave them without restraint and completely at the mercy of their own uncontrolled inclinations. . . . [The Founders] did not deny the existence of authority. They recognized it and undertook to abide by it, and through obedience to it secure their freedom. They made their appeal and rested their cause not upon earthly authority, but in the very first paragraph of the Declaration of Independence asserted [the authority of] the laws of nature and of nature's God. . . . [On this foundation the individual] is endowed with inalienable rights which no majority, however broad, can ever be justified in violating.[25]

III

Almost all sober-minded observers today, including those who insist that America's principle is Locke's calculating hedonism, agree that America is one of the most decent countries in existence. Does this mean that Locke's philosophy merits reassessment?

If Strauss is right, we cannot go back to Locke. Strauss's writings present Locke's philosophy as a way station on the road to twentieth-century historicism and nihilism. Locke and Hobbes tried to abandon classical natural right while retaining nature as a standard. The trap of natural teleology (which placed limits on man's freedom) was to be avoided by making nature a negative standard, an evil condition to escape from. Rousseau and his successors refuted Hobbes and Locke by showing that *any* retention of nature, even as a condition to be conquered, limits human freedom. Hobbesian nature is "crypto-teleological" because it in effect defines the right way of life as calculating, egoistic, bourgeois existence. Rousseau protested against

---

25. Coolidge, *Foundations of the Republic* (New York: Scribners, 1926), pp. 104–108.

this conclusion by going back to Locke's beginning point, man's freedom, which he understood more radically than Locke did. For Rousseau, man's distinguishing characteristic is his malleability, his ability to become almost anything through historical change.

Rousseau's successors abandoned natural right altogether. But if political philosophy was to retain any ability to say what the good society is, something had to take nature's place. That was reason (Kant) or a progressive historical process (Hegel and Marx). But how do we know that reason or historical change is good? Cut off from the standard of nature and natural right, such valuations come to seem quite arbitrary. Nietzsche drew the conclusion: The belief in "reason" and "progress" is no less a prejudice than the belief in religion or superstition. Therefore philosophy (as quest for knowledge of the good for man) is impossible.

Strauss was persuaded that Rousseau's critique of Lockean natural right on Locke's own premise was sound. The question remains whether Locke's theoretical insufficiency requires the rejection of liberal democracy, as Nietzsche held.

To repeat, Strauss never wrote thematically on America. His fullest statement on liberal democracy appears in the second chapter of *Liberalism Ancient and Modern*, in an essay on education. Judging from its first paragraph, Strauss produced that essay only as a dutiful response to a quasi-official request. Strauss evidently regarded the analysis of today's society as a distraction from his main task, "the education of the perfect prince, as it were."

In Strauss's view, as expressed here and elsewhere, liberal democracy is different in kind from other modern regimes, such as communism. Its spirit is closer to the classics because it retains an awareness of the ineradicable evil in man's nature and therefore of the need for morality. Strauss looked to America with hope. He encouraged Americans to understand themselves in light of what was highest in their tradition: democracy as originally meant is "the society in which all or most adults have developed their reason to a high degree, or *the* rational society. Democracy, in a word, is meant to be an aristocracy which has broadened into a universal aristocracy." He refused to endorse Heidegger's equation of American democracy with communism ("the same desperate frenzy of unleashed technology and the unrestricted organization of the average man"). On the contrary, the experience of totalitarianism helped Strauss "to understand again the old saying that wisdom cannot be separated from moderation and hence to understand that wisdom requires unhesitating loyalty to a decent constitution and even to the cause of constitutionalism." This led him to say that "liberal democracy, in contradistinction to communism and fascism, derives powerful support from a way of thinking which cannot be called modern at all: the premodern thought of our western tradition." Strauss went so far as to suggest that the fate of philosophy itself might depend on the outcome of the twentieth-century struggle between communism and liberal democracy.[26]

Nevertheless, Strauss's confidence in America was cautious and qualified. He could see that the old-fashioned elements in American life were under severe attack. "We must realize that we must hope almost against hope." America might not survive as an alternative to more radical modern regimes based on the annihilation of all remnants of nature. The politics of radical modernity may yet triumph. In light of this possibility, Strauss foresaw the possibility of a new Dark Age in which government would "suppress philosophy as an attempt to corrupt the young," forbidding especially "every teaching, every suggestion that there are politically relevant natural differences among men which cannot be abolished or neutralized by progressing scientific technology." (Consider the emerging consensus on what constitutes racism and sexism.) Strauss may have viewed his own teaching on exotericism in part as a preparation for this Dark Age, should it come.[27]

But Strauss did not intend to lose. He scorned those who preferred "surrender, that is, the abandonment of liberal democracy, to war." And if he was going to lose, it would not be with a whimper: "Resistance in a forlorn position to the enemies of mankind, 'going down with guns blazing and flags flying,' may contribute greatly toward keeping awake the recollection of the immense loss sustained by mankind, may inspire and strengthen the desire and the hope for its recovery, and may become a beacon for those who humbly carry on the works of humanity in a seemingly endless valley of darkness and destruction."[28]

---

26. *The City and Man*, p. 5; *Liberalism Ancient and Modern*, p. 4; Martin Heidegger, *Einführung in die Metaphysik*, 3rd ed. (Tübingen: Niemeyer, 1966), p. 28; Strauss, "Three Waves of Modernity," in *Political Philosophy*, ed. Hilail Gildin (Indianapolis: Pegasus, 1975), p. 98; *On Tyranny*, p. 226.
27. *On Tyranny*, p. 226. On exotericism, *Persecution and the Art of Writing* (Glencoe, IL: Free Press, 1952), pp. 24–25.
28. *Liberalism Ancient and Modern*, p. 223; *Natural Right and History*, p. 318.

A Return to Classical Political Philosophy and the Understanding of the American Founding

Christopher Bruell

I

What is the significance for the understanding of the American Founding of Leo Strauss's efforts toward the recovery of classical political philosophy? That this is a legitimate question to address to Strauss's work is suggested by the claims which he made in the introductions to a number of his most famous books (among other things). He opened his study on *Natural Right and History*, for example, by raising the question whether our nation "in its maturity still cherish[es] the faith in which it was conceived and raised," that is, whether it still holds the fundamental proposition of the Declaration of Independence to be true. In doing so, he gave warrant to the expectation that that study, which may be said to culminate in a treatment of classical natural right and make a case for its superiority to all alternatives, would contribute to the strengthening or restoration of our Founding faith. In similar fashion, the opening of *The City and Man* presents that work's turn "toward the political thought of classical antiquity" as dictated by "the crisis of our time, the crisis of the West," a crisis which it locates "in the West's having become uncertain of its purpose." The purpose spoken of in *The City and Man* is not identical to the Founding faith appealed to in *Natural Right and History*; but it is not hard to see the close kinship between the two. And, again, warrant is given for the expectation that the outcome of a successful return to classical political thought will be a recovery of the West's certainty as to its purpose. Indeed, the clear

This is a corrected version of a paper prepared for a conference on Classical Theory and Practice and the American Founding, John M. Olin Center for Inquiry into the Theory and Practice of Democracy, the University of Chicago, 16–18 June 1988. I've received invaluable help in thinking about the themes of the paper from several friends: Tom Pangle, Nathan Tarcov and especially David Bolotin whose questions, insights and judgment have drawn me back from many errors and set me again upon the track. I wish also to thank my research assistants, In Ha Jang and Michael Grenke, for their help in perfecting the manuscript and preparing it for publication.

and powerful meaning which Strauss thus attached to his efforts toward the recovery of classical political philosophy helps explain both the widespread influence his work has had on students concerned with the health of American politics and also the fact that it has inspired in many of them, as Gordon Wood has pointed out in a recent article,[1] a deepened interest in the American Founding. But clear and powerful as the bearing of Strauss's work may be on our most urgent concerns, that is, clear as it may be that his work has an important bearing on those concerns, the precise character of its bearing is a matter of some ambiguity. These ambiguities, moreover, are bound to affect students who have undergone its influence. That this is the case with those who have turned to the study of the American Founding has also been pointed out by Wood. It is on these ambiguities, then, insofar as they affect the study of the American Founding, that we must concentrate our attention if we are to answer the question with which we began.

"The crisis of the West," as Strauss saw it and as he led many others to see it, is constituted in large measure by the collapse of modern political philosophy or modern natural right—which had supplied to the West its universal purpose—into "historicism," the view that all doctrines are tied fundamentally to a particular time and place, that there can be no universal purposes or timeless truths. This philosophic doctrine, which denies to philosophy the possibility of reaching its essential goal, was characterized by Strauss as "the self-destruction of reason"; and he came to understand it as "the inevitable outcome of modern rationalism as distinguished from pre-modern rationalism."[2] A return to premodern rationalism (which meant ultimately to classical political philosophy) represented, then, the soundest hope for a recovery of rationalism, simply, as a "science" that, according to the formulation of Husserl which Strauss had recourse to, "would satisfy the highest theoretical needs and in regard to ethics and religion render possible a life regulated by pure rational norms."[3] Those who saw in Strauss's work the achievement of such a return might well believe themselves entitled, therefore, to entertain, with respect to the American Founding, a possibility

1. "The Fundamentalists and the Constitution," *The New York Review of Books*, 18 February 1988, pp. 33–40.
2. "Preface to the English Translation," *Spinoza's Critique of Religion*, trans. E. M. Sinclair (New York: Schocken, 1965), p. 31.
3. "Philosophy as Rigorous Science and Political Philosophy," *Studies in Platonic Political Philosophy*, (Chicago: University of Chicago, 1983), p. 34.

which many of their contemporaries had all but abandoned and consequently rarely permitted themselves to dwell on: the possibility, namely, of holding the guiding principles of the Founding to be simply true, as indeed they had been claimed to be, true not merely for "a decade or two" or for "several cultures at the same time,"[4] but everywhere and always. At the same time and in the same way, it became possible once again to take seriously the Founders' own understanding of what they were trying to accomplish.

But though Strauss's efforts supported and were no doubt intended to support these possibilities, though, for example, they truly vouched for the legitimacy of the *question* of the truth of the Founding principles, they were far from suggesting a simply positive answer to that question. The rationalism whose recovery Strauss aimed at or achieved was "premodern": his efforts conceded and indeed sought to confirm the inadequacies of modern rationalism. It was to modern rationalism, however, in its earlier forms, that he himself traced "the theory of liberal democracy,"[5] if not all aspects,[6] of the political order established by the Founders. The "undeniable fact" of the link between liberal democracy and early modern thought did not permit us, then, to return to that thought: "the critique of modern rationalism or of the modern belief in reason by Nietzsche cannot be dismissed or forgotten."[7] Or, as Strauss put it on another occasion, "All rationalistic liberal philosophic positions have lost their significance and power. One may deplore this [as, on a practical level, Strauss surely did], but I for one cannot bring myself to clinging to philosophic positions which have been shown to be inadequate."[8] (It is perhaps worth noting that both of the statements just quoted occurred in lectures, only one of which Strauss permitted to be published in his lifetime.) When Strauss claimed, therefore, that "liberal democracy . . . derives powerful support from . . . the pre-modern

4. Cf. Wood, "Fundamentalists and the Constitution," p. 34.
5. "The Three Waves of Modernity," typescript, 19 (published in *Political Philosophy: Ten Essays by Leo Strauss*, ed. H. Gildin ([Detroit: Wayne State Press], p. 98); cf. "On a New Interpretation of Plato's Political Philosophy," *Social Research* 13 (1946): 357.
6. Cf. "Liberal Education and Responsibility," *Liberalism Ancient and Modern* (New York: Basic Books, 1968), pp. 15–19.
7. "The Three Waves of Modernity," 20 (*Political Philosophy: Six Essays by Leo Strauss*, p. 98).
8. "Existentialism," typescript (probably from a tape and unedited), 4 (edited and published as "An Introduction to Heideggerian Existentialism," in *The Rebirth of Classical Political Rationalism*, ed. T. Pangle [Chicago: University of Chicago, 1989], p. 29).

thought of our western tradition,"[9] he cannot have meant by this such support as derives from a demonstration of the universal truth of the Founding principles as originally understood. The reason is not only that liberal democracy (whether or not the premodern thinkers would have preferred it to all currently available alternatives) is not the sort of political order considered best by premodern thought in general or classical political philosophy in particular. More important still is the fact that classical political philosophy did not intend to provide, or believe it possible to provide, a simply rational basis for *any* sort of political order, even the best: "it asserts that every political society that ever has been or ever will be rests on a particular fundamental opinion which cannot be replaced by knowledge and hence is of necessity a particular or particularist society."[10] It is in philosophy rather than politics that, according to classical political thought, true universalism is to be sought.[11]

We can sum up this point, then, by saying that Strauss's efforts toward the recovery of classical political philosophy—insofar as they raised again, in the face of the most powerful currents of modern thought, the question of the possibility of a genuine and viable rationalism—helped students of the American political order take seriously the Founders' claim as to the universal truth of the Founding principles; but those efforts did not thereby guarantee that that claim would be found valid in the final analysis.

The bearing of Strauss's work on the understanding of the Founding is ambiguous for a second reason, which has already been touched on in the discussion of the first reason. The classical political philosophers were not democrats, and still less liberal democrats. Strauss never sought to hide this fact: "I do not believe that the premises—democracy is good and Aristotle is good—lead validly to the conclusion that Aristotle was a democrat."[12] More than that, the acceptance of the premise that Aristotle is good calls into some question the premise that democracy is good. The recovery of classical political philosophy is at the same time a recovery of the clas-

---

9. "The Three Waves of Modernity," 20 (*Political Philosophy: Six Essays by Leo Strauss*, p. 98).

10. *Liberalism Ancient and Modern*, p. viii.

11. *The City and Man* (Chicago: University of Chicago, 1977), pp. 226–31; cf. "Philosophy as Rigorous Science and Political Philosophy," p. 29.

12. 'The Crisis of Political Philosophy," *The Predicament of Modern Politics*, ed. Harold J. Spaeth (Detroit: University of Detroit Press, 1964), pp. 93–94; cf. *The City and Man*, pp. 35–41.

sical critique of the democracy known to the classics; and, although ancient democracy was very different from our own, the classical critique is not without its contemporary applications. To put this point in another way, the crisis of liberal democracy, as Strauss understood it, is not due entirely to the loss of confidence in the truth of its Founding principles; nor can the aspects of contemporary America which are open to reasonable criticism all be traced to a falling away from those principles. In his analyses of the thought of the modern political philosophers, Strauss exposed the tendency of the principles in question with almost ruthless thoroughness; and he indicated his view of their contemporary consequences in occasional but telling remarks:

> If we look . . . at what is peculiar to our age or characteristic of our age, we see hardly more than the interplay of mass taste with high-grade but strictly speaking unprincipled efficiency.[13]

And, again, appropriating and explicating a remark of Nietzsche, in order to bring out the "dangers threatening democracy . . . from within":

> The reading of the morning prayer [has] been replaced by the reading of the morning paper: not every day the same thing, the same reminder of men's absolute duty and exalted destiny, but every day something new with no reminder of duty and exalted destiny. Specialization, knowing more and more about less and less, practical impossibility of concentration upon the very few essential things upon which man's wholeness entirely depends — the specialization compensated by sham universality by the stimulation of all kinds of interests and curiosities without true passion, the danger of universal philistinism and creeping conformism.[14]

Such remarks, together with his critique of the modern political philosophers, might seem to lend some weight to the suspicion that Strauss's return to classical political philosophy was politically motivated. He did, indeed, oppose to contemporary liberalism classical liberality,[15] and he wrote that "True liberals today have no more pressing duty than to counteract the perverted liberalism which contends 'that just to live, securely and happily, and protected but other-

---

13. "Liberal Education and Responsibility," p. 23.
14. "Existentialism," 7 (*The Rebirth of Classical Political Rationalism*, p. 31).
15. "The Liberalism of Classical Political Philosophy," *Liberalism Ancient and Modern*, p. 28ff.

wise unregulated, is man's simple but supreme goal' and which forgets quality, excellence, or virtue."[16] In opposing the new political science which had come to dominate the political science departments of major universities, he drew attention to its more or less unconscious harmony with "a certain version of liberal democracy," something he designated "its democratism";[17] his call for a restoration of the older political science was at the same time, therefore, a call to reopen the examination of "the very complex pros and cons regarding liberal democracy."[18] He approved of "setting up outposts which may come to be regarded by many citizens as salutary to the republic and as deserving of giving to it its tone."[19] But what Strauss meant by this, as the context of the last remark makes clear, was no more than that we should take advantage of the freedom democracy affords to all to "cultivate our garden"— that is, to pursue excellence on our own, so far as we are capable of doing so, while, if we are teachers (especially in political science departments or law schools), encouraging "whatever broadens and deepens the understanding" rather than "what in the best case cannot as such produce more than narrow and unprincipled efficiency."[20]

The deepest reason for this restraint is pointed to by the fact that the classical political philosophy to which Strauss would have us return — on the ground, among others, that its analysis of political life is superior to that of its modern alternatives[21] — is ultimately as harsh in its criticism of aristocracy as it is in its criticism of democracy. At most, the harshness of these criticisms differs only in degree. Aristocracy in its ideal (say, Platonic) form is devoted to the pursuit of excellence or virtue; but the adequate investigation of the question "What is virtue?" leads to the conclusion "that the ultimate aim of political life cannot be reached by political life, but only by a life devoted to contemplation, to philosophy."[22] Some of those who believe that they discern a political motivation behind Strauss's efforts toward the recovery of classical political philosophy are aware that, in Strauss's understanding of it, that philosophy is

16. *Ibid.*, p. 64.
17. "An Epilogue," *Liberalism Ancient and Modern*, p. 222 and context.
18. *Ibid.*, pp. 223, 222, and 205ff.
19. "Liberal Education and Responsibility," p. 24.
20. *Ibid.*, pp. 24 and 19.
21. See, for example, "An Epilogue," pp. 209–210, as well as *The City and Man*, pp. 10–11.
22. "On Classical Political Philosophy," *What Is Political Philosophy?* (New York: Free Press, 1959), pp. 90–91.

so far from calling for political action that it is concerned with bringing to light "the limits set to political life, to all political action and all political planning."[23] Yet they regard this fact as a confirmation rather than the definitive refutation of their thesis. They see in it or through it the conservatism of one who appealed to Plato's *Republic* as a critique of political idealism,[24] and attempted thereby to purge the best of contemporary youth of their longing for political action and political reform.[25] But the remarks quoted in the preceding paragraph are sufficient indication of Strauss's dissatisfaction with the present political situation in the West, however preferable it remained, in his view, to that in the East. Moreover, not given himself to undue despair, he was not inclined to encourage it in others, with regard to politics or anything else. For, since the outcome of serious conflicts is, generally speaking, unpredictable, "'men can always hope and never need to give up, in whatever fortunes and in whatever travail they find themselves.'"[26]

Still, it was not to political hopes of any sort that Strauss ultimately wished to address himself. Or, to return to our original question, it was neither reverence for the Founders' work—which he encouraged by opening up the prospect of recovering a genuine and viable rationalism—nor dissatisfaction with their work—a dissatisfaction bound to be deepened by the recovery of premodern thought—that was intended to be the final result of Strauss's return. These may well, however, have been intended to be way stations on a journey individuals as individuals were to be encouraged to make to solve a problem that only individuals can solve. The individuals in question were likely to be distinguished by the strength and purity of their devotion to liberal democracy as well as by the depth of their concern, or potential concern, with its plight; for the hope to which he ultimately addressed himself is all but certain to find its first expression, to make its first appearance in a more or less political guise.

II

Which hope, then, did he wish to address, after having first responded to it himself? The hope of an individual, in whatever

---

23. *Ibid.*, p. 91; *The City and Man*, p. 138.
24. *The City and Man*, p. 127.
25. Cf. M. F. Burnyeat, "Sphinx Without a Secret," *The New York Review of Books*, 30 May 1985, pp. 30–36.
26. "An Epilogue," p. 209; and "Liberal Education and Responsibility," p. 24.

circumstances he may find himself, to guide his life by a rational
or natural standard, or by reason. Considered in this light, the return to classical political philosophy reveals itself eventually as a return to a philosophy that attempted "to lead the qualified citizens,
or rather their qualified sons, from the political life to the philosophic
life."[27] Or, as he put it in an early article on Lessing which was published only after his death, "freemasonry," that is, philosophy, "came
into being, when someone who originally had planned a scientific
society which should make the speculative truths useful for practical and political life, conceived of a 'society which should raise itself from the practice of civil life to speculation,'" which is the same
thing as to say that "the intention of the good works of the free-
masons is to make good works superfluous."[28] Yet the difficulties or
ambiguities attending Strauss's return, when it is understood in this
way, are scarcely less massive than those we encountered in considering its significance for the understanding of the American
Founding. One example will probably suffice for showing that this
is the case. While Strauss gave frequent expression to the view that
the human or political science of the ancients is superior to the
modern alternatives, he was much more hesitant to assert the superiority of their natural science or metaphysics. Indeed, as he indicated on one occasion, "who can dare to say that Plato's doctrine
of ideas as he intimated it, or Aristotle's doctrine of the *nous* that
does nothing but think itself and is essentially related to the eternal
visible universe, is the true teaching?" But does this not mean, he
continued, that "those like myself who are inclined to sit at the feet
of the old philosophers [are] exposed to the danger of a weak-kneed
eclecticism which will not withstand a single blow on the part of
those who are competent enough to remind them of the singleness
of purpose and of inspiration that characterizes every thinker who
deserves to be called great?"[29] Strauss could not ultimately have accepted, in other words, as he may sometimes seem to have come
close to doing,[30] what he called, in *Natural Right and History* "a fun-

27. "On Classical Political Philosophy," pp. 93–94. This is one reason, though
not the only one, why it remains a return to *political* philosophy. Cf. "Exoteric
Teaching," *Interpretation* 14 (1984) :53 at the end of the first paragraph, as well as
note 47 below.
28. "Exoteric Teaching," pp. 52–53.
29. "Existentialism," 11 (*The Rebirth of Classical Political Rationalism*, p. 34).
30. Cf. *What Is Political Philosophy?* pp. 38–39; and Stanley Rothman, "The Revival of Classical Political Philosophy: A Critique," *APSR* 56 (1962): 350. Cf. "On
the Intention of Rousseau," *Social Research* 14 (1947): 487.

damental, typically modern, dualism of a nonteleological natural science and a teleological science of man . . . a position which presupposes a break with the comprehensive view of Aristotle. . . ." He traced "the fundamental dilemma, in whose grip we are," to "the victory of modern natural science." And he asserted that, "An adequate solution to the problem of natural right cannot be found before this basic problem has been solved."[31] Since he seems to have had little to say about such a solution, we might appear to be justified in concluding that he regarded the return to classical political philosophy as merely tentative; some of his remarks, moreover, seem to lend support to this view.[32] But other remarks leave no doubt that, at a relatively young age, he had already reached the conclusion that the decisive difficulties had been overcome, at least in principle.[33] We are thus forced to consider the question of how that conclusion was reached.

In order even to begin to approach this question, we must first try to see more clearly what exactly it was that led Strauss to regard a return to premodern philosophy as *desirable*—and this is the only aspect of the question which will be discussed here. In what context, in other words, did the thought of such a return present itself to him? His first book, *Spinoza's Critique of Religion*, "was based on the premise, sanctioned by powerful prejudice, that a return to premodern philosophy is impossible."[34] His second book, *Philosophy and Law*, which has the subtitle, "Essays Toward the Understanding of Maimonides and His Predecessors," all but begins with the assertion that "Maimonides' rationalism is the truly natural model, the standard that must be carefully guarded against every counterfeit, and the touchstone that puts modern rationalism to shame," or, more generally, that "medieval rationalism" is "the standard against which modern rationalism proves to be only apparent rationalism."[35] (The ground or grounds which sustain so harsh a judgment against modern rationalism are apparently sufficient to dispose also of "'irrationalism,'" which "is only a variety of modern rationalism."[36]) The

31. *Natural Right and History* (Chicago: University of Chicago Press, 1953), p. 8.
32. See, for example, *The City and Man*, p. 11. Cf. "On a New Interpretation of Plato's Political Philosophy," pp. 338–39.
33. *Philosophy and Law*, trans. Fred Baumann (Philadelphia: Jewish Publication Society of America, 1987), pp. 3, 11–16, 111–12; "Preface to the English Translation," p. 31.
34. "Preface to the English Translation," p. 31.
35. "Introduction," p. 3.
36. Note 1 to "Introduction," p. 111.

return to premodern philosophy takes place, then, in the course of Strauss's investigation of the problem to which each of these two books is devoted—what he called "the theological-political problem." It is true that the return in question here is a return to *medieval* philosophy and that the preeminence of Strauss's concern with classical philosophy becomes more visible in his work at a later stage, just as his concern with "the theological-political problem" becomes less visible there. But apart from the fact that he understood medieval philosophy from the beginning—that is, from the period to which *Philosophy and Law* belongs—in the light of "its classical (Aristotelian and Platonic) foundation,"[37] Strauss confirmed as late as 1965 that since his early work on Spinoza, "the theological-political problem has remained *the* theme of my investigations."[38] We must thus conclude that his mature concern with classical philosophy, too, grew out of and was sustained by his preoccupation with that problem.

In the 1962 "Preface to the English Translation" of his Spinoza book, by way of explanation of the context out of which the book emerged, Strauss has given us an account of the theological-political problem as he understood it and had confronted it. (The "Preface" may be supplemented by the "Introduction" to *Philosophy and Law*—a much earlier document from which it borrows whole passages virtually *verbatim*—as well as by a number of other statements, such as "A Giving of Accounts," the 1965 preface to the German edition of Strauss's Hobbes book, and "The Mutual Influence of Theology and Philosophy.") The problem has a "social or political" aspect (p. 6), as well as an aspect which concerns individuals as individuals. In his discussion of the latter aspect, Strauss begins from the case "of the Western Jewish individual who or whose parents severed his connection with the Jewish community." The individuals Strauss is concerned with admit that "their deepest problem would be solved" by "return to the Jewish community, the community established by the Jewish faith and the Jewish way of life," but "believe such a return to be altogether impossible because they believe that the

---

37. "Preface to the English Translation," p. 31; and , among other places, *Philosophy and Law*, p. 103ff.; "Quelques Remarques sur la Science Politique de Maimonide et de Farabi," *Revue des Etudes Juives* 100 (1936): 2-6.

38. Preface to the German edition of his Hobbes book, *Interpretation* 8 (1979): 1; cf. the remark of Avicenna which he prefixed to the last book he completed before his death, *The Argument and the Action of Plato's "Laws"* (Chicago: University of Chicago, 1975); cf. on the importance of that remark for Strauss, "A Giving of Accounts," *The College* 25 (1970): 3.

Jewish faith has been overthrown once and for all, not by blind rebellion, but by evident refutation . . . they assert that intellectual probity forbids them to sacrifice intellect in order to satisfy even the most vital need" (p. 7).

On the basis of an analysis of the alleged obstacles to return, as they were understood by his contemporaries and their predecessors, the young Strauss had apparently been tempted to draw the opposite conclusion:

> Considerations like those sketched in the preceding paragraphs made one wonder whether an unqualified return to Jewish orthodoxy was not both possible and necessary—was not at the same time the solution to the problem of the Jew lost in the non-Jewish modern world and the only course compatible with sheer consistency or intellectual probity (p. 15).

Yet, "Vague difficulties remained like small faraway clouds on a beautiful summer sky. They soon took the shape of Spinoza . . ." (p. 15). Some light is shed on this rather enigmatic remark by what Strauss says — more clearly, perhaps in the "Introduction" to *Philosophy and Law* than in the "Preface"—about "the most significant representatives" of "the movement of return," Hermann Cohen and Franz Rosenzweig. These men "did not unreservedly undertake the return to tradition"; in other words, they did not return to an undiluted orthodoxy ("Introduction," p. 8ff.; cf. "Preface," pp. 13–15 and 27). Their reservations could be traced back to the Enlightenment (to Spinoza among others), to a philosophy, that is, which had in the meantime allegedly been "overcome." These facts — the alleged overcoming of Spinoza or of Enlightenment thought, together with the continued reliance on that thought — made it necessary to reopen the question of whether Spinoza or the Enlightenment "had in fact refuted orthodoxy" ("Preface," pp. 27–28, "Introduction," pp. 9–10).[39] "Orthodoxy could be returned to only if Spinoza was wrong in every respect" ("Preface," p. 15).

Strauss summarized the results of his early examination of Spinoza — the examination which produced *Spinoza's Critique of Religion* — in both the "Preface" and the "Introduction." It appears from these summaries that he reached the conclusion that Spinoza was wrong, if not in every respect, in the decisive respect or that

---

39. Cf. Preface to the German edition of Hobbes book, 1, and "A Giving of Accounts," p. 3.

he had not refuted orthodoxy ("Preface," pp. 28–29, "Introduction," pp. 10–11). Yet, while this appearance is ultimately not misleading, it must be qualified. This is shown most simply by the fact that Strauss fails to present himself as having taken the step which only Spinoza's opposition, now apparently disposed of, had hitherto prevented.

As he indicates most clearly in the "Introduction," "even though the attack of the Enlightenment upon orthodoxy failed, the battle of the two hostile powers still had a highly consequential and positive result for the Enlightenment" (p. 11).[40] He even goes so far as to speak of what "justifies" the Enlightenment ("Introduction," pp. 13, 15, 16, 18, 19, and "Preface," p. 30). According to Strauss, "The quarrel between Enlightenment and Orthodoxy made clearer and better known than before that the presuppositions of Orthodoxy (the reality of Creation, Miracles, and Revelation) are not known (philosophically or historically) but are only believed and thus lack the peculiarly obligatory character of the known" ("Introduction," p. 12).[41] From this conclusion, accepted by Strauss, there is only a step to "the view . . . that the assertion of miracles is relative to the prescientific state of mankind and thus has no dignity whatsoever" ("Introduction," p. 15).[42] As we learn from the Spinoza book itself, the additional step was taken by "the positive mind" which "finds itself . . . unmovable by all reports on miracles, and therefore by all experience of miracles" because to it "it is plain that the prophets and the apostles did not view and analyze the events which they report with the same sobriety and severity which that mind brings to bear on events observed" (pp. 134–35); "miracles . . . are seen as occurring for a state of consciousness which is not capable of strict scientific investigation of experience" (p. 136). Comparing itself to such a state of consciousness, the positive mind, or "positive consciousness," which is "self-conscious of empirical awareness" (p. 126), regarded itself as having achieved a pure and decisive progress in openness to the world as it is. Abstaining from the more ambitious but flawed attempt to prove that miracles are impossible, it demanded only that they be "indubitably established" as such by being submitted to its own "precise observation and stringent analysis" (pp.

40. Cf. "A Giving of Accounts," p. 3.
41. Cf. "Preface," p. 28: Spinoza's refutation is therefore a failure only so long as orthodoxy "limits itself to asserting that it believes" the fundamental points.
42. Cf. "The Mutual Influence of Theology and Philosophy," *The Independent Journal of Philosophy* 3 (1979): 115.

213, 134). But Strauss came to see that that very demand or "the will to 'establish'" destroys the possibility of experience of miracles (pp. 213-14); and he therefore wondered whether that demand or will was "itself something to be taken for granted" (p. 214; cf. 145). Doubts on that score led him to see the issue as one "between the unbelieving and the believing manner of experiencing the world" (p. 198); and he drew the conclusion that "Just as the assertion of miracles is called in question by the positive mind, positive critique of miracles is called in question by the mind that waits in faith or in doubt for the coming of the miracles" (p. 214).[43] The openness to which the positive mind laid claim thus revealed itself to him as less than complete.[44]

Having reached this point, Strauss concluded at this stage that "the antagonism between Spinoza and Judaism, between unbelief and belief, is ultimately not theoretical but moral" ("Preface," p. 29; cf. "Introduction," pp. 15-16). His examination of that antagonism over the course of its history led him to the view that "The last word and the ultimate justification of Spinoza's critique is the atheism from intellectual probity which overcomes orthodoxy radically by understanding it radically . . ." ("Preface," p. 30, "Introduction," p. 19). But this solution to his problem, too, failed to satisfy him: "its basis is an act of will, of belief, and, being based on belief, is fatal to any philosophy" ("Preface," p. 30).[45] Just after speaking, therefore, of the overcoming of orthodoxy by "the atheism from intellectual probity," he refers to the same development as "the victory of

43. Cf. *ibid.*, p. 116; and especially "Introduction," p. 15.

44. It was on its way to becoming "probity," something which Strauss was to distinguish from "attentiveness" or "love of truth," from genuine openness to the world as it is. (Note 12 to the "Introduction," *Philosophy and Law*, pp. 113-14) — It is possible and even probable that Strauss was helped, in coming to understand this limitation of the positive critique of religion, by historicism, which "understands modern natural science as a historically conditioned form of 'world interpretation' along with others" ("Introduction," p. 14; cf. note 2 to the "Introduction," *ibid.*, p. 112). However that may be, his insight into this limitation of the positive critique must have confirmed for him the (limited) truth of the historicist critique of modern natural science ("Introduction," p. 15; cf. "On a New Interpretation of Plato's Political Philosophy," p. 338f.)

45. The most recent assessment of Strauss's work ("Truth for philosophers alone?" by Stephen Holmes, *Times Literary Supplement*, 1-7 December 1989, pp. 1319-24) gives no evidence that its author is aware of this dissatisfaction or, more generally, of Strauss's critique of probity. It thus in effect ascribes to Strauss a position — "dogmatic atheism" — whose denunciation by him had aroused the ire of an earlier generation of critics (see Strauss's "Reply" to Schaar and Wolin in *American Political Science Review* 57 (1963): 153).

orthodoxy through the self-destruction of rational philosophy" (p. 30).[46] Yet, as he goes on to point out, neither Jewish orthodoxy nor Nietzsche can dispense entirely with an appeal to reason or objective truth. Moreover, "Other observations and experiences confirmed the suspicion that it would be unwise to say farewell to reason." It was at this point that Strauss "began therefore to wonder whether the self-destruction of reason was not the inevitable outcome of modern rationalism as distinguished from pre-modern rationalism, especially Jewish-medieval rationalism and its classical (Aristotelian and Platonic) foundation" (p. 31).[47]

46. Cf., again, *Philosophy and Law*, p. 111 (note 1 to "Introduction"): "'Irrationalism' is only a variety of modern rationalism"; cf. also *Natural Right and History*, pp. 74–76, as well as "The Mutual Influence of Theology and Philosophy," pp. 117–18.
47. In the "Preface" itself, Strauss gives one hint as to what may have permitted "the change of orientation" that consisted in his coming to regard a return to premodern philosophy as not only desirable but also possible: he says that that change "found its first expression" in the article on Carl Schmitt reprinted at the end of the volume. In that article, Strauss says that, "In order to launch the radical critique" of modern political philosophy that Schmitt had in mind, he "must first eliminate the conception of human evil as animal evil, and therefore as 'innocent evil,' and find his way back to the conception of human evil as moral depravity" (p. 345). For the import of this remark, cf. the Spinoza book proper, when Strauss was still proceeding on the basis of the premise "that a return to pre-modern philosophy is impossible," 204, with *The City and Man*, pp. 38–40 and "On a New Interpretation of Plato's Political Philosophy," p. 344. Cf. *Natural Right and History*, p. 78.

Leo Strauss and American Democracy: A Response to Wood and Holmes

David Lewis Schaefer

Although Leo Strauss spent the better part of his scholarly career in the United States, his name remained essentially unknown in this country during his lifetime outside the rather restricted academic circles of political science and Judaic studies. Only in recent years — owing, positively, to the best-selling status achieved by a book by one of his students, Allan Bloom's *Closing of the American Mind*; and negatively, to several critical reviews of his thought and influence in the semi-popular media — has Strauss's name been publicized to a somewhat wider audience. This article is a response to two of the critiques: Gordon Wood's relatively moderate "The Fundamentalists and the Constitution," published in the *New York Review of Books* (18 February 1988), and Stephen Taylor Holmes's less restrained "Truths for Philosophers Alone?", which appeared in the *Times Literary Supplement* (1–7 December 1989).[1]

Unlike some of Strauss's critics, Wood, in his review of "Straussian" scholarship on the American Founding, concedes that "Straussians" have made a significant contribution to our understanding of the history of political thought. But he nonetheless presents a caricature of Strauss's and his students' work that is apparently intended to explain, or even to justify, what Wood describes as "widespread hostility and contempt towards the Straussians in academic circles" (33d).

Central to Wood's caricature is his account of Strauss's teaching as a "mysterious and occult," quasi-religious "faith," in which his followers "believe" less as students than as "disciples" (33d, 34c). Yet — beyond an aversion to "historicism," and an aspiration "to understand past political philosophers as they understood themselves" with which "any historian might agree" (33d) — Wood appears unable to articulate the content of this common "faith," or to demonstrate its influence on Straussian scholarship on the Constitution. He attributes to Strauss (without textual reference) the belief that the "eternal truth

1. For the reader's assistance, I have added letter references corresponding to the page columns being cited in each parenthetical reference to these reviews: hence "33d," for instance, refers to the fourth column of page 33 of Wood's essay; "1322b" to the second column of page 1322 of Holmes's review.

339

could ultimately be located in the writings of Plato," a truth which included the doctrine that "the right or the best political order was the highest ideal of man" (34a). But this questionable attribution leaves unclear why Strauss's students should have devoted so much attention to the (manifestly un-Platonic) foundations of the American regime.[2] Similarly, Wood acknowledges that Straussians do not necessarily "think alike about the Founding," and have in fact had disagreements among themselves "as bitter as any in academia" (35a). Yet he seems immediately to forget this point in attempting to identify an official "Straussian" conception of the Founding. While "welcom[ing]" the late Herbert Storing's seven-volume edition of Antifederalist writings, Wood observes that "on their face" these volumes "show little Straussian influence" (37a). He nonetheless contends that the edition "represent[s] a broadened definition by the Straussians of the important documents of the Founding," and explains this extension by reference to "the rise of conservative populism, rooted in anti-establishment feelings" (36b). He similarly claims that Philip Kurland and Ralph Lerner, by extending their edition of documents titled *The Founders' Constitution* through the end of the Marshall Court, adopt "a broader definition of the 'Founding' than many Straussians accept" (37a). Yet since (to the present author's knowledge) neither Strauss nor any of his students has issued a canonical definition of the "extent" of the Founding, either in chronological or in bibliographic terms, the basis of these remarks is obscure. Nor does Wood explain why "making sense" of the Kurland-Lerner collection requires "see[ing] it in Straussian terms" (37a), especially since Kurland, a prominent law professor, has had no particular scholarly connection with Straussians other than this collaboration. Is it not possible that such students of the Founding as

2. Wood's explanation of the spirit and motivation of Straussian studies of American political thought relies on a "conservative" critique of such studies by Charles Kesler (more accurately directed against George Will), with whose views one cannot imagine Wood to be otherwise sympathetic ("Is Conservatism Un-American?," *National Review*, 22 March 1985, pp. 28–37). For a corrective to Kesler's (and, *a fortiori*, Wood's) account, see Thomas Pangle, "Patriotism, American Style," *National Review*, 29 November 1985, pp. 30–34. For a misunderstanding of Strauss's own scholarly enterprise by another right-wing critic that is similar to Wood's (but more extreme), see Russell Kirk's claim that "for the past four decades the disciples of Leo Strauss have been declaring that they design 'to restore the polis'" ("What Did Americans Inherit from the Ancients?", *Intercollegiate Review* 24 [Spring 1989]: 43). Kirk supplies no source for his most unlikely quotation. Cf. Strauss's explicit denial of the possibility of any such restoration in a 1946 letter to Karl Löwith, published in *Independent Journal of Philosophy* 4 (1983): 107–108.

Kurland and Leonard Levy (a leading Constitutional historian and political liberal who co-edited another collection of documents reviewed by Wood) chose Straussian collaborators, not for some "occult" political or religious reason, but simply because the collaborators shared with them a dedication to sound scholarship, and a belief in the value of increasing the accessibility of important constitutional and historical documents? (Storing's own study of the Antifederalists began in the mid-1960's, well before, and in no evident connection with, the latest "rise of conservative populism.")

The artificiality of Wood's "Straussian" caricature is most clearly evident in his comments on Ralph Lerner's *The Thinking Revolutionary*. While praising Lerner's studies of the thought of the Founders for their insight and "historical sensitivity," Wood remarks that Lerner "does not always wear his Straussianism on his sleeve." But Wood's claim that Lerner's acknowledgment of the importance of historical circumstances in limiting or determining political action constitutes an apparent acceptance of "the historicism deplored by other Straussians" (38c) rests on a confusion between attentiveness to historical fact and adherence to the doctrine of historical *relativism* that runs throughout his essay. One of the central teachings of classical political philosophy, and of such modern thinkers as Montesquieu, as articulated by Strauss, was that varying circumstances necessarily constrain the possibilities of political improvement in any given situation; hence the cardinal political virtue, for Aristotle, is prudence rather than theoretical wisdom, and the craft of statesmanship can never be reduced to a science. Historical relativism, however — the doctrine that the truth about fundamental issues is inevitably inaccessible, because our minds are necessarily limited or biased by our historical era (which is what the term "historicism" originally meant, and what Strauss and his students have meant by it) — is, as Strauss stressed, not a historical, but a philosophic doctrine, one that can never be demonstrated by reference to the history it purports to explain.[3]

3. On the philosophical rather than historical ground of the historicist thesis, see Strauss's *Natural Right and History* (Chicago: University of Chicago Press, 1953), pp. 19ff. Wood's understanding of Strauss's conception of the relation between philosophy and history would have been enhanced by a consideration of the essay "Political Philosophy and History," reprinted in Strauss's *What Is Political Philosophy?* (New York: Free Press, 1959), pp. 56–77. He would also have benefited from a reading of Strauss's critique of R. G. Collingwood's philosophy of history (*Review of Metaphysics* 5 [1951–52]: 559–86), where — Myles Burnyeat's carping notwith-

Contrary to Wood's claim, the Straussians have not held that the Founders were "outside history," that they had "divine insight," or that their thinking was entirely "free of passion, ignorance, or foolishness" (38d). They would assert, however, that one cannot know that a given thought was ignorant or foolish, or the mere product of "its time," without thoroughly *weighing* that thought and the reasoning on which it is based. Precisely because of the tendency of contemporary historians (not all historians!) "to treat ideas," as Wood puts it, "as ideology" (38c), they have frequently ignored, or refrained from taking seriously, the claim of a thought to *be* true. The result, all too often, is a dismissal of the fundamental principles of natural right to which the Founders subscribed as a collection of antiquated prejudices (as in Carl Becker's influential study *The Declaration of Independence*), and an unjustified depiction of their thought as the product of a "distorting ideology" (the phrase is used by the non-Straussian historian Kenneth Lynn, apropos of Bernard Bailyn's *The Ideological Origins of the American Revolution*).[4]

Since Wood professes to share the Straussian aspiration of understanding past thinkers as they understood themselves, and since his own accomplishments as a historian have been acknowledged (albeit not uncritically) by Straussians themselves, it is curious that he should have chosen to publish this weakly grounded critique. The explanation, aside from the territorial imperative of a historian wishing to defend his discipline against the intrusions of political scientists, appears to lie in political partisanship, more specifically concern about "the growing influence of 'conservatism' in our national life." By "conservatism," Wood means the disposition of "many Americans [to] believe" that the Founding embodied "some perma-

standing—he would find Collingwood treated civilly, even sympathetically, even as the problematic assumptions that underlie his argument are uncovered. It is curious that Wood avoids any reference to Lerner's critical discussion of Wood's own historiography in the first chapter of his book.

4. Lynn, *The Air-Line to Seattle* (Chicago: University of Chicago Press, 1983), p. 188. Contrary to Wood's claim, however, it is not the case that "[b]elief in 'natural right' is crucial to the Straussian scheme of things" (34b); careful readers of Strauss's *Natural Right and History* such as Richard Kennington have emphasized the dialectical character of his treatment of that theme, consistent with Strauss's repeated statement that philosophy is properly characterized by the investigation of problems rather than the provision of, or dogmatic "belief in," solutions. See Kennington, "Strauss's *Natural Right and History*," *Review of Metaphysics* 35 (September 1981): 57–86; Leo Strauss, *On Tyranny* (Glencoe, IL: Free Press, 1963), pp. 209–10; *What Is Political Philosophy?* (New York: Free Press, 1959), pp. 38–40; "Farabi's Plato," *Louis Ginzburg Jubilee Volume* (New York: Academy for Jewish Research, 1945), pp. 392–93.

nent truths about politics" from which "we depart at our peril" (33a). In the last section of his essay, Wood contrasts the endeavor of such Straussians as Walter Berns to uncover the "original intent" underlying the Constitution with Justice Brennan's praise of that document's "adaptability" (39). While denying that the Constitution has any "timeless and universal meaning," Wood fails to respond to Berns's point that if such is the case, the very justification for judicial review disappears (39b).[5]

Wood's appeal to "history" to sanction Brennan's interpretation of the Constitution as infinitely flexible, and to dismiss Judge Robert Bork as a "radical" who rejected the Constitution's "inherited meanings" (40c), is disingenuous, since the judgments that Bork challenged were the quite recent creations of a group of Supreme Court justices, convinced that they possessed a unique insight into the meaning of justice that far surpassed the comprehension of the public or their elected representatives (to say nothing of the Founders). When the Court invented a "right" to abortion, purporting to have discovered it among previously unnoticed "penumbras" "emanating" from various amendments, for instance, it was arrogating to itself the most fundamental of the rights guaranteed to the people by the Constitution, the right to govern themselves through their elected representatives. Wood's accusation that Berns lacks a "feel for history" (39b) because he challenges such developments clearly reflects a political, not a historical, judgment.

Wood hopes to counteract the fears of opponents of judicial remaking of the Constitution by reassuring them that our culture's "inherited meanings" limit the possibilities of successful Constitutional innovation. But this assertion would seem to presuppose the very sort of popular reverence for the Constitution (as distinguished from rebellion against our "inherited" system of government) that he disparages (40b-d). Moreover, Wood fails to confront the consequences of the "restrictive" historicism he espouses (40b): that the dedication to preserve our political regime is, objectively, a groundless one; that man's fate is determined by a mindless historical "process"; and that freedom in its deepest sense, the liberation of the intellect from prejudice or bias, is unattainable. These consequences are hardly supportive of liberty or of liberalism, as Wood supposes.

---

5. See Berns, *Taking the Constitution Seriously* (New York: Simon & Schuster, 1987), pp. 207–208; cf. Hamilton, Madison, and Jay, *The Federalist*, ed. Clinton Rossiter (New York: New American Library, 1961), No. 78, pp. 466–68.

David Schaefer

Perhaps because his own scholarship has focused on early American history, Wood seems to have forgotten the variety of terrible regimes, both Left and Right, that have found their sanction in the dictates of "history" or in avowedly nonrational "commitments" during the twentieth century.[6] Whatever the dangers of an excessive reverence toward the text of the Constitution and the thought of its authors, the experience of our century surely shows them to pale before that of the faith in history.

Because we have no grounds for assuming the inherent benignity of the historical process, it has always been the aim of philosophy to enable its practitioners to transcend their "times" *in thought*, so far as is humanly possible, in order to judge political regimes in the light of reason and nature. It is this almost-forgotten quest that Leo Strauss and his students have sought to resuscitate. Precisely because of the essentially skeptical rather than dogmatic character of political philosophy as Strauss understood it, we may never be in a position to assert that a specific political doctrine *is* irrefutably true, or that its proponent entirely freed himself from prejudices reflecting a particular historical milieu, his own idiosyncrasies, or the human condition itself. But it would be the height of dogmatism, conversely, to take for granted, as Wood implies, that a genuinely transcultural or suprahistorical truth is inaccessible to us (34b).

For Wood, the observation by a student of Strauss's that "Straussians attract students because they are able to address the souls of students" demonstrates the essentially irrational nature of their pursuit — despite Strauss's remark that "a philosophy based on faith is no longer philosophy" (33d). But by presupposing that any teaching that addresses people's souls must have a nonrational ground, Wood exhibits the limitations of his own theoretical orientation. In assuming that a mode of teaching that appeals to the soul must be essentially nonrational, Wood evinces his apparent subscription to the Weberian view that the truth is in itself nonlovable; reason, therefore, cannot itself be a source of meaning or purpose in life. As Weber's teacher Nietzsche forewarned, this would be a truly damning consequence for the life ostensibly devoted to reason or science, and for the liberal political institutions that grew out of the Enlightenment, for it would

---

6. Cf. the quotation from Hans Kelsen in *Natural Right and History*, p. 4n., with Strauss's ironic comment on Kelsen's decision to omit the quoted remark from the (postwar) English translation of the work in which it appeared.

mean that we are doomed to be ruled by the irrational. Indeed, the widespread tendency of contemporary academicians to recruit followers by espousing partisan political causes in their classes or by flattering students' prejudices in favor of "idealism" or "compassion" demonstrates how, once the inherent attraction of truth is denied, the academy becomes the servant rather than the critic of unreflective passions.

Wood's charge that Straussian scholarship is insufficiently sensitive to the nuances of history is reiterated by Stephen Holmes (1324c). But Holmes's critique is far more indignant, since he believes Strauss to have been "undemocratic and illiberal" (1323c), and finds little or nothing of value in Strauss's scholarship to redeem its deleterious effects; indeed, in Holmes's judgment, Strauss wrote obscurely to conceal the fact that "he did not know what he was trying to say" (1324d). Like Wood, Holmes expresses concern at Strauss's capacity to "mesmerize" his students into "seemingly uncritical" "disciples" "by his passionate devotion to texts and his tireless effort to revivify what he called 'the Great Tradition'" (1319a). And like Wood, he is concerned that Strauss's teaching and influence threaten the properly "liberal" foundations of American politics. But for Holmes, Strauss's supposed discoveries never transcend the level of "banality," while the practice of esoteric writing to which he called attention did "irreparable damage" to philosophy itself (1322d, 1324d).

For someone who flaunts his devotion to logic, "clarity," and proof (1324c-d), Holmes is oddly opaque about the object of his criticism, in that he never makes clear whether he is taking Strauss to task for (1) misrepresenting what previous philosophers said; (2) repeating and supporting erroneous doctrines that they also maintained; or (3) stating *truths* that are at best "annoying" and at worst conducive to injustice and oppression. He notes, for instance, that Strauss's "theory of social change"— that is, his belief that philosophic ideas have had an enormous influence in shaping the character of modern political life — is "unfashionably elitist and intellectualist" (1324c); but does its unfashionableness demonstrate that the "theory" was *wrong*?[7] He treats as an arbitrary assumption (1324b) Strauss's claim that the philosophers sought to establish the superiority of their out-

---

7. For a massive philosophico-historical study that provides support for Strauss's "theory," see Hiram Caton, *The Politics of Progress: The Origins and Development of the Commercial Republic, 1600–1835* (Gainesville, FL: University of Florida Presses, 1988), reviewed by the present author in *Review of Politics* 52 (Winter 1990): 131–35.

look to that of the poets, as if this claim were not manifestly supported by Socrates' account of the "old quarrel between philosophy and poetry" in book 10 of Plato's *Republic*, as well as by the *Apology of Socrates*; but the next paragraph makes it clear that Holmes's real quarrel is with Socrates himself, who suffered from the "conceit that the philosopher is more noble than Achilles" and that his activity, despite its incomprehensibility to the multitude, is "'the ultimate aim of political life'" (1324b). Again: Holmes objects to Strauss's account of the tension between philosophy and the contentment of the multitude, given the dependence of the former on "urban civilizations" whose rise arguably "spells an end to the pre-philosophical happiness of most people" (1323b); but it appears that the real target of Holmes's complaint is Rousseau, who most clearly articulated the tension in those terms; can Holmes prove Rousseau wrong? And further: "why," asks Holmes, is "the desire to live," given centrality as the goal of political life by Hobbes, "low?" (1324b), as if this judgment were somehow an invention of Strauss or other philosophers. Can Holmes locate any civilization that ever regarded the desire to survive at all cost as particularly noble or admirable? Or is Holmes himself taking the part of Nietzsche's "last man," determined to suppress any challenge to his understanding of "happiness"? Finally, Holmes professes to be surprised by Strauss's "refus[al]" to celebrate the contribution of [modern] science and technology to the sedation of most citizens" (1323d), only because Holmes has previously attributed to Strauss and other philosophers the desire to "narcotize" the multitude (1322b). But should not this refusal—along with his reference to Strauss's lament at "'the oblivion of the most fundamental things'" (1323a)—have caused Holmes rather to doubt the validity of the attribution? (Should it not already have been cast into doubt by Plato's representation of Socrates' self-depiction at his trial as a "gadfly" seeking to stimulate the greatest possible *awakeness* among his fellow citizens?)

The same unclarity regarding the ground of Holmes's criticism is exhibited in his complaints about Strauss's interpretative methods. For instance, despite lamenting the notion that philosophers should have "played hide and seek" in their writings, Holmes's himself acknowledges "the existence of esotericism" in at least some thinkers' works (1324d). What, then, is the basis of Holmes's charge that Strauss "overtax[ed]" this theme, since he makes no attempt to demonstrate that philosophers whom Strauss identified as having practiced it didn't really do so? And why is Strauss's "hermeneutical principle" concerning the importance of the center of a philosophic work merely an "annoyance" (1322d): can Holmes demonstrate the falsity of the principle, despite its open acknowledgment by a number of philosophers?[8]

The underlying motive of Holmes's criticisms of Strauss, even more than of Wood's, seems to be chiefly a partisan one. Holmes judges Strauss's work "undemocratic and illiberal" because it denies "the fundamental premiss of democratic theory . . . that we cannot tell in advance who will contribute something important in a public debate"; Strauss's exaggeration of "the differences between the few and the many" denies that the philosophic few have anything to learn from the multitude (1323c). But what can this charge mean? Whether one holds the distinction between the few and the many, intellectually classified, to be one of "degree" or of "kind" (1323c), in neither case can the distinction be said to provide a ground for determining *in advance* who belongs to which category—or therefore for closing off "the free flow of information" (1324d). According to Strauss, the means by which the philosophers conveyed to the few and the many teachings that were appropriate for each, morally and/or intellectually, was a self-selecting one. That is, those who read serious books only carelessly or cursorily, because they lack genuinely philosophical motivation or competence, derive from esoterically written works an "exoteric" teaching that is at worst harmless and at best morally edifying. Those who read more carefully and thoughtfully learn more of the "dangerous" truths, but their very love of learning constitutes a self-enforcing safeguard against their abuse of the knowledge. (It is for this reason, Plato implies in the *Apology*, that Socrates behaved more rather than less justly than his fellow citizens, despite his unbelief in their religion and his refusal to take for granted the validity of the accepted Athenian morality: for someone who regards wisdom rather than power or wealth as the greatest good, not even tyranny, the apex of the unjust life, holds any particular attraction; it simply isn't worth the trouble).[9]

In *revealing* the character of the philosophers' esotericism, Strauss can hardly be said to have interfered with "the free flow of information," or the opportunity for members of the multitude (however

8. See, *e.g.*, Montaigne, *Essays*, trans.Donald Frame (Stanford: Stanford University Press, 1957), I: 28, p. 135; Michel Butor, *Essais sur les "Essais"* (Paris: Gallimard, 1968), pp. 125–30.
9. Cf.also Aristotle *Politics*, II.7, 1266a9–12, 32–36.

defined) to deepen their own education; quite the opposite. But it appears that, ultimately, Holmes's complaint is less the untenable charge that Strauss somehow restricted the educational opportunities available to his audience, than unhappiness about *what* things he taught them. For Holmes, simply to question or reveal doubts about the dogmas of contemporary liberal relativism—that a life dedicated to self-preservation is as "noble" as any other; that popular religious belief is in no way essential to the survival of civilization (1320a); that a social science which teaches that all "values" are equally arbitrary is the ally of liberal tolerance rather than a useless if not actually corrupting diversion (1321d)—is evidently to disqualify a thinker from serious consideration.

In contrast to Holmes's caricature, both the great philosophers of the Western tradition and Strauss himself appear to have held that, despite the difference in goals between the philosopher and most people, there exists a potential (if inevitably incomplete) harmony between them, such that the philosopher can best *serve* his society, as well as promote his own security, by acting as the society's moderate, diplomatic, yet profound critic. Prime instances of this role in antiquity are Socrates' account of his refusal to obey the unjust and unlawful commands of both democrats and oligarchs in Plato's *Apology,* and Aristotle's subtle modification or partial rationalization of the moral code of the Athenian gentleman in the *Nicomachean Ethics.* In modern times, no better model could be cited than Tocqueville, who in *Democracy in America* affirms the principle of the equality of men's natural rights, yet devotes much of his work to articulating the dangers that threaten modern democracy from within, and to considering how liberal democracy might somehow conserve elements of what was most valuable in the old, aristocratic order.

Among all human beings, Aristotle remarks, the virtuous might have the greatest justification for rebelling against an existing government, yet are least likely to do so, on account of their numerical weakness.[10] If we take this remark as applying above all, in Aristotle's mind, to the philosophers, it supplies the ground of the premodern philosophers' political moderation, or of their belief, "banal" to Holmes (1322d), that "not everything is possible." In assisting his students to recapture this ancient wisdom, Strauss, far from inducing them to despise political life, as Holmes implies (1322c), supplied

10. *Ibid.,* 1301a38–40, 1304b4–5.

them with the ground on which they might most beneficially contribute to it, whether from the academy or within the government
itself.[11] Despite Holmes's disparagement of the dangers posed to constitutional democracy both by political fanaticism and by moral relativism, it is this sobriety that helped Strauss's students to resist the
abject surrender of American universities to the dogmas of the irra-
tionalist Left during the 1960's, and that today gives them the intellectual self-confidence to oppose the rapid degeneration of the
liberal arts curriculum inspired by the pursuit of the "fashionable."

Contrary to Holmes's claim, Strauss never asserted that "the only
reason to study the great works of philosophy is to help defend civilization against its enemies" (1323b; contrast Holmes's sounder reference to Strauss's understanding of philosophy as "self-justifying"
or "an end-in-itself" at 1322b). Precisely because of his awareness
of the limited efficacy of reason in political life, Strauss never claimed,
as Holmes asserts he did, that the study of old books would itself
supply "a cure for the crisis of the West," let alone "that the only
reason to study the great works of philosophy is to help defend civilization against its enemies" (1323b). But Strauss referred to classical
philosophy rather than "ancient society and culture," as Holmes wishes
he had, for a diagnosis of the modern crisis (1324b) because, as Strauss
emphasized, our crisis *is* essentially an intellectual one, owing to
the overt deprecation by contemporary thinkers of the theoretical
principles of natural right on which the modern liberal regime was
expressly founded.[12] (It was never Strauss's claim that "ancient society
and culture" as a whole were simply healthy or unproblematic, or
even that they were unambiguously superior to modern liberal democracy; the various character types whom Socrates questions in
the dialogues of Plato and Xenophon may be said to exemplify the
characteristic defects and limitations of Athenian "culture.")

Holmes apparently believes he can refute "Strauss's insistence that

11. Contrary to Holmes, the fact that philosophers experience (in Strauss's words)
"contempt for the things which the non-philosophers hotly contest" (1323c) does
not entail that the philosophers feel only contempt for the nonphilosophers themselves: see Plato *Republic* 347a-b, where contempt for money and honor are said
to be prerequisites for just rule on behalf of the city's own well-being; to the extent
that philosophers might rule human beings indirectly through the influence of
their thought, their intellectual activity could simultaneously serve the good of
the multitude and themselves. Holmes supplies no evidence to support his denial
"that philosophers have ever effectively played such an educative role" for the nonphilosophers as Strauss attributes to them (1323d).

12. Cf. Nathan Tarcov, "Philosophy & History: Tradition and Interpretation
in the Work of Leo Strauss," *Polity* 16 (1983): 8–9.

scepticism is dangerous" simply by pointing out that "Montaigne, for example, was not a very dangerous man," and by citing the variety of possible forms that the danger might take ("listless despair," "frantic immoralism," or the replacement of "relatively harmless beliefs [such as patriotism and religion]" with "alternative dogmas [such as racial purity] that are much more harmful"), while complaining that Strauss "never explains how the seemingly contrary processes are related to one another" (1324c).[13] But it would not seem to require profound reflection to recognize that each of these evils, despite their "contrary" appearance, might result (among different people or at different times) from the same cause. Nor does the fact that Strauss explained how previous philosophers concealed their unbelief in the religion of their time entail, as Holmes implies, that his own attitude toward religion was hypocritical. While Strauss did not represent himself as a believer, his treatment of the religious issue as one that (from the standpoint of philosophy) must remain perpetually open[14] distinguished his position from the dogmatic atheism that typifies contemporary scholarship, as well as from the equally popular contemporary attempt to use the language of religion in support of dubious secular political causes. Among the students and readers Strauss attracted were a number of thoughtful clergymen and lay adherents of the Jewish, Protestant, and Catholic faiths, who recognized that he at least took the issues that concerned them more seriously than other scholars.[15]

13. Holmes's opinion of Montaigne's innocuousness was evidently not shared by the Catholic Church, which placed the *Essays* on its index, by Nietzsche, or, most importantly, by Montaigne himself: see Robert Eden, *Political Leadership and Nihilism* (Gainesville, FL: University of Florida Presses, 1984), pp. 59–61; Montaigne, *Essays*, I: 17, p. 51; I: 54, p. 227; II: 12, p. 379; II: 17, p. 498 (on the tension between freedom of thought and obedience to authority); I: 23, p.84 (on the consequences of tracing an established custom "to its origin"); II: 12, pp. 439–41; and, on the political influence and effects of the *Essays*, Richard Sayce, *The Essays of Montaigne: A Critical Exploration* (London: Weidenfeld and Nicholson, 1972), pp. 236–37, 259; Colette Fleuret, "Montaigne et la société civile," *Europe* 50 (1972): 107–23. Montaigne is also one of the most accessible sources of illumination about the practice of philosophic esotericism, for reasons other than the concern for self-preservation cited by Holmes: see, *e.g.*, *Essays*, II: 12, pp. 375–80, 408; III: 9, p. 757 (Solon); III: 10, p. 769.

14. See, *e.g.*, Strauss's "The Mutual Influence of Theology and Philosophy," *Independent Journal of Philosophy* 3 (1979): 111–18; "Jerusalem and Athens: Some Preliminary Reflections," reprinted in *Studies in Platonic Political Philosophy*, ed. Thomas Pangle (Chicago: University of Chicago Press, 1983), pp. 147–73; and Pangle's introduction to that volume, pp.18–26.

15. See, on Strauss's relation to Judaism, Milton Himmelfarb, "On Leo Strauss," *Commentary* 58 (August 1974): 60–66, with the clarification provided by the ex-

Despite charging Strauss with "a deplorable lack of clarity" reflecting his ignorance of "what he was trying to say" (1324c-d), and mocking his failure to provide "the intellectual and moral resources to resist Nazism" (1324b), Holmes himself, in his scatter-shot attack, fails either to demonstrate that he has spent much time studying (as opposed to cursorily surveying) Strauss's writings, or to articulate an alternative means of fortifying the liberal polity morally or intellectually. In this, as in other respects, he reminds one of Socrates' accuser Meletus, who charges Socrates with corrupting the young, but proves to have given no thought to how they may be improved, and hardly to have reflected about what Socrates actually taught, evidently never having regarded these issues as requiring deliberation (Plato *Apology* 24d-25b, 26b-27a).

In the end, perhaps what is most striking about the criticisms of Strauss leveled by both Wood and Holmes (along with numerous other academics) is their assumption that Strauss's work must have been *motivated* by a particular political agenda, or (according to Holmes) by the desire for recognition — rather than by the love of learning. Were this the case, Strauss surely chose an odd way to pursue fame and political influence: devoting his teaching and scholarship to commentaries on old books, and writing (as Allan Bloom has pointed out) in a way that was less accessible, or deferential to the conventions of contemporary scholarship, in his later works than his earlier ones.[16] As, for Wood, there is apparently no way of engaging in teaching and scholarship that is both based on reason and addressed to the concerns of the soul, for Holmes, there is no conceivable benefit to liberal democracy from the serious consideration of great books (or readings of those books) that would call into question the regime's underlying assumptions: those who aren't fully "with" us must be "against" us.[17] No better attestation could be provided of the continuing need for philosophical scholarship of the sort that Strauss practiced — lest the road out of the cave be entirely blocked.

---

change between Himmelfarb and Joseph Cropsey in the issue of January 1975 (pp. 14, 16).

16. Bloom, "Leo Strauss," *Political Theory* 2 (1974): 384-85.

17. Holmes's earlier allegation of "a kind of 'inverted agreement'" between "Leo Strauss and his followers . . . and the most brashly totalitarian of [contemporary] leftists" ("Aristippus in and out of Athens," *American Political Science Review* 73 [1979]: 113n.) is mirrored, in the essay under review, by the ominous hint that the "relationship" of "the Nazi theorist Carl Schmitt [of whose work Strauss published a critical review] . . . with Strauss is an interesting story in itself" (1320d). Such casual insinuations come perilously close to what used to be called McCarthyism.

Without Malice But with Forethought: A Response to Burnyeat

David Lawrence Levine

Everything that was said [was] directed to precaution — that those with whom one shares arguments are to have orderly and stable natures, not as is done nowadays in sharing them with whomever chances by and comes to it without being suited for it.

Plato *Republic* VII 539d

The work of Leo Strauss is not typical of American academics. He has explicitly rejected the premises and methodologies of modern scholarship. In its stead, he claims to have rediscovered other, more ancient methods of discovery to guide his research. As a result, his conclusions do not necessarily reconfirm what we think we already know. His work thus represents a challenge to current scholarship. For if Strauss's conclusions are true, then a radical rethinking of the history of philosophy, political philosophy and psychology is required. It would be much easier if we could simply say that Strauss's methods and conclusions are wholly misguided.

One such attempt is that made by Myles Burnyeat of Cambridge who brings the teaching and writing of Leo Strauss before the public tribunal of the popular intellectual press in his article "Sphinx Without a Secret" (*The New York Review of Books*, 32 [30 May 1985], pp. 30-36). Under the guise of a review of Strauss's book, *Studies in Platonic Political Philosophy* (Chicago: University of Chicago Press, 1985), Burnyeat lodges a comprehensive, fivefold accusation:

(1) The major fault of Strauss was that he was a teacher who rendered the minds of his students captive.
(2) Strauss was not a philosopher in the modern Anglo-American tradition.
(3) Strauss's view of the history of philosophy is contrived, the result of the forced imposition of a medieval doctrine on the principal texts of the tradition.
(4) This revisionism has the consequence that Plato is wrongfully interpreted as a conservative.
(5) The teaching of Strauss has dangerous political consequences.

The review is thus an indictment, indeed one with a familiar ring: Strauss has corrupted the young with his teachings, is no true philosopher but a sophist professing nonexistent wisdom, making the

David Lawrence Levine

weaker argument the stronger by introducing a mystifying hermeneutic of esotericism. What's more, he does not acknowledge the popular gods of academia and is thus an atheist. For these reasons, this modern day Meletus would have Strauss banished from academic respectability.

The differences between the reigning Anglo-American schools of interpretation and other, principally Continental, views have long been the subject of hallway derision. It is therefore good that one example of this simmering dispute comes into the open. With the subsiding of the immediate indignation that accompanied this review, it is time to consider the question of Strauss's contribution more dispassionately. My comments correspond to the fivefold accusation.

I

The major fault of Strauss was that he was a teacher who rendered the minds of his students captive.

As Gadamer has observed, most conspicuous about the life of Leo Strauss is that, unlike other recent Continental figures, Strauss has left behind students who are not ashamed to call themselves disciples. There are "Straussians." But more than this, this group has the trappings of a cult. Above all, there is a secret teaching and the extreme seriousness of those who are "initiates." Members of the inner circle cherish their transcripts of Strauss's lectures. Burnyeat is not alone in taking offense at such exclusiveness. However his review is more than a Socratic response to the unselfcritical confidence of those who think they know or, in the case of less distinguished epigone, those who think they know someone who knows.[1] Lest one precipitously judge a teacher by the excesses of his students, as was done in the case of Socrates, serious criticism must examine the work itself.

However, in this case this is inappropriate according to Burnyeat, since the reason that Strauss became "one of the most influential thinkers in the United States" is not his extensive *writings* (which

1. Surprisingly, however, for one who later accuses Strauss of blatant disregard of arguments, Burnyeat does not consider Strauss's arguments in defense of such circles of friends. It would be preferable, Strauss says in *On Tyranny* (Glencoe, IL: Free Press, 1963) if men did not fall into "schools of thought" but, maintaining their philosophical independence, remained open.

are "remote and rebarbative") but his *teaching*. This is not faint praise. For it is not the content of what Strauss said that accounts for this influence but the extralogical, captivating manner of his presentation alone. He was successful because he knew how to "establish an aura of reverence" difficult for young students to resist. Burnyeat here repeats the philosopher's accusation against the sophist. Strauss's success is a lie. Rather than imparting the wisdom of the ancients as he thought, Strauss only corrupted his young followers, requiring as the price of initiation that they surrender their intellectual integrity to perverse interpretations. Burnyeat therefore seeks to expose the impostor, this Sphinx without a secret.

That Burnyeat's indictment is motivated more by animus than by a clear sense of the philosophical differences between two points of view is apparent at the outset in his criticism of Strauss's central principle of interpretation. One ought not to criticize an author, Strauss urges his readers again and again, before one has sought to understand the author as he originally intended himself to be understood. This hermeneutic principle, clearly an ideal, is the indispensable precondition of understanding anyone and, we would think, undeniable. Above all, it keeps before the reader the problem of the superimposition of one's own prejudgments, leaving the reader open thereby to discoveries absent from existing interpretations. (Is this not Socrates' procedure in the *Theaetetus* where he first seeks to give Protagoras a fair hearing, seeking the utmost presuppositions and furthest consequences of his views?) Rather than requiring the suspension of one's critical intelligence as Burnyeat charges, this principle prepares its right employment and guards against its misuse. While one might justifiably be concerned with the possible mystification of the text that comes from excessive reverence, and while one might legitimately wonder whether it is ever possible to understand anyone as he understands himself, one must not be so carried away by the possibilities of obfuscation or the problems of intersubjectivity that one fails to see the prudent, moderating value of this hermeneutic caution.

Burnyeat's alternative is less worthy. He would have it that the "dialectical interaction of the student and the author" by itself leads to the truth. This seems to mean that criticism does not need to be preceded, as Strauss recommends, by careful, nonjudgmental (even sympathetic) discovery. Yet can we responsibly criticize what we have not taken the pains to understand? While one can be skeptical that a commentator has discovered "the truth,"[2] this does not mean that there is no original point of view there to be disclosed (unless, that is, one adopts a radically relativistic position [as in deconstructionism], in which case there is no revealing discussion possible, no "review" worth attending to).

Strauss's counterreply to Burnyeat is similar to Socrates' to the physiologists in the *Phaedo*: he is operating under a false sense of objectivity. What Burnyeat calls direct "criticism of arguments" is nothing more than detextualized, artificially constructed, fabrications of a predetermined intelligence, one that fails to see past its own biases and only leads to the dogmatic reinforcement of established scholarly opinions (committing the fallacies of editing, hasty generalization etc.). Nothing could be less philosophical or more cultish.

The issue, Burnyeat rightly sees, is "to whom is surrender [to be] made, the text or the teacher?" While his concern for intellectual transference or displacement is legitimate, he would have it that we surrender to neither, thus maintaining the independence of our "self." But while it is true that another human being cannot learn for us, it is also true that all we think is not knowledge. Is it not Socrates' principal critique that without the suspension of one's "self" and its cluster of preconceptions we cannot but fall victim to presumptuousness and conceit of wisdom? Dogmatic independence is not the same as intellectual integrity.

To make matters worse, Burnyeat then attributes the want of discrimination on the part of the lost and wayward students to the "psychology of conservatism." Again he refuses to grant that anyone could be attracted to Strauss for any good reason. No, in an age such as ours, so filled with uncertainties, the young need doxic security blankets and thus are attracted to authority. Not only does this tacitly admit that existing interpretations fail to provide a secure base for inquiry—in the words of the *Phaedo*, a raft to ride out the storms and vicissitudes of intellectual life—but it reveals the bankruptcy of a psychology based on caricature.[3] Just as it is true, as Burnyeat

---

2. Here too Burnyeat misreads Strauss. Too quick to judge, indeed to condemn, he is offended by Strauss's insistence that one must be open to the possibility that the author one reads speaks the truth. This applies not only to Plato, but to *all* authors, including Machiavelli, Descartes, Nietzsche, etc. This would require of Strauss that he take the time to first understand Burnyeat.

3. Burnyeat has adopted a partisan *political psychology* wherein the spectrum

rightly points out, that Strauss, continuing the Husserlian project, seeks to reclaim a presubjective mode of thought that does not explain away all significance by relegating it to its historical context (historicism), it is also true that he looked with equal suspicion upon arguments that would attempt to explain the attractiveness of an idea in terms of its psychological function only (psychologism). Like the ancient authors he explicates, Strauss seeks unconditioned truth. In this respect, Strauss is more faithful to the teaching of Plato than Burnyeat (*Phaedo, Phaedrus*).

II

Strauss was not a philosopher in the modern Anglo-American tradition. In a felicitous flight of imagination, Burnyeat compares Strauss's writings to a dialogue. The principal interlocutors are "the gentleman" and "the philosopher," figures that come out of the writings of Plato and, of course, Aristotle. Like Socrates in the *Republic* who speaks with the young gentlemen Glaucon and Adeimantus, Strauss seeks to have an influence on his readers. The writings of Strauss are thus rightly understood as conversations with political intent. Burnyeat objects to this ulterior intention.

Strauss's political program can be stated simply: he seeks to renew our appreciation for ancient aristocratic virtues in the face of "the tide of mediocrity" that is the consequence of our democratization of all things. Like Tocqueville and some of the Founding Fathers, he seeks to found a city within a city, an aristocracy within our democracy.[4] In thus educating his readers, Strauss seeks to be an "advisor to princes" in their choice of lives and political actions. Above all, this restoration of the ancient virtues means for Strauss that he must teach *sôphrosynê*. In political matters this means teaching "the limits of politics" or the difficulties in achieving a homogeneously just society. He thus teaches prudence and the moderation of political ambition.

Strauss is not alone in contending that much harm has been done

---

of soul-forms is reduced to two, fascists and liberals. This does not conform to the psychomorphology of any of Plato's writings.

4. Burnyeat is correct to point out that Strauss does not reject modern democracy but finds many aristocratic elements and possibilities therein. Modern representative democracies above all have sought through constitutional safeguards to moderate the extreme tendencies of ancient participatory democracies.

in the twentieth century in the name of political and philosophical idealism. Indeed the road to the modern world is lined with ideological tyrannies, left and right. He observed first hand what happens when philosophers enter politics. His teacher, Heidegger, embraced National Socialism. Philosophers, moreover, like other idealists, too often lack *phronêsis* and thus cannot deal with the practical impediments to their ideal with which the real world is replete. Is it not worth wondering why regimes founded on ideals so often have had recourse to repression to enforce their "idealism" and why ideologues so readily condone terrorism? Justice in theory is simpler than justice in practice. A moderation of unrealistic expectations thus does not seem unwise. Although Burnyeat may think otherwise, in politics second best is not bad. Burnyeat is offended by such aristocratic reserve and prudent politics. Would he have it that measured action not be preferred to committed engagement, that indiscriminate idealism go unchecked?

As such, it is to Strauss's unmodern notion of the role of the philosopher, one shared with Nietzsche, that the core of Burnyeat's critique is directed. Strauss's notion of the philosopher is, in his view, essentially a construction, indeed a most perverse one. The philosopher is one who "brings back reports from regions most of us are not privileged to enter." This is interpreted by Burnyeat to mean that the philosopher, after listening to "the conversations of the great philosophers," simply retells what he heard. They do not themselves, however, "engage in the active discussion of the central questions." Exposition of texts, not the analysis of arguments, becomes the medium of discussion. From Burnyeat's point of view this means that Straussians are not philosophers but false prophets. Under the guise of others' words they secretly insinuate their own unsubstantiated views. Burnyeat is sure that this is not what Socrates meant in the *Phaedo* by the "flight to the *logoi*."

This criticism of exegesis is surely excessive. Unless he thinks that his own article in the *New York Review of Books* is mere parody (and an opportunity to insinuate his own prejudices), Burnyeat likely sees it as a means of reviewing and critically assessing the opinions of Strauss, one that has philosophic legitimacy. Similarly, Strauss views his own writings not as secondary sources, but as mediated attempts to get at the truth in and through the opinions of others. As such the efforts of philosophical commentators are not derivative but alternative interpretations of the "flight to the *logoi*."

Burnyeat's criticism is thus really this: Strauss is not a contemporary analytic philosopher. His preoccupation with other concerns than argument form is proof of this indictment. Two examples are given. In one case, Strauss passes by the 26-step proof of the existence of God by Maimonides without looking at the details of the argument. Still more incredible is the second case. Strauss dismisses "the metaphysical doctrine, the Theory of Forms" as itself "utterly incredible." For Burnyeat and much of modern scholarship, the Theory of Forms is *the* foundational premise of their analyses, the basis of "any adequate interpretation of the *Republic*." Burnyeat's incredulousness prevents him, however, from seeing or remembering the reservations that Plato himself expressed concerning this "much babbled about theory" (as it is called in the *Phaedo*) or the very few dialogues in which it actually appears.

Risking further incredulity, allow me to suggest an alternative reading. In the *Republic*, it is rather the political premises of the conversation that lead to such epistemological and metaphysical views and alone make the defense of justice possible that Glaucon and Adeimantus desire. In the *Phaedo*, the original intention to establish a viable notion of immortality—even an ambiguous philosophical immortality—requires the chorismos (or separation) thesis and the "simple and artless" Theory of Forms. It is the requisite metaphysical raft that Simmias requested from which his greatest hopes will not fall victim to despair. Burnyeat cannot see how someone might hold that epistemology is not original nor absolutely prior. He is a modern for whom philosophy begins with a critique of reason and so must all those whom he reads. As a result he does not see that this is one interpretation of the Good being superordinate to the Forms or "beyond Being."

In Burnyeat's view, *nothing* in Strauss's work evidences any knowledge of what philosophy truly is, namely the analysis of arguments. Burnyeat countenances no other possibility than his own. What he does not realize is that his confidence that his is "the true philosophy" is no less outstanding than the Straussians' convictions about truths they are privy to.

Here we come to the question at the heart of the dispute, one that Burnyeat, in his rush to condemn, fails to raise: What is philosophy? Or in this context, how is *logos* to be understood? *Logos* in Greek is by no means coextensive with logical argument, for which there is no word. Is it to be understood after the model of contemporary analytic philosophy? Is Plato to be understood as some form of logical or linguistic analyst? Was the true Plato, then, not discoverable until the twentieth century? Yet Plato himself says that a *logos* has to be evaluated in more than logical terms. There should be a *threefold* criterion of evaluation: experience, prudence and argument. Hence to the above questions, Strauss answers *no*. Plato is rather a political philosopher of an ancient sort, the reclamation of whose opinions requires broader, more far reaching tools of interpretation than modern modes of analysis allow. Strauss therefore speaks of "logographic necessity" not only logical necessity, of "dramatic structure" not only logical structure.

Unlike Burnyeat, Strauss adopts Plato's teaching about *doxa* and *nomos*. We are prisoners in the cave of our unexamined, "given" opinions and customs. These screen and selectively focus our attention. Hence what we first see are but shadows of our own making. Therefore we cannot immediately and simply "criticize." To discover the truth, we must break out of our bondage to appearance and accepted opinions. Burnyeat finds it incredible that Strauss, not to mention Plato, could hold that this applies to the philosophic study of texts, that here too appearances can be misleading and that the discovery of the intended truth is the result of extensive reflection on what is not simply obvious.[5]

Indeed Strauss holds that reading ancient texts is now made doubly difficult because the opinions that we do hold are alien to those to be discovered. In general the modern philosophy with which Burnyeat is familiar is no sufficient key to ancient thought, although certain authors such as Rousseau, Nietzsche and Husserl can be a help, Strauss holds, if used with discrimination. Strauss thus revives the old distinction between the "ancients" and the "moderns" (see Swift's *Battle of the Books*). This distinction is not, however, an essentially historical one, but a transhistorical or regulative one (see Plato's *Sophist* for "moderns" among the "ancients").

Burnyeat is offended by it. He thinks that it degrades the modern, and therefore his own, world. He thereby misses the essentially Platonic criticism: *all* "todays" are degenerate, because *doxa* and *nomos* are not *alêtheia*. This was surely true of Plato's own "modern" world, as his criticism of the decadent Athens of Pericles makes plain. If indeed Burnyeat thinks otherwise and wants to embrace and defend today's world, then he must first establish its truthfulness and subject *Plato's criticisms* to honest analysis along with those philosophers

---

5. As such the indirect or depth construction promotes those very philosophical faculties necessary for all types of discovery.

from the Pre-Socratics to the modern day for whom philosophy begins in a critique of customary opinions. Rather than returning to the texts and probing the ancient authors anew, Burnyeat resorts to parody. The truth of Plato's cave image is thereby demonstrated in deed.

III

Strauss's view of the history of philosophy is contrived, the result of the forced imposition of a medieval doctrine on the principal texts of the tradition.

We know we are in for a treat when we read "It was Maimonides who started it." For Burnyeat, Strauss's reading of the history of philosophy exemplifies one gross violation of his own principle of interpretation, that of projecting or superimposing alien and secret views on authors whose views are plain enough as originally expressed. In *The Guide for the Perplexed* Maimonides instructs his readers "how to gather his meaning" from a work that is not immediately understandable, and deliberately so. Burnyeat begrudgingly grants that, in this case, esotericism many indeed be present. While it may be that Maimonides or Farabi had, for reasons of religious persecution, to adopt a mode of speech that is not simply open, this surely does not mean, in Burnyeat's view, that esotericism is true of most of the authors of the early tradition. Above all, in order to understand Plato, he is confident that we do not have "to read between the lines."

Burnyeat goes to some length to explain this preoccupation with esotericism in the light of Strauss's intellectual biography. Strauss's early work in Maimonides, and later Spinoza, allowed him to resolve the eternal conflict between reason and faith within himself. For Strauss, however, its validity was more than personal (biographism, after all, is a species of psychologism). Philosophy in its most fundamental form must always remain open to all things and thus cannot base its understanding on the unexamined principles of faith (*pistis*). Philosophy, to remain true to itself, in short, cannot ever be its handmaiden.[6] Yet doctrines of faith do represent possible interpretations of our experience and, for those who are

6. This has to be qualified in two respects. Plato was surely not averse to using the best in contemporary religion to bolster the authority of the city. In addition, Strauss's "defense" of religion is made despite its prejudices and history of persecution. Religious oppression, he seems to think, is easier to moderate than political oppression.

not philosophers, provide important political and moral foundations. Philosophy would thus be unjust to subject these beliefs ("values") to the analytical knife. Philosophy has therefore to respect the non-philosophical basis of political life by keeping silent, or at least being less than explicit about its teachings. Esotericism, thus understood, is an act of justice, if not piety.

One is surely justified in being mystified by any position that says that the truth is different than what it appears and therefore by all depth hermeneutic interpretations. But this does not of itself require that they be rejected as false. To an age such as ours in which free rational choice is thought to be the basis of political life and "values," Strauss's respectful insistence on the political and human importance of belief for nonphilosophers may seem disingenuous, indeed patronizing, and surely represents a double standard incompatible with universal, democratic principles. But does freedom of speech require absolute candidness?

People in pluralistic, democratic societies tend to think that the ancient conflicts between religion and philosophy, indeed between politics and philosophy, have been resolved. Strauss is not so sanguine. It was the same nation that gave birth to Bach and Goethe and to National Socialism. There the Enlightenment failed us. What is remarkable about Burnyeat's analysis is that, in restricting the phenomenon of esotericism to the Middle Ages and therewith to religious persecution narrowly conceived, he overlooks both the broader phenomenon[7] and specifically the fate of Socrates. Is it a projection of the peculiar medieval tension to think that Plato, reflecting on the Athenian accusation against Socrates, would take such a conflict seriously? The charges against Socrates, we have to remember, were first leveled against Anaxagoras before him and Aristotle following him. Strauss thus sees the Platonic corpus as an extended defense and guarded public representation of Socrates and philosophy (a Socrates made "young and beautiful"). In short it does not "start with Maimonides." Burnyeat simply refuses to consider as authentic the talk in the ancient world of other modes of teaching than simple straightforwardness.[8]

---

7. Esotericism need not be motivated by narrowly political considerations, see Thomas Aquinas, *Summa Theologica*, Q. 1 A.8.

8. He casts doubts on the *Seventh Letter* of Plato, does not make reference to those philosophers who have taken this seriously (namely Augustine, Farabi, Leibnitz and Shaftesbury etc.), nor does he acknowledge the works of non-Straussians Gaiser, Findley and Klein on the subject.

Plato's analysis of politics, in Strauss's view, confirms this. It is not some postwar inflammation of popular scapegoating that victimizes an innocent Socrates. Strauss understands the fate of Socrates to be the result of a conflict of two ever valid yet irreconcilable principles and hence to be a tragedy repeatedly played out on the world stage. The conditions are present always, though the outcome is not always necessary. The *polis* is the arena of this conflict, between *pistis* and *doxa* on the one hand and *philosophia* and *alêtheia* on the other. There is no political solution, no universal education or enlightenment, that can realistically put an end to it (though moderate it, perhaps). And until that comes about, philosophers must be circumspect. For this reason Plato, and thoughtful authors throughout our intellectual history, have taken precautions and written accordingly. Plato, in this view, has adopted a socially responsible mode of discourse, one that avoids the politically destabilizing consequences of philosophy.[9] Such a guarded speech is thus not undertaken simply out of self-interest. Burnyeat is correct, though, in concluding that Strauss follows what he takes to be Plato's example.

Ancient writings usually thought to be outside the domain of philosophy are understood by Strauss as sharing this understanding of political things. Indeed Aristophanes and Xenophon and Thucydides are now thought to be doubly worth reading, not only as comic writers and historians, but as themselves sources of insight into philosophical matters. Burnyeat objects strenuously to this general characterization of the "wisdom of the ancients" and objects above all to the corollary that the classics are unanimously anti-equalitarian or aristocratic. Burnyeat thus counters the sweeping contention that such a mode of discourse and disclosure obtains in many other authors with an equally sweeping counterclaim that it obtains in none.

So unreasonable is this characterization in his mind that he does not deign to dignify it with rational argument. By way of rejoinder he resorts to parody. Imitating what he believes to have discovered about the secret methods of Strauss, in particular his habit of looking at the overall design of a work to discern its broad intentions, Burnyeat gives a "Straussian analysis" of *Studies in Platonic Political Philos-*

---

9. There are philosophical reasons as well, ones which a careful rereading of the *Meno* and attention to Socrates' treatment of the slave-boy exhibit (see Klein's commentary thereon, *A Commentary on Plato's "Meno"* [Chapel Hill: University of North Carolina Press, 1965]).

ophy. This method, in Burnyeat's view, is bogus. Accordingly his parody does not even "indicate without fully revealing," it simply reveals nothing. It is Strauss's turn to be "dismembered with scorn and derision."

Whereas Burnyeat might not find it difficult swallowing Whitehead's famous remark that the history of philosophy is but a series of footnotes to Plato, Burnyeat has special difficulty giving any credibility to the implicit thesis of this book that "the history of political thought is the history of Platonic political philosophy." All of Strauss's work is simply "a tale of sound and fury and extraordinary inaccuracies" (presumably told by an idiot). Yet, inasmuch as it is generally held by philosophers that Plato, after some fashion, is the beginning of our tradition, setting out its problems and horizons, is it so incredible that Machiavelli and Descartes are seen as turning points, especially since they expressly reject the classical beginnings? And is it incredible that one might want to wonder about the objectivity of a science that from its inception and in its conception sought practical ends ("the obfuscation of the Enlightenment"), in Descartes' words, sought to make us "masters and possessors of nature"? There is nothing especially conservative about this issue. Further, it is surely faithful to Plato, and in itself not philosophically illegitimate, to seek out the sources of modern-day relativism.

Burnyeat's rejectionist attitude simply blinds him. Above all he refuses to consider Strauss's most serious challenge, the contention that our conceptual frameworks and methodological principles predetermine our results and predispose us to accept only certain conclusions as valid. This Strauss learned by studying the higher criticism of Spinoza, but it is nowhere more evident than in this article by Burnyeat. His position is no less polarized and exclusive than the caricature of Strauss he presents.

IV

Strauss's revisionism has the consequence that Plato is wrongfully interpreted as a conservative.

It is the interpretation of Plato that for Burnyeat is the linchpin of Strauss's entire scholarly "edifice." If this can be shown to be mistaken, Burnyeat believes, then the whole will come tumbling down. Above all "if Plato is the radical utopian that ordinary scholarship [and Burnyeat] believes him to be," then (a) the unanimity of ancient wisdom can no longer be maintained, then (b) there is no univocal teaching of "the philosopher" to be imposed on unsuspecting "gentlemen," and (c) the history of the West ceases to be a giantomachy, a battle between the ancients and the moderns. Burnyeat is convinced that Strauss's view is a tendentious distortion, his interpretation of Plato in particular "wrong from beginning to end." With the monstrous view of Plato gone, philosophy can resume its rightful function of debating "the nature and practicability of a just society." Such a "clash of reasoned views" is surely more "relevant" (only?) than the surreptitious insinuation of "anti-utopian teachings." With this Burnyeat's project of slaying the inscrutable Strauss comes to a head: he gets down to texts and arguments.

The battlefield he chooses is the *Republic*; the clash, the sense in which justice is to be understood as essential for happiness, individual or collective. This cannot be taken for granted in either sense, for injustice and tyranny are serious temptations as the eloquent defense of injustice by Glaucon and Adeimantus makes evident: secretly we all aspire to emulate the ancestor of Gyges. Burnyeat, though, is convinced of the infinite power of persuasion, is convinced, moreover, that the radical transformation necessary for justice — described by Plato as proportionate to the difference between Hades and the gods — is possible by means of words alone and without revolutionary violence. Idealistic youth, properly educated and inspired, can make over the city into what it is not now. Justice on earth is thus not only desirable but practicable. The city with no place (Utopia) will find its place. The political question therefore is whether such drastic change is possible in deed and whether logic, or even rhetoric, can ever replace force (the opening dramatic question of book 1). The philosophic question is whether human nature, especially as understood in the *Republic*, can ever admit of such a transformation even within its ruling class, a change that is at the very least against custom.

The refutation of Strauss focuses on a central passage of the *Republic*, the question of the rule of the philosopher-king. The issue is whether the philosophical guardians would want to take on this awesome task. Socrates has just described the preoccupation of the guardians with the things of the other world, the Forms. This makes them ideal candidates for rulers, since they have neither family nor worldly ambitions, neither money nor honor nor power. The problem is that, with their lives thus fully realized, they would not themselves therefore choose to rule. Why should they accept a lesser life, or as Glaucon puts it, an injustice done to them for the sake of the whole?

Burnyeat has no doubt about the possibility of persuading them to sacrifice their own good for the common good; they are "idealists." They look forward to "the coming of utopia" as much as they look up to the Forms. However, it is at this point in the text that Socrates shocks us. He says quite bluntly that the first guardians do *not* owe anything to their pre-utopian city, since it was in fact not responsible for their rearing and possibly, as in the case of Socrates himself, conspired to subvert their theoretical interests. For this reason, Socrates says on several occasions that the first guardians will have to be "persuaded and compelled." Burnyeat is sure that this means the compulsion of convincing speeches simply. There is no reason to doubt, in his view, the success of the founding.

Strauss, however, is not so sanguine. He interprets this ambiguous passage differently. His reasons are several, but above all the claim that the work as a whole is one extended disclosure of the extraordinary difficulties that must first be overcome in order that the right conditions for a city "as just as possible" to come about. Nothing short of a *total transformation* of imbedded custom must be undertaken. To secure this inversion of the traditional hierarchies, the political, social and educational system must be subjected to a radical reformation. For justice to be possible the founders have to "wipe clean the dispositions of men," that is, justice is possible only if the city and its citizens are *not* what they *are*: the weakest is supposed to rule the strongest, the irrational is supposed to submit to the rule of the rational. Therefore there are reasons for reservations about its possibility. Two stand out: justice rests on the fragile pillars of moral and civic education. (It is surprising that anyone today would not see any inherent difficulties here.) In addition, it requires the reversal of what one might call Plato's principle of political entropy, that the political order seeks the lowest level, power at the expense of principle. It is this latter that the *Republic* allows us to see. For this reason, Strauss, following Cicero, understands the dialogue to be not a utopian teaching, but a critique of the conditions of political reality. At best, justice is the rarest of exceptions.

This is not to say that it is not possible to improve one's own life and perhaps that of a few others. Whereas Burnyeat takes the education of Glaucon and Adeimantus as proof that *man* as such can improve and thus the ideal is not unreal, Strauss, by contrast, sees the education of these two gentlemen ("sons of the Best"), and even the education of Thrasymachus (whose persuasion is not logical but based on bad arguments) as evidence that only *exceptional men* can be molded and improved by the consideration of eternal truths. Despite Burnyeat's one-sided confidence of the contrary, there is at least a question whether Plato is an idealist or a realist.

Strauss's conclusion is that, though it is not theoretically impossible, justice on a political scale is practically very unlikely. The difference is not unimportant. Plato leaves a window of optimism open so as not to cause us to become corrupted by disillusionment and cynicism. The political function of the Theory of Forms is thus twofold: it introduces us to a higher standard, thereby providing us with a measure to gauge real world deficiencies. Moreover, in allowing us to see the contrast between the real and the ideal, our desire for the unconditioned is moderated at the same time as we realize that we do not have to take the popular standard as the standard of measure for ourselves.

By contrast, Burnyeat proposes his idealism as unquestioningly superior to Strauss's views. His rests on an uncritical acceptance that Plato means what he says. In the case of the *Republic*, however, this requires the endorsement of an explicitly authoritarian regime (IX 590 c–d). There, there is no universal franchise; no freedoms of speech, assembly, religion, or press; there is a radical restriction of choice, and a denial of personal and family autonomy; and its founding requires the forced expulsion of a majority of the population; moreover, its social engineering goes to the extreme of prescribing human breeding.[10] Justice of the whole, in short, requires that injustice be done, not simply to the few but to the many. Yet it is only to the "foreign policy" of the regime that Burnyeat objects.

Such measures taken literally are authoritarian, and should the rulers not be wise, indistinguishable from fascism. Should one become then, as Burnyeat recommends, "fired with ambition to help achieve justice on earth," if *this* is what justice really is? This is the same misguided thinking that leads some people to hold that Marx's teaching is the full development of the communalism of the guardian class. Indeed do we not see *ad oculus* confirmation of Strauss's earlier contention that idealism, when uncritical and naive, is dangerous? This is the reason why the *Republic* ends with an extended reflection

10. And are not the conclusions of the *Phaedo* similarly odious to a our equalitarian sensibility: philosophers alone are virtuous and alone achieve immortality?

on tyranny (books 8–9, confirmed in the myth of Er). By contrast, Strauss's conclusion allows us to say that the human price of such measures might be too high.

V

The teaching of Strauss has dangerous political consequences.

The dispute between Strauss and Burnyeat is, in the end, not a scholarly dispute. It is political, and thus we have the reason why scholarly means were not used to resolve it. A liberal is offended by the conservative conclusions that Strauss has managed to draw from Plato and the ancient tradition. Above all, as Burnyeat well understands, opinions do not only affect other opinions but determine actions as well. Here too Burnyeat wants the truth to be known: all of Strauss's talk of moderation is a facade. Beneath it lies a most intemperate teaching, Strauss's "ruthless anti-idealism" leading to a dangerously aggressive foreign policy.

This comes to view in the interpretation by Strauss of Polemarchus' definition of justice "to help one's friends and harm one's enemies." Strauss holds that it is not entirely refuted, indeed remains operative throughout the *Republic*. Polemarchus' opinion requires that one be generous with one's own friends but harsh with those who would seek to harm us. Burnyeat is convinced that this double standard of justice is adequately disposed of in book 1. We are not provided with Burnyeat's interpretation of the refutation of Polemarchus, only his incredulousness.[11] Burnyeat does not consider what to do with those who would *truly* harm us and thus his objections leave the city vulnerable (hence Thrasymachus' uneasiness).

Burnyeat would have to grant, though, that the apparent refutation does have the effect Strauss sees in the *Republic* as a whole: that of moderating the War Lord's (Polemarchus') convictions about getting back at those who do him harm, especially as he is not sufficiently thoughtful about the possibility of misidentifying those who truly harm and help him.[12] Plato could not allow such an indiscriminate partisanship (or reckless patriotism) to go unchecked. What Burnyeat does not see is that the refutation is not total and thus leaves

11. Burnyeat is right to wonder how Strauss's interpretation of the *Gorgias* (and the principle that one should never return wrong for wrong) would have turned out. We must go back to the text.

12. What of Strauss's observation that this is in fact the form that the education of the guardians takes? They are to be *double-natured*, like a noble puppy who is fierce to those he does not recognize yet friendly to those he knows. And, though

room for a proportionate defensiveness. Without his interpretation of books 1–4, and above all his response to Thrasymachus' contention that Socrates' refutation of Polemarchus is politically naive, if not deliberately so, we are left without a clear sense why a strong foreign policy is not part of the final understanding of justice in the *Republic* and why it should be considered so misguided a policy for today.[13] It simply remains an unargued presumption.

VI

What is most needed, clearly, is a considered and measured "review" of the work of Leo Strauss. His points of departure, his methodology, his conclusions are too different for us simply to juxtapose them to existing scholarship and, finding them wanting, to reject them *in toto* as wrong-headed. This, however, is what Burnyeat has done. He has "made his argument" and condemned Strauss. Surely without an effort of unpredisposed discovery, what is there that might contribute to our understanding of the ancient and modern traditions will not be admitted into the circle of respectable opinions. Thus what is most needed is not what we are given.

By contrast, in the name of greater logical faithfulness and analytical precision, this defender of academic authenticity has given us such well-known argument forms as the tit-for-tat, mockery, caricature, and guilt by association. Rather than reexamining the texts brought forth by Strauss in support of his alternative point of view, we are given the all-too-widely esteemed model of scholarship, the parody. With an illiberal sweep of the pen, proportionate discussion is replaced by "scorn and derision" (acceptable in this case but

---

they will plead developing country status to neighboring superpowers, they are, we must remember, to be as fierce as their size and trained abilities will allow. Lest they fall victim to those who would seek their harm or extinction, the guardians have to be strong if the new republic is to be more than a passing curiosity. Moreover, that the auxiliaries will be under the direction of the guardians does not make them any less needed. And that the ruling guardians come out of the ranks of the auxiliaries does not make them any less fierce.

13. It is not at all clear what Burnyeat is insinuating by citing the membership of one of Strauss's student's students on the National Security Council. Does he think, perhaps, we live in an age when we have no need of such councils and habits or that Strauss's philosophy leads to fanaticism, or patriotism, or that philosophy should not amount to more than an idle hobby? Our hopes notwithstanding, man has not changed. Moreover, that members of the Thatcher government read Strauss but philosophers in Britain do not, says as much about the present state of philosophy as it does of the relevance of Strauss.

not others). Above all, what we do not have is that much touted, but little practiced, "clash of reasoned opinions."

No, on Plato, and likely all else, we are told by Burnyeat that Strauss is simply wrong "from beginning to end." Strauss is given no credit whatsoever for reraising to the forefront of academic concern problems that occupy a lesser interest in the purview of contemporary philosophy. The "sound and fury" about the need for a renewed concern with civic and moral education, the search for a mode of thought not trivialized by historicism and psychologism, for a thoughtful evaluation of deeds as well as speeches, for increased attention to the political, rhetorical, and psychological dimensions of *logos*, these are but the perverted tale of a pathological imagination. Must one not wonder however about that state of a discipline that, while professing impartial, rational analysis, yet violates its own professions and canons? Thus, in spite of himself, Burnyeat has corroborated Plato's and Strauss's "dramatic interpretation" of human intentions: deeds are sometimes more revealing than speeches.

It is true, though, that Strauss, in his effort to articulate his own views, did little in general to build bridges that would make it possible for us to assess the comparative worth of his views and those of others. Rarely do we find a review of the literature or extended critical footnotes opposing his position with that of the reigning interpretation (there are, however, numerous separate reviews by Strauss of individual books). While this makes the reading of his works more difficult, it is not, however, damnable in itself. Indeed here is where Burnyeat fails us most of all. Rather than raising himself out of the cave of his own presuppositions and embedded outlook and articulating the fundamental principles that would make it possible for us to judge their respective positions, he dismisses Strauss's contentions at every turn. Indeed it is precisely the indiscriminate generality of his sweeping dismissal that proves obstructive in the end and prevents us from learning those things, perhaps many things, that do need correction or reconsideration in the work of Strauss. That there is nothing whatsoever redeemable here and, hence, no possibility of rapprochement (no complementarity theory) is most telling of all. Burnyeat thereby demonstrates for all to see the wrongheadedness of his objections to Strauss's advice to consider the possible truthfulness of all positions for purposes of discovery. Burnyeat's article is no model of impartial scholarship.[14]

14. It is hence revealing that Burnyeat's article was accompanied by a political caricature of the aging and ailing Strauss by my namesake.

Even more, Burnyeat has shown that philosophy is too often like the club or cult that he himself professes to detest. The guardians, he says, should be impartially motivated "for justice's sake," yet he is incited to parody by those who might suggest an opinion different from his own. His own conspicuous incapacity to treat Strauss's work judiciously disproves his contention and substantiates Strauss's measured view. Have we not here an instance of what he thinks has been and should be refuted, an instance that is of praising our friends and subjecting to public ridicule (harm) those whose work challenges our own opinions? Burnyeat, in short, has himself not attained to a higher level of judiciousness than Polemarchus. He has demonstrated how difficult it is to dispose of such a definition and how difficult justice is in individual cases. A refutation in speech does not eliminate the problem in deed. This however we need not have learned from Burnyeat.

Thus, after consideration of Burnyeat's article, the state of affairs is the same as it was before. The two separate worlds of discourse remain separate. A thoughtful and dispassionate evaluation of Strauss's challenging work remains to be undertaken.

It is appropriate that we end with a reference to the myth that gives Burnyeat's article its title. For those who would dismiss out of hand all opinions different from those held by one's own circle of friends, there are no riddles.[15] Indeed for Burnyeat there is, in the end, no riddle of the Sphinx and thus never any human truths worth shielding from the glare of public exposure. For the ancients, however, the riddle is man. Strauss has therefore not closed his mind to those dimensions that, though absent from the forefront of the contemporary discussion, might yet reveal man's innermost complexity. In this context we must remember too that the Sphinx was not slain by parody but by judicious words and that Oedipus was most wise when he thought he knew nothing, most fatefully ignorant, when he thought he knew.

Finally, perhaps it is true after all, as Descartes promised, that in the new age of enlightenment there will be no more riddles. Nothing more remains to be wondered at, then, than our own diminished capacity for wonder. But if philosophy loses its capacity for wonder, is it any longer philosophy?

15. This substantiates Strauss's contention that there can be no genuinely philosophical understanding of politics that excludes a political understanding of philosophy.

Strauss Read from France

David R. Lachterman

Leo Strauss has long had a "scholarly" presence among French orientalists and medievalists, thanks to his fundamentally important works on the *falāsifa* and Maimonides, two of which were published in France in the 1930's. To French political "thinkers," caught as they were for so long, like Laocoön, in the serpentine toils of Stalinism, Maoism and other variants of "Marxism," including its decadently ironic postmodern negations, Strauss seems to have been a largely unknown name. Some interpreters of the history of modern political philosophy have, of course, taken note of his analyses of Machiavelli, for example, and the French translation of *Natural Right and History* was in fact first published in 1954. In the main, however, it is only within the last dozen years that Strauss's work has come to the attention of a wider audience, through translations, expository articles and, very recently indeed, attempts at systematic criticism.[1] While the reception of Strauss has thus been delayed, it has also not been beclouded by the phenomenon of "Straussianism" and the accompanying rancor of internal debate among disciples and external fusillades against political "cultism" and elitism. The involutions of Sibylline style, to say nothing of the distinction between the many and the few, seem dearer to the French, than to the American, intellectual heart, the Enlightenment notwithstanding. (His essay "Persecution and the Art of Writing" and "On a Forgotten Kind of Writing" were published in French in *Poétique*, an avant-garde review of literary theory that has also published Derrida, Lacoue-Labarthe and Nancy, among other "postmodernists.")

The venerable *Revue de métaphysique et de morale* published in 1989 what I believe is the first issue of a French philosophical journal

---

1. In addition to *Natural Right and History* and *On Tyranny* (1954) the following works by Strauss have been published in French translation: *Pensées sur Machiavel* (1982); *La Cité et l'homme* (1987); *Maïmonide* (1988); and *La Persécution et l'art d'écrire* (1989). The most complete synthesis of Strauss's works and their interpreters is provided by an American expatriate Terence Marshall, "Leo Strauss, la philosophie et la science politique," *Revue française de science politique* 35 (1985): 605–638 and 801–839. Luc Ferry, *Philosophie politique 1. Le Droit: la nouvelle querelle des Anciens et les Modernes* (Paris: Presses Universitaires de France, 1984) [English translation, *Political Philosophy*, vol. 1 (Chicago: University of Chicago Press, 1990), Part One], ties together the Heideggerian and the Straussian critiques of modernity.

completely devoted to assessments of Strauss, under the collective title "Leo Strauss, historien de la philosophie."* A translation of his 1967 essay, "Remarks on Maimonides' *Book of Knowledge*," is followed by essays by Rémi Brague, Pierre Manent, Michel-Pierre Edmond, Michel Malherbe and Richard Bodéüs. Before turning to a précis and to brief comments on each of these articles I want to venture some reflections on the problematic significance of the title under which they are commonly yoked. In the most obvious sense the title is justified by the fact that all five contributions treat of Strauss's exegeses of particular traditions or figures in the history of political philosophy. Moreover, the French have a long-standing fascination, only sporadically imitated by English-language scholars, with the philosophy of the historiography of philosophy, that is, with the overt or tacit theoretical commitments at work in historical interpretations of philosophers and philosophies. A statement by the late Martial Gueroult, well-known for his systematic analyses of Descartes, Spinoza and Fichte, brings rather clearly to light what this fascination might lead to:

> to seek out independently of every previous system the conditions that make a priori possible the validity of philosophies and their worth as objects of a possible history of philosophy, without postulating in advance the prevalence of a system of philosophy that would impose its formula on the solution being sought.[2]

One might say that the relation between philosophy and the history of philosophy is less "charged" among the French than it has been for quite a while among English-speaking professors of philosophy. At the same time, Gueroult's formulation might remind one of von Ranke's claim that "every nation is equally close to God." In other words the philosophy of the history of philosophy is a more modest version of Dilthey's relativistic historicism, from which, indeed, Gueroult takes his inspiration.

Leo Strauss, "historien de la philosophie," sits uneasily in such company. This is not the place to review in detail Strauss's "historiographic" practices or his occasional remarks on the method of what he is doing in such texts as *The Political Philosophy of Hobbes* or *The Argument and Action of Plato's Laws*. Perhaps the most concise state-

---

* *Revue de métaphysique et de morale* 94 (No. 3, 1989).
2. M. Gueroult, *Dianoématique.1: Histoire de l'histoire de la philosophie* (Paris, 1984), p. 14. One will note that "systems," for Guerouit, are curiously apolitical. Thus, Spinoza's *Ethics* can be read without reference to the *Theological-Political Treatise*.

ment of principle can be found in his lecture "How to Begin to Study Medieval Philosophy": "The task of the historian of thought is to understand the thinkers of the past exactly as they understood themselves, or to revitalize their thought according to their own interpretation of it."[3]

Two things are fairly evident from this passage and its context: First, the dismissal of the Kantian claim to be able to understand a past thinker better than he understood himself and, second, the insistence that fidelity to the thinkers of the past is, or may be, of a piece with the effort to "revitalize" their thought. Strauss's "historiography" is always *engagé*, as the French say, never an affair of neutral doxography. His engagement may also be said to consist in the effort to awaken, even to create, certain prejudices or to combat countervailing prejudices. As he writes in the first paragraph of *Philosophy and Law* (1935): "The purpose of the present work is to arouse a prejudice in favor of this conception of Maimonides [*viz.*, as the truly natural model of rationalism] or, rather, to excite a suspicion against the powerful prejudice to the contrary."[4] It is obviously not immediately apparent whether all the "prejudices" Strauss attempts to arouse are compatible with one another. At all events, Strauss's historical investigations should be taken in the primordial sense of *historia*, of examining things at first hand. Far from trying, in the now-fashionable sense, to "keep the conversation going," Strauss seems to aim at dropping "conversation-stoppers"; at halting abruptly what passes for conventional wisdom. To put this differently, the "fusion of horizons" can only take place, if it ever does, once each competing horizon has been accounted for in its own terms.

1. Michel-Pierre Edmond, "Machiavelli and the Question of Nature," (pp. 347–52) touches quite briefly, but helpfully, on some of the major themes of *Thoughts on Machiavelli*, which he has translated into French with a much fuller exposition. His axial theme is Machiavelli's transformation of a theoretical (contemplative) political science into a new, nontheoretical science of the practical "conditions of the exercise of power" (p. 348). This change of orienta-

---

3. See *The Rebirth of Classical Political Rationalism* (hereafter = *RCPR*), ed. Thomas Pangle (Chicago: University of Chicago Press, 1989), p. 209. Other works by Strauss are abbreviated according to the scheme adopted in *Studies in Platonic: Political Philosophy* (hereafter = *SPPP*), ed. T. Pangle (Chicago: University of Chicago Press, 1983), p. 27, unless otherwise indicated.

4. *Philosophy and Law* (hereafter = *PL*), trans. F. Baumann (Philadelphia: Jewish Publication Society, 1987), p. 3.

tion "brings about, sooner or later, the abandonment of any reference to a nature of the political and to a nature *tout court*" (*ibid.*). "Political things do not have any 'nature'" (*ibid.*). Edmond proceeds to qualify and to clarify this view with respect to Strauss's Machiavelli. "Nature hides itself behind chance, better, nature is the putting in place of a *Deus sive fortuna*," where chance is potentially to be thoroughly mastered by human action. Machiavelli's "normative teaching," as construed by Strauss, implies that Machiavelli does not "suppress a philosophy of nature. To say it differently, Machiavelli is not Kojève" (p. 350). However, "the new conception of nature or of being," according to which nature (or *fortuna*) is "the radical absence of order" (p. 351) opens "the way to relativisms of every sort" (p. 352).

Among the many questions evoked by Edmond's resumé, the following may be singled out. (1) Does "nature" in Machiavelli in fact reduce to chance, "the radical absence of order"? A close study of all of the occurrences of *natura* and *naturale* and their contexts would be desirable here. For the moment, one might simply draw attention to the opening paragraph of the prologue to *Discorsi*, Book 1, where Machiavelli begins by referring to "the envious nature of men" that makes the discovery of "new modes and orders" as dangerous as the discovery of "unknown waters and lands" and then challenges this envy by adverting to the way "that natural desire . . . was always in me," namely the desire "to do [*operare*], without any respect, those things that I believe will bring common benefit to each person." Machiavelli's art of teaching effectively the "new modes and orders" seems to presuppose the clash between these congenital natures or natural desires, envy and fearlessness. Is "nature" used here equivocally or in a merely popular sense?

(2) Furthermore, of the three notions occupying "the empty place of nature" (p. 349) it is "foundation" in which *one* premodern sense of the natural is most tantalizingly audible. If "nature" must have governing beginnings (*archai*), then the search for, or the establishment of, such beginnings may be said to be according to nature. Can Machiavelli's emphasis on the primacy of "*fondatori*" or "*edificatori delle cittadi*," (see *Discorsi* 1. 1 and 1. 9) be read as the fruit of meditation, not simply on the actual exercise of political power, but, more fundamentally, on the question of how the political things get started at all? The founder-legislator, after all, is a *principe*, not just a prince, but also a principle, an *arche*. Or, should one rather say that Machiavelli's critique of classical political philosophy is a reversion to the prephilosophical equation of the ancestral with the good? In

the light of that equation, the "natural" always turns out to have been instituted or "customized."

(3) Finally, Machiavelli's semisuppression of the philosophy of nature is indissolubly linked to his critique of religion. As Strauss puts it in his essay on Machiavelli, "the heavenly is the natural; the supra-natural is human." Moses counts along with Solon and Lycurgus among the "infinite examples" of "founders of kingdoms and republics" (*Discorsi* 1. 9). Edmond does not comment on the route Strauss himself once traced from the apparently unresolvable conflict between Athens and Jerusalem to the study of "a kind of thought which is philosophic indeed but no longer Greek: modern philosophy. It is in trying to understand modern philosophy that we come across Machiavelli."[5] Does Edmond's useful emphasis on the question whether "a political philosophy can or cannot do without a reference to a philosophy of nature" (p. 351) reawaken, perhaps unintentionally, a sense for that premodern conflict and for its bearing on the advent of modernity?

2. Michel Malherbe, the author of an important recent book on Hobbes, submits Strauss's interpretation to a subtle exposition and critique in "Leo Strauss, Hobbes and Human Nature" (pp. 353–67).[6] He begins with a series of observations about the contemporary "humanist" return in France to values and the question of the best regime (*i.e.*, to the best-known dimensions of Strauss's work), after "the conceptual scaffoldings" of Marxism, positivism and the like have collapsed. Warning against an embrace of moral values when combined with a disdain for thought, he asks for the "liberating evidence that tears away the veil" of once-fashionable anti- or amoral philosophies (p. 354). For Malherbe, Hobbes makes the decisive case against any simplistic restoration of the moral as "the authentic source of political thought" (p. 355).

To reach this result he first analyzes Strauss's "antipathetically faithful" commentary on Hobbes, underlining or reworking several of Strauss's primary claims, *viz*.: (l) "it is not the method [*i.e.*, of Galilean analysis] that transforms the sense of the political, it is a certain moral judgment made about man that calls for the method" (p. 356); (2) "Hobbes surrenders political science to the metaphysical obsession with effectiveness [*l'effectivité*]" (p. 358); and (3) "Hobbes introduced Machiavelli's realism into the very heart

5. *SPPP*, p. 226; p. 211.
6. *Thomas Hobbes et l'oeuvre de la raison* (Paris, 1974).

of natural right; he destroyed the teleological ideality of the law by subordinating it to right; he confined human nature to the sole desire for power and gave as the reason for reason the fear of death" (p. 361). In sum, Hobbes's modern rationalism misses the opportunity provided by his own remark in the preface to *De cive* that modern natural philosophy is not the indispensable condition for civil philosophy. A person's introspective experience of human nature is a sufficient beginning, a beginning purportedly leading him to recognize the "finality" of human nature. Hence his affirmation of modern rationalism in the human sphere is the result of "the act of a philosophically wicked [*mauvaise*] will," a matter "less of an error . . . than a fault" (p. 363).

At this point Malherbe sets out to turn the tables against Strauss by assessing the "critical power of Hobbes' philosophy against the 'humanist' foundation of all civil philosophy" (*ibid.*). What, in truth, does introspection disclose about each individual's motivation and about the use of reason in the pursuit of the "ends" dictated by that motivation? To the first of these questions Malherbe's Hobbes answers "this natural man who presents himself to himself in the originary experience is living individuality, the pure determination of life, so urgent that each man, in relation to his very own individuality, is always already determinately caught up in the flow of his life, prior to all reflection" (p. 364; one cannot help but be reminded here of Hegel's analysis of living individuality in chap. 4 of the *Phenomenology*). Finality, or directedness toward ends as the result of deliberation or contemplation, is nothing other than a self-vitiating, not to say self-annihilating, "delay": or "distancing." The lives that we lead are "up close," not at any remove entailed by the distinction between potentiality and actuality.

Reason, always in the service of "the vital determination which is the *unique* principle of human nature" (p. 365), is consequently beset by an inherent paradox. As reflection and thus nonimmediate, it lacks "immediate effectiveness"; nonetheless, as a universal calculus inexorably joined to the life of *this* individual, it strives for an effectiveness beneficial to its possessor. "It is necessary that it produce a work [*qu'elle fasse oeuvre*], that it engender a real [*i.e.*, effective] principle" (*Ibid.*). Reason is not "the [teleological] order of human nature, but one of its powers" (p. 364). Its principal work and hence the confirmation of its validity as a calculus is the artifice of the commonwealth and the sovereign.

The Straussian appeal to the "moral" evidence furnished by Greek political philosophy, according to Malherbe, is countered by the Hobbesian demand that evidence as such be "incontestable, because it is absolutely prior [*viz.*, to philosophy]. And, for Hobbes, only the element of life satisfies this condition" (p. 367). His deft conclusion: "Hobbes' philosophy shows, if it needed showing,that it is very difficult for an 'honest man' of the 20th century to free himself from modernity or contemporaneity" (*ibid.*).

Readers of Strauss on Hobbes will be appropriately challenged by Malherbe. In this context I must limit myself to one observation regarding his defense of Hobbes and to one parenthetical remark concerning features of Strauss's interpretation which are tacitly endorsed by Malherbe himself.

The "original experience" of one's own irreducible vital or animal individuality is not altogether clear. Malherbe refers to the Preface to *De cive*, but in that text Hobbes speaks once of "the principle by experience known to all men" (*pro principio omnibus per experientiam noto*), which is that men naturally dread and distrust one another in the absence of some coercive power. On another occasion, when explaining his decision to publish *De cive* before completing the first two parts of his system, he claims that the third part was based on "its own principles known by experience" (*principiis propriis experientio cognitis*). In neither case is experience identical with the originary, first-person, experience of bodily vitality and desire; in both cases, on the contrary, experience assumes a maturity of exposure to political and historical "realities" (*e.g.*, international relations). Malherbe seems to have imported the Cartesian *ego cogitans* into Hobbes in the guise of an *ego desiderans*.

Perhaps more importantly, Malherbe's Hobbes would also have had to subscribe to the equally Cartesian notion that we are all, in principle, self-made men. In other words, all that is natal and native, including the opinions received willy-nilly from a linguistic community, goes by the boards, to be replaced by the simple sensation of the body as the locus of unremitting desires. When, then, Malherbe tries to turn the tables against Strauss's critique of Hobbes, we must assume that *this* philosophical fabrication (shared, in different ways, by Descartes and Spinoza,) is more "self-evident" than the moral "finality" of the reputable opinions, the *endoxa*. Since these, one could argue, are less fabricated and to this extent more prephilosophical, if not absolutely "natural," it would have been worth Malherbe's effort to explore Strauss's comments on Mendelssohn's excruciating attempt to secure "evidence" for moral propositions on a par with the putative evidence of metaphysical propositions. One key statement may be cited here from Strauss's "Introductions" to *Morgenstunden* and *An die Freunde Lessings*: "Therefore in the exercise of moral principles 'conscience and a felicitous sense of truth [*bonsens*]'— that is, the abilities correctly to distinguish good from evil or the true from the false through indistinct arguments — 'in most circumstances take the place of reason.'"[7] *Endoxa* and "evidence" name the arena of contention between the prephilosophical realm and the modern invention of radically deracinated individuality.

Furthermore, Malherbe seems to accept Strauss's "historical" thesis that Hobbes began from the study of Aristotelian rhetoric and Thucydidean history and only later marshaled the resources of inchoate natural science in his endeavor to create the very first political science. Malherbe does not remark on the strangeness, even the uniqueness, of Strauss's procedure in this case; as far as I know this was the only time he undertook to understand an author in, as it were, "developmental" terms.

The break from rhetoric and history and toward natural science is supposed to have been occasioned by Hobbes's concern for the *effectiveness* of means to reach moral ends, on the one hand, and for the *demonstrability* of causal relations, on the other. Two things seem to be missing, or underemphasized, in Strauss's account and in Malherbe's faithful rendition. First, it is not, strictly speaking, the axiomatic-deductive method of geometrical proof that captivated Hobbes, but the *constructive* power of geometrical problem-solving. Dispensing with the algebraic symbolism of Wallis and others, Hobbes saw in Euclidean definitions and postulates the power to generate figures whose features were, as a result, unmistakable. Hence, he reinterprets *apodeixis* as "placing the thing to be examined as it were before the eyes" or as "exposition to sense" (*Opera Latina* I, 76). Ratiocination rejoins sensation and fancy in geometry, since genetic definitions are "integral causes" of their effects. The sovereign is, in this respect, the visually potent solution to a geometrical problem.

In any event, Hobbes never abandons his preoccupation with rhet-

---

7. M. Medelssohn, *Gesammelte Schriften. Jubiläumsausgabe*, III, 2 (Stuttgart-Bad Canstatt: F. Frommann, 1974), p. lxv. Strauss's long introduction (xii-cx) demands close scrutiny. His editorial work on Mendelssohn leads him to Lessing and the *Atheismusstreit* and thence to Spinoza. The subject of his dissertation (1921) was Jacobi. As far as I know, no one has commented on Strauss's interpretations of Mendelssohn.

oric, history *and* heroic epic poetry, precisely because of his concern for "exposition to sense" and demonstrations *ad oculos*. Thucydides, in crafting his "deliberative orations," writes Hobbes, paraphrasing Plutarch, "maketh his auditor a spectator," thereby achieving both "perspicuity and efficacy." History in the Thucydidean manner "set[s] *before men's eyes* the ways and events of good and evil counsels."[8] Rhetorical and historiographic *enargeia* is political *energeia* or "effectiveness." Similarly, poetry, especially epic poetry, aims to *"exhibite* a venerable and amicable Image of Heroick virtue." The epic author must unite in himself "fancy" and "philosophy," since only the latter can "make both body and soul, colour and shadow of his poem out of his own store."[9] The next generation of students of Hobbes may want to trace the arc that links his "early" translation of Thucydides to his autumnal translations of Homer, an arc that also embraces the historical Behemoth, the poetic autobiography and the most transparently rhetorical exposition to sense, fancy and memory, the Leviathan itself.

3. Richard Bodéüs, whose recent book on Aristotle's political philosophy is very much worth reading, has produced a rather odd medley in his essay "Two Aristotelian Propositions on Natural Right Among the Continentals of America" (pp. 369–89).[10] By the "Continentals of America" he refers to the emigrés Strauss and Eric Voegelin, who are in turn allied with such German proponents of the "rehabilitation of practical philosophy" as Gadamer and Joachim Ritter. One thing they have in common is recourse to two Aristotelian passages taken as authoritative for the issue of natural right or, more exactly, for classical natural right. (In what follows I shall ignore the many affinities Bodéüs suggests between Strauss and Voegelin. Almost all of them strike me as ill-judged. In any case, Bodéüs overlooks Strauss's critique of Voegelin in "Restatement on Xenophon's *Hiero.*")

Bodéüs first examines how Strauss supposedly interpreted the two passages in question (*viz., Nicomachean Ethics* V, 1134b18–20; b28–33) in *Natural Right and History* and then presents his own reading, a reading at odds with what he takes to be Strauss's. The first propo-

8. *Hobbes's Thucydides*, ed. R. Schlatter (New Brunswick, NJ: Rutgers University Press, 1975), p. 18.
9. "Discourse upon Gondibert," in *Literary Criticism of 17th Century England*, ed. E. W. Taylor (New York: Knopf, 1967), p. 284.
10. *Le philosophe et la cité. Recherches sur les rapports entre morale et politique dans la pensée d'Aristote* (Paris, 1982).

sition, in "Strauss's free version," reads: "natural right is part of political right." The second proposition is that "all natural right is changeable" (*EN* 1134b30: *kinēton mentoi pan*). According to Bodéüs Strauss et al. have misread the texts called upon for support of these two propositions and have consequently been suspicious that the second gives rise to relativism or legal positivism, that is, to the disappearance or dilution of "classical natural right" (p. 379).

Bodéüs's philological arguments are both dense and subtle; their core, however, is relatively straightforward. When Aristotle speaks of *to politikon dikaion* —"the political right or just"— in *EN* V,7, he does *not* mean "political right" without restriction, but refers quite specifically to "the set of rules of the just properly speaking . . . that characterizes human relations within . . . the political society (of the type *politeia*) that unites free and equal men" (p. 381). "The adjective *politikon* in the expression *politikon dikaion* does not refer to the noun *politeia* insofar as it designates generically all sorts of constitutions, but insofar as it designates specifically one type of constitution, the one that bears 'the name common to all'" (p. 381 n.54). Several important consequences flow from this rather novel claim.

First, the "rightness [*la rectitude*] of the right" follows from the rightness of that regime characterized simply as *hē politeia*. Nonetheless, this makes sense only if there is a measure of rightness thanks to which regimes can be evaluated. For Bodéüs this measure is *to dikaion haplōs*, the right pure and simple. (See, *e.g.*, *Politics* III 6, 1279a17–21 and *EN* V, 6, 1134a 25–26.) However, Bodéüs seems to turn in a vicious circle when he writes "the absolute norm of the just is immanent, for Aristotle, in the rules of right" (p. 387 n.81). At the least he owes the reader an explanation of what "immanent" means here.

Second, the distinction between the natural (*physikon*) part and the legal (*nomikon*) part of "the political right" at the debut of *EN* V,7 is *not* the distinction between the just and the arbitrary. "They represent, respectively, that which in the laws [sic] imposes itself naturally or spontaneously on the legislator and that which the legislator himself commands in the precise terms of the law, in order to translate into the form of right what imposes itself upon him as natural" (p. 387). This is ingenious, but difficult to accept without reservations. If it is a matter of a founder-legislator the character of the laws of a still-absent regime cannot be a constraint on his natural "inclination." If it is a matter of a successor-legislator, his respect for already-instituted laws and their appropriate modifications stems from dispositions inculcated by the regime itself and thus is not spontaneous. Finally, Bodéüs wants to explain the variability or mutability of natural right in a nonparadoxical way. *Both* the legal *and* the natural aspects of the right "vary on an equal footing" (*de pair*); Aristotle's text cited here is more ambiguous: "if indeed they are both similarly changeable" [*EN* 1134b32]). The rule of right contains "the natural singularized by the legal as a function of circumstances" (p. 388). It is a nice finishing touch when Bodéüs, following Aristotle's simile, compares the legislator to the ambidextrous man; by nature his right hand is the stronger, but through law he can give his left hand equal dexterity.

The reader will have noticed that Bodéüs spends more time on his rendition of Aristotle than on an interpretation of Strauss. Only two supplementary remarks about the latter are in order here. (1) In *Natural Right and History* Strauss imitates Aristotle, whose "own view [of natural right] covers barely one page of the *Nicomachean Ethics*," by devoting barely six pages to the topic; it is of some interest that no references to the Aristotelian texts are provided on those pages, in marked contrast to the numerous reference to Plato and Cicero. It is as though "the Aristotelian natural right teaching," on first hearing, is an intermezzo between the Socratic-Platonic-Stoic teaching and "the Christian thinkers (especially Thomas Aquinas)."[11] Additional light is cast on Strauss's reading by the equally brief discussion of Aristotle in the essay "On Natural Law" from 1968. One will note, for example, that in the later text Strauss does cite the passage from *Rhetoric* I, 13, 1373b concerning "the law common according to nature" (to which Bodéüs links one of his counterarguments,) and comments ". . . it is not entirely certain that he takes that law to be more than something generally admitted and hence useful for forensic rhetoric."[12] The phrase "generally admitted" straightaway reminds us of the view of the Muslim and Jewish *falāsifa*, in contrast to the Christian Aristotelians.[13]

(2) Unlike Bodéüs, to judge by his laconic footnote (p. 384 n.67), Strauss does take monarchy to be, for Aristotle, the best regime by nature and thus the one in which natural right, but not positive

11. *Natural Right and History* (hereafter = *NRH*) (Chicago: University of Chicago Press, 1953), pp. 156 and 120.
12. *SPPP*, pp. 139–40.
13. *NRH*, p. 32; and *Persecution and the Art of Writing* (hereafter = *PAW*) (Glencoe, IL: Free Press, 1952), p. 47.

right, flourishes. Bodéüs cites *EN* VIII, 12, 1160a35–36, on monarchy as the best of regimes, but not, as does Strauss, *EN* V, 7, 1135a, where the identity of "the single regime everywhere by nature the best" is left open. This is not just a difference in detail, inasmuch as Strauss's "official" discussion of "the Aristotelian natural right teaching" takes place in a "twilight" analogous to "the twilight which is essential to human life as merely human."[14] If monarchy is, as he writes, "the maximum possibility of political society" and if the king "plausibly has the look of being a god among men" (see *Politics* III, 13, 1284a10–11), can one say that such a regime would be the civil equivalent or image of the philosophical life? Bodéüs, unlike Strauss, is not exercised by the tension between the best political life and the best human life *simpliciter*.

One general observation about the three essays just discussed. Edmond, Malherbe and Bodéüs all seem to take it for granted that Strauss himself had a "natural right/natural law teaching" and, consequently, a teaching about "nature." This is not the place to mimic those Delian divers Socrates alludes to when asked, according to Diogenes Laertius, what he thinks of Heraclitus, "the obscure one." It is an opportunity, nevertheless, at least to pose the question whether these alleged teachings are thoroughly exoteric, *pia*, rather than *vera*, *dogmata*. After all as Strauss remarks in *Philosophy and Law*: "The Islamic and Jewish philosophers of the Middle Ages are 'more primitive' than the modern philosophers because they are not, unlike the latter, guided by the derived idea of natural right but rather by the *original, ancient* idea of the *Law* as a unitary, total order of human life — in other words, because they are the disciples of Plato and not the disciples of Christians."[15] If Strauss was in any sense a disciple of Maimonides and the *falāsifa*, and hence of Plato, then natural right would seem to be a "derived," and possibly factitious, idea for him as well. At all events he does not dilute the force of this contrast between the derived and the original in subsequent writings such as "The Law of Reason in the *Kuzari*." One has to wonder in what measure the view ascribed to the *haver* (scholar) in the *Kuzari*, namely, "[the rational *nomoi*] are not natural precisely because they are nomoi" could be justly credited to Strauss himself.[16] Moreover, he reminds

        14. *CM*, p. 49; and *NRH*, p. 157. (Cf. P. A. Vander Waerdt, "Kingship and Philosophy in Aristotle's Best Regime," *Phronesis* 30 [1985]: 249–75.)
        15. *PL*, p. 53.
        16. *PAW*, p. 127 n. 103a.

his readers time and again that "the Hebrew term for 'nature' is unknown to the Hebrew Bible."[17] It would not be altogether exaggerated to say that the axis on which the perennial debate between Athens and Jerusalem turns is the question: Is there or is there not an underived, aboriginal Nature, as distinct from ways and customs, for instance, divinely instituted customs?

4. By its title perhaps the most inviting, Pierre Manent's essay "Strauss and Nietzsche" is in substance a bit disappointing (pp. 337–45). Manent casts his net more widely than his title would lead one to expect; indeed, he is intent on "trying to formulate in a synthesis the contrast between the Ancients and the Moderns" (p. 340). For him the pivotal contrast is between the Greek philosophers' "refusal to succumb to the authority or the charm" of any of the naturally founded opinions of the *polis* (p. 340) and the polemical "modern project," whose targets are variously ancient philosophy and Christianity. "This project is a construction. It takes as its elements aspects of the Greek experience, aspects of the Christian experience and, amalgamating them, in a way using one to neutralize the other, it makes them serve a construction contrary to the two experiences or to the two interpretations" (p. 341). Manent takes as an illustration the Hobbesian-Hegelian reinterpretation of the Christian sin of pride into vainglory or the desire for recognition. "The sin of the Christian, neutralized, has become the right of man" (*ibid.*).

Nietzsche, according to Manent, enters the scene at the moment the triumph of Christianity reveals "the power of its weak or low [*basse*] will." Nietzsche's idea of the will to power is "born from the historical experience of the Christian peoples" (p. 343).

As for Strauss's powerful attraction to Nietzsche, or so Manent conjectures, it can be explained by referring to "Nietzschean psychology . . . to the importance Nietzsche gives to human *types* (the philosopher, the saint, the scholar)" (p. 342). Of these types it is the *homo religiosus* who takes on capital importance in Strauss's reading of Nietzsche: Nietzsche as himself a new kind of *homo religiosus* brings to light his equivocal standing as a philosopher. Or, alternatively, Nietzsche's atheistic critique of Christianity in the name of probity itself rests on biblical (*i.e.*, Christian?) morality. Arch-critic of modernity construed as the triumph of Christianity, Nietzsche nonetheless reiterates or transfigures the characteristically modern attempt

17. *NRH*, p. 81.

to absorb theoretical reason into practical reason (morality). Hence, Strauss's implicit critique of Nietzsche (and Heidegger): "Strauss certainly admits that it is necessary to act morally. But precisely, to *act* morally, not to think morally" (p. 345). We return "in the last and most decisive part of his work [*oeuvre*] to the figure of Socrates," that is, "to the only human life capable of living morally without thinking morally" (*ibid.*).

If we leave aside Manent's estimation of the role of Christianity in preparing the way for the crisis of modernity, an estimation which would surely have seemed hyperbolic to Strauss, and if we overlook Manent's neglect of Nietzsche's own "preference" for the so-called Old Testament over the New, we are still somewhat struck by the paucity of his references to Strauss's own statements concerning Nietzsche. To be sure, "Notes on the Plan of Nietzsche's *Beyond Good and Evil*" is the only text wholly devoted to Nietzsche that Strauss published. Yet we can readily assemble a florilegium from which we may infer that something more than Nietzsche's psychology "powerfully attracted Strauss," even if the power of that psychology must also be duly acknowledged. To give just a few samples:

"The super-man is meant to unite in himself Jerusalem and Athens at the highest level."

"It is certainly not an overstatement to say that no one has ever spoken so greatly and so nobly of what a philosopher is as Nietzsche."

"I would not like to fail to draw attention to the curious conjunction of Muhammed and Plato in Nietzsche's *The Will to Power*, aphorism 972."[18]

The "philosophers of the future" must be, what the pre-Socratic (and Platonic?) philosophers already were, legislators. The remarkable string of partial synonyms at the heart of *Philosophy and Law*, viz., "the prophet as philosopher-statesman-seer-(miracle-worker)," might remind more than one reader of Zarathustra, at least before he despairs of teaching even "the higher men." A full-dress study of Strauss and Nietzsche will have to reckon with these and many other true or false resemblances.[19]

18. *SPPP*, p. 149; *RCPR*, p. 40–41; *PL*, p. 121 n.88.
19. Rémi Brague, in the essay discussed below, and in "Leo Strauss et Maïmonide," in *Maimonides and Philosophy*, ed. S. Pines and Y. Yovel (Dordrecht; Boston: M. Nijhoff Publishers, 1986), pp. 246–68, at pp. 258–60, makes fruitful suggestions about the alliance between Nietzsche and Strauss. Shadia B. Drury, *The Political Ideas of Leo Strauss* (New York: St. Martin's Press, 1988). Chap. 9 ex-

5. I have saved the initial essay, "Athens, Jerusalem, Mecca: The Muslim Interpretation of Greek Philosophy in Leo Strauss," for last because it seems to me that it is the richest and most provocative in this collection.[20] Rémi Brague, the author of three outstanding books on Greek philosophy and the translator of most of Strauss's work on Maimonides, furnishes, first of all, a treasure-trove of clarifications, updated references and scholarly emendations or hypotheses. Moreover, he brings to the center what has come to be seen as *the* focal point of Strauss's arts of reading and writing, and thus of his philosophical thinking as such, namely, esotericism. Acknowledging that Strauss practiced what he preached, Brague is also quick to confess: "It is impossible to say if one is penetrating the depth of his thought or if one is purely and simply groping on its surface, a brilliant and polished surface, in the double sense of those terms" (p. 310).

Adopting an "ascetic," historical attitude, Brague undertakes to show that "the model of reading that Strauss applies to the Greeks is not of ancient, nor of modern, origin, but of medieval origin: to be precise, of *Islamic* origin" (p. 316). The defense of this thesis leads him, first, to underscore the initially decisive and continuing importance of writers in the medieval Islamic community for Strauss's interpretation of the Greeks and, thus, for his critique of modern rationalism and its political manifestations. Brague makes al-Farabi "the central witness," while also emphasizing the parts played in Strauss's repertory by Abu Bakr al-Razi's *Kitab al-sirat al-falsafiyya* and Avicenna's puzzling pronouncement that "the treatment of prophecy and the divine law is contained in the books of Plato and Aristotle on the laws."[21]

This opening defense of his thesis subsequently leads him to his more fundamental and provocative attempt to relocate the matrix of Strauss's esotericism from "Jerusalem" to "Mecca." "The fact of esotericism in Islamic thought is manifest. In this respect, Straus-

---

presses some surprise in the face of this alliance or affinity. I have dealt with the question in "Hokmah Yenavit Reflections on Leo Strauss, *Philosophie und Gesetz*," delivered at The Hebrew University of Jerusalem, July 1990 (forthcoming).

20. Ironically, Brague's essay is translated from English; the English version will appear in A. Udoff, ed., *On Leo Strauss: Toward a Critical Engagement* (forthcoming).

21. Razi's text is available to English-language readers in a free translation by A. J. Arberry, "Rhazes on the Philosophic Life," *The Asiatic Review* (1949): 703–713. Brague is strangely silent about Averroes's *The Decisive Treatise*, which is the focus of chapter two of *Philosophy and Law*.

sian hermeneutics gets its support and finds its bastion in the exploration of this [Islamic] field" (p. 329). The existence of Islamic esotericism is not, according to Brague, a pure and simple fact, but stems rather from "an internal modality of the Islamic conception of revelation," a modality allegedly absent from, or less prominent in, Judaism (p. 330).[22]

Since the first part of Brague's thesis, namely that al-Farabi is the "central witness" summoned by Strauss in his exegeses of the Greeks, especially of Plato, seems to me eminently, if not totally, persuasive, I shall confine myself to one brief remark. Strauss's version of "Farabi's Plato" is divided into two apparently incompatible, or at least ambiguously juxtaposed, parts: "Plato's philosophy" as "essentially a political investigation" and Farabi's view of "what he considers the genuinely Platonic view." The latter is not identical with the philosophy of "the political things," so much so that the distinction between human perfection (the fully achieved science of beings *in toto*) and human happiness (the right way of life) is exacerbated. Farabi's Plato, the supposedly authoritative guide to Strauss's interpretation of the Platonic dialogues, is thus irremediably ambivalent. The synonymy briskly proposed in *Philosophy and Law* (1935), that is,"the prophet is philosopher-statesman-seer-miracle worker in one," is called into question in the essay "Farabi's Plato" (1945), as a result of the publication of the full Arabic text of *The Philosophy of Plato* in 1943. Strauss writes: "Since the legislator, as the founder of the virtuous city, creates the indispensable condition for the actualization of happiness, happiness would thus not be possible but on the basis of revelation. Farabi's Plato does not close that loophole by identifying the prophet, or the legislator, with the philosopher."[23]

All of the issues passed over in silence in *The Philosophy of Plato* and in Brague's account of Strauss's decisive dependence on al-Farabi return here with a vengeance. Which of Farabi's Platos are we to identify as Strauss's Farabian Plato? (A possible clue may be found in "Quelques remarques sur la science politique de Maïmonide et de Farabi," where Strauss, underscoring Maimonides' fidelity to al-

---

22. The grounds of Brague's point are unclear. Both Judaism and Islam arise from divine speeches and divine texts. It belongs to both traditions to claim that those texts are, after a fashion, eternal.

23. "Farabi's Plato," in *Essays on Medieval Jewish and Islamic Philosophy*, ed. A. Hyman (New York: Ktav Publishing House, 1977), p. 414.

Farabi's "platonizing politics," writes: "The true metaphysics — this is the ensemble of 'the opinions of the people of the perfect city.'")[24]

The second part of Brague's thesis — the relocation of esotericism from "Jerusalem" to "Mecca"— is more difficult to accept in its unmitigated form. Three sorts of objections or qualifications may be raised. (l) Brague points out that the toponymic metaphor "Jerusalem vs. Athens" first appears in the *Christian* apologist Tertullian (d. ca. 240 A.D.), to reappear only in the nineteenth century in Heine and Luzzatto. This is not yet equivalent to showing that the tension or antagonism encapsulated in that metaphor is not indigenous to the Jewish tradition, although it is certainly not exclusive to it. Brague cites one Talmudic and one Midrashic text to demonstrate that the opposition "appeared on the level of human types" (p. 312). But surely, if the opposition is one between "human types," that is, between mutually antagonistic ways of life, this corresponds to Strauss's own contrast between "a life of obedient love versus a life of free insight."[25] Moreover, in the particular Talmudic instance cited — R. Joshua b. Hananiah's defeat of the sixty wise men of Athens, Brague apparently fails to note that he wins by turning the articles characteristic of the Greeks — plays on words, enigmas, *double entendres* — against the Greeks themselves. He might also have cited the occurrences of "Greek wisdom" (*hokhmah yevanit*) in the Talmud (*bT Baba Qamma* 82b; *Sotah* 49b; *Menahot* 64b and 99b) in order to bring to light the existence of an essential tension in pre-Islamic Judaism. "Greek wisdom" is variously interpreted by later commentators; Rashi, for example, took it to mean "hinting gestures," a riddling body-language, while others identified it with philosophy.[26] Although the rabbis proscribed not the study of "Greek wisdom" on one's own, but the teaching of it to one's sons, this is already weighty testimony to the seriousness of the choice of lives. In a famous Talmudic phrase: "Cursed be the man who raises pigs or teaches his son Greek wisdom" (*bT Sotah* 49b). Pious Jews in *Jerusalem* in the second century B.C.E. opposed the "extreme of Hellenism" (*II Macc.* 4. 13), which featured

24. "Quelques remarques sur la science politique de Maimonide et de Farabi" *Revue des études juives* 100 (1936): 5. L. Strauss, *Maïmonide*, ed. R. Brague, pp. 147–48.
25. *NRH*, p. 74.
26. See Menachem Kellner, "Rabbi Isaac Bar Sheshet's Responsum Concerning the Study of Greek Philosophy," *Tradition* 15 (1975–76): 110–18. Cf. on *hokhmat yenavit.* JB. Septimus, *Hispano-Jewish Culture in Transition* (Cambridge, MA: Harvard University Press, 1982), pp. 85–86; 157–58; and Steven Harvey, *Falaquera's Epistle of the Debate: An Introduction to Jewish Philosophy* (Cambridge, MA: Harvard University Press, 1987), p. 39 n. 71.

the introduction of gymnasia, the reading of Homer and the reversal of circumcision by epispasm.[27]

(2) Brague's argument for the *Meccan* source of Straussian esotericism also depends on distinguishing between versions of "elitism," the vicarial elitism of the Jewish sages and the exclusionary or separatist elitism of the *falāsifa* in the Islamic environment. In the former, "the sages consider themselves as representing Israel, which itself represents the human species," while in the latter "the vulgar is always a means [*i.e.*, to the preservation or protection of philosophy], never an end" (pp. 334–35).Nuances are required if this beguiling distinction is to be maintained. One might, for example, refer to al-Farabi's *Paraphrase of Aristotle's Topics*: "We [philosophers] are political by nature. It is incumbent on us therefore to (a) live in harmony with the public, love them and prefer doing what is useful to them and redounds to the improvement of their condition (just as it is incumbent on them to do the same in our regard)."[28] Or, one might take note of the dictum ascribed to Aristotle in the Arabic *Book of the Treasury of Wisdom* compiled by someone close to al-Farabi's circle: "Withholding knowledge/science and philosophy is one of the cruelest acts and greatest sins."[29] The vicarial and the separatist versions of elitism do not appear to be separated *toto caelo*. Indeed, Maimonides, the disciple of al-Farabi, seems to bring the two into exquisite harmony by suggesting, in the final two chapters of the *Guide* (III, 53 and 54) that the philosopher-king, in imitation of divine governance, emanates the attributes of loving-kindness, judgment and righteousness to nonphilosophers, once he has achieved apprehension of the divine. Could it be that the "Straussian" teaching to the effect that the philosopher's sole political task is to render the city safe for philosophy is itself an exoteric teaching?

(3) I come, finally, to the topic of esotericism itself. Once more it is a question of nuances, not of outright opposition to Brague's second thesis. To his assertion: "Strauss, one can suppose, was conscious of the non-Jewish origin of esotericism such as he understood

27. See Martin Hengel, *Judaism and Hellenism*, trans. J. Bouden (Philadelphia: Fortress Press, 1974), I: 76; and the fundamental article by Saul Lieberman, "The Alleged Ban on Greek Wisdom," in his *Hellenism in Jewish Palestine* (New York: Jewish Theological Seminary of America, 1962), pp. 100–114.
28. Cited in M. Mahdi, "Man and His Universe in Medieval Arabic Philosophy," in *L'Homme et son univers au moyen age*, T. I. (Louvain-La-Neuve, 1986), p. 112.
29. Cited in Dimitri Gutas, *Avicenna and the Aristotelian Tradition* (Leiden: E. J. Brill, 1988), p. 231.

it" (p. 328), one could reply by asking "Esotericism in what sense?" In this setting I can merely suggest a threefold distinction among the pedagogical, the hermeneutical and the political sense of esotericism. The first two are undoubtedly anchored to (pre-Islamic) Jewish tradition; the historical status of the third is more ambiguous and elusive. A very few comments will have to suffice.

Pedagogical esotericism corresponds to the Talmudic emphasis on the special conditions required for successful *oral* teaching. The legal prohibition stressed by Strauss against teaching "The Doctrine of the Chariot" "even to one man, except he be wise and able to understand by himself" may have as much to do with a Rabbinical sense for the "realities" of teaching and learning as it does with the secrecy of the doctrines involved. A parallel may be seen in the ban against teaching the third class of "secrets/contradictions [*sitre*] of the Torah," namely forbidden sexual relations (*arayot*). The very same passage of the *Mishnah* (Hagigah 2: 1) invoked by Maimonides and Strauss to remind one of the interdiction against teaching physics and metaphysics except in restricted circumstances also says that "no more than two students can be present when the secrets of *arayot* are exposed . . . were three students present, two of them would be prone to argue between themselves and the content of the master's discussion might not be fully absorbed."[30] For the late-adolescents the *Mishnah* and Maimonides have in mind there is, we can suppose, little crucial difference among the topics of creation, metaphysics and eros.

By "hermeneutical esotericism" I am referring to the whole, endlessly complex, set of interpretive practices exhibited in the *Talmud* as well as in post-Talmudic legal and homiletical tradition. These practices have their ground in the character of the text itself, not in the necessity to protect the interpreter. The *Torah* as the word of an "infinite" God demands a multiplicity of exegeses; this is most familiarly registered in the image of the forty-nine faces (*panim*) of the *Torah*. Similarly, the ordering of the sections of the *Torah* is said to be improper from the human perspective, proper, from the divine perspective. The claim that the revealed text is multilayered and necessarily baffling seems clearly to antedate Arabic-language controversies over the appropriateness of allegorical interpretation

---

30. For the text, and commentary, see Moshe Idel, *"Sitre Arayot* in Maimonides' Thought," in Pines and Yovel, *Maimonides and Philosophy*, pp. 79–91.

(*ta'wil*) of the *Koran*. The secrets of the *Torah* are secret, not out of civic necessity, but in virtue of the gap between an infinite author and finite readers. That the text loves to hide itself was recognized long before the advent of the *falāsifa* and their Jewish disciples, including Maimonides, of whom Strauss once ironically suggested that he "was the first Kabbalist."[31]

"Political esotericism," the hiddenness of an author's true views in his publicly accessible texts, is a different affair once it is linked to the possibility or actuality of the persecution of philosophers (and others) for heresy or heterodoxy. Neither pedagogical nor hermeneutical esotericism, nor their combination, implies a threat to civic well-being; on the contrary, prudent observation of the abilities (and disabilities) of students, joined to incessant fidelity to the multiple meanings of the revealed text, is one of the principal guarantors of the integrity even of the dispersed community.[32] When the philosophical construal of the "same" text comes to be seen as antithetical to the consensus on which the perdurance of the community rests, then persecution, actual or merely "on the books," also becomes an unmistakable feature of the Islamic environment, as does esoteric dissimulation to avoid persecution. Al-Farabi, for example, analyzed John Philoponus' apparent conformity to Christian orthodoxy against Aristotle as his attempt to "avoid the fate of Socrates." "The fate of Socrates" is a constant refrain in the Islamic biographical and gnomological traditions.[33]

Does the legal persecution of philosophers *qua* philosophers have a counterpart in the Jewish tradition? Strictly speaking, the answer is "No," since Rabbinic law "stipulates no punishment for different beliefs."[34] And yet, Maimonides, toward whose premodern ration-

31. *PAW*, p. 51.
32. However, Maimonides himself entertained doubts whether adherence to scripture secures the community. In *Guide* I: 31 he adds to Alexander of Aphrocisias' three reasons for disagreement about things a fourth, vis. habituation to a sacred text. Cf. S. Pines, "The Limitations of Human Knowledge According to Al-Farabi, Ibn Bajja, and Maimonides," in *Studies in Medieval Jewish History and Literature*, ed, I. Twersky, vol. 1 (Cambridge, MA: Harvard University Press, 1979), pp. 100–104.
33. See M. Mahdi, "Alfarabi Against Philoponus," *Journal of Near Eastern Studies* 26 (1967): 233–60, at p. 257.
34. David Biale, *Power and Powerlessness in Jewish History* (New York: Schocken Books, 1987), p. 219 n. 51. Cf. also Menachem Kellner, *Dogma in Medieval Jewish Thought* (Oxford: Oxford University Press, 1986), esp. pp. 10–65. For Islamic counterparts, see, in addition to the essential study by Paul Kraus, cited by Brague,

alism Strauss wanted to arouse a "favorable prejudice," arguably followed Islamic models, perhaps that of al-Ghazali in particular, in insisting on capital punishment for deniers of the dogmas of belief, dogmas he himself articulated for the first time in the Jewish tradition! Thus, in his early *Commentary on the Mishnah* (Hulin 1: 2), he advocates capital punishment for the Karaites. In the later *Mishneh Torah* (Laws of Repentance, chap. 3) he treats in elaborate detail the twenty-four classes of sectarians (*minim*), "Epicureans" (*epikorsim*), deniers of the Torah (*kofrim ha-Torah*), apostates (*meshummed*), etc., although here the apposite punishment is said to be loss of a portion in "the world to come" (*olam ha-ba*). Moreover, philosophers are never mentioned by name, although some of the doctrines ascribed to the Epicureans echo directly al-Ghazali's charges against the philosophers, for example, rejection of God's knowledge of particulars.

It might well appear from these considerations that Maimonides *invented* the notion of persecution for dissent from the orthodoxy he had simultaneously fabricated. If so, then one could indeed say that "Mecca" has been transported to "Jerusalem." One would then have to wonder how deeply Maimonides' invention of persecution in the Jewish community affected Strauss's understanding of the philosopher *Überhaupt*, continually trying to keep the dogs of the city at bay. At all events, the public burning of Maimonides' *Book of Knowledge* and *Guide* in Montpellier by the Inquisition, at the instigation of French rabbis, may seem in retrospect an ironic ruse of history, confirming Strauss's political esotericism *post festum*.

The result of this partial survey of the evidence present and absent in Brague's essay is this: prior to Maimonides, pedagogic and hermeneutical esotericism were firmly entrenched in the tradition of "Jerusalem"; political esotericism may well have been Maimonides' adaptation of an Islamic motif. The modern esoteric authors, Spinoza and Lessing, for example, were equally under the pressure of ecclesiastical commonwealths. One might be tempted to conjecture that the issue of esotericism has *now* become a "red herring," leading the unwary down treacherously self-indulgent, but futile, trails, except when the interpretation of certain ancient, medieval and early-

---

Joel Kraemer, "Heresy Versus the State in Medieval Islam," in *Studies in Judaica, Karaitica and Islamica*, ed. S. R. Brunswick (Ramat Gan, Israel: Bar-Ilan University Press, 1982), pp. 167–80; and Bernard Lewis, *Islam in History* (New York, 1973), pp. 217–36.

modern texts is at stake. The real quarry ought, perhaps, to be Strauss's effort to resuscitate "pre-modern rationalism, especially Jewish-Medieval rationalism and its classical (Aristotelian and Platonic) formulation."[35] In our present circumstances the defense of premodernity can and ought to be philosophically outspoken.

A final comment about this collection as a whole. One name that does not appear in it is "Heidegger." Crudely put, one can divide the contemporary French philosophical world into "pious" and "impious" Heideggerians. The spate of recent publications on Heidegger's *Rektoratsrede* of 1933 and its implications should have made it plain that *Seinsrede* (or, *Seinsgerede*) never slips from its mooring in political philosophy. "Pious," but anxious, Heideggerians may be said to need Strauss more than "Straussians" need them.

35. *AP,* p. 31. Cf. S. Rosen, *Hermeneutics as Politics* (Oxford: Oxford University Press, 1987), pp. 87–140.

The Contributors

LEO STRAUSS (1899–1973) was one of this century's preeminent scholars of political philosophy. He joined the faculty of the University of Chicago in 1949 and was eventually named Robert Maynard Hutchins Distinguished Service Professor.

KENNETH L. DEUTSCH is professor of political science at the State University of New York at Geneseo. He has published several books including *The Crisis of Liberal Democracy: A Straussian Perspective.*

WALTER NICGORSKI is professor in the Program of Liberal Studies at the University of Notre Dame. Author of numerous articles in political philosophy, he is completing a book on Cicero's political thought.

CHRISTOPHER BRUELL is professor of political science at Boston College. He is the author of several articles on Thucydides and ancient political philosophy.

HILLEL FRADKIN is vice president for program development of the Lynde and Harry Bradley Foundation of Milwaukee. He is the author of a number of articles on Leo Strauss and Jewish thought.

DANTE GERMINO is professor in the University of Virginia's Woodrow Wilson Department of Government and Foreign Affairs. Among the many books he has published is *Political Philosophy and the Open Society.*

JOHN GUNNELL is professor of political Science at the State University of New York at Albany. Among his many books in political philosophy are *Political Philosophy and Time* and *Political Theory: Tradition and Interpretation.*

HARRY JAFFA is Salvatori Professor Emeritus at Claremont Graduate School. Among his publications are *The Crisis of a House Divided* and *Thomism and Aristotelianism.*

DAVID LACHTERMAN was a member of the Department of Philosophy and Classics at the Pennsylvania State University. He specialized in the field of early modern philosophy. He published a book titled *The Ethics of Geometry: A Genealogy of Modern Thought.*

DAVID LAWRENCE LEVINE is a tutor at the Sante Fe campus of St. John's College.

THOMAS PANGLE is professor of political science at St. Michael's College of the University of Toronto. He has published numerous books in political philosophy including *The Spirit of Modern Republicanism* and *The Ennobling of Democracy.*

DAVID SCHAEFER is professor of political science at the College of the Holy Cross. He is author of *The Political Philosophy of Montaigne.*

JAMES V. SCHALL, S.J., is professor of government at Georgetown University. Among his many publications are *The Politics of Heaven and Hell* and *Reason, Revelation and the Foundations of Political Philosophy.*

SUSAN SHELL is associate professor of political science at Boston College. A specialist in German idealist political thought, she has authored *The Rights of Reason: A Study of Kant's Philosophy and Politics.*

STEVEN B. SMITH is professor of political science at Yale University. Among his published works is *Hegel's Critique of Liberalism.*

WALTER SOFFER is professor of philosophy at the State University of New York at Geneseo. Co-editor of *The Crisis of Liberal Democracy: A Straussian Perspective,* he has also published a book titled *From Science to Subjectivity: An Interpretation of Descartes' Meditations.*

NATHAN TARCOV is professor of political science at the University of Chicago. He has authored a number of articles on Locke as well as a book titled *Locke's Education for Liberty.*

STEWART UMPHREY is a tutor at St. John's College of Annapolis. He is the author of *Zetetic Skepticism.*

THOMAS G. WEST is professor of politics at the University of Dallas. His publications include *Plato's Apology: An Interpretation, with a New Translation.*